BACKROAD BISTROS, FARMHOUSE FARE

A FRENCH COUNTRY COOKBOOK

BACKROAD BISTROS, FARMHOUSE FARE

A FRENCH COUNTRY COOKBOOK

JANE SIGAL

DOUBLEDAY

NEW YORK   LONDON   TORONTO
SYDNEY   AUCKLAND

PUBLISHED BY DOUBLEDAY

a division of Bantam Doubleday Dell Publishing Group, Inc.
1540 Broadway, New York, New York 10036

DOUBLEDAY and the portrayal of an anchor with a dolphin are
trademarks of Doubleday, a division of Bantam Doubleday Dell
Publishing Group, Inc.

Book design by Marysarah Quinn
Illustrations by Paula Munck

Library of Congress Cataloging-in-Publication Data
Sigal, Jane.
Backroad bistros, farmhouse fare / Jane Sigal. — 1st ed.
p.   cm.
1. Cookery, French.   I. Title.
TX719.S49   1994
641.5944—dc20   93-49926
CIP

To Paul Chutkow,
who pulled me from a class of
writer wanna-bees and said,
"You, do it."

ACKNOWLEDGMENTS

I was amazed, really, that of the scores of people I called for interviews while research-ing this book, only the butcher's wife in Pouldreuzie, Brittany, hung up on me. And even she just managed to do it. When I asked her about the specialties her husband still makes for traditional Breton weddings, she balked. "No, no, I can't talk to you," she protested before she put the phone down. "Really."

No one else declined to meet me. Apart from the butcher's wife, everyone re-sponded with enthusiasm to probing questions from a disembodied voice with an ac-cent. Yves Fantou, a butcher in Saint-Broladre, Brittany, invited me to join him in the salt marshes of Mont-Saint-Michel, and then he took me to meet his aunt, Thérèse Anger, who raises a herd of lambs there. He also introduced me to one of his cus-tomers, Olivier Roellinger, the two-star chef in Cancale.

Patrick Jeffroy, another chef in northern Brittany, agreed to see me for an early cof-fee and then showed me around the market in Morlaix. I curled my hands around end-less cups of coffee to get the story on rice farming from Jean-Pierre Clauzel, on cider making from Annie and René Lesur, on poultry farming from Jean-Claude Miéral, on growing carrots from Victor Letouzé.

Colette Giraud taught me about making *chèvre* and being a single mother in the French countryside. Thierry Rannou sat me down at his dining room table and told me how he came to make his grandmother's *kig ha fars*. Janine Chatel told me far more than how tripe is made in La Ferté-Macé. I also received a big-hearted welcome from Michel Bruneau, Jean-Robert Tiercelin, Pascal and Caroline Bernou, Franck Quinton, Didier and Michèle Militon, Michel Guillemot, Jean-François Vadot, Ludovic Alziari, Suzy Ceysson, Josiane Autrand-Dozol, Hélène Foltz, Christian and Muriel Eelson, Georges Hilliet, Monique Le Rhun, Jean-Marie Le Gall, Charles Vian, Gérard Salardaine, Nathalie Pelletier, Jacques Boudy, and Annick Collette.

Countless others shared their recipes with me. Recipes were dictated to me when I visited farmhouse kitchens, restaurant dining rooms, *charcuteries*, butcher shops, cheese-aging cellars. They poured in by fax and by mail, typed on word processors and handwritten on monogrammed stationery.

Besides the restaurateurs and food producers I went to see, several other people helped get this project done. Thank you Jackie Bobrow for your companionship and willingness to do whatever was needed, from traipsing through Brittany's salt marshes with me to recipe testing. Randall Price helped in many ways, as a source of restorative gossip and support as well as a marathon tester of apple recipes.

For having the bright idea to retire just in time to help as traveling companions and dining partners, I want to thank my parents, Barbara and Ronald Sigal. My mother tested and retested many of the recipes in this book, and they are immeasurably better for her comments and suggestions.

Thank you Michael Saklad for many things, not the least of which was giving me a room of my own.

I want to give special thanks to Patricia Wells, who taught me that the only way to write about food is to search out the farmers and bakers, fishermen and cheesemakers who produce it.

My agents, Maureen and Eric Lasher, approached me in 1990 with an idea they had for a French country cookbook, and I am grateful for their all-around guidance and support.

At Doubleday, I want to thank my editor, Judith Kern, and, for her lovely design, Marysarah Quinn.

There are some people who by their friendship and encouragement alone made this book possible. Among these are Judy and Michael Hill, Jay Kadampanattu, Martina and Hank Sigal, Claudie Massaloux, Joshua Sigal, Rajat Purkasthaya, Carole Clements, Jessica Palmer, Pierre and Isabelle Landau, and Marion and Aaron Yale.

Thanks to William Foster Lee for your smiles inside the kitchen and out, and to Bill Lee for loving everything I cook up.

CONTENTS

INTRODUCTION: KITCHEN WISDOM

Madame Guyon stood hunched over the stove. Waving a hand up and down like a one-armed conductor, she drew the pot-au-feu vapors to her nostrils and took a long drag. The steam made the wisps of white hair stir around her temples. When she shuffled into the dining room with the tureen, her face was still flushed.

Madame Guyon gave me my first lessons in living to eat. This widow of a university professor doled out Gallic rites along with boiled meat, vegetables, and bouillon.

Now, McDonald's is the largest restaurant service in France. But when I talked to people for this book, I still found the same ethos I had encountered fourteen years earlier in Madame Guyon's home in Aix-en-Provence.

In Normandy, Janine Chatel, whose husband, Gérard, is a tripe dresser, told me: "The palate, it's an education." Jean-Claude Miéral, a Bresse poultryman, set me straight on the difference between cooking and applied chemistry: "An egg is not cooking," he said. "It's either overcooked or undercooked or correctly cooked. It's an exact science. What distinguishes cooking is the creative element."

LOOKING FOR FRANCE'S COUNTRY COOKING

Unlike classic French cuisine, which evolved from the royal kitchens in Paris, the cooking I'm interested in here has its source in the countryside. There is, of course, considerable overlap between the two. Trends in *haute cuisine* have filtered down to provincial cooks, just as regional dishes have been refined for Parisian taste buds.

To get a cross-section of French country cooking, I traveled to four regions: Brittany, Normandy, Burgundy, and Provence. At first I was afraid that France's individualistic regions might have lost their quirks. But despite standardizing trends, I found regional integrity alive and well.

When Maurice Farine talked about "exporting" the *calisson* candies made in his family's factory outside Aix-en-Provence, he meant shipping beyond Avignon forty-five miles to the north. As Monsieur Farine sees it, there's a cultural divide between people who grew up eating *calissons*, the diamond-shaped almond-paste sweetmeat of Aix, and those who didn't. For him, where taste is concerned, Brest is as foreign as Boston.

It doesn't matter that today the almonds for *calissons* come from Spain because France's own crop has dwindled. These candies remain quintessentially Provençal, and loving them separates us from them.

As I continued to prowl, I was struck by the unfolding array of regional offerings and preferences. On the cheese front alone, I saw that Norman cheeses were made with cow's milk, while cheese makers in Burgundy, where North meets South, used either cow's or goat's milk. Once in Provence, local taste leaned heavily toward the goat and sheep varieties. In Brittany, although there have always been curd cheeses (made with cow's milk), along the lines of a fresh farmer cheese, I found no native tradition of making aged cheeses at all.

Cistercian monks who settled in Brittany brought cheese-making with them. Frère René, who now makes a cheese similar to Port-Salut at the Abbaye Nôtre-Dame de Timadeuc in central Brittany, told me that, ironically, nobody eats cheese where he comes from in western Brittany. "I only learned to like it by eating it," he said. "Here [at the abbey] it's the *plat de résistance*."

Aside from the cheese made in Timadeuc and at a sister abbey in Campénéac, today Brittany produces plenty of aged cheese, but mainly of the processed variety. Frère René suggested that industrial cheese makers got a foothold here because there were no indigenous ethics of cheese making to displace.

THE DIVERSITY MULTIPLIES

Even when I found certain foods in several regions, the combinations and permutations were endless. Provençal *charcutiers*, for instance, air-dried their hams after a salt-curing. Yet in Normandy, where the climate is too damp for drying meat, once a pig was killed, any meat not eaten fresh was salt-cured and then smoked in the chimney or, more commonly today, taken to a smokehouse.

Or take the case of salt farming in Brittany and Provence. I learned in the Breton salt marshes that to harvest natural salt from the Atlantic, independent salt farmers use the same tools and perform the same tasks, virtually unchanged, as they have for centuries. But in Provence, the Salins du Midi, the single salt harvester on the Mediterranean, uses modern industrial methods to produce standardized table salt.

Even within a single region, the *terroir*—the combination of soil and climate—and corresponding specialties vary as you move around. Burgundy, for instance, produces some of France's greatest wines. But the celebrated vineyards aren't everywhere. Marie-Thérèse Andriot, who runs a bed and breakfast on her cattle farm in Monthélon just outside Autun in Burgundy, recounted, "People come here and ask, 'Where are the vines?'"

Any wine maker will tell you that the style of a wine changes from one patch of land to another. Similarly, as I crossed Provence, the olive oils took on individual personalities from their *terroir*, as well as from the ripeness of the olives and the olive variety.

In Normandy, oyster farmers also told me about their "*crus*." Depending on where the oysters were raised—in Mont-Saint-Michel Bay or the waters off Saint-Vaast-la-Hougue or Isigny—each *cru* had its own character.

Besides finding distinctiveness resulting from geographic and geologic variations as well as from specific fruit varieties and animal breeds, it became clear from watching people at work that no two human beings do anything exactly the same way. "No peasant resembles another," said Monsieur Miéral, speaking of Bresse chicken farmers. "Know-how means differences."

ENDURING VALUES IN A CHANGING CULTURE

Still, I began to see connections wherever I went. Every corner of France had its sustaining porridge, I noticed, though in most places it's rarely eaten anymore: From oat flour, Bretons made *bouillie*; from cornmeal Burgundians made *gaudes*. And all regions—whether wine-rich or wine-poor—brewed a local brandy: Calvados in Normandy; *lambig*, another cider brandy, in Brittany; *marc*, or wine brandy, in Burgundy and Provence.

On another level, I found the same gestures repeated in different settings. Harvesting cider apples in Normandy resembled harvesting olives in Provence. And the labors involved in making cider, wine, olive oil, even mustard—the crushing, pressing, straining—did not change.

Also underlying the dizzying variety was the same passion. Roger Batteault, a *charcutier* in Beaune, couldn't wait to get to work in the morning. "Everyday there's something new to do," he said. "It's fascinating for someone who loves his work."

Poultryman Jean-Claude Miéral was matter-of-fact about the importance of passion in his work. "It doesn't interest me to live without passion," he said. "Passion makes you smile."

Colette Giraud, a cheese maker in Burgundy, was passionate but philosophic. She milked her goats by hand for six years before trying a milking machine. "I was disappointed," she said, patting a goat. "They took to the machine almost at once. They practically preferred to be milked by machine."

THE PASSION WANES

Still, how long does passion last? In the 1950s one out of four people was a farmer. Today farmers represent only 6 percent of the population. "Quality and passion are marginal," Jean-Claude Miéral lamented. "Bresse poultry farming interests only a few people because passion is not as productive as big business. I don't know where we're going. I don't understand."

I heard it over and over: People are more interested in low price than in quality. Janine Chatel, a shopkeeper in Normandy, told me about the time a doctor chided her about the cost of her tripe: "'Oh, it's expensive your tripe,' he said. Sure. People can spend fifteen dollars on a CD. Yet they're not willing to spend more than the supermarket price for good tripe."

But there's another side to the waning of gastronomic tradition. Old-fashioned quality and passion have a cost in human terms. Madame Chatel confided that her daughter reproaches her for not having spent enough time at home. In a pointed rejection of her mother's world, Madame Chatel's daughter abandoned the all-consuming family *triperie-boucherie-charcuterie* in favor of social work.

What's left after the shake-out? Only the most dedicated, high-minded, and off-the-wall market gardeners, mustard makers, salt farmers, olive-oil millers. Plus, nostalgia for authentic regional tastes and traditions is bringing back buckwheat in Brittany and farm cider in Normandy. New interest in the old ways is expanding the availability of goat (once the poor man's cow) cheese and putting such homely fare as *pieds et paquets*, a Provençal tripe dish, and chitterling sausages back on restaurant menus and in specialty shop windows.

WHAT'S COOKING IN THE FRENCH COUNTRYSIDE?

Today, with people spending less time in home kitchens, I found that it's often restaurateurs, *charcutiers*, bakers, and pastry chefs who keep yesterday's favorites alive.

Restaurant cooks are also looking to their gastronomic roots for inspiration. Their menus include stylish reinterpretations of heirloom recipes. The Breton chef Patrick

Jeffroy, for instance, still makes *bouillie*, or oatmeal porridge. But he fries it in butter and builds a salad around it. In Normandy, Régis Lecomte of Le Dauphin takes coffee and Calvados, the favorite Norman pairing, and flavors a witty frozen soufflé with them.

Some talented chefs deconstruct time-honored dishes and recombine the individual elements in new and whimsical ways. Jacques Thorel at L'Auberge Bretonne, who packs his menu with nods to traditional local cooking, steeps roasted oats (of *bouillie* fame) in a savvy *crème brûlée* mixture. At the Vintage Café in Nîmes, Paul Salvador takes the regulation basil-and-garlic *pistou* sauce from *soupe au pistou*, and uses it to perk up a light tomato tart.

WHAT IS AUTHENTIC?

But how do you sort out the countrified from the real McCoy? The middle-class cuisine from the farm variety? The classic from the contemporary?

You could eat hundreds of meals in the countryside. That would instill the taste education that French children receive from the cradle. It would familiarize you with traditional foods and dishes and, consequently, enable you to distinguish among bona fide, ersatz, personal, regional, and newfangled examples.

Another way to gauge how a recipe fits into the thicket of regional offerings is to apply what I call the fireplace test. Assume you have only a wood fire and a few earthenware or iron pots, like most people in the countryside at one time. How manageable is it to make any given dish? The easier it is, the nearer the dish is to authentic peasant fare.

By this reckoning, you work out that such dishes as *kig ha fars* and *potée*, two boiled versions of dinner, come closest to cooking as it was done on the farm as late as the twentieth century in some places. The first frying pan didn't reach the perched village of Puget-Rostang in Provence until 1925, let alone a stove. And a frying pan cost the equivalent of half a fattened pig.

To be sure, each community and larger farms had a bread oven. But families baked bread only every two weeks or so, and *tian*, or vegetable-and-meat loaf from Provence, roast leg of lamb, and *petits farcis*, or stuffed Provençal vegetables, were prepared only when the oven had been fired up for bread baking.

More prosperous households, though, had a *potager*. In Provençal museums you see examples of these early stoves, made of clay and often beautifully finished with glazed tiles. They were built at waist height next to the hearth or had a built-in hearth, and their "burners" consisted of indentations filled with hot coals. You can just imagine the *daubes* and *ragoûts* that would have simmered there.

Today, real French country cooking can be traditional or modern, fancy or rustic. Whatever the style, country cooking in France is rooted in the regions' fertile farms and coastal waters. Even as contemporary cooks overhaul the classics with a playful regard for tradition, they do it with serious respect for quality. And when you prepare these recipes, you share in their tantalizing dishes, rituals, and, sometimes, tongue-in-cheek pleasures. ✍

SOUPS AND STARTERS

What's happened to French soup? From limpid consommés to silky bisques, most fancy restaurants shun them. There was a time, however, when no respectable evening meal ever started without soup. In humble rural households, bouillon, remaining from Sunday's pot-au-feu, was poured over crusts of bread, and with an omelet, potatoes or chestnuts, and a bit of cheese, made supper.

Today you have to hunt to find soup, and when you do, it's often relegated to the price-fixed menu. Yet, for some reason, mussels are deemed the stuff of suitable soups, and in every region of France, whether seaside or landlocked, mussel soups come into view.

Modest establishments usually offer only one choice—the same choice—puréed vegetable soup, which is no less good for its familiarity. But in country restaurants with unabashed regional bias, you can still hit on a few traditional soups: *soupe au pistou* and garlic soup in Provence; cabbage soup in Burgundy; chestnut soup in Brittany; crab soup in Normandy.

Though soups may have lost ground in provincial France (and in the metropolises, too), tucking into a main course without some kind of introduction still gives pause. Just what is considered an hors d'oeuvre *comme il faut* depends on the region, the tenor of the meal, and the season.

If you're in Provence and the entrée consists of a rustic yet dramatic stuffed cabbage, the appetizer might appropriately be a few local snails in a zingy garlic-and-basil sauce. Michel Bruneau, a Michelin-starred chef with a passion for the ingredients of Normandy, serves a warm, elaborate mold of sliced chitterling sausage to begin a meal of *haute cuisine normande*. At any Burgundian bistro featuring wintry *coq au vin*, a slice of jellied ham is always a possible starter.

Whatever beginning you choose, it should rouse the appetite, not quash it. Keep the portions small. ↜

SOUPE DE LÉGUMES VERTS AUX POIS CASSÉS

(ALL REGIONS)

Green Vegetable Soup with Split Peas

6 SERVINGS

6 tablespoons unsalted butter
2 leeks, white and light green parts only, halved lengthwise and thinly
    sliced across
1 rib celery, cut into ⅜-inch dice
One ¼-pound zucchini, cut into ⅜-inch dice
¼ pound green beans, cut into ⅜-inch pieces
¼ pound broccoli, cut into ⅜-pieces
¼ pound Swiss chard leaves or spinach, shredded
Salt and freshly ground pepper
½ cup green split peas, washed (the younger the better)
6 cups water

CROUTONS (optional)
4 slices day-old firm white bread, crusts removed
¾ cup vegetable oil

*I*n a medium metal casserole, melt the butter over moderately low heat. Add all the vegetables except the split peas, season with a little salt, and stir until coated with the butter. Cover and cook, stirring occasionally, until tender, 10 to 15 minutes.

Add the split peas and water, cover, and bring to a boil. Lower the heat and simmer gently, covered, until the peas are tender, 35 minutes or more, depending on the age of the peas. Skim any foam regularly from the surface during cooking.

Meanwhile, if making croutons, cut the slices of bread into ⅜-inch cubes. In a frying pan, heat the oil until hot but not smoking. Test the oil by dropping in a cube of bread. If it browns instantly the oil is too hot; adjust the heat. Add the remaining bread without crowding the pan and brown the cubes on both sides, using wooden tongs or chopsticks to turn them. Drain on paper towels.

Purée the soup in batches in a blender or food processor and transfer it into a large saucepan. (For extra smoothness, work the purée through a food mill into a large saucepan. The soup can be made to this point a day or two ahead and chilled. If it thickens too much on reheating, thin it with a little water.)

To finish, bring the soup to a boil. Add pepper and taste for seasoning. Serve the soup, steaming hot, in a warmed tureen, soup plates, or bowls. Pass the optional croutons separately.

This is one unforgettable soup French housewives prepare out of half-forgotten leftovers. It is so much a part of eating habit throughout France that if not all home cooks still make it from scratch, they pile quarts of the ready-made stuff in their shopping carts to take home for dinner.

Anne Oudin's version is unconventional in that she adds split peas instead of the standard thickener, potato. Use the recipe more as an outline than sacred text, the idea being that any mix of green vegetables goes here. If you prefer a more spartan soup, cut the butter to 4 tablespoons or use half butter, half oil. And you could leave the soup chunky instead of puréeing it. But then it would be a different soup.

SOUPE AUX CHOUX

(BURGUNDY)

Cabbage and Cauliflower Soup

8 SERVINGS

6 ounces lard, cut into pieces
2 slices bacon, cut into tiny dice
1 green cabbage (about 3 pounds), cut into 8 wedges and cored
8 cups chicken stock, preferably homemade (page 369)
8 cups water
Salt and freshly ground pepper
¼ large cauliflower, cut into bite-size florets
8 slices country or rye bread
2 fat garlic cloves, peeled
1 cup crème fraîche (page 368) or heavy (whipping) cream (optional)
2 egg yolks (optional)

*I*n a large metal casserole, melt the lard and render the bacon over low heat, 5 to 8 minutes. Add the cabbage, stock, and water and season with a little salt. Bring to a boil, then reduce the heat and simmer, uncovered, for 30 minutes. Skim the fat and foam regularly during cooking. Add the cauliflower and continue cooking 30 minutes longer. Transfer the cabbage and cauliflower to a dish with a slotted spoon and keep warm. Continue simmering the soup until it reduces to 7 cups.

If you have the time, chill the soup until the fat rises to the surface and can easily be removed. Otherwise, skim off as much fat as you can. (The soup can be made to this point a day ahead and chilled. Reheat it and the vegetables before proceeding.)

Meanwhile, heat the broiler. Toast the bread slices on a baking sheet under the broiler, turning once, until golden, 2 to 3 minutes. Rub the toasts with the garlic and set aside.

If adding the cream and egg yolk enrichment, whisk ¼ cup of the *crème fraîche* or cream into the egg yolks. At the end of the cooking time, add the remaining *crème fraîche* or cream to the simmering soup. Whisk a little of the hot soup into the egg yolk mixture and then whisk this mixture into the soup in the pan over very low heat. Add pepper and taste the soup for seasoning.

Add a slice of toast to each warmed soup plate. Divide the reserved cabbage and cauliflower among the plates. Ladle the soup over them and serve, piping hot.

This recipe is the upshot of my long-standing infatuation with a fictional cabbage soup, one evoked in a novel called La Soupe au Chou *by René Fallet. In this funny portrait of the clash between old-time and modern-day rural France— with a few extraterrestrials thrown in—a couple of geezers inadvertently lure a cruising alien with the smells from their supper (cabbage soup). In the end, it's this symbol of French country cooking that saves them and their outmoded way of life.*

I always wanted to taste a soup capable of stopping a passing spaceship. I found a likely candidate at the Auberge de la Beursaudière in Burgundy. But with cream and egg yolks, Serge Lenoble makes over this plain-folks' soup into a dish with social aspirations. For the real flavor of soupe aux choux, *leave them out. (This soup is also excellent finished like onion soup. Omit the egg yolks and cream. Sprinkle each piece of toast with grated Gruyère or other Swiss-type cheese. Float each in a bowl of soup and broil until the cheese melts.)*

Don't be misled by the hunk of lard in the ingredient list. Regular skimming removes the fat, physically, from the soup, while the lard's unmistakable flavor remains.

SOUPE AU PISTOU

(PROVENCE)

Vegetable Soup with Basil and Garlic

Acchiardo, a workingman's preserve up the street from Nice's open market, is one place to sort out gastronomic fact from hooey. Is the almost mythical soupe au pistou today the fantasy of nostalgic food writers or a dish with a heartbeat? For the waitress at Acchiardo, the question seems a bit odd. "Of course we have soupe au pistou," she says. "Did you want some?"

So we can continue to chop and slice for this chunky vegetable soup in the comfortable knowledge that it's not some sort of Mediterranean fossil. In the version from Acchiardo, the vegetables simmer in water until soft but not falling apart, making a clean-tasting soup base. The addition of fragrant pistou, *here a purée of fresh tomatoes, garlic, basil, Parmesan, and olive oil, is pure southern genius.*

1 cup dried white beans, such as cannellini or Great Northern
 (the younger the better)
1 branch fresh thyme, or ½ teaspoon dried thyme leaves
1 bay leaf
Salt and freshly ground pepper
12 cups water
2 tablespoons extra-virgin olive oil
3 leeks, white and light green parts only, halved lengthwise and thinly
 sliced across
2 carrots (½ pound total), peeled and cut into ⅜-inch dice
1 rib celery, cut into ⅜-inch dice
1 or 2 zucchini (½ pound total), cut into ⅜-inch
½ pound green beans, cut into ⅜-inch pieces
2 all-purpose potatoes (½ pound total), peeled and cut into ⅜-inch dice
½ cup orecchiette, anelli, or other small dried pasta, or ½ recipe Pâte à
 Crousets (page 15)

PISTOU

2 tomatoes, cored and lightly cut with a cross on the bottom
4 garlic cloves, peeled
½ cup extra-virgin olive oil
Salt
1 cup packed basil leaves
⅓ cup freshly grated Parmesan cheese

Soak the dried beans in plenty of cold water for at least 6 hours or overnight.

After soaking, pour off the water. Put the beans in a large saucepan and cover generously with fresh water. Bring them to a boil and boil vigorously, skimming, for 5 minutes. Drain and rinse.

Return the beans to the pan with the thyme and bay leaf, cover again with cold water, and bring to a boil. Lower the heat and gently simmer the beans, uncovered, until tender, 1 to 1½ hours, depending on the age of the beans. Toward the end of the cooking time, add 1 teaspoon of salt. Drain the beans and set aside. Five minutes before serving, add the beans to the soup.

While the beans cook, in a large metal casserole, bring the 12 cups water to a boil with a little salt and the olive oil. Add all the chopped vegetables and drop in the *crousets*, if using. Bring the soup to a boil, reduce the heat, and simmer, uncovered, for 30 minutes.

If using dried pasta, add it to the soup about 15 minutes before the end of cooking and simmer until soft, *not* al dente. (The soup can be made to this point a day or two ahead and chilled. Reheat it before proceeding.)

Just before serving the soup, make the *pistou:* Immerse the tomatoes, whole, in the simmering soup until the skin begins to peel, 10 to 30 seconds. Using a slotted spoon, lift the tomatoes out, then peel and seed.

Combine the garlic, oil, and a little salt in a food processor and whir until the garlic is finely chopped. Add the basil and peeled tomatoes and process until smooth. Pulse in the cheese. Taste for seasoning and add more salt if needed.

Add pepper to the soup and taste for seasoning. Serve the soup, steaming hot, in a warmed tureen, soup plates, or bowls. Pass the *pistou* separately.

"Qui a de la sauce dans son jardin, n'a pas besoin de médecin," *says a Provençal adage. This is the herbal equivalent of "An apple a day keeps the doctor away," with sage standing in for the apple. With all its curative qualities, Nicole Vernerey's sage-infused soupe à l'ail resembles nothing so much as chicken soup.*

Most garlic soup recipes call for a few paltry garlic cloves and a smattering of sage. Most produce a pallid infusion more reminiscent of herb tea than soup. But with 40 cloves of garlic, bundles of herbs, and rich broth, Nicole's version has depth and flavor. (At her restaurant, instead of using chicken stock, she simmers two roasted duck carcasses with water and the rest of the ingredients to make the broth.)

One of the best touches in this soup is the little homemade dumplings, called crousets, *which are worth the extra trouble to make. Still, if you're put off by the additional work, substitute four ounces of fresh pasta in sheets, cut into ½-inch squares, or even tagliatelle, snipped into small squares.*
Don't let the impressive amount of garlic dissuade you from making the soup either. Keep in mind that cooking tames the raw flavor, leaving a well-behaved taste.

SOUPE À L'AIL DE NICOLE

(PROVENCE)

Nicole's Garlic and Herb Soup

4 SERVINGS

1 bay leaf
1 branch fresh thyme, or ½ teaspoon dried thyme leaves
2 branches fresh sage, or 1 teaspoon dried crumbled sage
40 garlic cloves, peeled
4 cups chicken stock, preferably homemade (page 369)
4 cups water
Salt and freshly ground pepper
½ recipe Pâte à Crousets (recipe follows)
2 tablespoons extra-virgin olive oil

*I*n a large saucepan, combine the herbs, garlic, stock, water, and a little salt. Bring to a boil over high heat. Reduce the heat to moderate and simmer the broth, uncovered, until it reduces to 6 cups, 30 to 40 minutes. Skim regularly during the cooking. Strain the broth into another saucepan, reserving the garlic. Discard the herbs.

Meanwhile, roll out the *pâte à crousets* on a floured surface to as thin a sheet as possible. Cut the dough into ½-inch squares with a pastry jagger. As the squares are cut, transfer them to a floured kitchen towel until ready to use.

In a small bowl, mash the soft reserved garlic. Add the mashed garlic, the *crousets*, and the oil to the broth. Cover the pan, bring to a boil, then lower the heat to moderate and simmer until the *crousets* float to the surface and are cooked through, 30 to 40 minutes. Add pepper and taste for seasoning. Serve the soup, steaming hot, in a warmed tureen, soup plates, or bowls.

PÂTE À CROUSETS

Egg Pasta Dumpling Dough

8 SERVINGS

1¼ cups all-purpose flour
1 egg
¼ cup lukewarm water, or more as needed
Pinch of salt

Sift the flour into a mixing bowl and make a well in the center. Add the egg, water, and salt to the well and work with your fingertips until the ingredients in the well are thoroughly mixed. Draw in the flour, tossing, to form coarse crumbs. If the crumbs seem too dry, add a little more water. Press the dough into a ball and knead on a floured work surface until smooth, 2 to 3 minutes. Transfer the dough to plastic wrap, flatten it into a disc, and wrap well. Set aside to rest at room temperature for at least 30 minutes or, chilled, overnight.

Following local ritual, Nicole serves this soup at La Table de Nicole to begin le gros souper, *Christmas Eve dinner in Provence (see also pages 216 and 138). "You weren't planning to attend midnight mass were you?" she probes a couple of diners. "I don't think dinner will finish in time. . . . We'll celebrate mass right here!"*

Dainty squares of this dough, which is close in spirit to spaetzle, are set adrift in the Provençal garlic soup served on Christmas Eve. According to custom, you make a hollow in each square with your index finger to give it the shape of a scallop shell (coquille Saint-Jacques) and add a religious flourish.

The following recipe makes enough to garnish 8 servings of soup—twice what is needed— but it's hard to work with smaller quantities. Instead of dried noodles, add any leftover dough, rolled out and cut into shapes as for the garlic soup, to Vegetable Soup with Basil and Garlic, or chicken soup.

SOUPE DE L'ÉCLUSIÈRE

(BRITTANY)

Chestnut Soup

4 SERVINGS

In France, chestnut soup appears in cooking repertoires wherever chestnut trees grow. In the peasant version from Brittany's Ferme de la Bintinais, a museum of rural life just outside Rennes, chestnuts are simmered with beef broth, while fresh bread crumbs add bulk. A ladle of milk (substituting for the cream of bourgeois cooking) is stirred in for the finish.

Though I enjoy a change from the usual swirl of crème fraîche added at the end, I find the rustic bread thickening superfluous. (A spoonful of crème fraîche, however, does no harm.) And, to my taste, chicken stock makes a finer soup. Low-key, woodsy, smooth, the following recipe keeps the original character but is classy enough to begin a special meal.

For a silken soup, use a blender or food mill. In a food processor, bits of chestnut escape the blades, although the soup is still tasty.

1½ pounds fresh chestnuts in the shell, more if some chestnuts are bad; or
   2 cups peeled unsweetened chestnuts
4 cups chicken stock, preferably homemade (page 369), or beef stock
Salt and freshly ground pepper
½ cup whole milk

*I*f using fresh chestnuts, peel them: Make a cut in the rounded side of each nut, being sure to cut all the way through the outer skin. Put the chestnuts in a saucepan, cover with water, and bring to a boil over high heat. Take the pan from the heat and let it stand for 5 minutes. Remove the chestnuts, a few at a time, and peel them, making sure to remove both the outer peel and the dark inner skin that is attached to the nutmeat. Once any bad chestnuts are discarded, you should have 2 cups of peeled nuts.

Add the peeled chestnuts, stock, and a little salt to a large saucepan and bring to a boil. Lower the heat and simmer gently, uncovered, for 35 minutes.

Purée the soup in batches in a blender or food processor and, using a rubber spatula, scrape the purée into a large saucepan. (For extra smoothness, work the purée through a food mill into a large saucepan. The soup can be made to this point a day or two ahead and chilled. If it thickens too much on reheating, thin it with a little water.)

To finish, bring the soup to a boil. Add the milk and pepper and taste for seasoning. Serve the soup, steaming hot, in a warmed tureen, soup plates, or bowls.

SOUPE AU POTIRON

(BRITTANY)

Pumpkin Soup

4 SERVINGS

One 1¼-pound wedge pumpkin or other hard-shelled squash
1 tablespoon unsalted butter
1 medium onion, finely chopped
1 medium all-purpose potato, peeled, quartered lengthwise, and thinly
    sliced across
4 cups water
Salt and freshly ground pepper
½ cup crème fraîche (page 368) or heavy (whipping) cream
Chervil sprigs, snipped chives, or scallion greens, for decoration

CROUTONS (optional)
3 slices day-old firm white bread, crusts removed
½ cup vegetable oil

Peel the pumpkin or squash with a knife and cut it into 1-inch chunks.

In a large saucepan, melt the butter over moderately low heat. Add the onion and cook, stirring, until translucent, 3 to 5 minutes.

Add the pumpkin chunks, potato, water, and a little salt to the saucepan and bring to a boil. Lower the heat and simmer gently, uncovered, for 35 minutes.

Meanwhile, if making croutons, cut the slices of bread into ⅜-inch cubes. In a frying pan, heat the oil until hot but not smoking. Test the oil by dropping in a cube of bread. If it browns instantly the oil is too hot; adjust the heat. Add the remaining bread without crowding the pan and brown the cubes on both sides, using wooden tongs or chopsticks to turn them. Drain on paper towels.

Purée the soup in batches in a blender or food processor and, using a rubber spatula, scrape the purée into a large saucepan. (For extra smoothness, work the purée through a food mill into a large saucepan. The soup can be made to this point a day or two ahead and chilled. If it thickens too much on reheating, thin it with a little water.)

To finish, bring the soup to a boil. Add the crème fraîche or cream and pepper and taste for seasoning. Serve the soup, steaming hot, in a warmed tureen, soup plates, or bowls decorated with the herbs, if you like. Pass the optional croutons separately.

In bourgeois homes throughout France, the evening soup was generally simple like this one from Brittany, in which pumpkin, onion, and potato are simmered in water and then puréed until smooth. But in these affluent kitchens, a dollop of thick cream (as here), or cream, butter, and egg yolks commonly enriched the soup base. Also, croutons replaced the bread crusts of peasant cooking.

If your pumpkin or other squash is particularly flavorful (taste the soup just before puréeing it and don't forget the salt), you can skip the puréeing and addition of cream. This makes easy diet fare you don't have to be slimming to eat. But for a lackluster vegetable, a whirl in the food processor plus cream make all the difference. Other vegetables, singly or mixed, also take well to this treatment. (Cut them into ⅜-inch dice.) Try the recipe also with tomatoes, turnips, carrots, and zucchini or any other vegetable that inspires you at the market.

SOUPE D'ÉTRILLES

(NORMANDY)

Blue Crab Soup

6 SERVINGS

2¼ pounds lively small blue crabs
4 tablespoons olive oil
1 leek, white and light green parts only, finely chopped
1 carrot, finely chopped
One 2-ounce wedge peeled celery root, finely chopped
6 shallots, finely chopped
1 large onion, finely chopped
4 garlic cloves, sliced
1 fennel bulb, finely chopped
Salt and cayenne pepper
4 tomatoes, peeled, seeded, and chopped
1 branch fresh tarragon, or ½ teaspoon dried tarragon
1 branch fresh thyme, or ½ teaspoon dried thyme leaves
1 bay leaf
4 cups water (my preference) or fish stock

CROUTONS (optional)
4 slices day-old firm white bread, crusts removed
¾ cup vegetable oil

Cut the crabs in half crosswise. In a large sauté pan or shallow metal casserole, heat 2 tablespoons of the olive oil over moderately high heat. Add half the crabs to the pan and cook, turning them once, until they turn red on both sides, about 2 minutes. With a slotted spoon, remove the crabs to a plate. Add the remaining 2 tablespoons of oil to the pan and repeat with the remaining crabs.

Reduce the heat to low and add all of the vegetables, except the tomatoes, with a little salt, and stir until evenly coated with the oil remaining in the pan from the crabs. Cover the pan and cook the vegetables, stirring occasionally, until tender but not brown, 10 to 15 minutes. Return the crabs to the pan with the tomatoes, herbs, water or fish stock, and a little cayenne pepper. Bring the liquid to a boil, lower the heat, and simmer gently, uncovered, for 30 minutes.

Meanwhile, if making croutons, cut the bread into ⅜-inch cubes. In a frying pan, heat the oil until hot but not smoking. Test the oil by dropping in a cube of bread. If it browns instantly the oil

---

While La Verte Campagne, a stone manor in the Cotentin Peninsula of Normandy, couldn't be more rustic and snug, don't look here for regional specialties to match the setting. Chef-owner Pascal Bernou's menu is dominated by inventive fare with allusions to traditional ingredients and recipes.

In addition to his à la carte offerings, Bernou does a model prix-fixe menu, one that doesn't feel like second best. From it I sampled this soup featuring the small, native étrille *with little meat but lots of flavor. Bernou starts with classic crab soup and then embroiders, adding fennel and celery root, pouring the olive oil freely, and banishing* crème fraîche.

Choose the smallest blue crabs you can find, the ones usually left behind as requiring too much effort. Chef Bernou calls for fish stock, but I like to add water instead. Fish stock gives the soup depth and body. With water, the crab flavor is purer, undiluted by the taste of other fish.

is too hot; adjust the heat. Add the remaining bread without crowding the pan and brown the cubes on both sides, using wooden tongs or chopsticks to turn them. Drain on paper towels.

Discard any fresh herbs from the soup. Remove the crabs and set them aside. Purée the remaining soup in batches in a food processor and, using a rubber spatula, scrape the purée into a large saucepan. (For extra smoothness, work the purée through a food mill into a large saucepan. The soup can be made a day ahead and chilled. If it thickens too much on reheating, thin it with a little water.)

To finish, if you have the patience, crack the crabs, remove any meat, and divide it among warmed soup plates. (The crabs will have given most of their flavor to the soup anyway.) Bring the soup to a boil. Taste for seasoning. Ladle the hot soup into the soup plates, or a warmed tureen or bowls. Serve it steaming hot and pass the optional croutons separately.

SOUPE DE MOULES AU CURRY

(BURGUNDY)

Curried Mussel Soup

4 SERVINGS

There's no denying that the curry powder in Jean-Pierre Billoux's mussel soup doesn't come from Burgundy. (Neither do the spices for pain d'épices, the local spice bread. Yet no confection could be more characteristic of Burgundy.) Call it a delicious lapse from Billoux's restaurant, the Bistrot des Halles in Dijon.

Take care to use all-purpose or fluffy potatoes not new potatoes or other firm boiling potatoes, or they will hold their shape when you want them to fall apart and thicken the soup.

2 tablespoons unsalted butter
1 shallot, finely chopped
2 cups dry white wine
1 branch fresh thyme, or ½ teaspoon dried thyme leaves
2 pounds lively small mussels in the shell, scrubbed and bearded
2 small all-purpose potatoes, peeled, quartered lengthwise, and thinly sliced
2 leeks, white part only, or the white part of 3 fat scallions, cut into 2-inch matchstick strips
¾ cup crème fraîche (page 368) or heavy (whipping) cream
½ teaspoon fresh prepared curry powder, or to taste
Salt and freshly ground pepper
1 tablespoon chopped fresh parsley

*I*n a large saucepan, melt the butter. When it foams, add the shallot and sauté until translucent, 1 or 2 minutes. Stir in the wine with the thyme and bring to a boil. Add the mussels and cover the pan. Cook the mussels, stirring once or twice, just until they open, 3 to 5 minutes. Take the pan from the heat. When the mussels are cool enough to handle, remove the mussel meat from the shells and set aside; discard the shells and any mussels that did not open (see Box).

Pour the cooking liquid through a fine strainer lined with a double layer of cheesecloth into another saucepan. Add the potatoes, cover the pan, and bring the liquid to a boil. Reduce the heat to low and gently simmer the soup, covered, for 20 minutes.

Meanwhile, cook the leeks or scallions in a pan of boiling salted water until tender, 1 to 5 minutes, depending on the age of the leeks, then drain. Rinse them in cold water and drain again thoroughly.

Purée the soup in batches in a food processor and, using a rubber spatula, scrape the purée into a large saucepan. (For extra smoothness, work the purée through a food mill into a large saucepan.) Stir in the *crème fraîche* or cream and heat gently. Whisk in curry powder and pepper and taste for seasoning.

Distribute the reserved mussels and leeks or scallions evenly among warmed soup plates. Ladle the hot soup over them and serve at once, sprinkled with parsley.

A WORD ABOUT MUSSELS

What are lively mussels, anyway? They are shut tight or show signs of life—that is, they close when you handle them. It's a good idea to beard your lively mussels just before cooking them because they die after bearding. On the other hand, I don't hold with the advice that says to discard any cooked mussels that remain closed when most have opened. Simply remove the open mussels and continue cooking any closed ones until they yawn. At this point, mussels still closed should be discarded.

SOUPE DE MOULES À L'ORANGE ET SAFRAN

(BURGUNDY)

Mussel Soup with Orange and Saffron

4 SERVINGS

You can hardly get a more springlike dish than Gérard Fillaire's mussel soup. Yet, it's easily prepared in the dead of winter. At the Moulin des Ruats in Burgundy, he sets the recipe's gastronomic tone less by seasonal ingredients than by the soup's delicate taste and appearance. (The sun-drenched flavors of orange and saffron are only hinted at.) If you're looking for something refined but not complicated to start off an elegant dinner, this fits the bill.

To continue in the same contemporary vein, serve Braised Pork Tenderloin with Sage as a main course, and Apple Pastries with Black-Currant Sauce for dessert.

2 pounds lively small mussels in the shell, scrubbed and bearded
1 cup dry white wine
2 shallots, finely chopped
1 bouquet garni (1 branch fresh thyme, or ½ teaspoon dried thyme leaves; 6 parsley stems; and 1 bay leaf, tied in a bundle with kitchen string or cheesecloth)
1 cup heavy (whipping) cream
Pinch of saffron threads
1 small carrot, cut into 2-inch matchstick strips
1 small leek, white part only, or 2 scallions, cut into 2-inch matchstick strips
1 orange
5 tablespoons unsalted butter, cut into small pieces
Salt and freshly ground pepper
1 tablespoon fresh chervil leaves (optional)

*I*n a large saucepan, combine the mussels, wine, shallots, and *bouquet garni.* Cover the pan and set it over high heat. Bring the wine to a boil and cook the mussels, stirring once or twice, just until they open, 3 to 5 minutes. Take the pan from the heat. When the mussels are cool enough to handle, remove the mussel meat from the shells and set aside; discard the shells and any mussels that did not open.

Pour the cooking liquid through a fine strainer lined with a double layer of cheesecloth into another saucepan. Add the cream and saffron and bring just to a simmer. Reduce the heat to low and barely simmer the soup, covered, for 10 minutes.

Meanwhile, cook the strips of carrot and leek or scallions, one vegetable at a time, in boiling salted water until tender, 1 to 5 minutes. Remove them with a slotted spoon as they are done.

With a vegetable peeler, cut the zest off half the orange, leaving as much as possible of the bitter white pith on the orange. Cut the zest into very thin strips. Or better yet, use a citrus peeler to remove strips of zest easily. Reserve the orange. Cook the strips for 1 minute in the same water used to cook the vegetables, and drain. Rinse in cold water and drain again.

Gradually whisk the butter into the soup over very low heat so the butter doesn't melt completely but softens to form a smooth mixture. Juice half the orange. Add 2 tablespoons of juice and a few grindings of pepper to the soup. Adjust the seasoning, adding more juice, salt, or pepper if needed.

Distribute the reserved mussels, strips of vegetables, and zest evenly among warmed soup plates. Ladle the hot soup over them and serve at once, sprinkled with chervil, if you like.

JAMBON PERSILLÉ

(BURGUNDY)

Jellied Ham with Parsley

12 SERVINGS

Jambon persillé, *a mold of ham chunks; chopped parsley; and piquant, jellied broth, is one of the masterpieces of Burgundian charcuterie. Its shape and size vary: it comes in terrine loaf pans, square bowls with rounded corners, and plain round crocks, big and small. A slice, a wedge, or a hunk is cut for serving.*

While most jambon persillé *accompanies a glass of white Burgundy in a bistro or wine bar, Jean-Pierre Silva offers the following recipe in his two-star hostelry. At the Hostellerie du Vieux Moulin in Bouilland, slivers of the jellied ham appear on the table as a predinner nosh. This genuine local specialty is rarely found outside the province, so if you have a yen for it at home, you'll have to prepare it yourself.*

To make jambon persillé, *Burgundian cooks don't in fact use* jambon, *or ham. They prefer a mixture of inexpensive pork cuts destined for braising, including hocks and blade. (The lordly ham is saved for special occasions.) Also, the pork is salt-cured only, not smoked as for our country hams. A good* jambon persillé *requires top-notch ingredients and infinite patience to remove all skin, fat, and gristle.*

You cannot tell the degree of saltiness by the look of the meat. Follow the directions on the meat wrapper or consult your butcher about the length of presoaking time needed to make the salt-cured or smoked pork palatable.

3 onions, peeled, 1 stuck with 1 clove
6 large carrots, peeled
2 leeks, trimmed
1 fat bouquet garni (2 branches fresh thyme, or 1 teaspoon dried thyme leaves; 12 parsley stems; and 2 bay leaves, tied in a bundle with kitchen string or cheesecloth)
10 peppercorns
4 cups dry white wine (Aligoté is traditional)
4 cups water
7-pound mix of salt-cured or smoked bone-in ham hocks, Boston butt, and picnic shoulder, presoaked if needed (see headnote)
2 pig's feet, split
Salt and freshly ground pepper
1 tablespoon unflavored gelatin
4 cups packed fresh flat-leaf parsley leaves, coarsely chopped

*I*n a large metal casserole, combine the vegetables, *bouquet garni,* peppercorns, wine, and water. Bring the liquid to a boil, lower the heat, and simmer, covered, for 1 hour. Skim.

Add the meats and pig's feet and bring back to a boil. (Add boiling water if the court bouillon doesn't quite cover the meats.) Reduce the heat to low and barely simmer the ingredients, covered, until the meat is very tender, 3 to 4 hours. Skim the fat and foam from the pot regularly.

Transfer the meats and pig's feet to a carving board with a well and cut the meat into ½- to 1-inch chunks, discarding all skin, fat, gristle, and bone.

Meanwhile, taste the cooking liquid; it should be full-flavored. Boil it to concentrate the taste, if necessary. Pour the cooking liquid through a fine strainer lined with several layers of cheesecloth into a large bowl. Discard the vegetables. Measure out 4 cups of cooking liquid and save the rest for another recipe. Season to taste.

Put ¼ cup of the measured cooking liquid in a small metal bowl. Sprinkle the gelatin over it and set aside until spongy, about 5 minutes. Set the bowl in a simmering water bath and heat until melted, shaking the gelatin gently without stirring. Stir the melted gelatin into the remaining measured cooking liquid.

In the bottom of a 3-quart terrine mold or a glass bowl, sprinkle about 3 tablespoons of parsley. Pack a layer of meat chunks on top. Pour in enough cooking liquid to barely cover the meat. Freeze the terrine until the jellied liquid sets lightly, 5 to 10 minutes. Continue layering the parsley, meat, and cooking liquid (ending with the liquid) and freezing briefly until all the ingredients are used. Cover and chill (do not freeze) until the jellied liquid is completely set, at least 6 hours or overnight. (*Jambon persillé* keeps for up to a week chilled, but should be eaten quickly once it is cut.) Serve sliced or cut into wedges.

GÂTEAU DE BLETTES AUX FOIES DE VOLAILLES

(NORMANDY)

Swiss Chard Custard with Sautéed Chicken Livers

4 SERVINGS

½ pound Swiss chard leaves
2 eggs, lightly beaten
⅔ cup crème fraîche (page 368) or heavy (whipping) cream
Several gratings of nutmeg
Salt and freshly ground white pepper
7 tablespoons unsalted butter
12 chicken livers
1 shallot, finely chopped
3½ tablespoons sherry vinegar
3½ tablespoons port

To eat this dish, from La Verte Campagne in Trelly, Normandy, balance a little of the baked custard and a piece of chicken liver on your fork, then dab it in the sherry sauce. It's at once creamy, earthy, rich—with a hint of acidity. Enjoy it as an opener to a special meal or serve the Swiss chard custard without the chicken livers as a side dish.

*H*eat the oven to 325°F. Generously butter four ½-cup ramekins or custard cups.

Cook the Swiss chard leaves in plenty of boiling salted water (as for pasta) until they are wilted and tender, 5 to 10 minutes, and drain. Rinse in cold water and drain again thoroughly. Press out most of the water by handfuls. Finely chop the leaves.

In a mixing bowl, combine the eggs, *crème fraîche* or cream, the nutmeg, ½ teaspoon of salt, and several grindings of pepper, then stir in the Swiss chard. Divide this mixture evenly among the ramekins and smooth the tops.

Put the ramekins in a roasting pan. Carefully add enough water to the pan to reach halfway up the sides of the ramekins. Bring the water to a boil on top of the stove, then transfer the lot to the heated oven. Bake until a knife inserted in the center comes out clean, 30 to 40 minutes. (Check the custards during cooking; if small bubbles appear, reduce the oven temperature to 300°F.) Remove from the oven; the custards will stay warm in the water bath.

Meanwhile, in a frying pan, melt 2 tablespoons of the butter. Season the chicken livers with salt and pepper. Add the livers to the butter without crowding the pan, and cook them over moderately high heat until they are brown on all sides but still pink in the center, 2 to 3 minutes in all. Remove the livers with a slotted spoon, leaving the butter in the pan.

To the same pan, add the shallot and cook over moderate heat, stirring from time to time, until translucent, 1 to 2 minutes. Add the vinegar and port, scraping up any browned juices. Simmer until the liquid reduces by half. Gradually whisk in the remaining 5 tablespoons of butter over very low heat so the butter doesn't melt completely but softens to form a smooth sauce. Add salt and pepper and taste the sauce for seasoning.

Run a knife around each custard and unmold it on a warmed plate. Arrange 3 chicken livers on each plate. Spoon the sauce around the custards and serve.

FEUILLETÉ DE LÉGUMES À LA FONDUE DE TOMATES

(NORMANDY)

Vegetables with Puff Pastry and Tomato Sauce

4 SERVINGS

Set on creamy tomato sauce, neat sticks of orange, white, and green vegetables alternate around a brown pastry rectangle. This artful recipe from the Château de la Salle in Montpinchon is not difficult, but cutting the vegetables into even pieces and cooking them separately takes patience.

If you prefer, prepare only one vegetable, but make it special, like asparagus tips or fresh morels. Large plates are useful here so the effect is generous and not crowded.

½ pound best-quality puff-pastry dough
1 carrot, peeled
1 zucchini, unpeeled
1 small cucumber, unpeeled
1 turnip, peeled
Small handful thinnest green beans, trimmed
12 small button mushrooms, trimmed
8 pearl onions, peeled
1 egg, lightly beaten with a little salt
2 tablespoons unsalted butter
Salt and freshly ground pepper
Chervil or parsley sprigs, for garnish

TOMATO SAUCE
1 ripe large tomato (about ¾ pound), peeled, seeded, and chopped
1 teaspoon olive oil
½ cup crème fraîche (page 368) or heavy (whipping) cream
3 tablespoons unsalted butter
Salt and freshly ground pepper

Sprinkle a baking sheet with water. Roll out the dough on a floured surface to a sheet ¼ inch thick. Cut the dough into 4 rectangles about 3½ × 2 inches. Transfer the rectangles to the baking sheet. Chill the dough until firm, at least 15 minutes. Heat the oven to 425°F.

Cut the carrot, zucchini, cucumber, and turnip into even sticks about 2 inches × ½ inch. Cut the beans into 2-inch lengths. You should have roughly the same quantity of each vegetable. Cook all the vegetables including the mushrooms and onions, one at a time, in plenty of boiling salted water (as for pasta) until tender, 1 to 3 minutes, depending on the vegetable. Remove them with a slotted spoon as they are done. Rinse in cold water and drain.

Make the sauce: In a medium saucepan, combine the tomato and oil. Set the pan over low heat and cook the tomato, partly covered, until tender and dry looking, 10 to 15 minutes. Stir the tomato now and then during cooking. Add the *crème fraîche* or cream and bring to a boil. Whir this mixture in a food processor until smooth. Return it to the saucepan and gradually whisk in the butter over very low heat so the butter doesn't melt completely but softens to form a smooth sauce. Add salt and pepper and taste the sauce for seasoning. (Both the vegetables and tomato sauce can be made several hours ahead and chilled.)

To finish, brush the dough rectangles with the beaten egg. Using a sharp knife, mark a design (such as leaves or stars) on the top of each one. Bake them in the preheated oven until risen and brown, about 15 minutes.

Meanwhile, melt the butter in a frying pan and add the cooked vegetables with a little salt and pepper. Toss the vegetables in the butter over moderate heat until they are warmed through.

To serve, set the pastry rectangles in the center of warmed dinner plates. Spoon the sauce around. Arrange the vegetables around the pastry like the spokes of a wheel, but tightly together, alternating the colors. Garnish with the chervil or parsley sprigs and serve.

TAPENADE

(PROVENCE)

Olive, Caper, and Anchovy Spread

MAKES 1¼ CUPS

3 cups black olives, preferably from Nyons, pitted
4 garlic cloves, peeled
6 cured anchovy fillets in oil, drained
1 tablespoon capers, drained
1 tablespoon extra-virgin olive oil
40 thin slices narrow French baguette

*I*n a food processor, purée the olives, garlic, anchovies, capers, and oil until smooth. Taste and add more garlic, anchovies, capers, or oil until the spread is seasoned as you like.

Heat the broiler. Toast the slices of bread on a baking sheet under the broiler, turning them once, until golden, 2 to 3 minutes in all.

Scrape the tapenade into a bowl for serving. Pass the toast separately.

Chef Michel Lecuyer's version of tapenade is so tasty that it won't languish in your fridge like the store-bought kind. A smooth paste with a husky flavor, tapenade is one of those dishes that's seldom made at home because, while it's easy, it's also fiddly (all those olives to pit). But, as with raking leaves, you get an inflated feeling of satisfaction when it's done.

That old kitchen gizmo, the olive/cherry pitter, takes the trauma out of pitting olives. But there's an effortless way to pit olives if you don't have a pitter: Slit one long side of the olive with a knife, then squeeze out the pit.

Besides spreading tapenade on toast to keep you going while you study the menu, as it's served at Le Mas de Cotignac, there are countless ways of using this Provençal condiment. Add a spoonful to halved hard-cooked eggs, an omelet, or boiled fingerling potatoes. Slather it on a free-style Provençal sandwich, or on fish or rabbit after baking or grilling. Or try it in Pan-Fried Red Snapper with Tapenade Vinaigrette and Tomato and Goat Cheese Salad with Tapenade Toasts.

SAUSAGE WITH A HEART

Guémené-sur-Scorff, Brittany—Sliced, the *andouille de Guémené* looks like an edible version of a psychedelic poster. Countless concentric rings of chitterlings surround a heart of scrunched chitterling strips.

How do you put together this artful layered sausage? For Madame Guillemot, whose husband, Michel, makes it here at the family butcher shop, the technique couldn't be more obvious. She states matter-of-factly, "It's like putting on socks."

Of all the French sausages, only the Guémené andouille has this quirky construction. Most are prepared with more or less finely chopped meat. Or in the case of Normandy's Vire andouille (in Brittany the same sausage is called *andouille de campagne* to distinguish it from *andouille de Guémené*), pork stomach and two kinds of intestine are cut into narrow bands and crammed into sausage casings.

Two sausage makers in Guémené-sur-Scorff, a small inland market town, still craft Guémené andouille from scratch. At his *boucherie-charcuterie*, Michel Guillemot employs two workers just to keep up with local demand for this regional specialty. Together they turn out thirty andouilles daily, five days a week, the old-fashioned way.

THE HEART OF THE MATTER

To make his Guémené andouille, Monsieur Guillemot first thoroughly cleans the pork chitterlings. Two thirds of them are left whole. He cuts the remaining third into strips for the center, or heart, and then scrapes out as much fat as possible. Next, the strips and the whole chitterlings are stirred in separate vats with coarse salt and pepper—Guémené andouilles, like all sausages generally eaten cold, pack a highly seasoned punch.

Assembling the sausage always starts with the heart, or *petit coeur*, as Monsieur Guillemot calls it. The seasoned strips are tied in bunches at the top with string. They look like the wet fringe of a rug.

While this sausage has no legal hallmark protecting it from impostors, in bona fide Guémené andouille, the heart makes up not more than a third of the sausage's diameter. This being the easy part of the operation, lazy sausage makers often devise an andouille where the heart takes up half of the sausage or more.

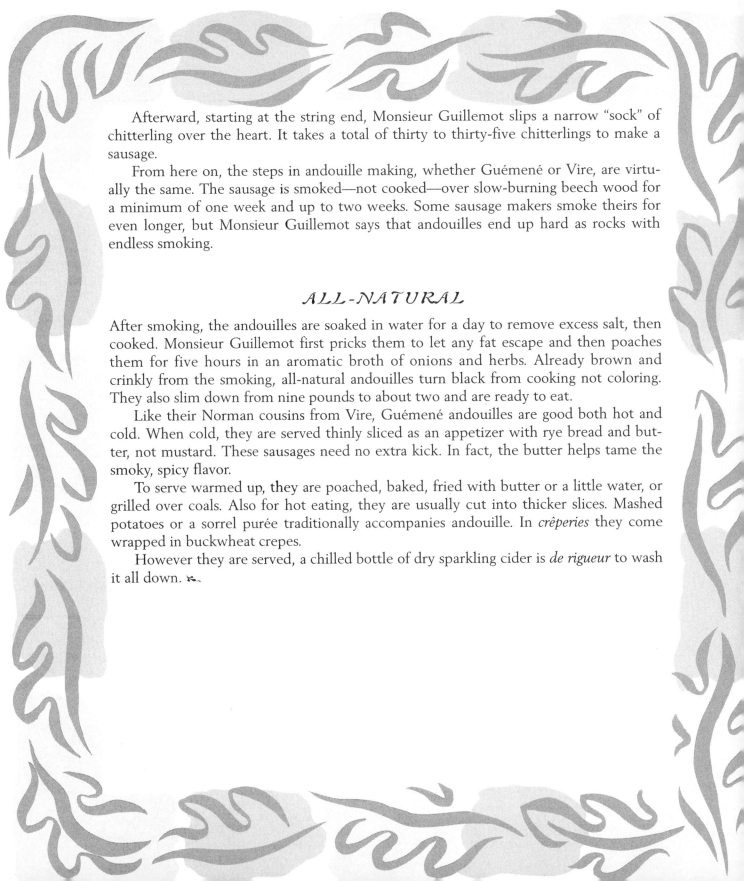

Afterward, starting at the string end, Monsieur Guillemot slips a narrow "sock" of chitterling over the heart. It takes a total of thirty to thirty-five chitterlings to make a sausage.

From here on, the steps in andouille making, whether Guémené or Vire, are virtually the same. The sausage is smoked—not cooked—over slow-burning beech wood for a minimum of one week and up to two weeks. Some sausage makers smoke theirs for even longer, but Monsieur Guillemot says that andouilles end up hard as rocks with endless smoking.

ALL-NATURAL

After smoking, the andouilles are soaked in water for a day to remove excess salt, then cooked. Monsieur Guillemot first pricks them to let any fat escape and then poaches them for five hours in an aromatic broth of onions and herbs. Already brown and crinkly from the smoking, all-natural andouilles turn black from cooking not coloring. They also slim down from nine pounds to about two and are ready to eat.

Like their Norman cousins from Vire, Guémené andouilles are good both hot and cold. When cold, they are served thinly sliced as an appetizer with rye bread and butter, not mustard. These sausages need no extra kick. In fact, the butter helps tame the smoky, spicy flavor.

To serve warmed up, they are poached, baked, fried with butter or a little water, or grilled over coals. Also for hot eating, they are usually cut into thicker slices. Mashed potatoes or a sorrel purée traditionally accompanies andouille. In *crêperies* they come wrapped in buckwheat crepes.

However they are served, a chilled bottle of dry sparkling cider is *de rigueur* to wash it all down. ⚮

FRICASSÉE D'ANDOUILLES AU VINAIGRE DE CIDRE

(NORMANDY)

Molded Chitterling Sausage with Potatoes and Cabbage

4 SERVINGS

2 tablespoons unsalted butter
½-pound wedge Savoy cabbage, finely shredded
1 shallot, finely chopped
Salt and freshly ground pepper
1 slice bacon, cut into tiny dice
1 pound fingerling potatoes, peeled and thinly sliced
¼ pound Vire andouille or other chitterling sausage
Chervil or parsley sprigs, for decoration

CIDER VINEGAR SAUCE

5 tablespoons cider vinegar
1 shallot, finely chopped
Reserved sausage skin
2 tablespoons crème fraîche *(page 368)* or heavy (whipping) cream
Reserved potato cooking liquid
8 tablespoons (1 stick) unsalted butter
1 teaspoon imported Dijon mustard
Salt and freshly ground pepper

An obsessive about Norman edibles, Michel Bruneau pampers rustic ingredients like spoiled movie stars. And it works. At La Bourride in Caen, he slices andouille de Vire, *the local smoked chitterling sausage, paper thin to use as a delicate shell for potatoes, cabbage, and bacon. The cider-vinegar butter sauce shares this dual nature, at once luscious and piquant.*

*I*n a medium saucepan, melt the butter. Add the cabbage, shallot, salt, and pepper. Press a piece of foil on top, cover the pan, and cook, stirring from time to time, over low heat, until the cabbage is tender, 8 to 10 minutes. Remove to a bowl.

Render the bacon over low heat in the same pan. Add the potatoes and stir to coat them with the fat. Add enough water to barely cover the potatoes, press a piece of foil on top, cover with a lid, and cook over low heat until they are tender, 5 to 10 minutes. With a slotted spoon, remove the potatoes and bacon to the cabbage and combine, tossing to distribute all the ingredients. Save the potato cooking liquid. Heat the oven to 325°F.

Peel the skin off the sausage and save it. Cut the sausage into very thin slices. Line four ¾-cup ramekins with the slices, overlapping them. Taste the cabbage and potato mixture and add salt and pepper if needed, remembering that the sausage is highly seasoned. Arrange layers of cabbage and potato mixture, slices overlapping in a neat pattern, in each ramekin until it is all used. (The chitterling molds can be made several hours ahead to this point and chilled. Return them to room temperature before proceeding.)

Set the ramekins on a baking sheet and warm them in the preheated oven, 8 to 10 minutes.

Make the sauce: In a heavy medium saucepan, boil 4 tablespoons of the vinegar, the shallot, and the reserved sausage skin until the vinegar reduces to 1 tablespoon. Stir in the *crème fraîche* or cream and, when it bubbles, add 1 tablespoon of the reserved potato cooking liquid. Gradually whisk in the butter over very low heat so the butter doesn't melt completely but softens to form a smooth sauce. Stir in the mustard, salt, pepper, and remaining tablespoon of vinegar. Taste the sauce; it should be pungent.

Run a knife around the ramekins and unmold them in the center of warmed dinner plates. Pour the sauce around the molds, decorate with the herbs, and serve.

HURRYING A SNAIL'S PACE

Blancey, Burgundy—Jean-François Vadot calls himself an antitraditionalist. "I always have to do things the wrong way round," he says.

But as a snail farmer in Burgundy, the land famous for *escargots de Bourgogne*, Monsieur Vadot sounds like a copycat. In fact, raising snails is little-explored territory. Snail hunters provide virtually all snails for the table.

As if to illustrate the scary novelty of snail farming, local banks balked at lending money to Monsieur Vadot. Yet in France, vineyard pesticides have so decimated the native snail population that Burgundy's canners must look to eastern Europe, Turkey, and North Africa for their supply.

So on his own, Monsieur Vadot became a snail-farming pioneer, making a viable enterprise out of a curiosity. Working on a vision and a hunch, he prodded and coaxed Mother Nature into speeding up the pokey developmental process.

Left to themselves, snails reach maturity in three years, with many drawn-out pauses for hibernation. With Monsieur Vadot's accelerated method, snails are ready to eat in three months. To achieve this feat, he stretches the snail season, which normally runs from June to October, to year-round.

HUMID HAVEN

In his nursery, Monsieur Vadot simply re-creates snail heaven—an eternally muggy summer day. The snails flourish in this greenhouselike setting, where light shines for eighteen hours at a stretch and humidity hovers around 100 percent.

For his breed of snail, Monsieur Vadot again defied tradition by shunning the local beige *escargot de Bourgogne* in favor of the *gros gris* from Algeria. Compared to the Burgundian variety, the Algerian snail thrives in a climate with less humidity. Plus, the *gros gris* is the only snail that lays eggs twice in its life, which makes it good for breeding.

Monsieur Vadot pampers newly hatched eggs, each measuring about the size of half a rice grain, in an incubator for ten days, then transfers them in batches of eighty to containers the size of a shoe box. After ten days, he removes half the snails to another container for ten more days so the developing snails have ample space to grow. Even at four weeks, a snail weighs only about 3½ grams.

At one month, Monsieur Vadot moves the baby snails to a noticeably unsmelly building with rows of ventilated nests, which look like mailboxes. Here he fattens up the snails for six to eight weeks. As Monsieur Vadot says, "You do your best to keep the snails happy."

How do you know if snails are happy? You watch them. Monsieur Vadot spends days and nights sitting in a chair studying his snails.

In nature, snails eat greenery. Constantly. Though they have no skeleton, they are solid creatures; the cellulose provides bulk. Monsieur Vadot feeds his snails with a mixture of flour, grains, and seaweed, plus "something special." While snails don't usually nibble at seaweed, Monsieur Vadot considers this fare to be the snail's return to its dietary origins. It's easy to digest, and the calcium beefs up the snail's shell.

ALL IN A DAY'S WORK

Just thinking about Monsieur Vadot's daily schedule would exhaust most people. Up at 5 A.M. to bed at 1 A.M., aside from tending his snails, Monsieur Vadot makes lunch for his children and looks after other farm chores. Fields still need plowing, planting, and harvesting. And there are the farm animals, too.

But today Jean-François sells all the snails he raises. Also, local scientists pester him for the secret. Another indication of his achievement: His snails are so good that Bernard Loiseau, pinned with three Michelin stars, buys them for his restaurant, La Côte d'Or, in nearby Saulieu.

When speaking of snail cuisine, a *sauce bourguignonne* means a composite butter flavored with garlic, parsley, and, sometimes, shallot. Every province in France has a version of Burgundy's snail butter. In Provençal cooking, basil may replace the parsley (see page 37). In Normandy and Brittany, the butter goes into broiled clams, mussels, and scallops on the half shell.

Although he's made a success of snail farming, it's not an occupation Jean-François would choose for his children. "I hope it doesn't interest them," he says. "This is no kind of life."

ESCARGOTS AU PISTOU

(PROVENCE)

Snails in Basil and Garlic Sauce

4 SERVINGS

BASIL BUTTER
4 tablespoons unsalted butter
2 garlic cloves, peeled
2 tablespoons chopped fresh basil
Salt and freshly ground pepper

1 tablespoon olive oil
1 small shallot, finely chopped
1 ripe large tomato (about ¾ pound), peeled, seeded, and chopped
1 small bouquet garni (1 sprig fresh thyme, or ¼ teaspoon dried thyme
   leaves; 3 parsley stems; and ½ bay leaf, tied in a bundle with kitchen
   string or cheesecloth)
¼ teaspoon dried herbes de Provence
Salt and freshly ground pepper
24 to 36 imported French canned snails, drained

*M*ake the basil butter: Combine the ingredients in a food processor. Process the mixture until smooth. Or finely chop the garlic and mash the ingredients together with a fork. Chill the butter until ready to use.

In a medium saucepan, heat the oil, add the shallot, and sauté until soft, 1 to 2 minutes. Add the tomato, *bouquet garni*, *herbes de Provence*, and a little salt, and cook, partly covered, over low heat until thick, about 20 minutes. Stir the tomato now and then during cooking. Discard the *bouquet garni*. (Both the basil butter and stewed tomato can be made a day or two ahead and chilled.) Add pepper and taste for seasoning.

Spoon the stewed tomato into four ¾-cup ramekins. Divide the snails among the ramekins. Top each with a tablespoon of the basil butter. (This dish can be assembled several hours ahead. Chill until serving time. Instead of broiling, as below, bake the snails in a preheated 450°F. oven until warmed through, about 5 minutes.)

Heat the broiler. Put the ramekins on a baking sheet and broil until the butter melts without browning, about 5 minutes. Serve sizzling hot with crusty bread.

To Grasse's floral scents (the town is famous for its perfumers), Maître Boscq contributes the aromas of relentlessly old-fashioned cooking à la grassoise. With his floppy chef's hat and pot belly, Maître Boscq prepares local specialties for twenty souls in his restaurant, Chez Maître Boscq, on a steep cobbled lane behind the flower market in the old town. If the sight of a man who demonstrably likes his own cooking isn't recommendation enough, certificates and awards hang around the dining room guaranteeing the quality of the master's hand. But why take anyone's word for it? Taste Maître Boscq's recipes for yourself.

MOUSSE DE SAUMON

(NORMANDY)

Fresh Salmon Mousse

4 APPETIZER SERVINGS

Philippe Potignon's salmon
mousse is good dinner-party
material for people you don't
know very well: It's a classic.
It works perfectly, and it's
tolerant—a few extra minutes
of cooking make no difference.
It looks like you've gone to
some trouble, but not overly so.
There's no fussing with bones.
And everybody likes salmon.

2 tablespoons unsalted butter
½ onion, thinly sliced
Salt and cayenne pepper
2 tablespoons fresh bread crumbs
¾ cup crème fraîche (page 368) or heavy (whipping) cream
1 tablespoon all-purpose flour
½ pound skinned salmon fillet
1 teaspoon Cognac, or to taste
1 tablespoon fresh lemon juice, or to taste
1 egg white
1 recipe White Butter Sauce (page 176)

*H*eat the oven to 325°F. Generously butter four ¾-cup ramekins.

In a small saucepan, melt 1 tablespoon of the butter over low heat. Add the onion, sprinkle with salt, and stir until coated with the butter. Press a piece of foil on top of the pan, cover with a lid, and cook, stirring from time to time, until the onion is very soft but not browned, 15 to 20 minutes. Remove the lid and foil and simmer to evaporate any liquid.

Stir the bread crumbs and 1½ teaspoons of the *crème fraîche* or cream into the onion.

In a small bowl, mash together the flour and remaining tablespoon of butter. Add this paste, the onion mixture, salmon, and Cognac to the bowl of a food processor and whir until puréed. Transfer the purée to a stainless-steel bowl set in ice water. Using a wooden spatula, beat in, one at a time, the lemon juice, egg white, remaining *crème fraîche* or cream, and salt and cayenne pepper. Cook a small piece of the mixture in a frying pan and taste. Adjust the seasoning in the rest of the mixture, adding salt, pepper, Cognac, or lemon juice as needed.

Using a rubber spatula, scrape this mousse into the prepared ramekins and smooth the tops.

Put the ramekins in a roasting pan. Carefully add enough water to the pan to reach halfway up the sides of the ramekins. Bring the water to a boil on top of the stove, then transfer the lot to the preheated oven. Bake until a knife inserted in the center of each mousse comes out clean, 25 to 30 minutes. Remove from the oven and the water bath. (If you're not ready to serve the mousses, they will stay warm in the water bath for a good half hour.) Unmold onto warmed plates. Pour the butter sauce around the mousses and serve as soon as possible.

SALADS

MÂCHE BEAUJE CAFÉ
8^F
200g

If good soup is hard to come by in France today, salads now appear here, there, and everywhere. No course is off-limits.

Once a salad accomplished small but important functions in the larger scheme of things. An integral part of the bourgeois repast, it teased the gastric juices into flowing for the entrée and vegetable. Afterward, as a palate cleanser, a plain green salad dressed only with oil and vinegar was *de rigueur*. Today a salad often *is* the meal.

The recipes in this chapter mirror the variety of salads now offered throughout the French countryside. Many of them, such as Salade Niçoise and Normandy's Potato, Celery, and Ham Salad belong to the old-time country repertoire. Others, like the upbeat Salad Greens with Warm Goat Cheese in a Hazelnut Crust from Provence, are a recent breed in France—both salad and cheese course in one. There are also elegant starters, like Artichoke Bottoms with Shrimp and Tarragon, and unglamorous ones, including Beet Salad with Vinaigrette.

Some cooks, seeking to lighten hearty regional dishes for modern taste buds, have recast those dishes into warm salads. François Lagrue's Green Salad with Blood Sausage-and-Apple Crown and Patrick Jeffroy's Salad of Greens, Fried Porridge Slices, and Bacon point up this kind of thinking.

In looking through this chapter, you'll find lettuce salads with all the fixings that can work like a meal in a dish. Oak-Leaf Lettuce with Mussels, Shrimp, Egg, Tomatoes, and Sardines is an example. You'll also see salads with endive or shredded cabbage instead of lettuce, and salads with no greens at all.

All the salads are for appetizer servings. An appetizer salad for four serves three as a main dish. ≽

SALADE DE CREVETTES SUR FOND D'ARTICHAUT

(BRITTANY)

Artichoke Bottoms with Shrimp and Tarragon

4 SERVINGS

Gérard Ryngel's recipe is just the type first-semester cooking-school students love to rail against. Why cut all the leaves off the artichokes? Why make over the spiky flower into an edible cup? Why not leave well enough alone? (Meanwhile, graduating students, flaunting technique, inevitably concoct edible treasure chests with the intricacy of nesting Russian dolls.)

The hard-to-strike balance between artless grub and overwrought packaging is one of the things that makes classic French cuisine the standard for inspired cooking. Tried-and-true flavor combinations are another. Only a genius could outdo the time-tested joining of steely artichokes with sweet shrimp (Chef Ryngel uses the local langoustines) *and aniselike tarragon.*

Tasting the dish at Gérard Ryngel's restaurant, Mon Rêve, in Brittany, a province where (especially on the northern coast around Roscoff) fields of globe artichokes stretch almost to the sea, and where small fishermen bring pink langoustines *to market still squiggling, you can only feel the classic dish has come home.*

ARTICHOKES
1 lemon, halved
4 large artichokes

VINAIGRETTE
½ tablespoon red-wine vinegar
Salt and freshly ground pepper
1 teaspoon imported Dijon mustard
2 tablespoons vegetable oil

40 medium shrimp, unpeeled
1 tablespoon chopped fresh tarragon
4 cups torn lettuce leaves, such as Boston or oak leaf
8 chives, cut into 2-inch lengths

Make the artichokes: Add the juice of a lemon half to a large bowl of cold water. Working with one artichoke at a time, break off the stalk. Then, with a sharp knife held with the blade flat against the side of the artichoke, cut off all large bottom leaves, leaving a cone of small soft leaves in the center. Lop off the cone level with the top of the artichoke bottom and discard all the small leaves. Trim the underside of the bottom to an even round shape. While you're working, rub the cut surfaces with a lemon half. As you finish each artichoke, drop it into the lemon water. Repeat for the remaining artichokes. Drain before using.

Cook the artichoke bottoms in plenty of boiling salted water (as for pasta) until they're tender when pierced with a knife, 15 to 20 minutes, and remove with a slotted spoon. Set aside to cool, then discard the choke.

Make the vinaigrette: In a small bowl, whisk together the vinegar and salt until the salt dissolves. Whisk in the mustard and pepper, then the oil until smooth.

Add the shrimp to the boiling salted water used to cook the artichokes. When the water returns to a rolling boil, drain the shrimp and peel them. Put the peeled shrimp and the tarragon in a bowl, add half the vinaigrette, and toss until evenly coated. Toss the lettuce with the remaining vinaigrette.

Line plates with the dressed leaves. Set an artichoke bottom on each. Mound 10 of the shrimp on each artichoke bottom. Strew each plate with the chives and serve.

SALADE DU PÊCHEUR

(BRITTANY)

Oak-Leaf Lettuce with Mussels, Shrimp, Egg, Tomatoes, and Sardines

4 SERVINGS

1 medium boiling potato, unpeeled
Salt
1 pound lively small mussels in the shell, scrubbed and bearded
12 medium shrimp, peeled

VINAIGRETTE
1 tablespoon red-wine vinegar
Salt and freshly ground pepper
2 teaspoons imported Dijon mustard
¼ cup vegetable oil

½ cup cooked rice
8 cups torn lettuce leaves, such as Boston or oak leaf
1 tomato, chopped
1 tender rib celery, thinly sliced
2 tablespoons chopped fresh herbs, such as parsley, chives, and tarragon
2 cured herring fillets in oil, drained and cut across into ½-inch slices
4 marinated sardine fillets, drained and halved
2 eggs, hard-cooked and quartered

*P*ut the potato in a medium saucepan, cover with water, add salt, and bring to a boil. Simmer until tender, 15 to 20 minutes, and drain. When the potato is cool enough to handle, peel it and cut into ½-inch dice.

Put the mussels in the same saucepan. Cover the pan, set over high heat, and cook the mussels, stirring once or twice, just until they open, 3 to 5 minutes. Take the pan from the heat. When the mussels are cool enough to handle, pull out the mussel meat, discarding the shells.

Put a shrimp flat on a work surface with the tail nearest you. Hold the shrimp flat with one hand. Using a sharp paring knife and beginning at the head end, slit two thirds of the way down the shrimp toward the tail, cutting about halfway through. Scrape out the exposed vein. Repeat with the remaining shrimp.

Set a nonstick frying pan over moderate heat. When the pan is

The Opéra de la Mer sits on a canal in Le Pouliguen, a stone's throw from Brittany's salt pans. A modern fish shack, it offers all the local seafood standbys: basic puréed fish soup, Moules à la Marinière, and a fisherman's salad—here a sampler of cured and marinated fish, steamed mussels and shrimp, with vegetables and rice thrown in for good measure. At this eatery, the salad practically makes an entrance: It arrives spilling out of a giant conch shell.

The haphazard heap loses none of its goodness for the lack of refinement. This sort of dish works well at home, probably better than at the average restaurant, because it requires no special talent, only fresh ingredients treated with care.

hot, add the shrimp and cook them without fat, turning once, until they are nearly opaque through, 2 to 3 minutes. Set aside.

Make the vinaigrette: In a small bowl, whisk together the vinegar and a little salt until the salt dissolves. Whisk in the mustard, pepper, and oil until smooth.

Combine all of the ingredients except the eggs and vinaigrette in a salad bowl. Add the vinaigrette and toss until evenly coated. Taste for seasoning. Arrange the salad on plates, setting 2 egg quarters on each.

SALADE BRESSANE

(BURGUNDY)

Warm Salad of Greens, Chicken Livers, Croutons, and Egg

4 SERVINGS

1½ cups ½-inch bread cubes

VINAIGRETTE
1½ tablespoons red-wine vinegar
Salt and freshly ground pepper
¼ cup plus 2 tablespoons vegetable oil

1 tablespoon unsalted butter
8 chicken livers, each cut into 3 or 4 pieces
Salt and freshly ground pepper
8 cups torn lettuce leaves, such as Boston or romaine
2 tablespoons chopped fresh flat-leaf parsley
1 fat garlic clove, finely chopped
2 eggs, hard-cooked and quartered

*H*eat the broiler. Toast the bread cubes on a baking sheet under the broiler, turning once, until golden, 2 to 3 minutes in all.

Make the vinaigrette: In a small bowl, whisk together the vinegar and salt until the salt dissolves. Whisk in the pepper and oil until smooth.

In a large frying pan, melt the butter. Sprinkle the chicken livers with salt and pepper. Add the livers to the butter without crowding the pan, and cook over moderately high heat until the livers are browned on all sides but still pink inside, 2 to 3 minutes.

Combine the lettuce, parsley, garlic, bread cubes, and livers in a salad bowl. Add the vinaigrette and toss gently until evenly coated. Taste for seasoning and add salt or pepper, if needed, until the salad is seasoned as you like. Arrange the salad on plates, setting 2 egg quarters on each.

Once you get past the rough bits at the Ferme-Auberge du Colombier in Vernoux—the hordes of French tourists, the sing-alongs—you find yourself face to face with Burgundy's farmhouse cooking. Catherine Debourg's salade bressane features the best of the Bresse barnyard. Chicken livers are cooked until pink, then tossed warm with lettuce, herbs, crunchy bread, farm eggs, and a smidgen of garlic. It's totally satisfying.

THE ART OF MAKING OLIVE OIL

Nyons, Provence—It is the day before Christmas, yet the Autrand olive-oil mill in northern Provence is running at full tilt. Stone wheels crush the ripe olives, and hydraulic presses squeeze out all the juice from the olive paste. You have to yell to be heard.

The olive-oil miller's labors peak in December and January when everyone else is celebrating, or recovering from holiday blowout. "We cram six months of work into two months," says Josiane Autrand-Dozol in a voice accustomed to combating noise. Madame Autrand-Dozol, a miller for twenty-two years, shouts cheerfully, "I was born in this atmosphere. I can't live without it."

Stacks of plastic crates filled with Verdales, Cayons, Souzins, or La Tanche, the official Nyons olive, begin blocking the Autrand mill's doorway in November, when the first olives are harvested. Lot by lot until the end of the season in February, Nyons's olives are pressed into the world's only oil with an *appellation d'origine contrôlée*.

"On Saint Catherine's Day," a Provençal saying goes, "the oil is in the olive." But around Provence, olives may be picked later than this November anniversary, depending on the variety, altitude, and whether the local taste is for a slightly bitter, fruity, or smooth oil.

MANY OILS, ONE METHOD

Whenever the olives are picked, the tools and the task remain the same. Pickers spread netting under designated trees. Armed with baskets and special combs, they lean their curious and characteristic wooden ladders—some are elongated *A* shapes, some are only a pole with steps and need to be gripped with the knees—against a tree. Then they climb aboard and rake the olives off the branches and into the nets.

Clients of Ludovic Alziari, Nice's most famous olive-oil miller, pay to press their crop of Cailletiers, the famous *olives de Nice*, in his 300-year-old olive-oil mill.

But in Maussanne-les-Alpilles near Les Baux, the 400-year-old mill with a vaulted ceiling works cooperatively. Over one thousand members take their olives to the

Coopérative Oléicole de la Vallée des Baux, which both presses the olives and sells the oil.

These olive growers must first weigh in their olives—a mixture of Salonenques, Grossanes, Picholines, Verdales, and Aglandaux. Then they receive a ticket for the amount, which determines what they will be paid.

Regardless of the arrangement between farmer and miller, and no matter which varieties of olives are used, to make *huile d'olive vierge extra*, the same basic procedure applies.

OLIVE JUICE

In the business, millers like to call extra-virgin olive oil, which undergoes only mechanical handling (i.e., no heating or chemical treatment), a fruit juice. The comparison is apt. To make homemade orange juice, say, you roll the oranges to break down the fiber and make them juicier, squeeze the oranges, and then strain out the pulp. The general operation is not unlike that for making olive oil.

For olive "juice," the olives are first washed and, in some mills like Maussanne's, stored in a loft for three days where they take on the temperature of the mill and develop special aromas.

Before being pressed, the olives are first crushed to boost the oil yield, a process called *triturer* in olive-oil parlance. Millworkers fill special tanks with 440-pound batches of unpitted olives. (The pits act like a natural preservative.) Double rotation takes place on a stationary millstone placed horizontally on the base of the tank. The vertical millstone turns on its axis around a central pivot, crushing the olives. Mills once harnessed water power to move the different wheels, which in turn moved the millstones. Today mills run on machine-driven hydraulic power.

Next, the workers spread the olive paste on two-foot-round mats of nylon, called *scourtins*, which both keep the paste in place and strain the oil. Traditionally, *scourtins* were shaped like *berets* and made of cocomatting, and the millworkers filled them with the olive paste. But the cocomats you see today are souvenir versions, which make unusual trivets.

To press the olive paste for oil, the miller piles the *scourtins* on the press, and the *margine*, or the olive's juice, a mixture of oil and water, collects in a tank. Modern millers separate out the oil using a centrifuge, but old-time millers, such as Monsieur Alziari, still decant the murky oil using a *feuille* or flat scoop.

Purists prefer nonfiltered oil, but many millers filter the oil through cotton to remove any *grignons*, or leftover olive paste. Factories buy the *grignons* to make cosmetic oil or soap. Horticulturists use it as fertilizer or as a nonpolluting fuel in greenhouses.

For one and a half to two months, the fresh "juice," or *huile primeur*, contains fleeting fragrances. When the oil matures, along with a gustatory change, it also turns from cloudy to limpid.

A MATTER OF TASTE

Though this process for making olive oil is common to all olive-oil millers in Provence, the resulting oils vary dramatically. In Maussanne, growers harvest olives *tournantes*, as they turn from green to violet, which produces a fruity oil (*huile fruitée*). Also, they mix olive varieties to make a well-rounded oil: Salonenques add fruity flavor, Grossanes lend a smoother taste, and Picholines intensify the characteristic green color.

The golden *huiles douces*, or mild-tasting oils, of Nyons and Nice are the product of pressing fully ripe olives. In the perched villages behind Nice, the olives are picked not only ripe, but already wrinkled. These wizened olives yield an oil that is clear as soon as it is pressed.

But the future of Provence's olive oils is increasingly clouded. "It's impossible to make a living from olive trees alone," says Suzy Ceysson, schoolteacher turned oil-cooperative director in Maussanne. "It costs too much."

There was a time when farmers didn't count the hours they spent as part of the oil's price. Today, farmers calculate differently.

Olive growers are only too aware that all the picking is still done by hand. They see that 220 pounds of olives produce only 20 quarts of oil, compared to grapes, which produce 70 to 80 quarts of wine for the same amount of fruit. To make ends meet, most farmers cultivate wine grapes or fruit trees, too.

Can a shaky olive industry endure? For Madame Ceysson the question is moot. "This is Provence," she says. "There's no Provence without olives." ✍

SALADE DE CHOUX

(PROVENCE)

Provençal Cabbage Salad

4 SERVINGS

*Winter comes even to Provence.
For a few months, icy air
chases the ubiquitous zucchini
blossoms and mesclun, that
stylish blend of infant greens,
from the farmers' markets.
People buy local cardoons or
just plain cabbage instead.*

*Jacques Mégean prepares a
cold-weather salad that makes
you forget winter's associations
with privation. When cabbage
is mixed with aromatic olive
oil, fresh herbs, and meaty
black olives—as at Le Vert
Galant in Carpentras—
chilly temperatures seem
quite manageable.*

*One 1-pound wedge green cabbage, shredded
Salt and freshly ground pepper
1 tablespoon red-wine vinegar
¼ cup extra-virgin olive oil
¼ cup chopped fresh herbs, such as parsley, chives, and tarragon
¼ cup black olives, preferably from Nyons, pitted and chopped
4 cherry tomatoes
1 egg, hard-cooked and quartered*

*A*rrange a layer of cabbage in a colander and salt generously. Continue layering until all the cabbage is used. Set the colander in a shallow bowl and leave for 3 to 4 hours. Press out the liquid by handfuls. Taste the cabbage. If too salty, rinse it, then press out the water by handfuls and dry in a salad spinner.

In a small bowl, whisk together the vinegar, oil, and pepper. (Salt probably won't be needed.) Combine the cabbage, herbs, and olives in a salad bowl. Pour the vinaigrette over the cabbage and toss until evenly coated. Taste the cabbage for seasoning.

Divide the salad among plates. Set a tomato and wedge of egg on each, and serve.

SALADE BRETONNE

(BRITTANY)

Tuna, Egg, and Potato Salad

4 SERVINGS

4 medium new potatoes (¾ pound total), unpeeled
Salt

MAYONNAISE
1 egg yolk, at room temperature, or hard-cooked if you prefer
2 teaspoons imported Dijon mustard
1 tablespoon white-wine vinegar
Salt and freshly ground white pepper
⅔ cup vegetable oil

One 6 ½-ounce can tuna, drained and coarsely chopped
2 eggs, hard-cooked and coarsely chopped
⅓ cup chopped fresh parsley
4 cups torn lettuce leaves, such as Boston or romaine

*P*ut the potatoes in a medium saucepan, cover with water, add salt, and bring to a boil. Simmer until tender, 15 to 20 minutes, and drain. While the potatoes are still warm, peel them and cut into ½-inch dice.

Make the mayonnaise: In a mixing bowl, beat together all the ingredients except the oil with an electric hand mixer or a whisk, or whir in the food processor. Slowly add a tablespoon of the oil and beat until incorporated. Gradually pour in the remaining oil in a thin stream, beating continuously. Taste and add more mustard, vinegar, salt, or pepper until the mayonnaise is seasoned as you like.

Combine the potatoes, tuna, eggs, and parsley in a salad bowl. Add the mayonnaise and fold the ingredients together with a large rubber spatula until they are evenly coated. Taste for seasoning.

Line a platter or plates with lettuce leaves and spoon the potato mixture into the center.

Along with every sort of pork preparation, charcuteries often sell salads like this one, plus rare roast beef by the slice, and a dependable plat du jour. Some dishes are the kind of thing better left to the professionals, such as eggs in aspic, or a terrine of foie gras. Many are home-style recipes, which housewives would make if only they had the time. Has some foreign dish become truly French? It has if the charcutier *makes it.*

We may dismiss the offerings (Burgundy beef stew, crepes) as old hat, but the French have never ceased to thrill to the charcutier's *repertoire. Besides being a fount of classic cooking, the* charcuterie *is today a chief source of regional fare. In Provence, for instance, you find the stuffed vegetables called* petits farcis *and* pissaladière, *the onion and anchovy tart. While in Brittany, I spotted the following salad in a Douarnenez charcuterie, across from the farmers' market. It's delightfully behind the times. For a speedy version, use ⅔ cup prepared mayonnaise instead of making your own.*

BOUILLIE D'AVOINE POÊLÉE EN SALADE

(BRITTANY)

Salad of Greens, Fried Porridge Slices, and Bacon

4 SERVINGS

VINAIGRETTE
2 teaspoons raspberry vinegar
Salt and freshly ground pepper
3 tablespoons vegetable oil

Vegetable oil, for frying
1 small leek, white part only, or 2 scallions, cut into 2-inch matchstick
* strips*
2 tablespoons lightly salted butter
4 slices bacon
4 slices cold Bouillie d'Avoine (page 147), ¼- to ½-inch each
4 cups mixed torn lettuce leaves, such as Boston, red leaf, arugula, and
* curly endive*
2 small tomatoes, peeled, seeded, and diced

*M*ake the vinaigrette: In a small bowl, whisk together the vinegar and salt until the salt dissolves. Whisk in the pepper and oil until smooth.

In a small heavy saucepan, heat ½ inch of vegetable oil. Add leek or scallion strips, a small handful at a time, to the oil, and fry until tinged with brown, 30 seconds to 1 minute. Using a skimmer, remove the strips to paper towels.

In a large frying pan, heat the butter. Add the bacon and render it slowly until golden, 5 to 8 minutes. With a slotted spoon remove to paper towels.

Add the slices of *bouillie* to the same pan and fry until brown on both sides, 2 to 3 minutes in all, and drain on paper towels.

Put the lettuces in a bowl, add the vinaigrette, and toss until evenly coated.

Line plates with the dressed leaves. Arrange a slice of bacon in the middle and set the *bouillie* slice on top. Sprinkle the tomatoes and fried leeks or scallions sparingly over all. Serve at once.

Even if you loathe oatmeal and refuse porridge in any form, you will still probably like Patrick Jeffroy's salad of something old and something new, served at the restaurant bearing his name in Plounérin, Brittany. The inspiration comes from the venerable Breton custom of frying leftover bouillie, *or oatmeal porridge, in butter. With meltingly soft* bouillie, *smoky bacon, the onion-garlic flavor of fried leeks, and a hit of fresh tomatoes and greens, Chef Jeffroy creates an appealing play of tastes, textures, and temperatures.*

Be warned that this is only for those willing to prepare the original bouillie *at least two days ahead, which includes standing over a hot stove for 1½ hours. (In Brittany you can buy the* bouillie *ready-made from special shops.) But if curiosity gets the better of your doubts, you'll be amply rewarded.*

SALADE DE PÉLARDON CHAUD AUX NOISETTES

(PROVENCE)

Salad Greens with Warm Goat Cheese in a Hazelnut Crust

4 SERVINGS

¼ cup hazelnut meats
6 ounces semifirm goat cheese log, cut across into 4 rounds
4 cups mixed torn lettuce leaves, such as Boston, red leaf, arugula, and curly endive

VINAIGRETTE
2 teaspoons red-wine vinegar
Salt and freshly ground pepper
3 tablespoons extra-virgin olive oil

*H*eat the oven to 350°F. Spread the nuts on a baking sheet. Bake until the nuts brown lightly, 10 to 12 minutes. Wrap the warm nuts in a rough kitchen towel and rub to loosen as much skin as possible. Discard the skin. Chop the nuts coarsely by hand or whir them in a food processor, pulsing, until they are coarsely chopped. Heat the broiler.

Press a scant tablespoon of chopped nuts onto each cheese round, covering all sides. Set aside the cheeses.

Combine the lettuces in a bowl.

Make the vinaigrette: In a small bowl, whisk together the vinegar and salt until the salt dissolves. Whisk in the pepper and oil until smooth. Add the vinaigrette to the lettuce and toss until evenly coated. Arrange on plates.

Put the hazelnut-crusted cheeses on a baking sheet and broil about 3 inches from the heat until the nuts brown and the cheese begins to melt, 2 to 3 minutes on each side. Watch the browning carefully, turning the baking sheet as necessary so the nuts brown evenly and don't burn.

Set each cheese on a plate of lettuce leaves and serve as soon as possible.

Grilled goat-cheese salads are almost a cliché today, but that doesn't make them any the less appealing. Usually I prefer plain goat cheese—without the fantaisie coatings of ashes, dried herbs, or spices you sometimes see. But I did like the following hazelnut-crusted version I sampled in western Provence. This is the land of Pélardon, as the local goat cheese is called.

The only trick to this salad is peeling the nuts. Don't worry about removing every bit of skin; some will stick inevitably. Other nuts can be substituted here, or you can use an assortment, like chopped almonds and macadamia nuts, though the latter isn't commonly used in France. And these varieties have the advantage of coming already peeled. Note that the short broiling time helps restore nuts that are less than fresh. You don't need to put these cheese rounds on toast while broiling because the nut crust prevents the cheese from melting onto your baking sheet.

SALADE DE PISSENLITS AUX LARDONS

(NORMANDY)

Salad of Spring Dandelions and Bacon

4 SERVINGS

Wild dandelions appear as early as February in the balmy maritime climate of Normandy's Marais-Vernier, the whorled sweep of marshland at the mouth of the Seine. These shoots are so tender and small (they're no bigger than a child's hand) that you can eat the whole plant, buds and all.

Near the Marais-Vernier in Pont-Audemer, Jacques Foltz adds these dandelions to a warm first-course salad at the Auberge du Vieux Puits. I think the slightly bitter greens are at their best here, set off by a zingy dressing, smoky bacon, and mild egg. Of course you can also use the larger, cultivated dandelion leaves you commonly find in the market.

8 cups dandelion greens
5 ounces slab bacon; or 5 slices bacon, cut across into ⅜-inch strips
2 tablespoons vegetable oil
¼ cup red-wine vinegar
Freshly ground pepper
2 eggs, hard-cooked and quartered

*P*ut the dandelion greens in a heatproof salad bowl.

If using slab bacon, cut off the rind. Cut the bacon lengthwise into ⅜-inch-thick slices, then across into ⅜-inch-thick strips called *lardons*.

In a frying pan, heat the oil. Add the bacon and render it slowly until golden, 5 to 8 minutes. Pour the bacon and fat over the greens. Quickly add the vinegar to the hot pan. (It will smoke and sputter so be warned.) Swirl it in the pan once, then pour it over the greens.

Add pepper and toss the salad until it is evenly coated with the dressing. Taste the salad for seasoning. Arrange the salad on plates, setting 2 egg quarters on each.

SALADE MOULIN DU PLATEAU

(BURGUNDY)

Ring Mold of Eggs with Mixed Vegetable Salad

6 SERVINGS

12 eggs
1 pound frozen macédoine of vegetables (diced mixed vegetables)
½ cup mayonnaise
½ cup chopped fresh herbs, including tarragon, chives, and parsley
Salt and freshly ground pepper
6 cups mixed torn lettuce leaves

VINAIGRETTE
½ tablespoon red-wine vinegar
Salt and freshly ground pepper
2 tablespoons extra-virgin olive oil

2 tomatoes, each cut into 8 wedges

Heat the oven to 350°F. Oil a 4-cup ring mold.

Break the eggs into the prepared mold, taking care to keep the yolks intact. Don't worry about spacing the yolks evenly. It will happen by itself.

Put the mold in a roasting pan. Carefully add enough boiling water to the pan to reach halfway up the sides of the mold. Transfer the lot to the preheated oven and bake until the whites and yolks are set, 20 to 25 minutes. Remove the mold from the oven and its water bath.

Meanwhile, cook the vegetable macédoine in boiling salted water until tender but not mushy. Drain them and rinse in cold water, then pat dry with paper towels or a kitchen towel. Put the vegetables in a mixing bowl with the mayonnaise and herbs. Using a rubber spatula, fold the ingredients together until they are evenly coated. Taste for seasoning, adding salt or pepper if needed.

Put the lettuce in a bowl.

Make the vinaigrette: In a small bowl, whisk together the vinegar and salt until the salt dissolves. Whisk in the pepper and oil until smooth. Add the vinaigrette to the lettuce and toss until evenly coated.

Line a platter with the dressed leaves. Run a knife around the mold to loosen the egg ring, then invert it onto the platter. Fill the ring with some of the vegetables. Arrange the tomato wedges around the ring. Pass the remaining vegetables separately.

There are some who would leave molded salads and all the fun of their presentation to French housewives (who have never tired of them). Not me. One evening at the Moulin du Plateau, a bare-bones lodge set on a hiking trail in Burgundy's Morvan forest, we were offered a hard-to-identify solid white ring whose center was filled with a classic macédoine—a colorful blend of vegetable dice in an herbed mayonnaise. The strange ring sliced into perfectly ordinary, perfectly done hard-cooked eggs.

This salade composée owes more to the tradition of French home cooking than to regional influences, but it makes an eye-catching display. What's behind the hocus-pocus? A dozen eggs are broken into a ring mold, then cooked in a water bath in the oven until the whites have set into an opaque ring, concealing the yolks.

You do not have to use frozen vegetables, as here, but it's easy and nothing to turn your nose up at. (French women have a knack for putting together fast and beautiful food.) By all means, use fresh peas plus equal amounts of green beans, carrots, and turnips cut into ⅜-inch dice, if you want to. You can get carried away experimenting with fillings other than a macédoine of vegetables, too. Serve the salad for brunch, lunch, or as a first course in a dinner menu.

SALADE CAROLINE

(NORMANDY)

Escarole Salad with Bacon, Mushrooms, and Cream

4 SERVINGS

Marie-Thérèse Jeanne prepares salads like this one, crepes, and more substantial food for the bird watchers, oarsmen, and ramblers who stop at the Auberge de l'Ouve, a riverside café in the Marais du Cotentin. There can be no more peaceful retreat from the usual hustle-bustle than these wetlands in Normandy, where the unhurried pace is set by grazing dairy cows and quarter horses.

I'm a fan of anything in a salad bowl, and I especially like the idea of a complete meal that includes fresh greenery. Marie-Thérèse combines smoky bacon and the delicate flavors of mushrooms, cream, and shallots with slightly bitter greens in this warm fall or winter salad.

8 cups torn escarole leaves, or other sturdy lettuce
2 tablespoons vegetable oil
¼ pound slab bacon, cut into lardons (page 56); or 4 slices bacon, cut
   across into ⅜-inch strips
½ pound button mushrooms (or chanterelles or oyster mushrooms), halved
   and sliced
2 shallots, sliced into rings
2 tablespoons red-wine vinegar
Freshly ground pepper
¼ cup heavy (whipping) cream

Put the escarole in a salad bowl.

In a large frying pan, heat the oil. Add the bacon and render it slowly until golden, 5 to 8 minutes. Push the bacon to one side of the pan.

Raise the heat to moderately high, add the mushrooms to the same pan, and toss them with the bacon until the moisture evaporates, about 5 minutes. Press a piece of foil on top and cover the pan if the mushrooms look dry to start. Push the bacon and mushrooms to the side and reduce the heat to low. Add the shallots and cook until translucent, 1 to 2 minutes. Stir in the vinegar and pepper. Add the cream and simmer a minute or two. Taste for seasoning.

Pour the hot mushroom mixture over the lettuce leaves. Toss the salad until it is evenly coated with the dressing and serve.

SALADE PAYSANNE

(NORMANDY)

Potato, Celery, and Ham Salad

4 SERVINGS

3 medium boiling potatoes (½ pound total), unpeeled
Salt and freshly ground white pepper
Juice of ½ lemon, or to taste
½ cup heavy (whipping) or light cream
¼ pound mushrooms, cut into ⅜-inch dice
⅓ pound best-quality boiled or baked ham, cut into ⅜-inch dice
1 rib celery, cut into ⅜-inch dice
¼ cup chopped fresh flat-leaf parsley

Put the potatoes in a medium saucepan, cover with water, add salt, and bring to a boil. Simmer until tender, 15 to 20 minutes, and drain. When the potatoes are cool enough to handle, peel them and cut into ⅜-inch dice.

In a small bowl, whisk together the lemon juice and a little salt until the salt dissolves. Whisk in the cream and a few grindings of pepper until smooth. (The cream will thicken dramatically.) Taste and add more lemon juice, salt, or pepper until the dressing is seasoned as you like.

Combine the potatoes, mushrooms, ham, celery, and parsley in a salad bowl. Add the dressing and fold the ingredients together with a large rubber spatula until they are evenly coated. Taste for seasoning and serve.

A ham-and-potato salad called salade cauchoise turns up in practically every book on Normandy cooking. But in my wanderings, I never saw this mythic title on a restaurant menu or in a charcuterie window. A virtually identical salad does, however, show up as salade à la crème or salade paysanne.

Never mind the name change. Tangy and bright yet creamy, the old favorite still pleases. I tasted the recipe here, not in Normandy but at Chez Marie-Louise, a bistro in Paris's out-of-the-way 11th arrondissement, where it's tagged as "salade maison."

IN THE OYSTER BUSINESS, CROSSING CASTE LINES

Plouharnel, Brittany—When Didier Militon turned his back on civil-engineering consulting to follow his passion into the oyster business, it was not at all what he expected. Today diplomas hang over the conveyer belt where he and his family sort the oysters, and he is considered the best oysterman in Quiberon Bay. But, asked if he would go through it all over, Didier, reflecting on his rough-and-tumble second career, shakes his head and laughs. He admits: "No, I'd never do it again."

Didier Militon's former work as a consultant kept him away from home for long stretches at a time. "I'd be gone three weeks, back one week," he says. "I never got to see my family. I made up my mind that before I turned forty I had to change my life."

So, at thirty-six, Didier started over. Like many white-collar professionals, he fantasized about the downwardly mobile jaunt back to nature. His grandfather had been a fisherman, and as a kid Didier had wanted to be one, too. "I've always loved it," he says. "I wore glasses, though. They told me real fishermen don't wear glasses."

BACK TO SCHOOL

In 1986, flouting convention, he registered for the degree necessary to raise oysters, a *brevet de conchyliculteur*. School was the first in a series of cultural stumbling blocks Didier would meet on his way to becoming an oysterman.

Since he did not grow up in an oyster-farming family, he had to take a grinding two-year course along with the normal run of sixteen-year-old vocational school students. By comparison, Didier says, not without a certain rancor, children of oyster growers take a shorter, lightweight course without all the theoretical science.

To make it through the marine-biology section, Didier was tutored by his wife, Michèle, a biologist at the hospital in Lorient. "We worked hard," says Michèle. "Every night. Weekends. We had to laugh when Didier, at age thirty-six, got his report card." He turned up at the top of his class.

As Michèle coached her husband, she learned about oyster farming herself. So it seemed natural when she decided to present herself as a degree candidate working independently. In the end, both the Militons passed their exams at the same time.

Armed with a pair of diplomas and the three-year-old oysters they had worked with at school, which were now ready to sell, the Militons were fixed to set up shop at Le Domaine de Kercroc in Plouharnel, overlooking Quiberon Bay on the south coast of Brittany. But the local officials denied them space in the oyster "parks" here.

OUTSIDERS GET COLD SHOULDER

Didier Militon read this rebuff as clannishness on the part of the oyster establishment. "We're not from around here, you see," he says, "and we had the audacity to succeed." What he means is that he and his wife were not raised in Plouharnel. He's from Quiberon, all of about nine miles to the south, and she's from Southwest France.

Still, they fought for space. There was no reason to keep them out and finally, they wrung one hectare, about two-and-a-half acres, out of the authorities. Getting a foot in the door meant no turning back for the Militons. Didier confides: "We couldn't allow ourselves to fail."

Like most oyster farmers, the Militons' work consisted of fattening up the one-year-old oysters (about the size of a child's fingernail) that come from nurseries and finishing them in special aging ponds.

France produces 140,000 tons of oysters a year, but not all these oysters are alike. Apart from the kind of oyster—and most today in France are the long *"creuse"* variety—oysters take their individual tastes from the bays in which they grow and the ponds or estuaries where they complete their aging. Variables include the degree of salinity in the water and the plankton that floats by on the tide as well as the sea bed beneath them.

REGIONAL WAYS WITH OYSTERS

Didier and Michèle Militon raise their oysters in plastic mesh sacks, called *poches*, laid in a single layer on metal "tables" about twenty inches off the bed. In Quiberon Bay, the bed is too soft to put the oysters directly on the ground (where they would sink in and disappear), as oyster growers do in other regions such as Cancale in northern Brittany.

Also because the bed is not firm enough, when the Militons go out to their farm, they use a *chaland*, a flat-bottomed boat. By contrast, the oyster growers in western Normandy, where the sea floor is hard-packed, wait for low tide and then putter to their farms on tractors; they are called fisherman-farmers and are considered farmers by the government for purposes of taxation and retirement.

But the differences between the Militons' oysters and those of Plouharnel's entrenched oyster growers run deeper than habitat. There's also the question of the oyster growers' divergent attitudes toward their work.

DEPARTURE FROM THE NORM

"I grow oysters as if they were all for my own table," Didier says. "There's no point in growing bad oysters. And you lose money with mediocre ones. But the people around here, they'll sell anything and sell them cheap. I wouldn't eat oysters from other people."

Their wildly differing backgrounds feed the conflict. As an oysterman who comes from another vocation, Didier can turn a dispassionate eye on old problems. When confronted with milky, spawning oysters, which customers didn't want to eat, he used his brains. "I applied science," he says. "Here when things go wrong they light candles at the church in Sainte-Anne-d'Auray. They're very backward in this profession."

To solve the spawning-oyster problem, he tricked the oysters into releasing their eggs by artificially mimicking natural conditions. Simply, he squeezed out the eggs by gradually raising the water temperature in a controlled environment as if it were summer.

Even after acquiring space in the local oyster park, however, the Militons still faced a problem. They had oysters to sell but no buyers. "Locals wouldn't buy from us," Didier says. "And wholesalers buy price not oysters."

In another act of defiance, Didier and Michèle shook up the closed oyster community by selling directly to people vacationing in the area.

Today, they even shuck oysters, grill a lobster, or prepare an entire shellfish platter on the spot for anyone who would like to enjoy seafood while enjoying a view of the oyster parks. Michèle also offers *far*, Brittany prune flan, for dessert.

"We like to have people here," says Michèle. "At least we get some compliments. Chefs come and taste our oysters when they're on vacation. In the winter, we serve in the work shed."

Michèle adds that their neighbors try to copy them. But their hearts aren't really in this newfangled way of selling oysters. She explains, "They won't even buy rye bread and butter for the tasting."

NO ICE PLEASE

In addition to selling their oysters at Le Domaine de Kercroc, the Militons do a mail-order business, which peaks around Christmas and New Year's when 70 percent of all oysters are eaten in France. They recommend eating the oysters raw, on the half shell. And when you prepare them at home, Didier counsels keeping them in the vegetable drawer of the refrigerator. "Don't put them on ice," he cautions. "Iced oysters have no taste."

As far as oyster cuisine goes, the Militons have a tepid appreciation of the idea. If an oyster is really good, their thinking goes, it's too good to cook.

Michèle and Didier's first crop of oysters amounted to two tons. Today the yield has climbed to forty tons, and they feel they are getting somewhere. "We made it through this thing," says Didier. "We're very happy with the work we have done. We sleep well at night. It's gratifying."

But with painful recollections still fresh, Didier has a hard time separating the business of growing oysters from the pleasures of eating them. While he snacks on them now whenever he's feeling peckish, he says, "If we ever stop, I'll never eat another oyster." ❧

BARBECUE D'HUÎTRES D'ISIGNY AUX GÉSIERS CONFITS

(NORMANDY)

Lamb's Lettuce with Grilled Oysters and Preserved Gizzards

4 SERVINGS

24 medium oysters in the shell

VINAIGRETTE
½ tablespoon red-wine vinegar
½ tablespoon sherry vinegar
Salt and freshly ground pepper
2 tablespoons vegetable oil
2 tablespoons extra-virgin olive oil
1 tablespoon chopped fresh tarragon

3 garlic cloves, peeled
2 tablespoons vegetable oil
1 tablespoon duck fat or additional vegetable oil
8 preserved duck gizzards, sliced; or ¼ pound slab bacon, cut into lardons (page 56); or 4 slices bacon, cut across into ⅜-inch strips
Salt and freshly ground pepper
8 cups lamb's lettuce or other salad greens torn into pieces
2 small tomatoes, peeled, seeded, and diced

Scrub the oyster shells. Open an oyster. Free the oyster from the shell by loosening the muscle in the top and bottom shells. Put the oyster on a plate lined with a double layer of paper towels and discard the shells. Repeat with the remaining oysters. Cover with plastic wrap and chill for 1 hour.

Make the vinaigrette: In a small bowl, whisk together the vinegars and salt until the salt dissolves. Whisk in the pepper, then the oils until smooth. Add the tarragon and taste for seasoning.

Slice the garlic cloves into the bowl of a mini food chopper. Add the oil and whir until you have a coarse paste. With a rubber spatula, scrape the paste into a dish.

Heat the duck fat or oil in a large frying pan over moderately high heat. Add the gizzards, season with salt and pepper, and sauté until lightly browned, 2 to 3 minutes, then remove. (If using bacon,

Set on the truck route between Lisieux and Deauville is a village dining room done up with sprays of fresh flowers, exposed beams, and antique finds (there's a wonderful enameled stove). Here, at the Auberge du Dauphin in Le Breuil-en-Auge, Régis Lecomte is rethinking Norman cuisine.

Monsieur Lecomte's à la carte menu contains mostly contemporary fare based on local ingredients. But from his menu du terroir comes some of the most interesting regional cooking around, such as this salad.

It combines, from nearby farms at Isigny-sur-Mer, oysters dabbed with garlicky oil and passed under the broiler, meaty preserved gizzards, flecks of tomato, and tender lamb's lettuce. To this mixture, Chef Lecomte adds a handful of sliced, sautéed mushrooms—button, oyster, or a wild variety—though I prefer the following streamlined version without the mushrooms. Preserved duck gizzards are available in fancy food shops, or substitute bacon.

render it slowly in 1 tablespoon vegetable oil until golden, 5 to 8 minutes, and remove.)

Heat the broiler.

Put the lamb's lettuce or other greens in a bowl. Add the vinaigrette to the lettuce, and toss until evenly coated with the dressing. Arrange the dressed greens on plates.

Turn the oysters in the garlic paste until they are evenly coated. Put the oysters on a foil-lined baking sheet and broil them about 3 inches from the heat until just warmed, about 30 seconds.

Scatter the gizzards and tomatoes on top of the salad. Arrange the oysters in a ring around the salad and serve at once.

SALADE DE BOUDIN NOIR AUX POMMES

(NORMANDY)

Green Salad with Blood Pudding-and-Apple Crown

4 SERVINGS

François Lagrue's salad, from the Moulin de Villeray in the Perche region of Normandy, doesn't try to hide its debt to the area's famed ingredients: apples and blood pudding. Yet, this chef rejuvenates the super-regional dyad, alternating them in a crown atop a refreshing green salad.

If you'd like to try boudin noir, or give it a second try, this recipe for blood-pudding beginners is a good place to test the waters of down-to-earth Norman cooking. Blood pudding can be found at German, Polish, and other eastern European butcher shops.

VINAIGRETTE
1 tablespoon red-wine vinegar
Salt and freshly ground black pepper
2 teaspoons imported Dijon mustard
¼ cup vegetable oil

4 small firm apples, such as Granny Smith
3 tablespoons unsalted butter
Salt and freshly ground pepper
1 pound blood pudding
4 cups torn lettuce leaves, such as Boston or oak leaf
2 tablespoons chopped fresh herbs, such as parsley, tarragon, and chives

Make the vinaigrette: In a small bowl, whisk together the vinegar and salt until the salt dissolves. Whisk in the mustard and pepper, then the oil until smooth.

Core and peel the apples. Halve them through the stem and cut top to bottom into ½-inch-thick wedges. Melt the butter in a frying pan over moderately high heat. When the butter foams, add the apples in batches, sprinkle with salt and pepper, and cook, turning once, until they begin to brown and are tender but not limp, 3 to 5 minutes.

Meanwhile, heat the broiler. Prick the blood pudding in several places with a fork. Put the blood pudding on a rack about 4 inches from the heat and broil, turning once, until sizzling, about 10 minutes in all. Cut the blood pudding into ¼-inch slices.

Put the lettuce and herbs in a bowl, add the vinaigrette, and toss until evenly coated.

Line plates with the dressed leaves. On them, alternate slices of apple and blood pudding, overlapping, in a crown around each plate. Serve as soon as possible.

A CANNY CANNER'S
VINTAGE SARDINES

Quiberon, Brittany—Canned sardines typically conjure up a ho-hum pick-me-up, useful only when the cupboard's bare. But vintage sardines, stamped with a date and aged like wine, were once so prized that classy restaurants served them still in the can so diners could inspect the label.

"Sardines get better with age," says Georges Hilliet. Monsieur Hilliet and his brother, Bernard, run La Belle-Îloise, one of two remaining fish canneries in Quiberon, a fishing port, resort, and link to Belle-Île, the largest of Brittany's charming islands with whitewashed houses and small farms.

"One year of aging is good," he says. "Two years is even better. It works by osmosis like a good wine."

According to legend, fish canning started in Nantes in the nineteenth century, the brainchild of a transplanted Parisian *confiseur*, or candymaker, named Colin. He applied his candy-preserving skills to the sardines and tuna fish that migrated to southern Brittany in the summer, and a new industry was born.

Soon *confiseurs*, here meaning canners instead of candymakers, appeared wherever independent fishermen brought in a daily catch—Belle-Île, Quiberon, Lorient, and Concarneau, to name several ports. The industry peaked quickly and then fizzled out in the 1950s and '60s with competition from cheap labor and fish prices in Portugal and Morocco.

Monsieur Hilliet's father, Georges senior, launched the family business in 1932, canning's heyday. But La Belle-Îloise slumped in the sixties along with Quiberon's thirteen other *confiseurs* and the rest of the Breton canners, leaving them to scramble for customers in the face of cheap imports. "We couldn't sell to distributors working with the supermarket chains," says Monsieur Hilliet. "All they care about is price. Quality is an afterthought."

FOR LOVE NOT MONEY

Eventually, the family moved into a newly minted market niche. They decided to stick to traditional canning ways and offer a topflight sardine. "We hesitated," says Monsieur Hilliet. "We chose quality."

Instead of selling their canned fish to distributors, they chose the novel route of direct sale to the many vacationers who come to Quiberon and Belle-Île each year.

Clinging to the old ways means putting up the fresh catch each day as it arrives and following the fishing season. In sync with the migrating fish, the work force at La Belle-Îloise drops from a hundred people in the summer to twenty off-season. By comparison, most canneries operate steadily year-round, using frozen fish. But as Monsieur Hilliet explains, small fatty fish like sardines oxidize easily and don't take well to freezing.

With the decline of sardines off the Breton coast, the search for fresh fish has forced Monsieur Hilliet to work with fish pulled in from the Mediterranean as well as off Brittany. Sometimes there's no fish at all. In bad weather, for instance, small fishermen stay home when turbulent water could wreck their fishing nets.

Apart from using fresh sardines, Monsieur Hilliet makes better canned fish because at La Belle-Îloise much of the work is still done by hand.

MANUAL LABOR

Sardinières here still begin by removing the guts with their fingers. This way the flesh remains intact. In most canneries, machines take care of the evisceration. This does save labor, but for connoisseurs of canned sardines, the result isn't satisfying. Part of the innards always stays in the fish, and the fish looks battered.

At La Belle-Îloise, machinery kicks in after evisceration. Workers put the fish on a conveyer belt of grill racks, which passes through a tunnel of water jets for washing the sardines, through a hot-air tunnel for drying, and into a deep-fryer.

When the sardines emerge, workers are ready with scissors to snip off the head, and the tail if needed, so the sardines fit neatly into the cans. They arrange them silvery side down so the presentation is perfect. The cans are then sterilized, and the prepared sardines cure in extra-virgin olive oil or in nine other sauces.

In the canning process anywhere else, raw sardines go directly into cans with salt and vegetable oil and then they are steam-cooked.

With so much hand labor, the sardines at La Belle-Îloise take four times longer to process than in the average cannery. "There were difficult years," admits Monsieur Hilliet. "Our way was more expensive."

Still, some people recognized a difference between canned sardines from La Belle-Îloise and the supermarket variety. And they told their friends and relatives.

Today, in summertime, the boutique here is packed with tourists in bathing suits stocking up on not only sardines in extra-virgin olive oil, but hand-packed germon tuna, mackerel, fish soup, fish mousses, and sauces to accompany fish.

But you don't have to go to Quiberon to taste La Belle-Îloise products. They are also sold by mail order and, in Paris, Fauchon stocks La Belle-Îloise brand under their house label.

What about aging the canned sardines? "Sardines keep almost forever," says Monsieur Hilliet. He explains that the problem is the cans. The metal eventually oxidizes, so you should hold canned sardines no longer than four or five years. (Turn them from time to time.) But to get the special vintage taste, Monsieur Hilliet considers a year of aging the minimum.

For La Belle-Îloise, the gamble to cultivate a more sophisticated niche in the marketplace worked. Says Georges Hilliet: "We're still here." ⌦

SALADE POUL-FÉTAN

(BRITTANY)

Bread Salad with Tomatoes and Greens

4 SERVINGS

The 16th-century granite houses of Poul-Fétan near Quistinic in eastern Brittany were no more than rubble heaps until a band of dedicated locals fought to save their crumbling heritage. Today, during the summer months, you can visit this restored village of farmers and weavers and envision a vanished way of life.

At the auberge in Poul-Fétan, you can actually taste the kind of food that was once daily fare here, such as Bouillie d'Avoine, an oat porridge, and this bread salad. Although it sounds like hardship food, bread salad really grows on you. If you've ever swished a crust of bread in a puddle of salad dressing, you know what I mean. (To be sure, in its heyday, farm wives used homemade sourdough bread not baguette, which hadn't yet been invented.)

To make the salad into a more substantial meal—and more "gourmet"—accompany it with a dish of vintage cured Brittany sardines, aged at least a year. This canned fish has cachet.

4 cups narrow French baguette or Italian bread cut into ¼–½-inch slices

VINAIGRETTE
2 tablespoons red-wine vinegar
Salt and freshly ground black pepper
½ cup vegetable oil

4 cups mixed torn lettuce leaves, such as Boston, red leaf, arugula, and oak leaf
4 small tomatoes, each cut into 6 wedges

*H*eat the broiler. Toast the bread slices on a baking sheet under the broiler, turning once, until golden, 2 to 3 minutes in all.

Make the vinaigrette: In a small bowl, whisk together the vinegar and salt until the salt dissolves. Whisk in the pepper and oil until smooth.

Cover a platter or plates with the lettuces. Arrange the tomatoes around the edge. Pile the toasts in the center. Pour the vinaigrette over the salad and serve.

SALADE LA STRADA

(BURGUNDY)

La Strada's Salad with Herbs and Garlic

4 SERVINGS

VINAIGRETTE
1 tablespoon red-wine vinegar
Salt and freshly ground pepper
2 teaspoons imported Dijon mustard
2 tablespoons extra-virgin olive oil
2 tablespoons vegetable oil

*6 cups mixed torn lettuce leaves, such as Boston, red leaf, arugula, and
    curly endive*
1 cup shredded red cabbage or a mix of red and green
*¾ cup fresh whole herb leaves, such as basil, thyme, tarragon, parsley,
    chervil, chives*
1 tomato, halved and sliced
1 garlic clove, finely chopped
½ cup freshly grated Gruyère or other Swiss-type cheese
4 cured anchovy fillets in oil, drained and halved
¼ cup black olives, preferably from Nice
One 3¼-ounce can tuna, drained and coarsely chopped

Imagine a dining room set in a Burgundian flea market and you've got La Strada. Ancestral portraits hang next to the chimney, flowered oilcloth covers the tables, and shelves hold dried flowers, soup tureens, sugar canisters, and Grandma's plates. As for the cooking, the style is friendly, not fussy, such as this tossed salad. With Northern cabbage and Gruyère cheese, Provençal olives and anchovies, it's a crossroads collection of ingredients, much like Burgundy itself.

*M*ake the vinaigrette: In a small bowl, whisk together the vinegar and salt until the salt dissolves. Whisk in the mustard and pepper, then the oils until smooth. Taste for seasoning.

Combine the remaining ingredients in a salad bowl. Add the vinaigrette and toss until evenly coated. Taste again, adjust the seasoning if necessary, and serve.

SALAD DAYS IN PROVENCE

You can't love salads without loving Provence. Provence's markets are the best place to indulge in a salad shopping spree.

In old Nice, on the Cours Saleya, merchants hawk a roster of possibilities for the salad bowl: sweet red peppers; mesclun (a mixture of salad sprouts rather than full-fledged leaves); purple-tipped asparagus; piles of braided pink garlic; green, cracked olives flavored with rosemary; tiny black olives swimming in barrels of brine; artichokes the size of a child's hand; fat bunches of basil; tomatoes that taste like tomatoes.

But why stop with salad? Zucchini blossoms soak in plastic buckets. The bright orange flowers turn up on menus in the neighborhood, deep-fried or stuffed with fresh Brousse (sheep-milk cheese), along with polenta, ravioli, and pizza—all edible reminders that Nice was once part of Liguria.

In fall and winter, Swiss chard, cardoons, wild mushrooms, walnuts, chestnuts, clementines, quinces, pumpkins, fennel, and wrinkled black olives to cure at home all crowd the market stalls.

Niçois cooks still prepare age-old specialties, including *soupe au pistou* (vegetable soup with basil and garlic), *trouchia* (Swiss-chard omelet), *farcis* (stuffed vegetables), *brissauda* (Provençal cheese and olive oil toasts), and *pissaladière* (onion and olive pizza). With these Provençal names, even the average Frenchman needs a food glossary to read a local menu.

WORLDLY FISH

In Cannes, the fish section at the Forville market spotlights this sophisticated town's taste. A dozen fishwives, in makeup and high heels, sell the morning's catch. It's a small yield but glorious. The fish was caught just three to five hours ago by the twenty or so local fishermen in the Bay of Cannes, beyond the sleek yachts. Within hours, local cooks will serve the fish for lunch.

The tiny rockfish and scorpion fish will go into *bourride* (a local fish soup). The stiff salt cod will be soaked and pounded for *brandade*, a silken purée flavored with olive oil and garlic. One restaurateur waits around for enough *rougets*, a tiny version of red snapper, to be able to serve it for lunch, sautéed in olive oil, with a black-olive vinaigrette.

Away from the glittering Riviera, in the mountains behind the coast, the earth is dry, the sun unrelenting. Lavender, planted in straight rows, seems to grow everywhere, filling the air with its scent and making you sneeze. Sheep and goats graze in the foothills on sparse grass, rosemary, and thyme. Naturally, markets here are full of lavender honey and sheep and goat cheeses, pressed with sprigs of fresh summer savory.

The Provençal repertoire boasts dozens of lamb dishes, including *gigot à la crème d'ail*, a roast leg of lamb with creamy garlic toasts, *aillade d'agneau*—sometimes lamb roast patted with garlic, bread crumbs, and parsley, sometimes a garlicky lamb casserole—and *daube d'agneau*, a stew of lamb, herbs, and red wine.

OF BULLS AND BULLFIGHTING

In the Camargue's wild marshlands, where the Rhone River meets the Mediterranean, there's yet another Provence. *Manadiers* breed bulls and horses on ranches here, and bullfighting buffs fill the local Roman amphitheaters in Arles and Nîmes. The love of bullfighting is matched by a passion for bull's meat. Butchers in the Camargue sell *saucisson d'Arles*, a spicy sausage made with pork and bull's meat, as well as fresh bull's meat for making *gardiane*, a local stew.

As noon approaches, the merchants' shouts grow louder and more strident. Now's the time to pick up a crate of figs for a song or down the last of your pastis before puttering home along the sycamore-lined lanes. If you have to battle the frosty Mistral, the wind that barrels down the Rhone Valley, at least you can look forward to a warming lamb *daube* or, if the sun is shining, a salad of Provence's incomparable ingredients. ❧

À LA PROVENÇALE

Ingredients that Make a Dish Typically Provencal

Mesclun
Asparagus
Garlic
Olives
Olive oil
Capers
Artichokes
Basil
Herbes de Provence
Tomatoes
Eggplant
Zucchini blossoms
Cavaillon melons
Figs
Brousse (fresh sheep's cheese)
Banon (sheep's or goat's cheese wrapped in chestnut leaves)
Polenta
Chick-peas
Swiss chard
Cardoons
Truffles
Rockfish
Scorpion fish
Squid
Salt cod
Lavender honey
Calissons d'Aix
Montélimar nougat
Candied fruit from Apt
Lamb
Bull's meat
Linden blossoms
Orange-flower water
Côtes du Rhône wines
Côtes de Provence wines
Pastis

SALADE DE TOMATES MAS DE COTIGNAC

(PROVENCE)

Tomato and Goat-Cheese Salad with Tapenade Toasts

4 SERVINGS

2 tablespoons pine nuts
12 thin slices narrow French baguette
¼ cup Tapenade (page 30)

VINAIGRETTE
1 tablespoon red-wine vinegar
Salt and freshly ground pepper
¼ cup extra-virgin olive oil

8 cups mixed torn lettuce leaves, such as Boston, red leaf, arugula, and oak
   leaf
4 small tomatoes, each cut into 6 wedges
4 ounces soft goat cheese, sliced
8 large basil leaves, torn in half

One bite of Chef Michel Lecuyer's sophisticated-peasant salad makes you think of a whirl through a Provençal market. Tapenade toasts ring a mélange of tossed greens, basil, toasted pine nuts, ripe summer tomatoes, and soft goat cheese. (Monsieur Lecuyer also adds the local Brousse, or sheep-milk cheese.) This cool summer salad seems to taste best poolside, in a silvery olive grove—as at the Mas de Cotignac.

*H*eat the oven to 350°F. Spread the pine nuts on a baking sheet. Bake until the nuts brown lightly, 3 to 5 minutes.

Heat the broiler. Toast the bread slices on a baking sheet under the broiler, turning them once, until golden, 2 to 3 minutes in all. Spread the toasts with tapenade and set aside.

Make the vinaigrette: In a small bowl, whisk together the vinegar and salt until the salt dissolves. Whisk in the pepper and oil until smooth.

Combine the lettuces, tomatoes, cheese, toasted pine nuts, and basil in a salad bowl. Add the vinaigrette to the salad and toss gently until all the ingredients are evenly coated. Taste for seasoning and add salt or pepper, if needed.

Arrange the salad on plates, set 3 tapenade toasts in a ring around each salad, and serve.

SALADE NIÇOISE

(PROVENCE)

Anchovy, Pepper, and Olive Salad

4 SERVINGS

Many cafés across France serve a version of Nice's famed salad—both legitimate and wayward. Some make a tossed green salad of the vegetable platter and add, variously, cooked rice, corn, tuna, or green beans. On its home turf in Provence, however, salade niçoise is normally just another way of saying assorted crudités. In the name of salade niçoise, I've been served piles of shredded carrots, mixed greens, radishes, endives, and cubed beets along with the classic makings, namely black olives, anchovies, peppers, and tomatoes. But I can't join the doomsayers wailing over the demise of the rightful salade niçoise. As long as the ingredients are top-notch, I'll eat the salad in all its permutations.

Still, if you care about such matters, Mimi's recipe from Les Arcades in Biot is about as close to the time-honored formula as you get. Rather than providing a major ingredient, the few lettuce leaves serve as an edible base. And, the egg wedges aside, Mimi uses all raw ingredients. Her vegetables appear not in small mounds but layered. Furthermore, the salad comes on a platter as opposed to a salad bowl. One other thing. Besides being authentic, Mimi's salad is delicious.

6 large romaine lettuce leaves
1 red bell pepper, halved and thinly sliced
1 bulb fennel, halved and thinly sliced lengthwise
4 ripe plum tomatoes, each cut into 8 wedges
¾ cucumber, peeled and sliced
½ small red onion, sliced and separated into rings
¼ cup black olives, preferably from Nice
2 eggs, hard-cooked and quartered
6 cured anchovy fillets in oil, drained and halved
8 large basil leaves, torn in half

VINAIGRETTE
1 tablespoon red-wine vinegar
Salt and freshly ground pepper
¼ cup extra-virgin olive oil

Line a platter (not a salad bowl) with the lettuce leaves. Layer all the remaining salad ingredients on the lettuce.

Make the vinaigrette: In a small bowl, whisk together the vinegar and salt until the salt dissolves. Whisk in the pepper and oil until smooth. Taste for seasoning.

Pour the vinaigrette over the salad and serve.

PLEUROTTES EN SALADE

(BURGUNDY)

Sautéed Oyster-Mushroom Salad

4 SERVINGS

¼ cup vegetable oil
1¼ pounds oyster mushrooms, cut into ⅜-inch slices
1 tablespoon extra-virgin olive oil
1 tablespoon unsalted butter
Salt and freshly ground pepper
2 tablespoons raspberry vinegar, or to taste
1 fat garlic clove, finely chopped
2 tablespoons snipped fresh chives
4 cups torn escarole leaves, or other sturdy lettuce
8 cherry tomatoes
4 slim scallions, trimmed to 3-inch lengths

*H*eat the vegetable oil in a large frying pan over high heat. Add the mushrooms and toss them in the oil until the moisture evaporates, about 5 minutes. Pour the mushrooms into a colander to drain them. Discard the oil from the pan.

Heat the olive oil and butter in the same pan. When the fat is very hot, return the mushrooms to the pan and lightly brown them, tossing repeatedly, 3 to 5 minutes. Reduce the heat to low and add salt, pepper, the raspberry vinegar, garlic, and chives and cook until the garlic is fragrant, about 30 seconds. Take the pan from the heat. Taste the mushrooms for seasoning and add more vinegar, salt, or pepper if needed.

Line a platter or plates with lettuce leaves. Spoon the hot mushrooms in the center. Decorate with the tomatoes and scallions and serve.

The Restaurant-Bar Les Minimes is a savvy village bistro in Semur-en-Auxois, Burgundy. (You don't have to be a shutterbug to crack for this pinkish-brown stone village set above the Armançon River.) Les Minimes' brief menu offers a sampling of all the Burgundy mainstays like Boeuf à la Bourguignonne *and Poached Eggs in Red Wine Sauce, but there are always a few new ideas here, too, such as this mushroom salad.*

This recipe raises the status of oyster mushrooms from side dish to centerpiece. The mushrooms are sliced and tossed in oil, then drained and quickly fried again in a mixture of olive oil and butter for flavor. I don't know why the splash of raspberry vinegar added at the end works so well, but it does.

SALADE DE BETTERAVES

(BURGUNDY)

Beet Salad with Vinaigrette

4 SERVINGS

The nouvelle vague of the polite bistro has rolled from Paris into the French countryside. Most of these places lack soul—the decorators cleaned up the gritty bistro act with new banquettes (no cigarette holes) and well-preserved collectibles—but they have brought back food on the verge of extinction.

Le Quai, waterside in Auxerre, Burgundy, has resurrected dishes like Rapée de Pommes de Terre *(potato pancakes) and isn't too proud to serve this everyday beet salad. A cinch to put together, all you have to do is think of it when you're looking for a no-frills opener.*

VINAIGRETTE
1 tablespoon red-wine vinegar
Salt and freshly ground pepper
2 teaspoons imported Dijon mustard
¼ cup vegetable oil

1 pound cooked beets (page 132), cut into ½-inch dice
1 small shallot, finely chopped
4 cups lamb's lettuce, or other salad greens torn into pieces

Make the vinaigrette: In a small bowl, whisk together the vinegar and salt until the salt dissolves. Whisk in the mustard and pepper, then the oil, until smooth. Taste for seasoning.

Combine the beets and shallot in a bowl.

Line a platter or plates with lamb's lettuce or other salad greens. Spoon the beets in the center. Drizzle the vinaigrette over the beets and serve.

SALADE D'ENDIVES AUX BETTERAVES, POMMES FRUITS, ET NOIX

(NORMANDY AND BURGUNDY)

Endive Salad with Apples, Beets, and Walnuts

4 SERVINGS

VINAIGRETTE
1 tablespoon red-wine vinegar
Salt and freshly ground pepper
1 teaspoon imported Dijon mustard
3 tablespoons vegetable oil
1 tablespoon walnut oil

1 medium apple, cored, peeled, cut into 8 wedges, and sliced crosswise
1 small cooked beet (page 132), cut into ⅜-inch dice
1¼ pounds small Belgian endive, sliced across on the diagonal
¼ cup broken walnut meats
1 tablespoon snipped fresh chives or scallion greens

*M*ake the vinaigrette: In a small bowl, whisk together the vinegar and salt until the salt dissolves. Whisk in the mustard and pepper, then the oils, until smooth. Taste for seasoning.

Combine the remaining ingredients in a salad bowl. Add the vinaigrette and toss until evenly coated. Taste and add more salt, pepper, or walnut oil, if needed, until the salad is as seasoned as you like.

While endive salad isn't typical of one region in particular, you are more likely to come across it in the North, say, in Burgundy or Normandy. To vary the salad, substitute cubes of cheese, such as Roquefort or Cantal, for the beets. You could also leave the endive leaves whole, which makes a prettier presentation but means cutting the leaves on your plate.

SALADE DE CHÈVRE ET JAMBON DU PAYS

(PROVENCE)

Goat Cheese and Cured Ham Salad

4 SERVINGS

Cured ham, goat cheese, olives, and garlic—here's a hodgepodge of Provençal flavors tossed in a salad bowl. That's not to say that they don't harmonize, but they're not usually combined in this way. The inspiration for this salad comes from the Relais de la Vignette in Provence.

When fresh thyme is not available, use one teaspoon dried thyme and steep it first in the vinaigrette to bring out its flavor. If making the chapons (garlic toasts) seems like too much trouble, leave them out and rub the salad bowl with the garlic clove instead.

8 thin slices narrow French baguette
1 garlic clove, peeled

VINAIGRETTE
1 tablespoon red-wine vinegar
Salt and freshly ground pepper
¼ cup extra-virgin olive oil

4 ounces semifirm goat cheese, cut into ½-inch dice
1 tablespoon snipped fresh thyme sprigs
¼ cup black olives, preferably from Nice or Nyons
8 cups mixed torn lettuce leaves, such as Boston, red leaf, arugula, and curly endive
4 thin slices salt-cured, air-dried, prosciutto-type ham

*H*eat the broiler. Toast the bread slices on a baking sheet under the broiler, turning once, until golden, 2 to 3 minutes in all. Rub the toast with garlic.

Make the vinaigrette: In a small bowl, whisk together the vinegar and a little salt until the salt dissolves. Whisk in the pepper and oil until smooth.

Combine the cheese, thyme, olives, and lettuces in a salad bowl. Add the vinaigrette and toss until the ingredients are evenly coated. Taste for seasoning, remembering that the cheese, olives, and ham are all salty.

Lay the slices of ham, overlapping, on top. Or, arrange the salad on plates, setting a slice of ham on each serving.

SALADE DE POIVRONS GRILLÉS

(PROVENCE)

Roasted Red Pepper Salad

4 SERVINGS

2 large red bell peppers

VINAIGRETTE
1 tablespoon red-wine vinegar
Salt and freshly ground pepper
¼ cup extra-virgin olive oil
1 garlic clove, mashed in a garlic press
2 tablespoons chopped fresh flat-leaf parsley

*H*eat the broiler. Set the peppers on a foil-lined baking sheet and broil about 4 inches from the heat until the skin is charred and blistered in patches on all sides, 15 to 30 minutes, depending on the broiler. (You will see a distinct skin when the peppers are ready.) Take a look at the peppers from time to time, turning them as necessary.

Remove the baking sheet from the oven. Transfer the foil and peppers to a plate and wrap the peppers well in the foil to steam the skin loose, 10 to 15 minutes. Unwrap the peppers, peel off and discard the skin. (You can use your fingers for this.) Pull out the stem end. Most of the seeds and ribs will come away with the stem. Cut the peppers into thick strips. Scrape off any remaining seeds and ribs. Put the peppers in a serving dish.

Make the vinaigrette: In a small bowl, whisk together the vinegar, salt, and pepper until the salt dissolves. Whisk in the oil, garlic, and parsley until smooth.

Pour the vinaigrette over the peppers and set aside to marinate at room temperature for an hour or more. (These peppers can be made a day or two ahead and chilled. Bring to room temperature before serving.) Taste for seasoning before serving.

I probably picked up more about French cooking in the six weeks I stayed with Madame Guyon in Aix-en-Provence than in all the years I've been in France. As part of this crash course in French living, Madame Guyon fed me rabbit (I'm supposed to eat this!?), bloody steak (to ask for even medium-rare was humiliating), and just-peeled, boiled-in-oil french fries (I'll never forget . . .).

Another dish that sticks in my mind is this salad of roasted red peppers. I remember the peppers marinating in Madame's broad earthenware bowl—they looked lost in that roomy dish. I worried vaguely that the food was sitting out on the kitchen table in warmish fall weather. But it tasted real good so I relaxed and got with it, à la provençale. Pass a dish of cured anchovies alongside for amateurs.

SALADE RASCASSON

(PROVENCE)

Spicy Marinated Fennel, Tomato, Red Pepper, and Olives

4 SERVINGS

Straight out of an authentic Provençal restaurant—right up the street from my Paris home. Le Rascasson recently moved its formula for fresh, fresh seafood dishes (and its rustic Provençal pottery) from Saint-Tropez to make its fortune up North.

This spicy mélange, really a Provençal health salad, is always set out while you choose from the chalkboard menu. Despite being a giveaway, this salad rates its own course in a meal. It also makes a great addition to a simple buffet of, say, homemade Tapenade; Mussels in Pastis Sauce; and Salt Cod Purée with Herbs, Olive Oil, and Garlic.

1 small fennel bulb, trimmed
1 small red bell pepper, halved and thinly sliced
2 ripe small tomatoes, cut into ⅜-inch pieces
16 spicy marinated green olives
2 tablespoons chopped onion

VINAIGRETTE
1 tablespoon red-wine vinegar
Salt
¼ cup extra-virgin olive oil
1 teaspoon crushed fennel seeds
Pinch of cayenne pepper, or to taste

Cut the fennel bulb in thirds lengthwise, then thinly slice lengthwise. Combine the fennel with the bell pepper, tomatoes, olives, and onion in a serving bowl.

Make the vinaigrette: In a small bowl, whisk together the vinegar and salt until the salt dissolves. Whisk in the oil, fennel seeds, and cayenne until smooth.

Toss the salad with the vinaigrette until it is evenly coated. Set aside the salad to marinate at room temperature, stirring occasionally, for at least 1 hour. Taste for seasoning before serving.

TARTS, CREPES, CHEESE, AND EGGS

This chapter will be anathema to the health-conscious. French cooks, after all, frivolously mix an egg yolk into their pie dough. In Burgundy, *pâtissiers* think nothing of pinching turnovers around a cheese filling. Norman *crêpiers* stuff their crepes with ham, and in Brittany they roll smoked sausages in a buckwheat version. Dubious at best. Only the olive-loving cuisine of Provence gets the dietitian's seal of approval—unless you count the omelets. Those scornful of eggs and cheese would probably be happier skipping the whole thing.

Ironically, though, what is considered a life-threatening diet today—a hunk of cheese; a bit of bacon, sausage, or ham; a few eggs; and dough of some kind—helped some poor rural populations to survive before the 1950s. Many of the recipes here, although some have been enriched for wealthier times and palates and others show updating, draw on peasant cooking.

So it's not surprising that much of this food seems to come out of a time warp. Even in the hands of a contemporary cook, Pissaladière and Burgundy cheese puffs still taste pleasantly old-fashioned. And there's little crossover cooking from distant places because, traditionally, one ate what one produced. Even today you don't find *crêperies* in Provence without a Breton proprietor.

Adjacent regions, however, spawn similar recipes. To keep up their energy, workers in Provence still make *brissauda*, open-face melted cheese sandwiches doused with olive oil. In Burgundy, the favorite pick-me-up is a related sandwich drizzled with white wine. Some classic dishes turn up all over France, with local variations. Surely no one has gone so far with the art of egg cookery as the French, and in each province cooks bring to it the bounty or barrenness of what grows close by. An omelet in Provence contains Swiss chard and garlic. One from Normandy uses native smoked ham.

For the less cowed and less priggish, those of open mind and unclogged arteries, here is a collection of French creations to serve as finger food, to begin a feast, or to make a light meal. ❧

TARTES À LA TOMATE ET AU PISTOU

(PROVENCE)

Tomato Tarts with Garlic and Basil

4 SERVINGS

Hidden on a cobbled pedestrian street in old Nîmes, Paul Salvador's lively Vintage Café offers local dishes without being a temple of tradition. These light tarts, for instance, aren't in the standard Provençal repertoire. Yet, with slices of ripe tomatoes on golden puff pastry, finished with a spoonful of fresh basil sauce, they couldn't be from anywhere but the sunny South. Serve the tarts as a first course or as a light meal with a tossed salad.

TOMATO SAUCE
2 tablespoons extra-virgin olive oil
1 small onion, chopped
2 fat garlic cloves, chopped
Salt and freshly ground pepper
2 ripe medium tomatoes (about 1 pound), chopped; or 1 cup chopped canned Italian plum tomatoes, with their juice

PISTOU
2 tablespoons pine nuts
2 garlic cloves, peeled
½ cup extra-virgin olive oil
Salt
1 cup packed basil leaves
⅓ cup freshly grated Parmesan cheese (optional)

¾ pound best-quality puff-pastry dough
4 ripe medium tomatoes, thinly sliced
Salt and freshly ground pepper
2 teaspoons snipped fresh thyme, or ½ teaspoon dried thyme leaves

*M*ake the tomato sauce: In a medium saucepan, heat the oil. Add the onion and garlic with a little salt and stir until evenly coated with the oil. Cover the pan and cook over low heat, stirring occasionally, until tender, about 10 minutes. Add the tomatoes and cook, partly covered, until thick, about 20 minutes. Stir the tomatoes now and then during cooking. Work the sauce through a food mill into a bowl to remove skin and seeds. Add pepper and taste the sauce for seasoning.

Make the *pistou:* Heat the oven to 350°F. Spread the pine nuts on a baking sheet. Bake until they brown lightly, 3 to 5 minutes. Remove from the oven and raise the oven temperature to 425°F.

Combine the garlic, oil, and a little salt in a food processor and whir until the garlic is finely chopped. Add the basil and toasted nuts and process until smooth. Pulse in the cheese, if using it. Taste for seasoning and add salt if needed. (The tomato sauce and *pistou* can be made a day or two ahead and chilled.)

Sprinkle 2 baking sheets with water. Roll out the dough on a floured surface to a sheet ⅛ inch thick. Cut the dough into 4 rounds about 8 inches across, using a pan lid or plate as a guide. Transfer the rounds to the baking sheets. Prick the dough all over with a fork about every ½ inch. Chill until firm, at least 15 minutes.

Spread 2 tablespoons of the tomato sauce on each chilled dough round, leaving a narrow border of plain dough. Arrange the slices of 1 tomato, overlapping and in concentric circles, on each. Sprinkle with salt, pepper, and thyme.

Bake the tomato tarts in the preheated oven until the pastry has risen around the edges and is golden brown, 15 to 20 minutes. Serve the tarts hot, with a spoonful of *pistou* on each. Pass the remaining *pistou* separately.

TARTE COLETTE GIRAUD

(BURGUNDY)

Goat-Cheese Tart with Leeks

8 SERVINGS

Colette Giraud takes her forty goats out for a stroll whenever she can. "They follow me like dogs," she says. "We walk through neighbors' fields, after the barley has been harvested, of course. They nibble the hedges. Nobody minds."

A one-woman band, when she's not off on a trek with her goats in the Burgundy countryside, Colette takes care of cheese making, aging, and delivering, plus she milks the goats twice each day. With the milk, she crafts seventy crottins *daily in the fall and twice that many in the spring when the milk is more abundant. Her cheese is so good that Bernard Loiseau, pinned with three Michelin stars, buys it for his restaurant in Saulieu.*

After spending the whole day with her goats and elbow-deep in their milk, can Colette face eating her own creations? Sure thing. In fact, saving them for the cheese course isn't enough. Goat-cheese tart, anyone?

Buttery Pastry Dough for one 10- to 11-inch tart shell (page 361)
6 small leeks (about 1½ pounds), white and light green parts only
2 tablespoons unsalted butter
3 eggs
¾ cup heavy (whipping) cream
½ teaspoon salt
Freshly ground pepper
6 ounces semifirm goat cheese, cut into chunks

Roll out the dough on a floured surface to a round that is 2 inches wider than a 10- or 11-inch tart pan and about ⅛ inch thick. Line the pan with the dough, building the tart shell slightly higher than the sides of the pan to allow for shrinkage. Prick the tart shell all over with a fork about every ½ inch. Chill until firm, at least 30 minutes. Heat the oven to 400°F.

Blind-bake the tart: Line the tart shell with foil and fill it almost to the top with dried beans. Bake in the preheated oven for 15 minutes. Remove the foil and beans and continue baking until the shell looks dry, but not yet fully cooked, 5 to 10 minutes. Take the tart shell from the oven and reduce the oven temperature to 375°F.

Slice the leeks in half lengthwise almost through the root end and wash them to remove all grit. Thinly slice the leeks crosswise. In a frying pan, melt the butter over moderately high heat. Add the leeks, and sauté them until translucent, 3 to 5 minutes, or longer for winter leeks. Set aside.

In a food processor, whir the eggs, cream, salt, and pepper until smooth. Add the cheese and pulse until it is coarsely chopped.

Spread the leeks evenly over the bottom of the partially baked tart shell. Add the cheese mixture.

Set the tart on a baking sheet and bake in the bottom third of the preheated oven for 15 minutes. Raise the tart to the top third and continue baking until the top of the tart is golden and a knife inserted in the center comes out clean, 15 to 20 minutes. Remove the tart from the oven and let it cool for 5 minutes on a rack. Serve warm or at room temperature.

PISSALADIÈRE

(PROVENCE)

Thin-Crusted Onion, Anchovy, and Olive Pizza

MAKES 6 SLICES

3 tablespoons extra-virgin olive oil
1½ pounds onions, halved and thinly sliced
3 fat garlic cloves, crushed
½ teaspoon dried herbes de Provence
4 to 6 cured anchovy fillets in oil, drained and chopped
1 recipe French Bread Dough (page 357) made with all-purpose flour
Freshly ground pepper
12 black olives, preferably from Nice

*H*eat the oven to 450°F.

In a large saucepan, heat the oil over low heat. Add the onions, garlic, herbs, and anchovies and stir until coated with the oil. Press a piece of foil on top, cover with a lid, and cook, stirring from time to time, until the onions are very soft but not browned, about 20 minutes. Remove the lid and foil and simmer the onions to evaporate any liquid.

Meanwhile, roll out the dough on a floured surface to a rectangle about 10 × 15 inches. Transfer the dough to a heavy baking sheet and cover with a floured kitchen towel until ready to use.

Spread the onion mixture over the dough, without leaving a border. Sprinkle with pepper. Scatter the olives over the top. Bake the pizza in the preheated oven until the crust is crisp and brown, 15 to 20 minutes. Serve hot or warm, cut into 5-inch squares.

Throughout Provence, bakeries sell this wafer-thin (or bready, depending on the cook), rectangular onion pizza by the slice to warm up at home. But it's infinitely better when you make it yourself.

The pile of sliced onions that accumulates when you prepare this recipe looks like a small mountain. But after 20 minutes of cooking over low heat, they practically melt into a sauce and turn cloyingly sweet. Sassy cured anchovies and olives balance out the flavor. Just how many anchovies you add depends on whether you like them or not. If you use 4 small anchovy fillets you'll scarcely be able to detect them. Still, without them something would be awry. If you like the taste of anchovies, add as many as 6.

Serve pissaladière as a first course or as a light main dish with a tossed salad. Or cut it into bite-size squares and pass as an hors d'oeuvre with Fortified Orange Wine or another aperitif. Also, you can press the recipe for French Bread Dough into service for any pizza.

IN NORMANDY, SMILE AND SAY CHEESE

When I think of cheese I inevitably think of Normandy. Seven-hundred-fifty-thousand dairy cattle chew the cud in Normandy. Local farmers and dairies transform their abundant milk into the province's famous cheeses: smooth-tasting, crumpled Camembert in the familiar wood-chip box; rounds of pungent Livarot, wrapped in strips of orange paper or grass; fragrant Pont-l'Evêque squares and its chunky cousin, Pavé d'Auge; the salty, variously shaped (hearts, logs, squares, and bricks are all popular) Neufchâtel.

The cream of Normandy's rich milk is turned into sweet butter as well as ripened to make tart *crème fraîche*. (In the region of Isigny, both are designated with an *appellation d'origine contrôlée*.) Butter goes into such specialties as *moules à la marinière* and the region's buttery pastry doughs. Whatever doesn't contain butter probably has cream—whether it's meat, fish, vegetable, or poultry. Also, a pot of *crème fraîche* traditionally accompanies the ubiquitous apple tart.

APPLES, CIDER, CALVADOS

Apple trees are as common as cows in Normandy. In the fall, farmers pick tons of eating apples, which flavor fritters, tarts, doughnuts, cakes, puddings, sorbets, and just about any other dessert you can imagine. But Norman cooks also use them as a vegetable, sautéing or baking them to serve as a side dish.

Farmers press any apple varieties too sour to eat to make sparkling, low-alcohol (maximum 5 percent) cider. Cider is the region's traditional thirst quencher and the basic ingredient in the apple brandy Calvados. *Pommeau*, Normandy's apple aperitif, is a brew of fresh apple juice and Calvados aged together in oak.

In Normandy, farmers also made a delicate pear cider, called *poiré*, little-known outside the province. Apart from its popularity as a beverage, *poiré* is mixed with apple cider to make a local Calvados.

Besides producing wonderful dairy products, the Norman breed of cattle has a particularly fine, marbled flesh as well as high-butterfat milk. And beef tripe, along with aromatic vegetables and herbs, stars in one of Normandy's great soulful dishes: *tripe à la mode de Caen*. From Norman pigs, *charcutiers* prepare countless specialties, including smoked ham, rustic terrines, *andouilles de Vire* (smoked chitterling sausage), and blood sausages.

Restaurant chefs seek out *canards de Duclair*, ducks strangled and not bled, for such gastronomic dishes as *canard à la rouennaise*, or pressed duck. Housewives roast barnyard chickens or, in season, feathered game with apples and cream for poultry *vallée d'auge*.

SEA CATCH

Normandy's three-hundred-mile coast along the English Channel provides a wealth of fish and shellfish. With these marine assets and Normandy's cream, it's not surprising to find countless versions of fish in cream sauce, whether a complicated, classic *sole normande* garnished with mussels and shrimp, or a simply poached fish sauced with fresh seasoned *crème fraîche*.

From the abbey of Mont-Saint-Michel and up through the western Cotentin Peninsula, a few farmers still pasture their lambs in the salt marshes. *Pré-salé* lambs cover nine to ten miles a day, a regimen that adds little fat to the flesh, and salt grasses give the meat a delicate sea flavor. The place to sample this lamb remains La Mère Poulard, also famous for omelets that puff up like soufflés.

But nothing stays the same forever. In this land of the cheese platter, farmers have begun fattening ducks for luxurious *foie gras*, a tradition once reserved for eastern Alsace and the Southwest.

Norman *foie gras* now appears on menus throughout the region. And during the holiday season in December and January, *foie gras* producers even organize special markets to peddle their rich, home-bred livers. Today's Norman cuisine has expanded to include *foie gras*, just as it once grew to include the new arrival, Camembert.

RIPE FOR A
CHEESE FAIR

Livarot, Normandy—Philippe Meslon, the boyish president of the dairy Le Domaine de Saint-Loup, urges samples of his Camembert on the sunburned locals and Parisians who have come to the annual Livarot cheese fair.

When one visitor objects to the chalky streak running through the center of his cheese, Meslon simmers under his cap of brown curls. "Is cheese aging a continuous process or a fixed result?" he quizzes.

"A continuous process," mutters the visitor.

"Ah!" says Meslon, satisfied. "So you see. There's a range of ripeness for enjoying cheese. Here we prefer a delicate, fruity flavor. In Paris they only want Camembert that's creamy all the way through."

Meslon is one of thirty cheese makers from Normandy, the Loire Valley, and even Corsica to have gathered in this quiet market town, a two-hour drive northwest of Paris, for the cheese fair held every year on the second weekend in August.

Unswayed by cheesy odors and the ripe carnival smells of grilled sausages and greasy french fries, the cheese makers carry on offering pamphlets and samples from plastic ice chests and talking about the art of cheese making. A group of Livarot shopkeepers, dressed in regional costume, lend boisterous support to the event. The men wear black smocks and wooden clogs. The women model long skirts and tall white coifs, the headdress of Marie Harel, the countrywoman credited with inventing Camembert cheese in 1791. Down the street from the cheese stands, a local marching band kicks off the afternoon with the music of John Philip Sousa followed by a regiment of baton twirlers.

Livarot's fair typifies the small country festivals throughout France where you can meet the artisans who keep French traditions alive. The tourist office here—population, 2,759—launched this fair in 1988 to spur interest in cheese and revive tourism in rural Normandy, away from the province's crowded beaches.

But the idea of a cheese fair is hardly new. In the nineteenth and early twentieth centuries, these fairs served as distribution networks. Farmers sold their freshly drained cheeses to roving merchants, who aged them. With the appearance of the railroad, though, these cheese fairs vanished.

CHEESE THREAT

The cheese makers at the fair today run the gamut from farmers with a few cows and small creameries to the industrial dairies that produce 80 percent of Normandy's cheese. Often the cheese makers strain their voices to be heard above the rock music piped over the makeshift P.A. system. This seems symbolic. The muffling of their voices is echoed by what some traditional cheese makers have to say.

"I don't think we'll be around in five or ten years," says Henri Waroquier, a third-generation Camembert maker says. Waroquier, who manages his family's small dairy, Le Moulin de Carel, explains, "We can't compete with the industrial giants." His traditional Camembert loses out because the average Frenchman prefers the bland, and cheaper, mass-produced variety.

But other cheese makers have hope for the future of handcrafted cheese. "We sell all the Neufchâtel we can make," says Daniel Binet, speaking of the variously shaped cheese with a downy rind made in eastern Normandy. "And now, since there's a milk surplus in the Common Market, farmers who had been raising cows for milk are returning to cheese making."

A CLUTCH OF CHEESE MUSEUMS

Pays d'Auge, Normandy—To witness cheese making without rising with the cowherds, visit a cheese museum. Here you can watch cheese making on video or walk through the process with a recording. Three museums in the heart of cheese-producing Normandy document this traditional craft, and they can easily be visited in a leisurely weekend tour.

Livarot's Musée du Fromage stands, aptly, down the street from a dilapidated nineteenth-century Camembert cheese factory. (Note the building's rare faience-tiled Camembert Georges Bisson sign and the characteristic narrow windows, which regulate incoming air and shield the interior from the sun.) This homespun museum, housed in the basement of a manor, collects, catalogs, and displays old dairy artifacts. Here you can see milk churns, cream separators, draining cups, cheese labels, and vintage 100-liter tubs for clabbering milk. Because of its location in Livarot, the primary cheese-making process illustrated here is that of Livarot cheese, from collecting the milk to aging the young cheeses.

By way of contrast, the snazzy Museum of Cheese-Making Techniques in neighboring Saint-Pierre-sur-Dives occupies a restored thirteenth-century convent. Even if its technological charms are folksy (this is no Euro Disney), the museum is a good place to learn about cheese making. Under the soaring medieval roof, a flashing plastic cow illustrates how grass becomes milk. Next to the model cow, you'll find a display of old wooden cheese molds and pottery ladles.

A video in French with English subtitles explains how modern dairies make Livarot, Camembert, and Pont-l'Evêque cheeses. Charts show all aspects of cheese making, including a cheese time-line and the molecular and chemical makeup of milk.

Originally a temporary exhibit set up under a tent in 1985, the Musée du Camembert found a permanent home in the Vimoutiers tourist office after it drew record crowds. "They laughed at us in the beginning," admits Paulette Thomas, director of the museum. "No one believed that such a small town could attract so many people with a cheese museum."

During the first year, 14,000 visitors came to Vimoutiers, a few miles south of Livarot and a stone's throw east of the village of Camembert, to learn about one of the world's most popular cheeses.

A recording (in French or English) guides the visitor through this grass-roots museum, identifying the antique utensils and explaining the venerable method for making Camembert. The earthenware bowl at your feet is really the first cream separator. A farmer left fresh milk in the bowl until the cream rose to the surface. Then he skimmed off the cream and let it ripen to make tart *crème fraîche*.

FARM CHEESE

To make Camembert, he curdled the skimmed milk and ladled the uncut curd, one scoop at a time, into perforated cheese molds, such as those set on the sloping wooden table on display in the next room. As the molds were filled in five successive passes (it takes five scoops to make true Camembert even today) and the whey trickled out, the cheese became more compact and the molds were turned.

In the next few days, the farmer unmolded the cheese and rubbed it with coarse salt. Now the cheese was ready for the *hâloir*, a drafty room where the cheese developed its characteristic white bloom.

In the past, the bloom grew naturally from invisible fungi in the air and on the wooden planks where the cheese sat. Today plastic is favored over wood, and cheese makers must spray the young cheese with liquid *Penicillium candidum* to hurry its development.

Finally, the farmer moved the cheese to a cool, humid cellar, where he turned and tended it daily for a month until it was ripe for eating.

The museum also displays an unusual collection of cheese ephemera—1,400 Camembert labels. Most labels portray idealized scenes of flowering apple trees and blushing milkmaids. One humorous label depicts a gourmet kitten about to polish off a cheese. If you are a label collector, this is the place to add to your collection. The museum sets out baskets of duplicate labels for interested visitors. Also, ask at the information desk, where the staff keeps their supply. ✒

CRÊPES FOURRÉES

(NORMANDY)

Gratin of Crepes Stuffed with Ham and Cheese

4 FIRST-COURSE OR 2 MAIN-COURSE SERVINGS

CRÊPES
½ cup all-purpose flour
¼ teaspoon salt
1 egg
½ cup milk
¼ cup water, or more as needed
1 tablespoon vegetable oil
Clarified unsalted butter (page 199)

FILLING
4 thin slices best-quality boiled or baked ham
½ cup crème fraîche (page 368) or sour cream
¼ cup freshly grated Gruyère or other Swiss-type cheese
Freshly ground pepper

TOPPING
½ cup crème fraîche or heavy (whipping) cream
¾ cup freshly grated Gruyère or other Swiss-type cheese, or to taste

After five days of serious eating during one trip to Normandy, my father and I had reached our limit. We pined for a cure, for something light. Still we soldiered on, planning yet another four-course meal at a village restaurant.

Once in Beaumont-en-Auge, though, we dawdled over aperitifs at the Café des Arts, enjoying the balmy spring evening and postponing the inevitable. In the end we headed for dinner. But, for once, I hadn't reserved and we were turned away. We gratefully stole back to our café table and ordered the perfect supper: crepes and a great big salad.

To be sure, "light" is a relative term. What seems reasonable at a café in Normandy appears swimming in cream and cheese at home, so this is a trimmer version of the original. Use light cream in the topping if this still looks like overkill, but reducing the quantity only makes a dry crepe.

Make the crepe batter: Sift the flour with the salt into a mixing bowl and make a well in the center. Break the egg into the well and add a little of the milk. With a whisk, beat the egg and milk to mix. Gradually beat the flour into the central ingredients while pouring in the remaining milk, the water, and the oil. Set the batter aside at room temperature for at least 1 hour. (Cover and chill the batter if leaving it for longer.)

Heat the oven to 400°F. Butter a gratin dish just the size to hold the crepes, once stuffed and rolled, in a single layer.

Make the crepes: Set a 9-inch crepe pan, lightly brushed with clarified butter, or a nonstick frying pan, over moderately high heat. It's hot enough when a drop of batter sizzles in the pan. Pour in 3 or 4 tablespoons of the batter and quickly swirl it around so the batter covers the bottom of the pan. (If the batter doesn't coat the pan easily, add another tablespoon of water to the remaining batter.) Cook for 1 to 2 minutes, then flip the crepe with a thin-bladed spatula and cook until the crepe is spotted with brown on the other side, about 1 minute. Repeat for the remaining crepes. As the crepes are done, stack them on a plate. (You'll have about 4 crepes.)

Fill the crepes: Lay a ham slice on the spotted side of each crepe. Spread with 2 tablespoons of the *crème fraîche* or sour cream. Sprinkle with a tablespoon of cheese and a little pepper. Roll up like a carpet and arrange in the prepared baking dish.

Top the crepes: Spread the *crème fraîche* over the crepes or pour on the cream. Sprinkle with the cheese and bake in the preheated oven until bubbling and golden, 15 to 20 minutes. Serve as soon as possible.

PROOF OF THE PUDDING

According to food lore, medieval cheese-making communities grappled with the quest for truth in a spooky way: Anyone suspected of a crime was forced to eat cheese. In this unusual lie-detector test, the inability to digest cheese provided evidence of guilt!

CRAFTING CREPES THE BRETON WAY

Douarnenez, Brittany—The pair of crêpe makers at Ty Krampouz (that's Breton for house of pancakes) don't have a moment to let their four revolving griddles get cold. Working two griddles at a time, each *crêpière* pours on the batter, spreads it handkerchief-thin and then coolly tosses the crepes with a thin-bladed spatula to brown the other side.

To watch these crêpe makers in Douarnenez' covered market, you'd think that griddle crepes required all the skill of filing nails. In fact, the art of crêpe making has gotten easier. "I learned to fry crepes over a wood fire," muses Monique Le Rhun, a second-generation miller in Pont-l'Abbé who grinds buckwheat to make flour for crepes. "We didn't have gas griddles then."

But making crepes on a griddle or *pilig*, *galetier*, or *tuile*, as it's known in Brittany, still isn't as effortless as it might appear. First the batter must be just right: thin enough to flow easily over the griddle yet dense enough once fried to sink your teeth into. Second, there's the matter of heating the griddle to the right temperature and learning to spread the batter over the griddle using a *rozell*, a kind of small wooden hoe, and then flip the crepe over with a *spanell* or thin spatula.

Also, crepes made with buckwheat flour are harder to carry off than the plain wheat variety. Without gluten to hold it together, the batter spreads less evenly, and the finished crepes tend to have holes, giving them a rustic, lacy look.

RHYMING CREPES

The perils of crepe making recall an old Mardi Gras song:

Shrove Tuesday, Shrove Tuesday, poor Jack went to plow,
His mother made pancakes, she scarcely knew how;
She tossed them, she turned them, she made them so black
With soot from the chimney, that poisoned poor Jack.

Still, Madame Le Rhun encourages *crêpière* wannabes to give it a whirl. "Even if it's not perfect, put some butter on it," she says. "It's still good to eat." To her way of thinking, successful griddle crepes are largely a question of motivation: "Those who want to, manage it."

Only crepe makers in Brittany use the wide, round *pilig*. In classic French cuisine, cooks fry crepes in small crepe pans. But besides frying on a griddle, it's the use of buckwheat flour, called *farine de sarrasin* or *blé noir*, that separates the crepes of regional cooking from those of classic cooking.

Buckwheat reached France from China and Nepal in the fifteenth century, and its cultivation spread from central France all the way to Brittany. In Brittany, taking the shape of *bouillie*, or porridge, as well as crepes, it made up the bulk of peasant fare, along with oat porridge and dairy products.

But in the second half of the nineteenth century, buckwheat farming bottomed out as wheat took over, and, to a large extent, bread replaced crepes and *bouillie*. As a result, thirty years ago buckwheat flour was as scarce as hens' teeth. Instead of growing buckwheat, farmers preferred pasturing animals because it paid the bills every month.

BUCKWHEAT COMEBACK

Today, however, milk quotas make dairy farming less appealing, and some farmers are coming around again to growing buckwheat. This hardy cereal (though not a true cereal, it is usually classed as such), which grows without fertilizers or insecticides in the acidic soil of central Brittany, is giving new life to once-abandoned fields and offering young farmers a place to start. It also allows farmers in wobbly circumstances to grow a crop without huge investments.

In most cases, farmers cultivate a plot of buckwheat in addition to other activities. "Might as well make the most of what you have," says Monique Le Rhun, who farms a patch of buckwheat near her flour mill. "Anyway, it's part of the traditions here."

So, if you travel in the Breton heartland between mid-June and October, you're likely to spot fields of wispy plants with heart-shaped leaves and small white blossoms. Breton farmers today grow 1,500 tons of this unlikely crop, and the dark honey made from the flowers' nectar is a prized specialty. Still, this hesitant yield represents only 15 percent of French consumption. France imports the remainder from Canada, Latin America, China, and Turkey.

GALETTES

But all this talk of crepes and buckwheat is only part of the story. When is a crepe not a crepe? Answer: When it's a *galette*. Definitions of these thin pancakes vary as you move around Brittany. In the eastern part of the province, called Upper Brittany, locals know crepes as the ones made with wheat flour, reserved for dessert. For them, buckwheat flour means a galette, the wrapping for a savory filling.

In western Brittany, especially Finistère—the most Celtic of Brittany's *départements*—they distinguish crepes from galettes by thickness. Crepes, whether made of plain wheat or buckwheat, measure not quite 1 millimeter, less than $\frac{1}{16}$ inch. Galettes rise to 3 millimeters, about $\frac{1}{8}$ inch.

Aside from eating crepes and galettes for Mardi Gras as a pre-Lenten treat, Bretons traditionally ate them with cider or buttermilk for the meatless Friday meal.

But people also relished leftovers through the week, cold or cut up in soup. At markets and fairs, too, crepes sustained shoppers, traders, and market gardeners, much as they do today in Douarnenez and at other markets throughout Brittany.

Contemporary crepes wrap everything from smoked salmon to a soufflé mixture, in addition to the customary fillings of fried egg, bacon, and sausage. But for the crepe lover, the best crepe is a plain one, spread only with a little salted butter. Then you can really taste the crepe itself.

Some cooks, like Madame Le Rhun, still serve them every Friday. Although the meal is no longer meatless, Madame Le Rhun likes to hew to tradition as far as fillings are concerned. She wraps her crepes around local smoked sausage, and her extended family flocks to get 'em.

"Everybody loves crepes," she says. "Big eaters can swallow a dozen at a sitting."

À LA NORMANDE

Ingredients that Make a Dish Typically Norman
Camembert cheese
Livarot cheese
Pont-l'Evêque cheese
Pavé d'Auge cheese
Neufchâtel cheese
Butter
Crème fraîche
Créances carrots
Apples
Apple cider
Pear cider (*poiré*)
Calvados
Pommeau (apple aperitif)
Tripe
Vire andouille
Smoked ham
Blood pudding
Pressed duck
Poultry
Mussels
Oysters
Lobsters
Dover sole
Herring
Scallops
Salt-marsh lamb
Benedictine

GALETTE PAYSANNE

(BRITTANY)

Bacon and Egg Galette

4 SERVINGS

GALETTES
¾ cup buckwheat flour
¼ cup all-purpose flour
½ teaspoon salt
1 egg
1¼ cups water, or more as needed
Clarified lightly salted butter (page 199)

FILLING
4 slices bacon
2 tablespoons lightly salted butter
4 eggs
Salt and freshly ground pepper
¼ cup crème fraîche (page 368) or sour cream

The Lamour family packs them in at their ferme auberge-*meets-Disneyland in northern Brittany. (This is the only place in France I can think of that books several seatings for dinner.) Even if the Char à Bancs bursts at the seams on weekends and holidays with French families flocking to this ersatz farm for pony rides and a wide-eyed look at the rusting scraps of their grandparents' lives, the Lamours do offer a Breton menu that could scarcely have been better when people still ate it by necessity not choice.*

Along with a potée—here vegetables, smoked pork, sausage, and bacon simmered together in a giant iron cauldron—they serve this galette. It's a rustic crepe made with a good proportion of buckwheat flour on a round, wide griddle called a pilig. *The egg cooks on top of the galette, then a spoonful of cream and a slice of crisp bacon are added, and the galette is folded around the filling.*

$\mathcal{M}$ake the galette batter: Sift the flours with the salt into a mixing bowl and make a well in the center. Break the egg into the well and add a little of the water. With a whisk, beat the egg and water to mix. Gradually beat the flour into the central ingredients while pouring in the remaining water. Set the batter aside at room temperature for at least 30 minutes. (Cover and chill the batter if leaving it for longer.)

Cook the galettes: Set a 10-inch crepe pan, lightly brushed with clarified butter, or a nonstick frying pan, over moderately high heat. It's hot enough when a drop of batter sizzles in the pan. Pour in ⅓ cup of the batter and quickly swirl it around so the batter covers the bottom of the pan. (If the batter doesn't coat the pan easily, add another tablespoon or two of water to the remaining batter.) Cook for 30 seconds to 1 minute, then flip the galette with a thin-bladed spatula and cook until the galette is spotted with brown on the other side. Repeat for the remaining three galettes. As they are done, stack them on a plate.

Prepare the filling: In a frying pan, cook the bacon gently until golden, 5 to 8 minutes.

Replace a galette, spotted side up, in the crepe pan or frying pan over moderately high heat. Spread with ½ tablespoon of the salted butter. Break an egg in the middle, sprinkle with salt and pepper, and cook until the white sets but the yolk is still soft, 1 to 2 minutes. Top the egg with a tablespoon of *crème fraîche* or sour cream and set a slice of bacon next to the egg. Fold the galette in half and slide it onto a warmed plate. Repeat for the remaining galettes. Serve as soon as possible.

GALETTE MOULIN DE L'ÉCLUSE

(BRITTANY)

Buckwheat Crepe with Country Sausage

4 SERVINGS

Once the emblem of backwardness and hard times in Brittany, buckwheat now means regional chic. Fashion blows hot and cold, but the Moulin de l'Écluse on the road to Pont-l'Abbé has ground "black wheat" for flour since 1760. "We've always had some," says Monique Le Rhun, second-generation miller. Seated at her desk, her skin, clothes, and hair dusted with flour, Madame Le Rhun talks about the changes she's seen in thirty years. "Today, though, we get enough to sell an all-Breton buckwheat flour in the stores. I can't say how much that represents. It's never the same. Varies year to year."

Madame Le Rhun makes the kind of buckwheat galettes that were standard fare in Brittany before they were rehabilitated into gourmet wrappings. This batter makes enough for a few extras. The first galette, which never seems to come out right, is traditionally fed to the dog.

GALETTES
1 cup buckwheat flour
½ teaspoon salt
1 egg
¾ cup water, or more as needed
½ cup milk
Clarified lightly salted butter (page 199)

FILLING
4 smoked pork sausages (about 1½ pounds in all)
2 tablespoons lightly salted butter

*M*ake the galette batter: Sift the flour with the salt into a mixing bowl and make a well in the center. Break the egg into the well and add a little of the water. With a whisk, beat the egg and water to mix. Gradually beat the flour into the central ingredients while pouring in the remaining water and the milk. Since there is no gluten in buckwheat flour there's no need to set this batter aside to rest. (Cover and chill the batter if not using it right away.)

Make the galettes: Set a 10-inch crepe pan, lightly brushed with clarified butter, or a nonstick frying pan, over moderately high heat. It's hot enough when a drop of batter sizzles in the pan. Pour in ⅓ cup of the batter and quickly swirl it around so the batter covers the bottom of the pan. (If the batter doesn't coat the pan easily, add another tablespoon or two of water to the remaining batter.) Cook for 30 seconds to 1 minute, then flip the galette with a thin-bladed spatula and cook until the galette is spotted with brown on the other side. Repeat for the remaining galettes. As they are done, stack them on a plate.

Prepare the filling: Add ¼ inch of water to a frying pan, bring to a simmer and add the sausages. Prick the sausages to release the fat. Cook until the sausages are brown all over and cooked through, about 15 minutes. Discard the fat from the pan.

Replace a galette, spotted side up, in the crepe or frying pan over moderately high heat. Spread with ½ tablespoon of the salted butter. Put a sausage in the center and fold the galette around it. Slide it onto a warmed plate. Repeat for the remaining galettes. Serve as soon as possible.

TRUE BLUE BRETON GALETTES

Monique Le Rhun's actual recipe for galette batter recalls a time before the nuclear family, when home cooking meant turning out food for many mouths. She leaned across her desk and reeled off the ingredients: 2 pounds buckwheat flour, 4 teaspoons salt, 1 whole egg, 6 cups water, and 4 cups milk. Then she settled back in her chair, content. "That's the real thing."

BRISSAUDA

(PROVENCE)

Provençal Cheese and Olive Oil Toasts

4 SERVINGS

It's 9:30 A.M. a week before Christmas at the Alziari olive mill in Nice. The mill workers, Pascal Lambert and his assistant, have already labored several hours and are ready for a restorative casse-croûte. But instead of doughnuts and coffee, they prepare these brissauda *in the old stove at the back of the mill. The bread, doused with scented, murky olive oil straight from the press, is washed down with a no-name red wine poured from a thick-bottomed bottle. Then it's back to work.*

These toasts are so obvious they hardly require directions. Still I find it helpful to suggest amounts, even though quantities will vary according to your taste and available ingredients. If cheesy toasts seem off-putting for coffee break, try them as a special bread with a tossed salad or alongside a bowl of soup, a simple grilled chicken, or a steak. And don't forget the wine.

1 narrow French baguette
8 teaspoons fruity extra-virgin olive oil, or to taste
¾ cup crumbled Roquefort or other blue cheese, or to taste
3 ounces thinly sliced Gruyère or other Swiss-type cheese, or to taste
Salt and freshly ground pepper

*H*eat the broiler.

Cut the bread into 4 even lengths, then in half lengthwise. Toast the bread lightly on a baking sheet under the broiler, 1 to 2 minutes per side.

Drizzle about 1 teaspoon of the olive oil over each piece of toast. Sprinkle half the toasts with the Roquefort. Arrange the Gruyère slices, overlapping, on the remaining toasts. Broil the toasts until the cheese melts without browning, 1 to 2 minutes.

Sprinkle the Gruyère toasts with salt and pepper and the Roquefort toasts with pepper only. Serve hot.

PAIN BEURRÉ VINCELOTTOIS

(BURGUNDY)

Burgundian Cheese, Wine, and Garlic Bread

4 SERVINGS

2 half-baked ("brown-and-serve") baguettes (1 pound total)
2 fat garlic cloves, mashed in a garlic press
4 tablespoons unsalted butter, thinly sliced
¼ pound Comté or other Gruyère-type cheese, thinly sliced
4 tablespoons dry white wine, such as a Burgundy Aligoté
Grating of nutmeg
Salt and freshly ground pepper

*H*eat the oven to 400°F.

Cut the baguettes lengthwise almost in half, and open like a book. Spread each cut half with ½ teaspoon mashed garlic. Dot each half with 1 tablespoon butter. Arrange 4 slices of cheese, overlapping, on top. Sprinkle with 1 tablespoon wine and a little nutmeg, salt, and pepper.

Put the baguettes on a baking sheet. Bake until the cheese melts without browning, 10 to 12 minutes.

After an early morning in the vineyard, wine makers know they can sidle up to the bar at Les Tilleuls for pain beurré and a glass of Aligoté de Saint-Bris-le-Vineux. Alain Renaudin serves this old-time snack at ten o'clock at his auberge in Vincelottes before gearing up for the noontime service. Says Monsieur Renaudin, "Never use grated cheese. The texture once melted won't be the same."

LES GOUGÈRES D'ISABELLE

(BURGUNDY)

Isabelle Landau's Cheese Puffs

MAKES ABOUT THIRTY-TWO 1-INCH PUFFS

1 cup water
4 tablespoons unsalted butter, cut into pieces
½ teaspoon salt
1 cup all-purpose flour
4 eggs
¼ pound Gruyère or other Swiss-type cheese, cut into shavings

Gougères are a fixture at wine tastings and other gatherings in Burgundy. They range in size from dainty puffs to fist-size specimens. (At Les Gourmets in Marsannay-la-Côte, Chef Joël Perreaut offers gougère samples flecked with bacon while you contemplate the menu.)

Isabelle Landau, who comes from an old Burgundy wine clan, learned to make them from her mother. The family recipe calls for a minimum of butter, half of what other recipes suggest. If you want a richer dough, double the amount of butter. Isabelle also specifies shavings of cheese, not grated cheese. Says Isabelle, "It makes all the difference."

Heat the oven to 325°F. Butter and flour 1 or 2 baking sheets.

Combine the water, butter, and salt in a medium saucepan. Set the pan over moderately high heat until the butter melts and the water boils, then take the pan from the heat. Add all the flour at once and beat to combine with a wooden spoon. Set the pan over low heat and continue beating until the mixture is smooth and comes away from the sides of the pan in a ball, about 1 minute.

Off the heat, beat in 3 of the eggs, one at a time, beating well after each addition. Whisk the last egg until mixed. Now beat enough of this egg into the dough to make a mixture that is just soft enough to fall from the spoon but firm enough to hold its shape. Stir in the cheese shavings.

Either put the dough in a pastry bag and pipe 1-inch mounds on the prepared baking sheets, spacing the mounds well apart, or use 2 spoons to shape the dough. Bake for 5 minutes, then raise the heat to 375°F. and bake until golden and crisp, 30 to 40 minutes. *Gougères* are best freshly baked, though they can be stored a day or two in an airtight tin, or frozen, and reheated.

COMTÉ AUX RAISINS

(BURGUNDY)

Comté Cheese Tidbits Speared with Grapes

MAKES 16 HORS D'OEUVRES

¼ pound Comté, Appenzell, or other best-quality Swiss-type cheese
1 teaspoon imported Dijon mustard, or to taste
16 green seedless grapes

Cut the cheese into ½- to 1-inch cubes. You will need 32 cubes for 16 hors d'oeuvres. Make "sandwiches," spreading mustard sparingly between each pair of cheese cubes. Set a grape on top of each sandwich and spear with a toothpick.

Joël Perreaut sets out these palate teasers for guests to nibble while they decide the serious matter of what to eat. Chef-owner of Les Gourmets in Marsannay-la-Côte, just outside Dijon on the wine route, Monsieur Perreaut could hardly assemble a more regional mouthful to begin a meal. Comté cheese comes from the Franche-Comté, bordering on eastern Burgundy; mustard is a hallmark of Burgundy cooking; and eating-grapes act as stand-ins for the Chardonnay variety, which are pressed to make the Côte de Nuit's prestigious wines.

The fresh fruity grapes and pungent mustard offset the dense, rich cheese. One caveat: There's no hiding shabby ingredients here.

LES CORNIOTTES MORVANDELLES

(BURGUNDY)

Savory Cheese Pastries from the Morvan

MAKES 8 PASTRIES

At Serge Lenoble's folkloric institution La Beursaudière (beursaude *is the word for cracklings in local dialect*), energetic waitresses in regional costume serve up platters of Burgundy soul food, including these three-cornered turnovers from the Morvan.

If you are thinking cheese pastries, as in sweet Danish to eat with coffee, note that Monsieur Lenoble's recipe is a savory one for serving as an appetizer or as a light meal with salad. (For a dessert version, see Apple Pastries with Black Currant Sauce.) He blends drained *fromage blanc with* crème fraîche *and grated Gruyère cheese for the filling, then pinches puff pastry dough around the cheese to make triangles.*

2 cups fromage blanc, or 1 cup ricotta cheese
1 pound best-quality puff-pastry dough
¼ cup crème fraîche (page 368) or sour cream
2 eggs
1 cup freshly grated Gruyère or other Swiss-type cheese
Salt and freshly ground pepper

If using *fromage blanc*, pour it into a strainer lined with several layers of cheesecloth and set over a bowl. Chill until thickened, at least 8 hours or overnight.

Sprinkle 2 baking sheets with water. Divide the dough in half. Roll out each portion of dough on a floured surface to a sheet ⅛ to ¼ inch thick. Cut each portion into 4 rounds 5 inches across, using a pan lid or plate as a guide. Transfer the rounds to the baking sheets. Prick them all over with a fork about every ½ inch. Chill until firm, at least 15 minutes.

Meanwhile, in a mixing bowl, beat together the thickened *fromage blanc* or the ricotta cheese with the *crème fraîche* or sour cream, 1 egg, ¾ cup of the Gruyère, and salt and pepper.

Spoon a scant ¼ cup of the cheese mixture in the center of a chilled round. Brush a little of the remaining egg, lightly beaten, around the filling. Pull the dough up and pinch it into a triangular shape so the filling is completely enclosed. Repeat for the remaining dough rounds.

Chill the *corniottes* on the baking sheets until very firm or they will open during baking, at least 30 minutes. (The *corniottes* can be prepared to this point 2 or 3 hours ahead of time.)

Heat the oven to 425°F.

Brush the *corniottes* with additional beaten egg and bake in the preheated oven until puffed and lightly browned, about 15 minutes. Sprinkle each with ½ tablespoon of the remaining Gruyère and continue baking until the cheese melts and browns, 5 to 10 minutes longer. Serve as soon as possible.

OEUFS EN COCOTTE À LA CRÈME DE MOULES

(NORMANDY)

Eggs en Cocotte with Mussels

4 SERVINGS

24 lively small mussels in the shell (about ½ pound), scrubbed and
    bearded
4 eggs
¼ cup crème fraîche (page 368) or heavy (whipping) cream
Freshly ground white pepper
½ tablespoon snipped fresh chives or scallion greens

*H*eat the oven to 375°F. Butter four ½-cup ramekins.

Put the mussels in a medium saucepan, cover, and set over high
heat. Cook the mussels, stirring once or twice, just until they open,
3 to 5 minutes. Take the pan from the heat.

When the mussels are cool enough to handle, remove the mussel meat from the shells and set aside. Discard the shells and any
mussels that did not open. Pour the mussel liquor through a fine
strainer lined with a double layer of cheesecloth into a bowl.

In each ramekin, put 3 of the mussels. Break in an egg and add
a teaspoon of the strained mussel liquor, a tablespoon of *crème
fraîche* or cream, and a little pepper. Top with 3 more mussels and
a sprinkling of chives or scallion greens. (The eggs can be prepared
to this point 2 or 3 hours ahead and chilled.)

Fill a roasting pan halfway with water and bring it to a boil on
the stove. Set the ramekins in this simmering water bath and transfer it to the preheated oven. Bake the eggs for 10 minutes. Take the
ramekins from the water bath and serve them *tout de suite*.

Nothing has changed the love affair Normans and Bretons have with the poached egg-and-mussel duo. (There are mussel farms in the coastal waters off both provinces.) I've sampled the pairing set on little toasts and, once, nestled in a small brioche. Classic chefs add a butter and flour–based velouté sauce, while modern cooks finish the dish with a reduction of mussel cooking liquid and cream. The following version, with eggs en cocotte, is easier, speedier, and just as wonderful. With little effort you have an oh-so-French first course.

In such a simple dish, you taste every ingredient. Using crème fraîche or fresh cream instead of ultra-pasteurized cream, for instance, makes a big difference. (You need only a tablespoon per serving so it won't tip any high-fat scales.) And don't even think about buying cooked mussels. Preparing such a small quantity of fresh ones is no trouble, and the result more than makes up for the brief task.

As for the cooking time, you have to take my directions on faith or you'll overcook the eggs. Baking the eggs, set in a simmering water bath, for 10 minutes produces soft yolks and whites that are just set. Set out spoons and crusty bread for scooping up every drop.

RATATOUILLE À L'OEUF

(PROVENCE)

Baked Eggs with Ratatouille

4 SERVINGS

6 tablespoons olive oil
1 medium onion, chopped
2 garlic cloves, chopped
½ teaspoon dried herbes de Provence
Salt and freshly ground pepper
3 ripe medium tomatoes (about 1½ pounds), chopped; or 1½ cups chopped canned Italian plum tomatoes, drained
1 small red bell pepper, halved and thinly sliced
¼ pound small, young zucchini, halved lengthwise and thinly sliced across
¼ pound small eggplant, quartered lengthwise and cut across into ¼-inch slices
4 eggs

If you like Mexican huevos rancheros *and Basque* pipérade, *you will also like this Provençal version of eggs* sur le plat *from Le Rascasson. Here, an egg is broken onto a velvety stew of Provençal vegetables, then baked in an individual gratin dish until the white sets but the yolk is still soft. I love the way the egg yolk spills into the ratatouille and mixes with the tomatoes, pepper, zucchini, and eggplant.*

If you don't have individual gratin dishes, substitute a shallow baking dish. Spread the ratatouille on the bottom and make 4 hollows in it for the eggs. When serving, take care not to break the yolks. Try this dish for brunch, a light lunch, or as a first course.

In a large saucepan, heat 1½ tablespoons of the oil. Add the onion, garlic, and *herbes de Provence* with a little salt, and stir until evenly coated with the oil. Cover the pan and cook over low heat, stirring occasionally, until tender, about 10 minutes. Add the tomatoes and cook, partly covered, until thick, 20 to 30 minutes. Stir the tomatoes now and then during cooking.

Heat the oven to 375°F.

In a frying pan, in 1½ tablespoons of oil for each vegetable sauté the red pepper and zucchini, one at a time, with a little salt. Cook, stirring now and then, over moderate heat until tender, 5 to 15 minutes, depending on the vegetable, then transfer to the tomatoes. In the same pan, sauté the eggplant in the remaining 1½ tablespoons of oil until tender. Press a piece of foil on top and cover the pan if the eggplant looks dry. Add to the tomatoes.

Stir the vegetables into the tomatoes, cover, and cook gently for 10 minutes to blend the flavors. Add pepper and taste for seasoning. (The ratatouille can be made a day or two ahead and chilled.)

Butter 4 individual gratin dishes. Spread a quarter of the ratatouille in each dish. Make a hollow in the center and break an egg into it. Cover the dishes loosely with foil.

Set the dishes on a baking sheet and bake in the preheated oven until the egg white sets but the yolk is still soft, 8 to 12 minutes. Discard the foil and serve the ratatouille as soon as possible.

OEUFS BROUILLÉS À L'OSEILLE

(BURGUNDY)

Creamy Scrambled Eggs with Sorrel

4 SERVINGS

8 tablespoons (1 stick) unsalted butter, cut into pieces
¼ pound sorrel, stemmed and shredded
Salt and freshly ground pepper
1 tablespoon heavy (whipping) cream
10 to 12 eggs

*M*elt a tablespoon of the butter in a large saucepan. Add the sorrel and a little salt and cook, stirring, over low heat until the leaves wilt and the liquid evaporates, 3 to 5 minutes. Stir in the cream and cook until it thickens slightly, 1 to 2 minutes. Set aside.

Break the eggs into a mixing bowl, add a pinch of salt and pepper, and whisk to mix them.

In a large heavy saucepan, melt the remaining 7 tablespoons of butter. Set the pan in a barely simmering water bath. Pour the eggs into the pan and cook very gently, stirring constantly with a wooden spoon. As the eggs thicken on the bottom and sides of the pan, scrape them with the wooden spoon so they mix into the remaining uncooked eggs. Continue stirring until the egg mass thickens but remains soft and moist, at least 15 minutes. Taste for seasoning and add salt or pepper if needed. Take the pan from the heat.

Spoon the eggs into warmed soup plates. Add a dollop of the creamy sorrel to each plate. Stand a spoon in the sorrel and draw a spiral to form a swirl pattern in the eggs. Serve as soon as possible.

Olivier Robert's buttery dish of eggs is strictly for those who
1) still eat eggs, including the yolk,
2) eat eggs that are not hard-boiled,
3) can think of scrambled eggs as sophisticated,
4) fulfill the first 3 conditions and will eat eggs as a first course,
5) like the sour taste of sorrel.

If you're still with me, it's because you've been eating in France for years and you inherited low-cholesterol genes. This being the case, the following ethereal dish from La Bouzerotte in Bouze-lès-Beaune needs no hype to sell it.

OEUFS EN MEURETTE

(BURGUNDY)

Poached Eggs in Red Wine Sauce

4 SERVINGS

Burgundy's reputation for stodgy wine sauces can be a gastric turnoff. Yet in the right hands those sauces, studded with mushrooms and cubes of bacon, are so wonderful they can make you drop your spoon.

No question, this is a lot of trouble for eggs. But what eggs! Taste the yolk mixed with richly smoky (bacon) and slightly tart (wine) flavors, then dip a garlic-rubbed toast in the sauce. Some things are worth taking time for.

Serve oeufs en meurette as a first course (1 egg per person will do, and halve the other ingredients) or make it a meal.

5 tablespoons unsalted butter
¼ pound slab bacon, cut into lardons (page 56); or 4 slices bacon, cut across into ⅜-inch strips
4 shallots, finely chopped
3 garlic cloves, finely chopped
2 leeks, white and light green parts only, thinly sliced
2 carrots, thinly sliced
Salt and freshly ground pepper
3 cups red wine, preferably a Burgundy
1 bouquet garni (1 branch fresh thyme, or ½ teaspoon dried thyme leaves; 6 parsley stems; and 1 bay leaf, tied in a bundle with kitchen string or cheesecloth)
¼ cup marc de Bourgogne (the local brandy) or Cognac
2 tablespoons all-purpose flour

GARNISH

2 tablespoons unsalted butter
¼ pound button mushrooms, thinly sliced
Salt and freshly ground pepper
16 thin slices narrow French baguette
1 fat garlic clove, peeled

2 tablespoons distilled white vinegar
8 eggs

*I*n a medium saucepan, heat 3 tablespoons of the butter over low heat. Add the bacon and cook gently until golden, 5 to 8 minutes. Remove the bacon with a slotted spoon and set aside. To the same pan, add the shallots, garlic, leeks, carrots, and a little salt and stir until the vegetables are evenly coated with the butter. Cover the pan and cook over low heat, stirring occasionally, until tender, 10 to 15 minutes.

Stir the wine into the vegetables and add the *bouquet garni.* Heat the *marc* or Cognac in a small saucepan and light it. (It will flare up so take care.) Pour the flaming liquor into the vegetable pan and shake until the flames subside. Cover the pan, bring to a boil, then reduce the heat to moderate and simmer for 25 minutes.

Discard the *bouquet garni*. Pour the vegetables through a fine strainer, pressing to extract all their juice, back into the same pan. Discard the vegetables. (The sauce can be made a day or two ahead to this point and chilled.)

In a small bowl, mash together 2 tablespoons of butter and the flour. Bring the sauce to a boil and skim off the fat. Whisk in just enough of the butter-and-flour paste, a little at a time, to thicken the sauce lightly. Add the reserved bacon and simmer for 10 minutes. Add pepper and taste for seasoning. Take the pan from the heat and keep warm. Reheat the sauce to boiling before serving.

Meanwhile, make the garnish: In a frying pan, melt the butter. Add the mushrooms with salt and pepper. Toss them in the butter over moderately high heat until they lose all their moisture, about 5 minutes. Press a piece of foil on top and cover the pan if the mushrooms look dry to start. Add the mushrooms to the sauce.

Heat the broiler. Toast the bread slices on a baking sheet under the broiler, turning once, until golden, 2 to 3 minutes. Rub the toasts with the garlic and set aside.

If you have an egg poacher, poach the eggs according to the manufacturer's instructions. Alternatively, fill a sauté pan two thirds full of water and bring it to a boil with the vinegar. Break 4 eggs, one at a time, into a patch of bubbling water. Regulate the heat so the water barely simmers and poach the eggs until the white sets but the yolk is still soft, 3 to 4 minutes. Remove the eggs with a slotted spoon to paper towels. Poach the remaining eggs.

Arrange the eggs in warmed soup plates or bowls. Pour ½ cup of sauce over each serving. Set 4 garlic toasts around each dish, and serve as soon as possible.

OMELETTE MORVANDIAUDE

(BURGUNDY)

Potato Omelet with Mushrooms, Bacon, and Cheese

4 SERVINGS

3 medium boiling potatoes (½ pound total), unpeeled
Salt and freshly ground pepper
4 tablespoons vegetable oil
¼ pound slab bacon, cut into lardons (page 56); or 4 slices bacon, cut
    across into ⅜-inch strips
6 ounces mushrooms, halved and sliced
2 tablespoons chopped fresh flat-leaf parsley
10 to 12 eggs
3 tablespoons unsalted butter
¼ cup freshly grated Gruyère or other Swiss-type cheese

*P*ut the potatoes in a medium saucepan, cover with water, add salt, and bring to a boil. Simmer until tender, 15 to 20 minutes, and drain. While the potatoes are still warm, peel and cut them into ½-inch dice. Put in a bowl.

In a large frying pan, heat 2 tablespoons of the oil. Add the bacon and render it slowly until golden, 5 to 8 minutes. Remove with a slotted spoon and drain on paper towels.

Add the diced potatoes to the same pan and sauté over moderately high heat, stirring often, until crusty brown on all sides, 3 to 5 minutes. Add the potatoes to the bacon.

Heat the remaining 2 tablespoons of oil in the same pan. Toss the mushrooms in the oil until the moisture evaporates, about 5 minutes. Press a piece of foil on top and cover the pan if the mushrooms look dry to start. Discard any liquid from the pan. Take the pan from the heat and add the bacon, potatoes, and parsley to the mushrooms.

In a mixing bowl, whisk the eggs with a little salt and pepper until mixed. In a 10-inch omelet pan or a nonstick frying pan, melt the butter over moderately high heat. Add the eggs. When the omelet starts to cook on the bottom, pull the cooked egg from the sides to the center of the pan and tilt the pan to allow the uncooked egg to run underneath. When the mixture is set on the bottom but still runny on top, sprinkle the cheese evenly over the eggs, then top with the mushroom mixture. Leave the omelet on the

---

Before pizza dough became a worthy canvas for inspired taste buds, there was the omelet. Chefs to archbishops, royalty, and the merely rich once exercised their considerable talents on the garnished omelet, folding in asparagus tips, truffle slices, and crayfish tails. Meanwhile, down on the farm, where laying hens were plentiful, farmers' wives stuffed their eggs with ingredients near at hand. (You are what you fill your omelet with.)

In Burgundy's Morvan region, where the rugged hillsides are turned over to the business of growing Christmas trees, the local omelet still means a stuffing based on what was easily raised, grown, and hunted. This recipe comes from La Strada, where there's a woman in the kitchen and the food is unmistakably homemade.

heat until lightly browned on the bottom and still a little runny on top if you like a moist omelet, or until almost set if you prefer it well done.

Fold the omelet, tipping the pan away from you and turning the edge with a spatula. Half roll, half slide the omelet onto a warmed platter, guiding it to land folded in three. Serve it at once.

OMELETTE NORMANDE

(NORMANDY)

Smoked-Ham Omelet

2 SERVINGS

Thinly sliced and served with bread and butter or folded into a tender omelet, smoked ham is one of Normandy's best-kept secrets. Most of the smokehouses cluster in the Cotentin, in western Normandy.

I first tasted this omelet at the Auberge des Grottes, one of those end-of-the-world places on the windswept Cap de la Hague, at the western tip of the Cotentin Peninsula. The Auberge des Grottes shouldn't even be there on Jobourg's Nose, as this rugged promontory is called—the site should be left to hikers (one of the most beautiful trails in France crosses the Nez de Jobourg) and the spotted cows that graze in sight of the sea. But, somehow, you're grateful for this solitary, no-frills lodge, serving basic omelets made with local smoked ham, seafood platters, and roussin, *native lamb roasted until pink.*

2½ tablespoons unsalted butter
1 thin slice raw smoked ham (1½ ounces), cut into strips
5 or 6 eggs
Salt and freshly ground pepper

*I*n a frying pan, melt ½ tablespoon of the butter. Add the ham and cook gently until the fat runs, 1 or 2 minutes. Set aside.

In a mixing bowl, whisk the eggs with a little salt and pepper until mixed. In a 9-inch omelet pan, melt the remaining 2 tablespoons of butter over moderately high heat. Add the eggs. When the omelet starts to cook on the bottom, pull the cooked egg from the sides to the center of the pan and tilt the pan to allow the uncooked egg to run underneath. When the mixture is set on the bottom but still runny on top, add the ham. Leave the omelet on the heat until lightly browned on the bottom and still a little runny on top if you like a moist omelet, or until almost set if you prefer it well done.

Fold the omelet, tipping the pan away from you and turning the edge with a spatula. Half roll, half slide the omelet onto a warmed platter, guiding it to land folded in three. Serve it at once.

OMELETTE LA TROUCHIA

(PROVENCE)

Flat Swiss Chard Omelet with Garlic and Parmesan

2 SERVINGS

4 cups chopped Swiss chard leaves
5 or 6 eggs
Salt and freshly ground pepper
1 small garlic clove, finely chopped
¼ cup freshly grated Parmesan cheese
2 tablespoons unsalted butter

Cook the Swiss chard in plenty of boiling salted water (as for pasta) until wilted and tender, 5 to 10 minutes. Drain, rinse in cold water, and drain again thoroughly. Press out the water by handfuls.

In a mixing bowl, whisk the eggs with salt and pepper until mixed. Stir in the greens, garlic, and cheese. In a 9-inch omelet pan or a nonstick frying pan, melt the butter over moderately high heat. Add the egg mixture. When the omelet starts to cook on the bottom, pull the cooked egg from the sides to the center of the pan and tilt the pan to allow the uncooked egg to run underneath. Leave the omelet to cook until lightly browned on the bottom but still runny on top.

Take from the heat, set a heatproof plate over the top of the pan, and invert the pan to turn out the omelet. Slide it back into the pan and brown the other side. Using a spatula, guide the omelet onto a warmed platter. Cut the omelet into wedges and serve either hot or at room temperature.

Searching for Nice's unembellished soul? Settle into one of the ten tables at Lou Pistou. Madame la patronne, a wiry woman with short, frizzled blond hair and glasses, looks after you in the unfussy dining room, while Monsieur, in shorts and white apron, tends to the cooking.

For his trouchia, Michel Vergnaud first boils the leafy green tops of Swiss chard (a favorite vegetable in Nice), then mixes it with garlic, whisked eggs, and cheese. But not just any cheese. "Use Parmesan," Madame Vergnaud told me. "Gruyère cooks into strings."

At Lou Pistou, trouchia is served as a first course. It makes a good luncheon dish, too. And if you are amenable to bending the rules, this flat omelet also works well as a sandwich filling. I recommend lightly basting homemade bread, hard rolls, or even pita with vinaigrette first.

OMELETTE LA MÈRE POULARD

(NORMANDY)

La Mère Poulard's Puffy Omelet

2 SERVINGS

It's easy to be scared off by a dish with a rep. And the soufflélike omelet from La Mère Poulard comes with more hoopla than most. At this sentiment-tugging landmark on Mont-Saint-Michel, omelets have been made in the same way, watched over by a string of proprietors, for more than a century.

Still, the mystery surrounding this omelet puzzles me. Anyone—you don't even have to be a customer—can watch them being made at the restaurant. Cooks gussied up in nineteenth-century peasant garb whisk eggs by hand, then cook them in a long-handled pan over a log fire. Neck kerchiefs and bonnets aside, the recipe is Omelet Making 101: 2 eggs per serving plus 1 for the pan. The only funny business here is beating the eggs, whole, until they triple in volume, and this can be done without shame using electricity instead of elbow grease. The result is a cross between an omelet and a cloud.

5 eggs
1 teaspoon salt
Freshly ground pepper
3 tablespoons unsalted butter

*H*eat the broiler.

In a large stainless-steel or unlined copper bowl, whisk the eggs with the salt and pepper until mixed. Using an electric beater or a balloon whisk, whip the eggs until they triple in volume, 5 to 7 minutes.

In a 9-inch omelet pan or a nonstick frying pan, melt the butter over moderately high heat. Add the eggs. Cook for 1 minute then remove the pan from the heat for 15 seconds. Return the pan to the heat for another minute. Remove from the heat for 15 seconds. Return the pan to the heat until the omelet has puffed up like a soufflé, 30 seconds to 1 minute more.

Set the pan on a rack just under the broiler for a few seconds—just until the top begins to brown lightly. The omelet should be set but not dry inside.

Fold the omelet, tipping the pan away from you and turning the edge with a spatula. Slide the omelet onto a warmed platter, guiding it to land folded in half. Serve as soon as possible.

VEGETABLES
AND
SIDE DISHES

Although Provençal cooking is a gastronomic heartthrob at the moment, those who grew up eating it can be surprisingly disdainful of its virtues. "*Cuisine provençale* is poor man's cooking," sniffed Ludovic Alziari, a retired olive-oil maker from Nice. "It's cheap. All those tomatoes, peppers, and potatoes. You could feed a family with two pounds of vegetables. Now Southwestern cooking . . . *confit, foie gras* . . . there's something to write about."

This dismissal of Provençal cooking—and, by extension, of vegetables—is partly a longing for what's available somewhere else, partly the sloughing off of hungry memories. Only the well-fed can wax poetic about what, for others, is merely filling when the wolf is at the door.

Still, as a rule, the French have rehabilitated their vegetables, their beans, and their grains—going so far as to give cabbage and lentils a certain chic. Even so, it is unthinkable to have a dish of carrots, say, as the centerpiece of a meal. To be sure, you may begin a Provençal dinner with braised artichokes. And flageolet beans were made for roast lamb, according to the Norman way of thinking. But a whole supper of vegetables and dried beans? "Well," says Pierre Landau, a record industry executive, "it's not cuisine."

While there are no main dishes in this chapter, if you want to make a vegetarian feast, do it. Baked Endives with Apple and Clove from Normandy goes well with Beet Salad with Vinaigrette, and dried beans and millet or barley round out the meal. Although a menu of Braised Cardoons with Cheese (made with vegetable stock instead of chicken stock) and a mixed bean salad together with Polenta with Wild Mushrooms couldn't be called truly Provençal, it nonetheless has the feel of Provence.

Whether you're looking for a side of something or a basic element, this chapter offers all manner of regional recipes from the French countryside to suit. ✍

CÔTES DE BLETTES CIGALOUN

(PROVENCE)

Swiss Chard with Bacon and Tomatoes

4 SERVINGS

½ tablespoon olive oil
2 slices bacon, cut across into ⅜-inch strips
10 ounces Swiss chard stems, halved lengthwise and sliced across
　(2½ cups)
4 small plum tomatoes, peeled, seeded, and chopped (½ cup)
Salt and freshly ground pepper

*I*n a medium saucepan, heat the oil. Add the bacon to the pan and render slowly without browning it, 3 to 5 minutes. Add the Swiss chard and stir until coated with the fat. Mix in the tomatoes. Cover and cook over moderate heat, stirring now and then, until the Swiss chard is tender, 10 to 25 minutes (timing varies wildly). Add pepper and taste for seasoning. Salt may be unnecessary if the bacon is salty.

In Saint-Antonin-du-Var, Denise and Jean-Pierre Chevraux run the kind of unprepossessing country auberge you hope to find all over France but rarely do. Lou Cigaloun's front door opens directly into the bar, its bedrooms look out over the vineyards, and the restaurant, adorned with old gardening tools and tanks for fresh lobster and trout, serves up far better cooking than you'd expect in such an unsung place. (From the guide books you'd never make a detour to Lou Cigaloun.)

This Swiss chard dish was one of three generous, down-home accompaniments—no wilted lettuce leaves here—Monsieur Chevraux prepared for us, setting the tone for a cozy Provençal evening. If the stems of the Swiss chard are tough and stringy, you may need to peel them. (Save the leaves to make Flat Swiss Chard Omelet with Garlic and Parmesan, or use them in a typical Provençal stuffing for pasta or cabbage.) Vary the vegetable to suit the season and what you have on hand, substituting green beans, zucchini, or even okra for the Swiss chard.

ÉCHALOTES GLACÉES AU MIEL

(BRITTANY)

Honey-Glazed Shallots

4 SERVINGS

1 tablespoon unsalted butter
1 tablespoon honey
1 pound shallots, peeled
1 cup chicken stock, preferably homemade (page 369)
Salt and freshly ground pepper

In a saucepan big enough to hold the shallots in a single layer, melt the butter. Add the honey and stir until it melts. Add the shallots, stock, and a little salt, and cook, uncovered, over low heat, stirring occasionally, until the shallots are tender and the liquid reduces to a coating glaze, 20 to 30 minutes. Add pepper and taste for seasoning. Serve hot.

As summer winds down in western Brittany, the shallot harvest is in full swing. Around Plougastel (also famous for its early strawberries) everybody takes part in the harvesting: cousins, neighbors, kids on vacation, and students from the area. They all kneel in the dirt and pull plant by plant, working their way down the furrow as quickly as possible.

Many of the Plougastel farmers haul their crates of shallots to SAVEOL, a local cooperative that markets and distributes the crop as far as the USA. During a visit to SAVEOL in Plougastel, I was offered this easy recipe by President Jean-Marie Le Gall. Now that shallots are readily available in American supermarkets, try this sweet version with smoked meats, poultry, or pork.

POMMES SAUTÉES AUX RAISINS

(BURGUNDY)

Autumn Fruit Sauté

4 SERVINGS

Pierre Landau, a record industry executive, sometimes calls just to tell what he found in the market and what he's going to do with it for dinner. If I'm lucky, he and his wife, Isabelle, also invite me to join them for the meal. (Pierre the dinner guest is something special, too. He's been known to bring the cheese course uninvited—Americans can't always be counted on to serve Camembert at its peak, and what's a meal without cheese?)

Utterly simple, yet uncommon, this fruit sauté typifies Pierre's cooking. The Landaus had just returned from a visit to Isabelle's grandmother in Burgundy wine country, laden with apples and grapes. As a side dish for his Turkey Drumsticks in Red Wine, Pierre sliced the apples and tossed them in sweet butter with the grapes.

4 large apples (about 1½ pounds)
½ pound seedless red grapes
3 tablespoons unsalted butter
Salt and freshly ground pepper
Squeeze of lemon juice, or to taste

*P*eel, halve, and slice the apples. Halve the grapes.

In a frying pan, melt the butter over moderately high heat. When the butter foams, add the apples, salt, and pepper, and cook, stirring occasionally, until the apples are tender and beginning to brown, 5 to 10 minutes. Add the grapes and toss until warm, about 1 minute. Add lemon juice and taste for seasoning. Transfer to a warmed bowl and serve at once.

POMMES CUITES AU FOUR

(NORMANDY)

Savory Baked Apples

4 SERVINGS

4 baking apples, cored, peeled, and halved
½ large lemon
Salt and freshly ground pepper
Granulated sugar, for sprinkling (optional)

Heat the oven to 425°F.

Rub the apple halves with the cut lemon, and put the apples, rounded side down, in a shallow heavy baking dish just big enough to hold them. Squeeze any remaining lemon juice over the apples and sprinkle them with salt, pepper, and, if using, sugar.

Bake the apples in the preheated oven until they are tender when pierced with a knife but still hold their shape, 20 to 30 minutes.

Denis Chartier, a charcutier in Le Mêle-sur-Sarthe, Normandy, likes to serve these apples as a side dish with boudin blanc, a fine-textured pure pork sausage. He prepares them simply, with only salt, pepper, and a sprinkling of sugar if the apples are tart. The lemon juice is my addition, to discourage the fruit from browning and to boost the apples' own flavor. These pommes could accompany most Norman main dishes— ones that don't already include apples, that is.

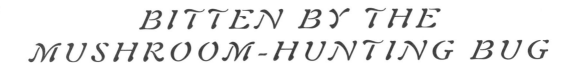

BITTEN BY THE MUSHROOM-HUNTING BUG

Bagnoles-de-l'Orne, Normandy—Twenty-nine-year-old Franck Quinton has the enthusiasm of a puppy combined with the philosophic acceptance of a man twice his age. "Did you bring boots?" he asks. "And long pants?"

Franck, whose family runs the Manoir du Lys, a comfortable *auberge* in the Andaines forest, has seen more than a few wild outfits for mushroom hunting. Shaking his head, Franck says: "I've known some to show up in high heels and mini-skirts."

Here in the Bocage region of southwestern Normandy, where farmers keep a few cows, grow hay, and press the apples and pears in their mixed orchards for cider, locals hold the secret of their wild-mushroom trove close to their chests. "There are many more cepes here than in Périgord," Franck explains, referring to *Boletus edulis*, a celebrated staple in France's southwestern cooking. "But nobody realizes it."

For those in the know, the Quinton family organizes mushroom weekends in September and October from the Manoir du Lys. During the hunts, groups of twenty track down wild mushrooms in the Andaines forest with the help of a mycologist.

Besides waterproof boots for mucking around in damp forests and long pants to protect against slaps from wet branches, no self-respecting mushroom hunter leaves home without a lucky woven basket (not a plastic bag) in the back seat of the car.

THE MUSHROOM TRAIL

Suitably attired and armed with the proper holder, the chase is on. But where to start? "Mushrooms grow all over the forest," says Franck, "but it's not everywhere that you find quantities of them." Franck explains that every mushroom gatherer has a private corner, which he keeps under his hat.

Franck plots the course: From the Manoir du Lys, head out the D235 toward Bagnoles-de-l'Orne. At the first crossroad, keep left—this is the D53. Follow the road past the golf course, then make a left in front of a white iron gate onto the D335. Drive by a half-timbered manor house on the right into a forest of beech and oak trees until you come to a picnic sign. Park here.

Diagonally across the road from the picnic sign is a packed dirt path. Remember to take your mushroom basket and walk up the path until you see the low-bush European blueberries, or *myrtilles*, on the right. The blueberry bushes are the first promising sign. *Myrtilles* like the same quality of light, the same soil and humidity as many wild mushrooms. Make for the stand of pine trees beyond, where the boletes and *girolles* (chanterelles) hide.

And cross your fingers. While Franck now has the route down pat, for a beginner out in the forest the markers are hard to spot. "I've taken friends mushroom hunting here once or twice," Franck says. "After that they wanted to come back on their own. They've never been able to find the right place. Even I end up taking a different route back through the forest every time I go. I never seem to find the same one twice."

The *myrtille* bushes you come across will bear small intensely flavored berries next July and August. But in October the animals have eaten the fruit, and the lush ferns of summer have turned from green to yellow and brown. The ground is soft and squishy underfoot. "Very pretty," says Franck, glancing around appreciatively. "That's what attracts me the most. It's nature."

He spots the first mushrooms growing on a log, *petits violets*, a slender, dusty-purple variety. "They're edible," he says, handing them over. "Good in an omelet."

GETTING HOOKED

Now you scramble to find your own and turn up only roots and logs. Suddenly, you happen on to something. What are they? Are they edible? "I'm sure it's a real *girolle*," Franck confirms. "Good sautéed, with roast pheasant or partridge."

Adding these mushrooms with a brown, slightly depressed cap and yellow stalk to your basket, you continue prowling. Next thing you know, you can hardly take a step without crushing a mushroom.

With the find, the world changes. If you've been chattering, you stop. Wet branches whack your cheek as you walk, bent over, concentrating on mushrooms. But who cares?

Franck, picking up on this change of heart, laughs and says, "People, as soon as they find their first mushrooms, they're hooked. They'll go anywhere. They don't notice the rain, the cold, how long they have walked."

But what about the cepes? Where are those fleshy mushrooms with the bulbous white stalk and golden-brown cap? Under the low pine trees, Franck points out a *montre cepe*, the local name for a mushroom with a milk-white stem and a broadly convex, Day-Glo red cap spotted with white. These deadly mushrooms signal that cepes grow close at hand.

Near the *montre cepe*, the ferns are well trampled. Other mushroom pickers have been here recently. Unlike Franck Quinton, not everyone enjoys mushroom hunting solely for its natural charms. Fresh cepes sell for about twenty dollars a pound, a strong economic draw.

Still, it takes only a day or a day and a half for cepes to grow to eating size. Since the last mushroom sweep new cepes have already sprung up. You discover one beautiful example, then another a foot from the first one. At your elbow, there's a carpet of *girolles*.

Franck gives a lesson on proper mushroom-picking technique: Clear the ground around the mushrooms of dead leaves and twigs. To avoid breaking off the stem too high up, put your fingers as close to the base of the mushroom as possible before pulling.

HITTING THE JACKPOT

You feel giddy faced with such bounty. Thirty species, not all edible, is the minimum spotted on a mushroom hunt in the Andaines forest. On a good day, you can collect sixty to eighty pounds of cepes in just two hours.

But the giddiness quickly changes into shrewd appraisal. Not just any cepe wins a good word now. You glance at a giant one and sniff. Big cepes aren't very tasty. A slug or frog has clearly nibbled another, and you snub that one, too. But at least you know it's edible. Animals won't touch the poisonous varieties.

What exactly are you looking for in superior cepes? "It should feel firm, like a balloon," says Franck. The best earn the name *bouchons de champagne* because they're roughly the size and shape of Champagne corks.

From mid-September, even August sometimes, until November when the first frost comes, you can find cepes in the Andaines forest. But at different seasons other mushrooms come into view. Yves Fairier, a math and science teacher with a passion for the microscopic mushrooms that grow on logs, leads groups around for the Manoir du Lys. "We've collected as many as eighty varieties in a weekend," he says. He estimates that there are close to a thousand varieties in this forest.

For Franck Quinton that's the beauty of the mushroom hunt. "You never know what you're going to find," he says. "It's the chase that counts."

POMMES FARCIES AUX PLEUROTTES

(NORMANDY)

Apples Stuffed with Oyster Mushrooms

4 SERVINGS

4 large baking apples, preferably Cortland
½ lemon
3 tablespoons unsalted butter
2 garlic cloves, finely chopped
½ pound oyster mushrooms or wild mushrooms, cut into ⅜-inch slices
Salt and freshly ground pepper
¼ cup crème fraîche (page 368) or heavy (whipping) cream
¼ cup chopped fresh flat-leaf parsley
½ cup chicken stock, preferably homemade (page 369), or water

*H*eat the oven to 350°F. Butter a small shallow baking dish just big enough to hold the apples.

Cut off the top of each apple about an eighth of the way down. Using a grapefruit knife or melon baller, hollow out the apples, leaving a thin but sturdy "cup." Rub and moisten the apple "cups" with the cut lemon to discourage browning, and set aside. Pick over the apple tops and insides. Discard skin and seeds. Chop any apple flesh.

In a large frying pan, melt the butter over moderate heat. Add the garlic and stir until fragrant, about 1 minute. Add the chopped apple and the mushrooms with salt and pepper. Toss them in the butter over moderately high heat until the mushrooms lose all their moisture, about 5 minutes. Press a piece of foil on top and cover the pan if the mushrooms look dry to start. Stir in the *crème fraîche* or cream and the parsley and simmer to evaporate most of the liquid. Taste for seasoning.

Sprinkle the apple "cups" with salt and pepper. Spoon the mushroom mixture into the apples, mounding it slightly. Arrange the apples in the prepared baking dish and pour the stock around them. Bake, uncovered, in the preheated oven until tender when pierced with a knife, 45 minutes to 1 hour, depending on the size and variety of the apples. If the apples begin to brown during cooking, cover them with foil. Serve hot.

When at La Rançonnière, a fortified farm-hotel in Normandy's Bessin region, opt for the least complicated offerings on the hit-or-miss menu. These apples, stuffed with a blend of apple insides, garlic, parsley, cream, and mushrooms, then baked until tender, are a bull's-eye. They could team up with Roasted Pheasant with Calvados and Cream, Chicken in Cider Vinegar Sauce, or a plain roast bird or pork chops. If you like grilled sausage, either a fresh pork variety or blood pudding, it's a love marriage. This recipe is easily halved to serve two.

PURÉE DE BETTERAVES
À L'ORANGE

(BURGUNDY)

Red Beet Purée with Orange

4 SERVINGS

1 pound cooked beets (recipe follows), cut into 2-inch chunks
1 cup orange juice
Salt and freshly ground pepper

*W*hir the cooked beets in a food processor until puréed.

Put the purée in a medium saucepan and stir in the orange juice and a little salt. Cook over moderately low heat, stirring now and then, until the purée thickens and holds a soft shape, about 30 minutes. Add pepper and taste for seasoning before serving.

BETTERAVES CUITES

Baked Red Beets

4 SERVINGS

2 large or 8 small fresh beets with tops (1¾ pounds in all)

*H*eat the oven to 325°F. Cut the leaves off the beets, leaving 1 inch of stem, and save them for another recipe. Trim the roots. Scrub the beets in cold water.

Wrap the beets all together in a double sheet of aluminum foil. Set the package on a baking sheet, seam side up, and bake in the preheated oven until the beets are tender when pierced with a knife, 1 to 2 hours, depending on the size. When they are cool enough to handle, peel off the skin. Serve warm like baked potatoes, or let cool before using in another recipe.

Sweet and earthy, beets appeal more than ever to French cooks. Bistrotiers cut them into slices or chunks and add them to crudité platters. Fancy chefs like beets especially for their flamboyant color. At Les Gourmets in Marsannay-la-Côte (Burgundy wine territory), Joël Perreaut purées beets and blends them with orange juice to make a familiar yet elusive-tasting side dish. Every time I make it someone asks, "It's delicious, but what is it?"

In France, truck farmers cook up beets, en masse, to sell cooled and ready to eat at the market. At home it's either beets from scratch or settling for the canned variety. Baked beets require more time than toil. You can also steam or boil beets, about 30 minutes or more, depending on the size. Alternatively, cook them in a 600-watt microwave oven for 15 minutes on High. Save the beet tops. Cook both stems and leaves like spinach.

SALADE DE HARICOTS VERTS ET TOMATES

(BRITTANY)

Warm Salad of Green Beans and Tomatoes

4 SERVINGS

VINAIGRETTE
1 tablespoon red-wine vinegar
Salt and freshly ground pepper
¼ cup vegetable oil or a mixture of vegetable and olive oil

1 pound green beans, preferably haricots verts, *ends trimmed*
2 small tomatoes, peeled, seeded, and diced

*M*ake the vinaigrette: In a small bowl, whisk together the vinegar and salt until the salt dissolves. Whisk in the pepper and oil until smooth. Taste for seasoning.

Cook the beans in plenty of boiling salted water (as for pasta) until crisp-tender, 5 to 8 minutes, and drain. Rinse in cold water and drain thoroughly.

Transfer the cooked beans to a bowl. Toss with the vinaigrette and tomatoes until evenly coated. Serve still slightly warm.

I'm not a fan of undercooking vegetables (my French training), but in this recipe a bit of crunch is nice to reinforce the saladlike quality. To be sure, the beans must be tender and garden-fresh, the tomatoes ripe and just-picked, as at the Auberge Bretonne in La Roche-Bernard, where I tasted these beans as an accompaniment to a roasted saddle of rabbit.

In this luxurious auberge *on Brittany's southern coast, the dining room is arranged around a small courtyard planted with green beans, zucchini, leeks, tomatoes, and celery. Naturally I wanted to know if the same decorative vegetables appeared in the restaurant kitchen or whether they were simply for show. "I assure you," said Madame Thorel, "the beans you ate at noon came from our kitchen garden."*

CÉLÉRI À LA CRÈME

(NORMANDY)

Creamy Cubed Celery Root

4 SERVINGS

1 largish celery root (2 pounds)
½ lemon
Salt and freshly ground white pepper
½ cup crème fraîche *(page 368) or heavy (whipping) cream*
Grating of nutmeg, or to taste
1 tablespoon chopped fresh flat-leaf parsley (optional)

The scruffy appearance of untrimmed celery root (celeriac) belies its delicacy when pared and cooked. Most people who eat this vegetable for the first time are pleasantly surprised. "If I'd known celery root was this good," one taster remarked, "I wouldn't have waited so long to try it."

At the Moulin de Villeray, in southern Normandy, this creamy celery root accompanies Marinated Duck Stew with Bacon. This side dish also suits any creamless poultry or meat recipe.

Thickly peel the celery root. Quarter the peeled root and rub and moisten the cut surfaces with the lemon half. Cut the pieces into 1-inch chunks.

Cook the celery root in plenty of boiling salted water (as for pasta) until tender, 15 to 20 minutes. Drain.

Combine the celery root, *crème fraîche* or cream, nutmeg, and a little salt in a medium saucepan. Simmer, stirring from time to time, until the mixture thickens, 5 to 10 minutes. Add pepper and taste for seasoning. If needed, add more nutmeg, salt, or pepper until the dish is flavored as you like. Spoon the celery root into a warmed serving dish and sprinkle with the parsley, if you like.

ENDIVES ET POMMES AU CLOU DE GIROFLE

(NORMANDY)

Baked Endives with Apple and Clove

4 SERVINGS

4 large Belgian endives, trimmed
8 cloves
4 tablespoons unsalted butter
2 apples, peeled, halved, and thinly sliced
Salt and freshly ground pepper
½ cup dry white wine
½ cup water

It is difficult to imagine baked endives as anything other than boring. But once you've tried Simone Monneron's recipe, it will be harder still to imagine them any more wonderful than prepared in this way, perfumed with cloves and apples. Simple to make and satisfying, this vegetable goes well alongside roasted pork, game, or poultry, or as part of a vegetarian meal.

*H*eat the oven to 350°F.

Cut each endive in half lengthwise. Stud the core of each half with a clove.

Using 1 tablespoon of the butter, generously butter a shallow lidded casserole just the size to hold the endives in a single snug layer. Arrange half the apples in the bottom of the casserole. Fit the endives on top. Push the remaining apple slices into the spaces between the endives. Sprinkle with salt. Pour in the wine and water. Dot with the remaining 3 tablespoons of butter.

Cover with the lid and bake in the preheated oven for 1 hour. Remove the lid and raise the oven temperature to 400°F. Continue baking, uncovered, until the endives are very tender and the juices have reduced, 20 to 30 minutes. Season the endives with pepper. Serve hot. Warn diners about the cloves.

ARTICHAUTS À LA BARIGOULE

(PROVENCE)

Braised Artichokes with Onions and Garlic

4 SERVINGS

1 lemon, halved
8 baby globe artichokes, or 4 medium artichokes
4 tablespoons extra-virgin olive oil
1 onion, halved and sliced
2 garlic cloves, thinly sliced
3 ounces slab bacon, cut into lardons *(page 56)*; or 3 slices bacon, cut
    across into ⅜-inch strips
2 imported bay leaves, broken into pieces
Salt
½ cup dry white wine
½ cup water

*H*eat the oven to 350°F.

To prepare the artichokes, add the juice of ½ lemon to a large bowl of cold water. For baby artichokes, snap off the tough outer leaves. Trim the stalk with a stainless-steel knife and cut 1 inch from the top of the remaining leaves. Cut the artichokes in half lengthwise. While you're working, rub the cut surfaces with a lemon half. Drop the finished artichokes into the lemon water.

For medium artichokes, snap off 15 of the tough outer leaves. Using a stainless-steel knife, trim the bottom to an even round shape and cut 1½ inches from the top of the remaining leaves. Quarter the artichoke lengthwise and cut each quarter into 2 wedges. Cut out the fuzzy choke. Rub with lemon and add to the lemon water as for baby artichokes.

Put 2 tablespoons of the oil, the onion, garlic, bacon, bay leaves, and a little salt in a shallow lidded casserole just big enough to hold the artichokes in a snug layer. Toss the ingredients to coat them in the oil. Fit the artichokes, lying down, into the casserole. Drizzle the remaining 2 tablespoons of olive oil over the artichokes. Pour in the wine and water.

Cover with the lid and transfer the casserole to the oven. Bake for 1 hour. Increase the oven temperature to 400°F. Remove the lid

---

Two sisters, Jeanne and Simone Laffitte, run a magical rabbits' warren of shops called Les Arcenaulx. This is the place in Marseilles to find a play by Marcel Pagnol or a cookbook, to pick up damask linens for the table, and, at lunch or dinner, to sample tasty Provençal fare such as these braised artichokes.

In classic French cooking, artichauts à la barigoule is a substantial dish with a meat stuffing. But, originally, it's supposed to have been a whole artichoke, cooked on the grill and basted with olive oil. Today the term is used to mean just about any artichoke dish with a Provençal accent.

Whatever the source, the version of braised artichokes from Les Arcenaulx is delicious. Resist cutting short the cooking time. Even though the artichokes are tender after an hour of cooking, the flavors need the extra half-hour to mingle. Serve these artichokes as a first course or side dish.

from the artichokes and continue baking, uncovered, until the artichokes are very tender and the juices have reduced, about 30 minutes. (The artichokes can be cooked a day ahead and chilled; the flavor improves with time. Reheat gently, adding a little water if the dish is dry.) Serve hot, warm, or at room temperature.

CARDONS AU GRATIN

(PROVENCE)

Braised Cardoons with Cheese

4 SERVINGS

In December the boules courts at La Table de Nicole, which provide reliable entertainment in Valaurie most of the year, stand empty. The tables that fill the courtyard of this good-time auberge are vacant, too. But even with this off-season scene, it looks like a party could start here any minute.

This is the season Nicole Vernerey, like most Provençal cooks, puts cardoons on her menu. She prepares this vegetable, which looks like celery but tastes faintly of artichokes, in the simplest possible way—braised in chicken stock and then gratinéed with cheese. At La Table de Nicole, it arrives as an accompaniment to roast turkey on Christmas Eve, but it can be served as a side dish with any hearty winter meal.

Juice of 1 lemon (about 3 tablespoons)
Salt and freshly ground pepper
2 pounds cardoons, trimmed
4 tablespoons unsalted butter
1½ cups chicken stock, preferably homemade (page 369)
1 cup freshly grated Gruyère or other Swiss-type cheese

Heat the oven to 350°F. Bring a large pot of water to a boil. Add the lemon juice and salt.

While the water boils, cut the cardoons across into 4 even lengths, then halve the wider parts lengthwise. Cook in the boiling water (as for pasta) until barely tender, about 15 minutes. Drain, rinse the cardoons in cold water to cool slightly, and drain thoroughly again. Using a knife, zip off the tough strings as for green beans.

Using 1 tablespoon of the butter, generously butter a shallow lidded casserole just the size to hold the cardoons snugly. Arrange the boiled cardoons in the casserole. Pour in the stock. Dot with the remaining 3 tablespoons of butter. Cover with the lid and bake for 1½ hours. Remove the lid and increase the oven temperature to 400°F. Season the cardoons with pepper. Sprinkle the cheese over the top and continue baking, uncovered, until the cardoons are very tender and the tops are golden, 20 to 30 minutes. Serve hot.

CAROTTES À LA CRÈME

(NORMANDY)

Baked Carrots in Cream

4 SERVINGS

3 tablespoons unsalted butter
1½ pounds carrots, grated
Salt and freshly ground pepper
Grating of nutmeg, or to taste
¾ cup crème fraîche *(page 368)* or heavy *(whipping) cream*

*H*eat the oven to 400°F., or, if you are already roasting something, simply bake the carrots at the set temperature.

In a large frying pan, melt the butter. When hot, add the carrots and a little salt and cook, stirring, until they lose their raw look, 3 to 5 minutes. Stir in some pepper, the nutmeg, and *crème fraîche* or cream, and cook until it boils. Taste for seasoning.

Transfer the carrots to a small shallow casserole, cover with the lid, and bake in the preheated oven until the cream has been absorbed and the carrots brown around the edges, 30 to 45 minutes. No harm is done if the carrots cook longer; they will simply continue to caramelize. But undercooked they're just ordinary. Serve hot.

Without fail, every time I make these carrots someone asks me for the recipe. Full credit goes to Carole Clements, friend and colleague extraordinary, who developed this dish with typically Norman ingredients. (Near the heart of crème fraîche country—the area around the "landing-day" beaches—farmers cultivate some of France's best carrots.) One evening after work, I stood at her elbow grating carrots as she tossed together a four-course dinner for company. (Carole is very organized.) My jaw dropped when I tasted the unpromising carrots sautéed in butter and baked with a little nutmeg and cream.

The best time to make these carrots is when you have dinner already roasting in the oven (such as Roast Lamb on a Potato Gratin) and need something to round out the meal. Besides lamb, serve these alongside roast poultry, game, or pork loin.

TOMATES À LA PROVENÇALE

(PROVENCE)

Golden Garlicky Tomatoes

4 SERVINGS

This is a forgiving recipe and one that easily adjusts to your timetable and dinner menu. If the oven is going at 400°F. for roast lamb, the higher temperature does the tomatoes no harm. They can also wait in the oven an extra 10 or 15 minutes if you're held up. In some recipes, only sun-ripened tomatoes will do. But even the hothouse variety tastes uncharacteristically good this way.

The main thing to remember is that these tomato halves sprinkled with bread crumbs, garlic, and parsley shouldn't bake so long that they collapse entirely (though they should wilt in a dignified way). Also, the crunchy topping shouldn't burn. Cover the tomatoes with foil if they threaten to darken too much.

1½ slices sourdough or other country bread, crusts removed (to make ½ cup fresh bread crumbs)
2 fat garlic cloves, peeled
¼ cup chopped fresh flat-leaf parsley
4 medium firm tomatoes, halved crosswise
Salt and freshly ground pepper
2 tablespoons extra-virgin olive oil

Heat the oven to 350°F.

Tear the bread into pieces. Drop the pieces into the bowl of a food processor and pulse into large crumbs. Slice the garlic into the food processor. Pulse until the garlic is coarsely chopped. Add the parsley and pulse until everything is finely chopped.

Arrange the tomatoes, cut side up, in a shallow baking dish just big enough to hold them. Sprinkle them with salt and a little pepper. Spoon the bread topping over the tomatoes. Moisten each tomato with some of the oil.

Bake the tomatoes in the middle of the preheated oven for 30 minutes. Raise the tomatoes to the top of the oven and continue baking until the bread crumbs are golden and the tomatoes are soft but still hold their shape, about 15 minutes.

A PROVENÇAL MENU UNDER THE CLIPPED PLANE TREES

When everyone else in France has fished woolen scarfs and gloves out of drawers smelling of mothballs, in Provence they're still wearing sunglasses. "Cold, you say?" goes the arch query.
"We're dining alfresco."
The meal in question, if it's at someone's mother's house, could very well be the following. With a game of *pétanque*, it's standard fare in the Provençal Sunday repertoire. The red wine from Bandol was made for the occasion.

Salade de Poivrons Grillés (page 81)
Roasted Red Pepper Salad

Gigot à la Crème d'Ail (page 272)
Roast Leg of Lamb with Garlic Toasts

Tomates à la Provençale (page 140)
Golden Garlicky Tomatoes

Goat Cheeses

Tarte aux Noix (page 307)
Walnut Tart
or
Tartelettes aux Framboises (page 312)
Warm Raspberry Tartlets

RÂPÉE DE POMMES DE TERRE

(BURGUNDY)

Potato Pancakes from Burgundy

4 SERVINGS

4 large baking potatoes (about 2 pounds total), peeled
2 eggs
2 tablespoons fromage blanc or ricotta cheese
3 to 6 tablespoons all-purpose flour
2 teaspoons salt
Freshly ground pepper
Vegetable oil, for frying

Grate the potatoes by hand using the largest holes on a grater, or in a food processor, again using a grating disc with the largest holes to prevent a gluey mess.

Press out the liquid by handfuls and transfer the grated potatoes to a mixing bowl. Beat the eggs and *fromage blanc* or ricotta cheese into the potatoes. Then beat in just enough flour to make a light batter. Add the salt and a few grindings of pepper.

In a large cast-iron skillet or heavy frying pan, heat ¼ inch of oil. For each pancake, drop about 1 tablespoon of batter into the oil and flatten with the back of a fork. Fry for 1 to 2 minutes on one side, then turn and fry for 30 seconds or so on the other side. As they are ready, remove the pancakes to a baking sheet lined with paper towels or, even better, brown paper bags. Keep the drained pancakes warm in a 200°F. oven while frying the rest. Serve as soon as possible.

One retired specialty to make a comeback with the revival of regional food is the potato pancake. A relative of the popular pommes paillasson, *or grated potato cake, this petite version includes some fresh cheese. While they are often served as part of a first-course platter of hot appetizers such as* Les Corniottes Morvandelles, *they also make a good accompaniment to roasted meat and poultry.*

GRATIN DE POMMES DE TERRE AUX LARDONS

(BRITTANY)

Scalloped Potatoes with Bacon from Brittany

4 SERVINGS

4 tablespoons unsalted butter
6 slices bacon
2 pounds all-purpose potatoes, peeled and thinly sliced
Salt and freshly ground pepper
Several gratings of nutmeg
1 cup whole milk
½ cup crème fraîche *(page 368)* or heavy (whipping) cream
1 cup freshly grated Gruyère or other Swiss-type cheese

The inspiration for this dish comes from Entre Deux Verres, a spunky wine bar in the heart of Saint-Malo's old walled city. Savory and satisfying, these potatoes typify the simple Breton fare served here to set off the wine available by the glass. They suit any plain roast, or sautéed veal or pork chops.

*H*eat the oven to 375°F. Butter a 6-cup shallow baking dish with 1 tablespoon of the butter.

In a nonstick frying pan, render the bacon slowly until golden, 5 to 8 minutes. Drain on paper towels.

Arrange a third of the potatoes in a layer, slices overlapping, in the bottom of the baking dish. Season with salt, pepper, and nutmeg. Cover with 3 slices of the bacon. Layer the potatoes, seasoning, and bacon until all the ingredients are used, finishing with a layer of potatoes.

Whisk together the milk and *crème fraîche* or cream and pour over the potatoes. Sprinkle with the cheese and dot with the remaining 3 tablespoons of butter.

Bake in the preheated oven until the potatoes are perfectly tender and the top is golden, 45 minutes to 1 hour.

POMMES DE TERRES BRAYOISES

(NORMANDY)

Baked Potatoes Filled with Neufchâtel Cheese

4 SERVINGS

These baked stuffed potatoes may be retro but they still seem to satisfy the longing we all have for homey foods. I found the recipe in a booklet published by the Groupement Féminin de Développement Agricole du Pays de Bray, a group of farm women who beat the drum for their fragile livelihood.

In the Pays de Bray, a strip of dairy land in eastern Normandy, one of the ways farmwives help make ends meet is by making Neufchâtel cheese at home with the surplus milk that doesn't go to the local dairies. Neufchâtel, a salty cow's-milk cheese with a downy rind and a light crumbly texture, reminds me of goat cheese (which you can use to replace the Neufchâtel). Neufchâtel takes well to cooking, as here, mashed into baked potato with cream and butter, then scooped back into the potato skins.

4 baking potatoes
4 ounces young Neufchâtel or soft goat cheese, cut into small pieces
2 eggs, separated
2 tablespoons crème fraîche (page 368) or sour cream
2 tablespoons unsalted butter
Salt and freshly ground pepper

Heat the oven to 450°F. Prick the potatoes and bake them in the oven until tender, about 45 minutes. Reduce the oven temperature to 425°F.

When the potatoes are cool enough to handle, cut them in half lengthwise. Scoop out the insides into a bowl. Mash together the potato insides, cheese, egg yolks, crème fraîche or sour cream, butter, salt, and pepper until fairly smooth. In a mixing bowl, whip the egg whites until they hold stiff peaks, then fold them lightly into the potato mixture. Taste; it should be highly seasoned.

Spoon this mixture into the potato skins, set them on a baking sheet, and bake in the preheated oven until heated through, about 15 minutes.

PURÉE À LA VINAIGRETTE D'HERBES

(BURGUNDY)

Mashed Potatoes with Herbed Vinaigrette

4 SERVINGS

1¼ pounds baking potatoes, unpeeled
Salt and freshly ground white pepper
2 tablespoons lemon juice
½ cup extra-virgin olive oil
½ cup milk
2 tablespoons unsalted butter, cut into small pieces
1 tablespoon finely chopped shallot
2 tablespoons chopped fresh herbs, such as parsley, tarragon, and chives or
  scallion greens

*P*ut the potatoes in a medium saucepan, cover with water, add salt, and bring to a boil. Simmer until tender, 20 to 25 minutes, and drain. While the potatoes are still warm, peel them, cut into chunks, and work through a food mill back into the saucepan.

While the potatoes boil, make the vinaigrette: In a small bowl, whisk together the lemon juice and a bit of salt until the salt dissolves. Whisk in a few grindings of pepper, then the oil until smooth.

In a small saucepan, heat the milk until bubbles appear around the edge. Beat the hot milk and the butter into the mashed potatoes until smooth. Beat in the vinaigrette until absorbed, then the shallot and herbs. Taste the mashed potatoes for seasoning. Serve them at once.

This side dish combines the silky texture of mashed potatoes with the oomph and fragrance of a French potato salad. The potatoes are boiled, then peeled and mashed with a little milk and butter as for traditional mashed potatoes. Next, a lemon-and-olive oil vinaigrette and fresh herbs are beaten in. The idea for this recipe comes from La Côte d'Or in Burgundy, where Bernard Loiseau serves a version of these potatoes with steamed salmon. They are also good with grilled poultry, cured ham, and roasted meats.

FLAGEOLETS CAFÉ DES SPORTS

(NORMANDY)

Café des Sports' Flageolet Beans

4 SERVINGS

1¼ cups dried flageolet beans (the younger the better)
1 onion, quartered and stuck with 2 cloves
2 imported bay leaves
1 large branch thyme, or ½ teaspoon dried thyme leaves
Salt and freshly ground pepper
3 tablespoons unsalted butter
½ cup crème fraîche (page 368) or heavy (whipping) cream
¼ cup chopped fresh flat-leaf parsley

Soak the beans in plenty of cold water for at least 6 hours or overnight.

After soaking, pour off the water. Put the beans in a large saucepan and cover generously with fresh water. Bring them to a boil and boil vigorously, skimming, for 5 minutes. Drain and rinse.

Return the beans to the pan with the onion, bay leaves, and thyme; cover again with cold water, and bring to a boil. Lower the heat and gently simmer the beans, uncovered, until tender, 1 to 1½ hours, depending on the age of the beans. Toward the end of the cooking time, add 1 teaspoon of salt. Drain the beans.

In a medium saucepan, melt the butter. Add the cooked beans, and sauté them, stirring, until they are evenly coated. Stir in the crème fraîche or cream and cook until it thickens slightly. Add pepper and taste the beans for seasoning. Stir in the parsley and serve hot.

Ry, set in Normandy's Crevon Valley, is known mostly as the spot that inspired the stultifying "Yonville-l'Abbaye," home of Gustave Flaubert's unhappy Emma Bovary. The half-timbered village appears virtually unchanged since the nineteenth century, and the scene in the Café des Sports— the town's lone café—is timeless: locals buying rounds of drinks, whiling away a Saturday afternoon in the company of the café-owner.

But the way I see it, Ry's chief draw is its proximity to Martainville, where the town's elegant brick château houses Normandy's finest collection of traditional arts and crafts. One lunchtime, while waiting for the museum to reopen, I ordered a plat du jour at the Café des Sports and was served these delicate gray-green beans to accompany slices of rare roast beef and sautéed potatoes. They were tender and flavorful, as only freshly dried beans can be. Flageolets traditionally accompany lamb, too. If you are roasting lamb, try these beans without the cream. Serve them with sweet butter and the lamb juices.

BOUILLIE D'AVOINE

(BRITTANY)

Oat Porridge from Brittany

8–10 SERVINGS

2¾ cups oatmeal flour
5 cups water
2 cups whole milk
Salt
Unsalted butter, to taste (optional)

The day before you plan to serve the *bouillie*, combine the flour and 4 cups of the water in a bowl. Cover with plastic wrap and set aside overnight, chilled or not.

The next day, discard the foamy water from the bowl, leaving only the soaked flour. Using a rubber spatula, scrape the flour into a large heavy saucepan. Stir in the remaining cup of water, the milk, and salt. Set over moderately low heat and cook, stirring continuously with a wooden spatula, until the mixture looks like thick cake batter, 1¼ to 1½ hours. It will form a crust inside the pan, which should be tolerated but not allowed to burn. Take the pot from the heat and stir in the butter, if using it. Taste for seasoning. Serve hot.

If making *bouillie* to fry, omit the butter, scrape it into a buttered 4-cup loaf pan, and smooth the top. Brush the top with melted butter to discourage a skin from forming. Chill overnight until firm enough to cut.

CORNMEAL-MUSH MEMORIES

Gaudes, the roasted cornmeal mush that once filled empty bellies in eastern Burgundy, doesn't get much airplay today. But Josette Batteault remembers. One of seven children brought up on the farm, Madame Batteault ate homemade salami flavored with *marc*, the local brandy, for an afternoon snack. She says, "I can still taste it." And instead of soup they often ate *gaudes*.
A few mills still grind corn to make *gaudes* and provide a generation that didn't grow up on the stuff with recipes, including sweet variations. The rustic, textured *gaudes* is not for everybody.
But it should please all connoisseurs of "ethnic" cornmeal dishes like polenta and mamaliga.

Polenta gets all the good press as far as mush is concerned. Yet in Brittany, there's an oatmeal version every bit as humble and soulful. "I gotta have bouillie," announces Patrick Jeffroy. The chef-owner of restaurant Patrick Jeffroy in northern Brittany says, "I crave the stuff. It's part of my history, my personal history when I was growing up." He's so crazy about this Breton soul food that he puts it on the menu at his starred restaurant. And even skeptics gobble it up.

Bouillie, *however, will probably never win the audience polenta has acquired: It takes too long to cook—1½ hours of constant stirring. Not that it requires heaps of dexterity or strength. Older women used to sit by the fire stirring the* bouillie *while younger ones attended to the more arduous chores. But unless you've actually tasted this smooth, earthy porridge in Brittany, it's unlikely you'll be tempted to prepare it. Note that, like polenta, it can be chilled until firm, then fried in butter.*

THE BLACK TRUFFLE,
DIAMOND OF THE KITCHEN

Carpentras, Provence—At the heart of the truffle business, with its rarefied prices, erratic harvest, and flagrant snub to humanism (in the truffle quest, the hunter's intelligence counts for nothing compared to the pig's keen snout), there's a hook that can't be entirely explained by the truffle's beguiling taste.

Charles Vian, who cans prized, white Provençal asparagus as well as the local black truffles, could be expected to appreciate both equally. Yet, though he loves spring's vegetable spears, truffles have the edge. "I get tired of asparagus," he says. "But with truffles, it's a different story."

Perhaps it's because truffles, unlike asparagus, can't be taken for granted. Truffle merchants like Monsieur Vian talk about the golden age of truffles, from the 1880s to early 1900s, when the truffle harvest in Tricastin, Provence's northern tip, topped 240 tons a year. Today the annual crop has plunged to 20 tons.

NUDGING NATURE

Although truffles can't be cultivated like asparagus—that is, you can't plant a seed and get a truffle—farmers can help nature along. Besides growing wild in the woods, truffles can be prodded into growing under nurturing conditions.

Truffle plantations first spread through northern Provence after 1865, when phylloxera wiped out the region's vineyards, and farmers needed an alternative to survive. These plantations led to the truffle's heydey, which lasted until 1914, when in the upheaval of World War I and its aftermath, the declining plantations were not replanted as farmers looked for faster and easier ways to make a living.

But Monsieur Vian remains optimistic about the truffle's prospects. He says, "It's starting to come back." To encourage farmers to cultivate truffle plantations, the government exempts the land from taxation until after it starts producing truffles.

Still, tax incentives don't take the sweat and risk out of truffle culture. First, truffle plantations don't thrive just anywhere. Most of Monsieur Vian's coaxed truffles come from the Tricastin, home of the *Tuber melanosporum Vittadini*, pinned with the *appellation truffe noire du Tricastin contrôlée*.

This northern patch of Provence offers just the stormy summers and mild winters truffles need, and the porous, calcareous soil here, once it is planted with "truffle oaks" or other suitable truffle hosts, such as hazelnut, linden, chestnut, pine, and cedar trees, gives the Tricastin truffle the right environment to prosper.

AN UNCERTAIN WAIT

But that's not all. Farmers must correctly prune their trees, prepare the soil, wait, and hope. A truffle plantation takes anywhere from ten to fifteen years before truffles begin to crop up, out of view, amid the truffle trees' roots, if it produces at all.

Whether wheedled or wild, truffles ripen from November to March. At the end of March, any remaining truffles are left to seed next year's crop. Inconveniently for the holiday season, the best truffles don't appear until January, February, and March. "Everyone wants truffles in December," says Monsieur Vian. "But they only start to be good then. They're much better later."

Also, while farmers can create a coddled setting that brings forth truffles (sometimes), they still can't get at the mature ones without a pig or a dog. A barren patch of ground, called a *brûlé*, points to a developing truffle in the vicinity underground, and certain flies, the *Suillia tuberivora*, signal ripe, aromatic truffles by laying their eggs above them. But compared to a dog or pig, these are fallible indicators.

In Provence, hunters prefer dogs for sniffing out truffles because, even though they are harder to train than pigs, dogs don't mind eating a biscuit as a reward for work well done. And truffle hounds can always be reined in. Pigs frankly prefer the truffles themselves. Try holding back a full-grown sow.

In season, truffle hunters must check the terrain every week or so for ripe truffles because they soften in the ground as they mature. For farmers, with an average five acres of land devoted to truffles, the task is a relatively brisk one. Wild-truffle hunters, on the other hand, start early in the morning and spend the whole day shank's mare on the search. "People don't realize how much work it is," says Monsieur Vian. "You can't be afraid of walking. You've got to love it."

On a good day, an experienced hunter can unearth 4½ to 6½ pounds of truffles. Most take their spoils to a truffle market, like the one in Carpentras on Friday mornings, where they get the best price. The truffle market in Carpentras starts at 9 A.M. and continues until 10:30 or 11. There is no auctioneer for the 300 to 400 sellers. Face to face with a seller and his offerings, the buyer sets the price.

On the average, a pound of truffles goes for $194, but the rate goes up week by week. You'd think that with the amount of money traded, hi-tech electronic scales would be in evidence. But the truffles are weighed in old-fashioned hand-held scales.

What are you looking for in a superior truffle? According to Monsieur Vian, the truffles should not have too much clinging soil, even though they are sold with the dirt still on. A truffle can lose 20 percent of its weight once the dirt is brushed off. They should not feel soft either. "We know the good ones," he states.

TREAT THEM RIGHT

If you are able to get your hands on and pay for a fresh truffle, Monsieur Vian says that they keep for eight days in a jar stored in the vegetable drawer of the refrigerator. The definitive warning is: Don't keep them in plastic. Truffles soften in plastic. If he hears the word plastic, Monsieur Vian cringes and says, *"Plastique, c'est la catastrophe."*

While nothing tastes like a fresh truffle, canned truffles can be very good. The best ones are *truffes entières extra de 1ère ébullition*—whole truffles brushed and washed of every speck of dirt, then sterilized once in the can. Canned truffles lose about 25 percent of their weight but ooze truffle juice, which is loaded with truffle flavor.

Monsieur Vian's favorite truffle recipe is *ragoût de truffes*, really a truffle sauce (count ten grams (⅓ ounce) of truffle per person) flavored with sautéed ham and red Côtes-du-Rhône, then poured over grilled country bread.

But even truffle merchants like Monsieur Vian can't eat as many truffles as they want. "People used to make it often to serve with aperitifs," says Monsieur Vian. "But not so much anymore. Now it's too expensive. We made it last when my daughter got married."

POLENTA AUX CÈPES

(PROVENCE)

Polenta with Wild Mushrooms

4 SERVINGS

1 ounce dried cepes or other boletus mushrooms
1 cup boiling water, plus 2 cups water
Salt
½ cup plus 2 tablespoons yellow cornmeal
3 tablespoons unsalted butter
½ cup freshly grated Gruyère or other Swiss-type cheese

To prepare the mushrooms, put them in a heatproof bowl and pour the cup of boiling water over them. Set a small saucer that just fits inside the bowl on top to keep the mushrooms submerged. Set aside for at least 30 minutes. When you are ready to use the mushrooms, pour them and their liquid through a fine strainer lined with a double layer of damp cheesecloth into a bowl. Discard the liquid or save it for a soup or stew. Wash the mushrooms well to remove all the grit. Chop the mushrooms.

In a heavy medium saucepan, bring the 2 cups of water to a boil. Add salt. Stir in the cornmeal in a thin stream. Cook, stirring constantly to prevent sticking, until thickened and coming away from the sides of the pan, about 10 minutes. Take the pan from the heat and stir in the butter, cheese, and plumped mushrooms. Taste for seasoning.

Pour the polenta into a buttered shallow baking dish just the size to make a ¼- to ½-inch-thick layer of polenta. Set aside until firm enough to cut, 25 to 30 minutes. (Polenta can be made a day or two ahead and chilled.)

Heat the oven to 350°F.

Cut the firm polenta in its dish into 16 triangles. Or turn it out onto a work surface, stamp out rounds with a decorative 2-inch cookie cutter, and set on a baking sheet. Bake in the preheated oven until warmed through, 15 to 20 minutes. Serve hot.

The inroads Italian specialties made over a century ago into Provençal cooking can be seen in dishes like polenta, which local cooks adopted wholesale. For today's chefs, who are reclaiming regional castoffs, polenta is a recovered prize.

Polenta has a special affinity for musky mushrooms like cepes, and at La Fenière in Lourmarin, Reine Sammut uses this polenta flavored with wild mushrooms instead of pasta or potatoes to garnish her Beef Stew with lemon.

PÂTES AU CITRON

(PROVENCE)

Lemony Orzo with Black Olives

4 SERVINGS

1 cup (½ pound) orzo pasta
2 tablespoons fresh lemon juice
Salt and freshly ground pepper
¼ cup plus 1 tablespoon extra-virgin olive oil
¼ cup black olives, preferably from Nyons, pitted and chopped

Schoolteacher turned olive-mill director, Suzy Ceysson offers olive-oil fans this easy-to-make pasta side dish. It's wonderful with other Provençal dishes that don't already include olives, such as Roast Guinea Hen in Sweet Red Pepper Sauce or Beef Stew with Wild Mushrooms.

Cook the pasta in plenty of boiling salted water until al dente, 10 to 12 minutes. Drain.

While the pasta cooks, make the dressing: In a small bowl, whisk together the lemon juice and salt until the salt dissolves. Whisk in the pepper and oil until smooth. Stir in the olives.

Combine the warm pasta with the dressing in a bowl and toss until the pasta is evenly coated. Taste for seasoning and, if needed, add salt or pepper. Serve warm.

SEAFOOD

While most of France's sea catch is rushed from port to Rungis, the wholesale market outside Paris, people still head for the shore to eat fish and shellfish. It may be deluded nostalgia to prefer *moules à la marinière* out by the mussel farms, with the briny sea smells wafting in on the breeze, but only in part. You do come across flapping fresh seafood in a handful of bow-and-scrape restaurants in Paris. Yet at the water's edge in France, even family restaurants serve fish of this quality.

Servicing wealthy Paris with the fruits of the countryside has been a thriving industry for hundreds of years. Before refrigerated trucks and trains were ever imagined, the *chasse marée*, a relay of horse-drawn coaches, hauled fish from Dieppe to the Boulevard Poissonière, or "fish boulevard," in the capital.

But within the provinces, speed and its gastronomic dislocations didn't arrive until relatively recently—until the twentieth century in some cases. In 1800 it took half a day to get from the Provençal perched village of Puget-Rostang down to Puget-Théniers in the valley below, about four and a half miles away. Travel to Nice and back required more than three days. Today a trip between the two villages in the Rodoul valley can be done in fifteen minutes.

What was the result of such hampered movement? All seaside provinces had two cultures: along the coast, fishing and, inland, farming and raising livestock. (In the Breton language, there are even words for the two—*armor* and *argoat*, respectively.) Only coastal folk made a diet from the catch of the sea. Farmers near a river or lake ate freshwater fish. When they couldn't fish they ate salted or smoked fish, especially on Fridays.

Today, while it may be a few hours or days older than at the waterfront, you can find good and varied seafood practically anywhere in France. Young regional cooks—in the hills as well as on the beach—have poured make-over madness into traditional preparations, and so this chapter offers some new specialties, which combine local ingredients in original ways, including Golden Gratin of Cod with White Beans and Pan-Fried Red Snapper with Tapenade Vinaigrette, as well as recipes from the old fishing communities, such as Provençal Fish Stew and Normandy's Dogfish Stew. ❧

MOULES À LA MARINIÈRE

(NORMANDY AND BRITTANY)

Mussels in Buttery Broth

4 SERVINGS

4½ pounds lively small mussels in the shell, scrubbed and bearded
2 large shallots, finely chopped
½ onion, finely chopped
½ cup dry white wine, such as Muscadet
2 tablespoons distilled white vinegar
7 tablespoons unsalted butter, cut into pieces
Freshly ground pepper
¼ cup chopped fresh flat-leaf parsley

In a large metal casserole, combine the mussels, shallots, onion, wine, vinegar, and butter. Cover the pot, set over high heat, and cook the mussels, stirring once or twice, just until they open, 3 to 5 minutes. Take the pot from the heat.

With a slotted spoon, dish the mussels into a warmed serving bowl or soup plates. Pour the cooking liquid through a fine strainer lined with a double layer of cheesecloth over the mussels. Add pepper, sprinkle with the parsley, and serve hot.

Moules à la marinière *are typically prepared in Normandy and Brittany, but they also come into view anywhere in France you find a coast and a café. I found the best at Les Vapeurs, a brasserie in Trouville-sur-Mer, on Normandy's Côte Fleurie. Gérard Bazire's version calls for a spoonful of distilled white vinegar, which adds, well, a certain* je ne sais quoi.

This basic preparation is quick, easy, and irresistible all by itself. But it's the foundation for endless spin-off recipes, too. Add 1 cup crème fraîche *to half the cooking liquid, simmer for 2 minutes, and you have mussels in cream sauce.*

In France no one thinks to treat other tender shellfish in this fashion, but Manila, butter, and razor clams, and pink and spiny scallops in the shell also taste good this way. Serve them with crusty bread, sweet butter, and a dry white wine such as Gros Plant, Muscadet, or Sancerre.

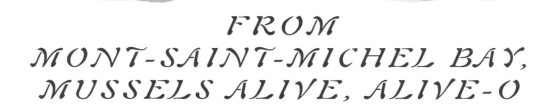

FROM MONT-SAINT-MICHEL BAY, MUSSELS ALIVE, ALIVE-O

Le Vivier-sur-Mer, Brittany—Wader-clad musselmen hose down mussels gathered early this wet August morning. By 11 A.M. the mussels, bundled in sacks and ticketed, will be on the road. And by tomorrow morning, they'll be heaped on fish-stall counters all over Paris.

For Gérard Salardaine, second-generation mussel farmer here, these are no ordinary bivalves. Called blue mussels or *moules de bouchot*, they grow twirled around rows of aligned stakes—or *bouchots*—planted deep in the offshore sand. Suspended above the ocean floor, *moules de bouchot* are noticeably free of sand, sea mud, and tiny fiddler crabs. And thanks to the plankton-rich waters of Mont-Saint-Michel Bay, which wash over the mussels twice a day, they have a deep yellow color and a special briny flavor.

"We're lucky to have the bay," says Monsieur Salardaine. "The mussels here, they're the Château Margaux of mussels."

A thriving profession, mussel growing off Le Vivier-sur-Mer employs a total of 300 workers in 65 different family businesses. With *"boucholeurs"* here today harvesting 10,000 tons of mussels each year, nearly a quarter of France's production, it's hard to believe that before 1954 not a single mussel was farmed in Mont-Saint-Michel Bay.

A SURPRISE START

Until a mysterious disease in the early 1950s wiped out mussel farming off the Atlantic coast south of the Loire River, Charentes was the mussel capital of France. In fact, the technique of growing mussels on rows of oak stakes, each 12- to 18-feet high, originated in the bay of Aiguillon near La Rochelle. According to legend, a shipwrecked Irishman, Patrick Walton, happened on the method in 1235.

Had the mussels not suddenly died, the *moule de bouchot* might well have stayed in its home waters. But when disaster struck, mussel farmers like Gérard Salardaine's father moved with their families to Mont-Saint-Michel Bay and started over.

While Brittany's northern coast produces France's largest crop of *moules de bouchot* today, the mussels farmed here still begin their lives in the Atlantic. Near the Île de Ré, in April, mussel nurseries collect *Mytilus edulis* the size of sand grains on wire cords stretched between poles. After a month or two, the nurseries sell these baby mussels for fattening to farmers like Monsieur Salardaine on the Atlantic coast and on the English Channel.

MUSSEL FARMING

By September or October, the young mussels are ready for the *bouchots*. Mussel farmers pour them into dissolvable tubular netting, wrapping 9- to 12-feet worth around each stake. After two weeks, when the netting melts away, the mussels have attached themselves by their wiry beards.

If their various predators—seagulls, starfish, and periwinkles—don't make lunch out of them, the fast-growing mussels reach legal eating size, 1½ to 2 inches, in twelve to eighteen months. The first mussel harvest usually takes place in June or July.

Around Mont-Saint-Michel Bay, the vehicle of choice for working the *bouchots* looks like a cross between a military tank and a barge. Fifty of these amphibious boats easily shuttle *boucholeurs* between the work sheds and mussel farms at high tide or low.

After July, when the mussels are fully grown, they bunch into clusters and easily detach themselves. To keep them in place until needed, musselmen wrap the mussels in another kind of netting—this one doesn't dissolve—so the mussels don't drop off.

With mussel farming now a flourishing occupation in the bay, Monsieur Salardaine worries about the threat of overproduction and slipping standards. To keep up the high quality of mussels from Le Vivier-sur-Mer, farmers here voluntarily stick to a production target of 10,000 tons of mussels a year. New mussel farmers must wait for an established farmer to retire.

When is the best season to eat *moules de bouchot* from Mont-Saint-Michel Bay? According to Monsieur Salardaine, July to the end of February is prime mussel-eating time. From March to June, the mussel first swells with milky spawn. Then as it empties itself, there's not much to eat.

A TASTE FOR MUSSELS

Monsieur Salardaine finds the raw mussel delicious, but salty. "You don't realize it until you've swallowed five or six of them," he says. "Then you feel it in the back of your throat." He prefers his plain, just grilled over a wood fire. However you like your mussels, don't forget to uncork a bottle of chilled Muscadet to go with them.

So Monsieur Salardaine the mussel farmer is also a mussel lover? "I can't get enough at the beginning of the season," he admits. "But as time goes on, I kind of lose a taste for them." ✍

MOULES VIVARAISE

(BRITTANY)

Garlicky Mussels in Wine Sauce

4 SERVINGS

1½ slices sourdough or other country bread, crusts removed (to make ½
cup fresh bread crumbs)
1 fat garlic clove, peeled
⅓ cup freshly grated Gruyère or other Swiss-type cheese
1 recipe Moules à la Marinière (page 156), without pepper and parsley
½ cup crème fraîche (page 368) or heavy (whipping) cream
Freshly ground pepper

*T*ear the bread into pieces. Drop the pieces into the bowl of a
food processor and pulse into large crumbs. Slice the garlic clove
into the food processor. Pulse until the garlic is coarsely chopped.
Add the cheese and pulse until everything is finely chopped.

Make the *moules à la marinière*. When the mussels are cool
enough to handle, discard one of the shells from each mussel.
Arrange the mussels on the half shell in a gratin dish, layering as
needed. Reserve the cooking liquid.

Heat the broiler. Into a medium saucepan, pour the cooking
liquid through a fine strainer lined with a double layer of cheesecloth. Discard (or save for another recipe) half the cooking liquid.
Add the *crème fraîche* or cream to the remaining liquid and bring to
a boil. Reduce the heat to low and simmer this sauce for 2 minutes
to concentrate the flavor. Add pepper to taste.

Pour the sauce over the mussels. Sprinkle the bread-crumb
mixture evenly over the top. Put the gratin dish on a broiler rack
about 3 inches from the heat and cook until the top is lightly
browned, 3 to 5 minutes. Watch the browning carefully, turning
the dish as necessary so the topping browns evenly and doesn't
burn. Serve at once.

On the August morning
I interviewed Gérard
Salardaine, a mussel farmer in
Le Vivier-sur-Mer, fog hid
Mont-Saint-Michel. Usually
the Mont dominates the
seascape on Brittany's
northeastern coast.

It was raining so hard my
rented car wouldn't start when
it was time to leave, and I was
soaked. But it was business as
usual in the bay, and
musselmen on their
amphibious tractors harvested
mature mussels, thinned
growing ones, and wrapped
new cords of baby mussels
around empty stakes. For me,
too, the day was far from
spoiled. When I finally left
Monsieur Salardaine, I had a
notebook full of information on
mussel farming and a recipe
for these sweet mussels on the
half shell with a golden
garlicky topping.

You could knock down the fat
in the following recipe by using
a light cream or by dropping
the cream altogether, but these
mussels are already light
(though feisty). The crème
fraîche *adds flavor above
anything else: The sauce is
more an enriched broth than a
coat-the-spoon cream sauce.
Set out finger bowls as well as
small forks and soup spoons.
This is definitely finger food.*

MOULES AU PASTIS

(PROVENCE)

Mussels in Pastis Sauce

4 SERVINGS

2 tablespoons unsalted butter
2 large shallots, finely chopped
2 fat garlic cloves, finely chopped
4½ pounds lively small mussels in the shell, scrubbed and bearded
¾ cup dry white wine, such as a southern Côtes-du-Rhône
¼ cup pastis
¼ cup crème fraîche *(page 368)* or heavy (whipping) cream
Freshly ground pepper

In a large metal casserole, melt the butter over moderate heat. Add the shallots and garlic and cook, stirring, until soft, 1 or 2 minutes. Add the mussels, wine, and pastis. Cover the pot, raise the heat to high, and cook the mussels, stirring once or twice, just until they open, 3 to 5 minutes. Take the pot from the heat.

With a slotted spoon, dish the mussels into a warmed serving bowl or soup plates. Into a medium saucepan, pour the cooking liquid through a fine strainer lined with a double layer of cheese-cloth. Discard half the cooking liquid. Add the *crème fraîche* or cream to the remaining liquid and bring it to a boil. Reduce the heat to low and simmer this sauce for 2 minutes to concentrate the flavor. Pour the sauce over the mussels. Add pepper to taste. Serve hot.

Dinner at La Table de Nicole, a country auberge straight out of a Marcel Pagnol stage set, always kicks off with a tureen of soup, followed by a hot shellfish starter like this one. In her kitchen near Montélimar in northern Provence, Nicole Vernerey pulls a bottle of pastis off the shelf to give a whiff of anise to her variation on Moules à la Marinière.

Though you may think of pastis as a summertime aperitif, when used to flavor a mussel broth, as here, it makes for a warming appetizer or a light meal in chilly temperatures. This is my version of Madame Vernerey's recipe, and one taste instantly transports you to the South of France.

ROUSSIN D'ÉPINARDS AUX MOULES

(PROVENCE)

Mussel and Spinach Gratin

4 SERVINGS

Another Provençal best-seller, more than a few years old, from Bernard Dumas who runs two restaurants in Arles. While Monsieur Dumas experiments with regional ingredients at Le Vaccarès, creating an ever-changing, personal cuisine, at the Brasserie Nord-Pinus, he's not afraid to oversee a menu that pleases by the fact of its familiarity.

For this popular gratin, sweet mussels are layered between spinach and a creamy sauce made with the mussel cooking liquid. A handful of grated cheese is sprinkled over the top and the whole kit and caboodle is passed under the broiler until browned and bubbling.

2 pounds spinach, stemmed
3 tablespoons extra-virgin olive oil
Freshly ground pepper
3 pounds lively small mussels in the shell, scrubbed and bearded
2 shallots, finely chopped
1 garlic clove, finely chopped
1 branch fresh thyme, or ½ teaspoon dried thyme leaves
1 bay leaf
1 cup dry white wine
Juice of ½ lemon
1½ tablespoons unsalted butter
1½ tablespoons all-purpose flour
¾ cup crème fraîche *(page 368)* or heavy (whipping) cream
1 cup freshly grated Gruyère or other Swiss-type cheese

Cook the spinach in plenty of boiling salted water (as for pasta) until wilted, 3 to 5 minutes. Drain. Rinse in cold water and drain again thoroughly. Press out most of the water by handfuls. Coarsely chop the spinach. In a frying pan, heat the oil over moderately high heat. Add the spinach with a little pepper and cook, stirring, until it dries out, 1 or 2 minutes. Set aside.

In a medium metal casserole, combine the mussels, shallots, garlic, thyme, bay leaf, wine, and lemon juice. Cover the pot and set it over high heat. Bring the wine to a boil and cook the mussels, stirring once or twice, just until they open, 3 to 5 minutes.

Take the pot from the heat. When the mussels are cool enough to handle, remove the meat from the shells and add the meat to the reserved spinach; discard the shells. Pour the cooking liquid through a fine strainer lined with a double layer of cheesecloth into a measuring cup. Discard (or save for another recipe) all but ½ cup of this cooking liquid.

In a heavy medium saucepan, melt the butter over low heat. Whisk in the flour and cook for 30 seconds without letting it color. Pour in the reserved cooking liquid, whisking, and bring to a boil.

Whisk in the *crème fraîche* or cream, then reduce the heat and simmer the sauce until thickened, about 5 minutes.

Stir half the sauce into the spinach and mussels, then spoon this mixture into a 6-cup gratin dish. Spread the remaining sauce over the top and sprinkle with the cheese. (This dish can be assembled several hours ahead. Chill until serving time. Instead of broiling, as below, bake the dish in a preheated 450°F. oven until browned and bubbling, about 10 minutes.)

Heat the broiler. Put the dish on a rack about 3 inches from the heat and broil until the top browns lightly, 3 to 5 minutes. Watch the browning carefully, turning the dish as necessary so it browns evenly and doesn't burn. Serve as soon as possible.

SEA SALT ON THE ATLANTIC COAST, A STEP BACK IN TIME

Batz-sur-Mer, Brittany—The only thing that has changed in hundreds of years of salt farming here is the introduction of the wheelbarrow. Women no longer carry on their heads fifteen-pound baskets of salt from the salt pans to the drying area.

Here in the alluvial soil at the mouth of the Loire river—within shouting distance of La Baule, one of Brittany's best-known seaside resorts—about two hundred families still trap ocean water to make salt.

Since 1992, the salt marshes attached to the towns of Batz-sur-Mer, Guérande, La Turballe, Le Pouliguen, Le Croisic, and Mesquer have been officially protected so that the ancient ways of cultivating sea salt may continue. Other salt fields exist west of here in Carnac and La Trinité-sur-Mer as well as on the islands of Noirmoutier and Ré. But the Guérande peninsula is the salt capital of the Atlantic coast.

Looking like a series of bas-relief labyrinths modeled in mud, the peninsula's *salines*, or salt fields, produce 10,000 tons of salt in the space of a summer. A pittance. By contrast, mined salt in France accounts for 5 million tons annually.

SEASONAL WORK

In the fall and winter, the clay walls of the salt fields cave in and the ponds fill with rain water. So before the salt season resumes, the salt farmers, or *paludiers*, go to work repairing ditches and dikes, cleaning the ponds of algae, and bailing fresh water. Then the ponds are left to dry out for a month.

In June, when the egrets and herons return to this marshland along with sunshine and longer days, the *paludier* reopens the sluice gate separating the salt field from the ocean, and the tide flows into a canal, filling a first large pond, or *vasière*.

Together the sun and wind warm and evaporate the water as it travels through the shallow canal and ponds. For about five days the ocean water, regulated by the *paludier* with gates, creeps through progressively smaller ponds dug barely one and a half inches deep in the native clay and becomes increasingly salty.

The *paludier* channels the brine into the salt pans, where in twenty-four hours the salt concentration climbs above eight ounces per quart and crystallizes. On a good day, each salt pond can produce 120 to 150 pounds of salt.

A spell of thunder showers, however, can throw off the delicate balance of the salt field by diluting the briny water. When this happens, the *paludier*, like all farmers, simply hangs tough. Hardships and wild swings in the weather come with the territory. He shuts the gates against the incoming tide and delays harvesting until the combined action of sun and wind again boost the water's salt content.

SUPERIOR SALT

In fact, two kinds of salt precipitate. First, fine crystals of naturally white salt float to the surface. This is gourmet salt. Each day barefoot salt farmers pad along the low mud walls to the salt pans and with a *lousse*, a kind of wooden shovel, lift off this salt, known as *fleur de sel*.

One hundred times more productive is the grayish, coarse salt, which settles on the bottom of the pan. The art of harvesting this salt consists of detaching as much salt as possible from the bottom without mucking up the clay. With a supple *lasse*, a wide toothless rake stuck on a spindly ten-foot pole, the *paludier* pulls the crystallized salt to the edge of the salt pan, working it onto the *ladure*, a small platform where the salt dries overnight.

The next day the *paludier* shovels the salt onto a wheelbarrow and hauls it to a *tremet*, another spot where all the salt collected from the pans dries thoroughly. In September, at the end of the salt season, this salt is taken to the *salorges* (salt docks or barns), owned cooperatively by 180 of the salt farmers, for packaging and shipping. Inside these barns, salt suffuses the air with a violet perfume, lent by the dried phytoplankton *Dunaliella salina* absorbed in the salt.

The salt from the Guérande Peninsula is not washed or refined, but is made up of pure salt crystals, retaining all the ocean's natural smells, flavors, and mineral salts, such as magnesium and potassium. The special qualities of this top-of-the-line salt so impressed local government that in 1991 the authorities awarded the salt a regional label, *sel de Guérande*, which guarantees the consumer that the salt comes from that area and meets certain standards.

VISIT THE SALT PANS

Traveling around the salt fields in summer, you pass roadside stands selling the local salt. If you do buy salt here, you will be advised not to keep it in its plastic bag. Store it in an earthenware or wooden saltcellar to allow it to "breathe," as they say.

To make ends meet, *paludiers* turn to traditional farming off-season and sell this additional harvest at their stands, too. Besides salt, they offer braids of garlic; onions; potatoes; shallots; and pickled glasswort, an edible seaweed that grows in the marshland. (Use it like any tart pickle.) Some *paludiers* also do a little fishing on the side.

As background to a *saline* visit, two museums, the Maison des Paludiers in Saillé and the Musée des Marais Salants in Batz-sur-Mer, chronicle the history of salt farming and the lives of the people here who, until the 1950s and the influx of tourists along the Breton coast, still wore their native costume.

Unlike most old-time trades, which are disappearing throughout France, salt farming holds its own on the Guérande Peninsula. Farmers who want to stay on the land can still make a living in the salt fields. Yet, not content with the comfortable status quo, older folks here actively favor restoring neglected salt fields, and with advantageous financing they encourage the young to carry on the trade.

In a bit of optimistic planning, local vocational schools even offer courses in the thousand-year-old business of salt farming.

GRATINÉE DE COQUES AUX HERBES

(BRITTANY)

Gratin of Cockles with Spinach, Tomatoes, and Herbs

4 SERVINGS

2 tablespoons unsalted butter
½ pound spinach, stemmed and chopped
Freshly ground pepper
1 recipe Moules à la Marinière (page 156) using cockles, small clams, or mussels
½ cup crème fraîche (page 368) or heavy (whipping) cream
4 small tomatoes, peeled, seeded, and chopped
2 tablespoons chopped fresh herbs, such as parsley, chives, and tarragon
2 tablespoons sliced blanched almonds

*I*n a frying pan, melt the butter over moderately high heat. Add the spinach and cook, stirring, just until it wilts. Season with pepper.

Make the *moules à la marinière* without the pepper and parsley. When the shellfish are cool enough to handle, remove the meat from the shells and set it aside; discard the shells.

Into a medium saucepan, pour the cooking liquid through a fine strainer lined with a double layer of cheesecloth. Discard half the cooking liquid. Add the *crème fraîche* or cream to the remaining liquid and bring to a boil. Reduce the heat to low and simmer this sauce for 2 minutes to concentrate the flavor. Add pepper to taste.

Divide the shellfish, spinach, tomatoes, herbs, and sauce evenly among 4 individual gratin dishes or heatproof soup plates. Sprinkle the sliced almonds over the top. (This dish can be assembled several hours ahead. Chill until serving time. Instead of broiling, as below, bake in a preheated 450°F. oven until heated through, 5 to 7 minutes.)

Heat the broiler. Put the gratin dishes on a baking sheet about 3 inches from the heat and broil until the almonds are lightly browned, 3 to 5 minutes. Watch the browning carefully, turning the dishes as necessary so the almonds brown evenly and don't burn. Serve as soon as possible.

At the Jardin Gourmand in Lorient, a major fishing port on Brittany's south coast, Nathalie Pelletier prepares this fragrant, colorful seafood gratin. She uses tender, juicy coques, *or cockles, which are cheap and plentiful at the fish market, but Manila or butter clams and mussels are perfect here, too.*

The shellfish, cooked à la marinière *with a little cream, are shelled and combined with spinach, tomatoes, and herbs, then sprinkled sparingly with sliced almonds and browned under the grill. (Lacking individual gratin dishes, use heatproof soup plates or a 6-cup gratin dish.) When mussels are used, the effect is like a fauve painting with blotches of orange, red, and green.*

NAGE DE COQUILLES SAINT-JACQUES AU BEURRE NANTAIS

(BRITTANY)

Steamed Sea Scallops with Butter Sauce

4 SERVINGS

2 tablespoons lightly salted butter
1 pound spinach, stemmed
Salt and freshly ground white pepper

BUTTER SAUCE
2 shallots, finely chopped
1 cup dry white wine, such as Muscadet
10 tablespoons lightly salted butter, cut into tablespoon-size pieces
Freshly ground white pepper
1 tablespoon chopped fresh flat-leaf parsley or snipped chives

1 small carrot, cut into 2-inch matchstick strips
1 small leek, white part only, or 2 scallions, cut into 2-inch matchstick
   strips
16 even-size sea scallops, tendons removed

*I*n a frying pan, melt the butter over moderately high heat. Add the spinach and salt and cook, stirring, just until the spinach wilts, 1 or 2 minutes. Set aside. Reheat the spinach and season with pepper before serving.

Make the sauce: In a heavy medium saucepan, combine the shallots and wine and simmer over moderately high heat until the liquid reduces to 3 tablespoons, 10 to 15 minutes. Reduce the heat to very low and gradually whisk in the butter to make a smooth sauce. Strain, if you like, add pepper, and stir in the parsley or chives. Keep the sauce warm in a water bath.

In a steamer or a steaming basket, steam the carrot and leek strips separately until tender, 2 to 4 minutes, depending on the vegetable. Sprinkle the scallops with salt and pepper and steam them until nearly opaque, 2 to 3 minutes.

Arrange a quarter of the spinach on each warmed plate, mounding it slightly. Set 4 scallops around the edge. Spoon the sauce over the scallops and sprinkle with the vegetables. Serve as soon as possible. Pass any remaining sauce separately.

Half the year, Erquy, home of the restaurant L'Escurial, is a quiet port on Brittany's Bay of Saint-Brieuc. But from November to March, scallop-fishing season, the sleepy place comes to life with fishermen sailing their loaded boats into port for the fish auction.

In this recipe, Véronique Bernard, chef at L'Escurial, combines Erquy's sweet scallops with more of Brittany's fine ingredients: tender spinach, Muscadet wine, and salty Breton butter. She treats them simply yet luxuriously. The only tricky part is the sauce: Set the pan over very low heat to ensure that the sauce thickens creamily without separating.

BY THE SEA IN BRITTANY

With something like 750 miles of coastline, Brittany is the place the French flock to for seafood.

On the *armor*, Breton for "coast," the protected gulfs and coves supply much of the sea urchins, mussels, and crabs that Breton chefs pair with creamy egg recipes, toss into shellfish salads, and purée into soup.

Scallop and lobster fishermen sailing into the northern port of Erquy provide the ingredients for seafood feasts—fat sea scallops doused with white butter sauce and grilled blue lobsters that require a battery of utensils for extracting every succulent morsel.

Plankton-rich waters in the southern Gulf of Morbihan and in Mont-Saint-Michel Bay to the north nourish the common *creuses*, or long oysters, and, increasingly, *les plates*, the flat, rounded oysters of Brittany now making a comeback. On home ground, oysters are swallowed raw and very cold (but not iced). They can be squirted with lemon juice or splashed with red-wine vinegar and shallots, but purists prefer them absolutely plain.

Brittany's ports remain lively testaments to the province's thriving fishing industry. In the smaller fishing ports in Le Guilvinec, Loctudy, and Lesconil, you can watch the independent fishermen offload their daily catch, including *langoustines*—the sweet, pink prawns—sardines, mackerel, tuna, bass, monkfish, and skate.

STOCKING BRITTANY'S LARDER

The sea provides salt, too. Salt farmers trap water to make salt in ancient salt pans, and canners use the salt to preserve the fisherman's catch. In Brittany's salt marshes bordering Mont-Saint-Michel, farmers pasture their lambs, called *agneaux de pré-salé*, which are famous for their slightly salty flavor.

Salt also gives Breton butter its unmistakable taste. Everything made with this butter, from the butter sauce served with fish to Brittany's frivolously buttery cakes and pastries, obliquely recalls the sea.

Once considered a nuisance, seaweed now has a tentative place in the Breton pantry. Seaweed-based fertilizer has transformed local agriculture. Ironically, much of the enriched soil is too fertile for growing buckwheat, the source of Brittany's famed crepes, *far* puddings, and infamous *bouillie* or buckwheat mush. Crepes are largely made instead with imported buckwheat or with wheat flour.

The sea, warmed by the Gulf Stream, also means surprisingly mild, almost Mediterranean winters along the coast. With this temperate climate and rich soil, Brittany's fruits and vegetables appear early for such a northern locale. There are Breton recipes for artichokes stuffed with *langoustines;* shallots glazed with honey; pumpkin soup, to name a few.

BEYOND THE BRINY DEEP

But Breton gastronomy draws on more than the sea. In the *argoat,* or inland Brittany, *charcutiers* use every part of the pig and craft the famous Guémené *andouilles,* or chitterling sausages, smoked pork sausages, bacon, and blood sausages.

Though there's a huge dairy industry in Brittany—cheese of the commercial Port-Salut type is produced today—there's no history of cheese making here. With their cows' milk, Breton dairymen traditionally made delicious butter, cream, curd cheese, and buttermilk.

This is apple, not grape, country, and Breton farmers make cider and their own version of cider *eau-de-vie* called *lambig.* In cider regions, cooks add the sparkling brew to the pot instead of wine.

Brittany's cooking offers just the right mix of fresh, straightforward tastes and earthy, long-simmered flavors. If you're in the mood for rib-sticking food, there's Thierry Rannou's Kig Ha Fars (page 236), a Breton version of pot-au-feu. Or if the green beans ripening in your garden threaten to submerge you, there's always the simple Warm Salad of Green Beans and Tomatoes from L'Auberge Bretonne (page 133). Somehow, the recipes from this corner of France seem to satisfy the appetite we all have for good country cooking.

À LA BRETONNE

Ingredients That Make a Dish Typically Breton

Mussels
Scallops
Lobsters
Oysters
Langoustines
Sardines
Cod
Tuna
Sea salt
Salt-marsh lamb
Salted butter
Seaweed
Buckwheat flour
Oatmeal flour
Crepes
Galettes
Far
Bouillie
Artichokes
Cauliflower
Dried beans
Potatoes
Onions
Shallots
Strawberries
Guémené andouille
Buttermilk
Cider
Lambig (cider brandy)
Muscadet wine
Gros Plant wine

BOURRIDE

(PROVENCE)

Provençal Fish Stew

6 SERVINGS

For Mimi, bourride *is the name of the fish soup she cooks Wednesdays at Les Arcades in Biot. She wouldn't know about the creamy, garlicky versions some cooks claim as the genuine article. The way this Provençal* cuisinière *sees it, bourride is a meal in a bowl, complete with soup, chunks of fish and potatoes, plus such essential accompaniments as spicy rouille and grated cheese for mounding on toasts and adding to the soup bowl.*

If you're still hungry after this feast, try Mimi's Sweet Swiss Chard Tart for dessert.

STEW BASE

8 tablespoons olive oil
2 pounds whole white sea fish, cleaned, cut into 1-inch steaks, heads reserved, plus any additional bones the fishmonger has to offer
Salt and freshly ground pepper
1 large onion, halved and thinly sliced
2 fat garlic cloves, crushed
1 large bulb fennel, halved lengthwise and thinly sliced across
1 rib celery, thinly sliced
1 leek, white and light green parts only, thinly sliced
2 carrots, quartered lengthwise and thinly sliced
1 tomato, chopped
2 tablespoons tomato paste
10 cups water
1 fat bouquet garni (2 branches fresh thyme, or 1 teaspoon dried thyme leaves; 12 parsley stems; and 2 imported bay leaves, tied in a bundle with kitchen string or cheesecloth)

ROUILLE

1 egg yolk, at room temperature, or hard-cooked if preferred
2 teaspoons tomato paste, for coloring (optional)
1 teaspoon cayenne pepper, or to taste
2 garlic cloves, peeled
Salt
½ cup vegetable oil
¼ cup extra-virgin olive oil

6 medium new potatoes
Salt and freshly ground pepper
Pinch of saffron powder or threads, or to taste
Pinch of cayenne pepper, or to taste
1½ pounds mixed white sea fish fillets, skinned and cut into 3-inch pieces
40 thin slices narrow French baguette, toasted
1 cup freshly grated Gruyère or other Swiss-type cheese

𝒩ake the stew base: In a large metal casserole, heat 6 tablespoons of the oil. Add the fish steaks, heads, and bones to the oil without crowding the pot. Sprinkle them with salt and sauté over moderately high heat until the fish is opaque on both sides, 5 to 10 minutes, then remove fish, heads, and bones to a plate.

Heat the remaining 2 tablespoons of oil in the same pot. Add the onion, garlic, fennel, vegetables, and salt and stir until evenly coated with the oil. Cover the pot and cook over low heat, stirring occasionally, until the vegetables are tender, 10 to 15 minutes.

In a small bowl, dilute the tomato paste with a little of the water. Replace the fish, heads, and bones in the pot with the diluted tomato paste, the remaining water, *bouquet garni*, and a little salt and bring to a boil. Boil, stirring to break up the fish, for 15 minutes. Lower the heat and simmer gently until the broth reduces by half, 45 minutes to 1 hour. Skim the broth regularly.

While the broth simmers, make the rouille: In a food processor, whir together all the ingredients except the oils. Slowly add a tablespoon of the oil and whir until incorporated. With the blades turning, add the remaining oils in a thin stream. Taste and add more cayenne pepper or salt until the rouille is seasoned as you like.

Prepare the potatoes: Put them in a medium saucepan, cover with water, add salt, and bring to a boil. Simmer until tender, 15 to 20 minutes, and drain. When the potatoes are cool enough to handle, peel them and cut into large chunks.

Add the stew base in batches to the bowl of a food processor. Pulse to grind the vegetables and bones as finely as possible. (The food processor will balk at this endeavor.) Work each batch through a food mill into a large saucepan or pour it into a fine strainer set over a large saucepan and press hard to extract all the purée.

Add the saffron and cayenne to the soup and simmer for 2 minutes. Reduce the heat to low. Sprinkle the fish fillets with salt and pepper. Cook the fish with the peeled potatoes in the soup until the fish is opaque through and the potatoes are reheated, 5 to 10 minutes. Taste the *bourride* and add more saffron, cayenne, salt, or pepper until it is seasoned to your liking.

Serve the *bourride* in a warmed soup tureen or soup plates. Pass the rouille, toasts, and cheese separately.

POISSON À LA CRÈME

(NORMANDY)

Fish and Mushrooms in Cream Sauce

4 SERVINGS

1 onion, halved and thinly sliced
1 carrot, thinly sliced
1 bouquet garni (1 branch fresh thyme, or ½ teaspoon dried thyme leaves;
    6 parsley stems; and 1 bay leaf, tied in a bundle with kitchen string or
    cheesecloth)
4 cups water
1 teaspoon salt
2 cups dry white wine
1½ pounds skate or other skinned fish fillets, or four 5-ounce salmon steaks
6 black peppercorns, crushed
4 medium boiling potatoes, unpeeled
Sea salt and freshly ground white pepper
½ pound mushrooms, halved if large, thinly sliced
¼ cup water
Juice of ½ lemon
1 cup crème fraîche (page 368)
1 tablespoon finely chopped fresh flat-leaf parsley

*M*ake the court bouillon: In a large sauté pan or shallow metal casserole, combine the onion, carrot, *bouquet garni*, water, and salt. Set the lid on top, bring the water to a boil, then reduce the heat and simmer for 15 minutes. Add the wine and continue simmering, covered, for another 15 minutes.

Add the fish and peppercorns and bring the liquid to a simmer. Cover and reduce the heat to low. Poach the fish until opaque through, about 5 minutes. Remove the fish and drain on paper towels. Transfer to a warmed serving dish and keep warm. Discard the bouillon.

Meanwhile, put the potatoes in a medium saucepan, cover with water, add salt, and bring to a boil. Simmer until tender, 15 to 20 minutes, and drain. When the potatoes are cool enough to handle, peel them and cut in half. Set aside with the fish.

In a saucepan, combine the mushrooms, water, lemon juice, and a little salt. Bring the liquid to a boil over high heat. When the liquid boils to the top of the pan, take the pan from the heat and discard any liquid.

In a heavy medium saucepan, simmer the *crème fraîche* with a

In Normandy, crème fraîche country, cream sauce consists not of a butter-and-flour roux whisked with milk or stock, then enriched with a spoonful of cream. It is cream, full stop—simmered with a little sea salt.

"The cream must be fresh and thick and without added butter or milk," says Madame Orange of La Chaumière in Le Quettehou, on Normandy's Cotentin Peninsula. Madame Orange, who gave me this recipe, adds: "We call this cream crème fraîche de Normandie."

With a cream-only sauce and just-out-of-the-water fish poached separately in an aromatic broth, this dish embodies Norman country cooking at its best. A word of caution: If your fish is not really fresh, you'll end up scraping the cream off the fish and eating it instead with the potato accompaniment.

little salt, stirring from time to time, until the cream thickens slightly, 5 to 10 minutes. Add the drained mushrooms and a few grindings of pepper and taste for seasoning.

Pour the cream sauce with mushrooms over the fish and potatoes, sprinkle with parsley, and serve.

J. P. Gloanec's contemporary salmon dish isn't meant to stir up thoroughgoing notions of Breton food. It's true that at the Hôtel de la Plage in Sainte-Anne-la-Palud, Chef Gloanec uses olive oil, a southern import, to sauté the fish, and the dish is conceived for a plate not a platter. Yet with Brittany's incomparable butter sauce, using Brittany wine, and a classic purée of celery root—it's both starch and vegetable—he clearly relishes the old ways.

Serve Chef Gloanec's recipe to company. While the fish needs to be sautéed and the sauce made at the last minute, both are quick and easy. The celery root purée can be made up ahead of time. Begin dinner with Artichoke Bottoms with Shrimp and Tarragon and finish with Caramelized Apple Tartlets.

CÔTELETTES DE SAUMON AU GROS PLANT

(BRITTANY)

Salmon in Brittany Wine Sauce

4 SERVINGS

CELERY ROOT PURÉE
1 small celery root (about 1 pound)
½ lemon
1 tablespoon unsalted butter
¼ cup crème fraîche (page 368) or heavy (whipping) cream
Salt and freshly ground white pepper

WHITE BUTTER SAUCE
2 shallots, finely chopped
½ cup dry white wine, preferably Gros Plant
Salt and freshly ground white pepper
2 tablespoons crème fraîche (page 368) or heavy (whipping) cream
10 tablespoons unsalted butter, cut into small pieces
Fresh lemon juice, to taste

Four 5-ounce salmon steaks
Salt and freshly ground pepper
2 tablespoons olive oil

*M*ake the purée: Thickly peel the celery root. Quarter it and rub and moisten the cut surfaces with the lemon half. Cut the pieces into 1-inch chunks. Cook the celery root in plenty of boiling salted water (as for pasta) until very tender, about 20 minutes. Drain.

Purée the celery root in a food processor. Scrape the purée into a medium saucepan. Set the pan over moderately low heat and beat in the butter, *crème fraîche* or cream, and salt and pepper. Taste for seasoning and set aside. Reheat before serving. (The purée can be made ahead of time.)

Make the sauce: In a heavy medium saucepan, combine the shallots and wine with a little salt and simmer over moderately high heat until the liquid reduces to 3 tablespoons, 5 to 10 minutes. Add the *crème fraîche* or cream and bring to a simmer. Reduce the heat to very low and gradually whisk in the butter to make a smooth sauce. Add the pepper and lemon juice and taste the sauce for seasoning. Keep warm in a water bath while you cook the fish.

Sprinkle the salmon with salt and pepper. In a large frying pan, heat the oil over moderately high heat. (Or use 2 smaller frying pans, splitting the ingredients between the pans.) When hot, add the steaks. Cook, turning once, until opaque through, about 5 minutes in all. Cut each steak in half lengthwise to make 2 *côtelettes* or "chops," discarding the skin and bones.

Arrange 2 *côtelettes* on each warmed plate. Add a dollop of celery-root purée. Spoon some sauce over the salmon and serve as soon as possible. Pass any remaining sauce separately.

SOLE BOURGUIGNONNE

(BURGUNDY)

Sole Poached in Red Wine with White Butter Sauce

4 SERVINGS

The restaurant Le Bareuzai, which means "vintner" in local dialect, sits on the highway between Dijon and Beaune, flanked by some of the world's most famous vineyards. The Burgundian twist on this sole recipe is that red wine replaces white in the aromatic poaching liquid.

COURT BOUILLON
1 onion, halved and thinly sliced
1 carrot, thinly sliced
1 bouquet garni (1 branch fresh thyme, or ½ teaspoon dried thyme leaves;
  6 parsley stems; 1 bay leaf; and 3 leek or scallion greens, tied in a
  bundle with kitchen string or cheesecloth)
4 cups water
1 teaspoon salt
2 cups young red wine, preferably a Burgundy

1½ pounds skinned sole fillets
6 black peppercorns, crushed

SAUCE
3 tablespoons heavy (whipping) cream
2 shallots, finely chopped
Salt and freshly ground white pepper
10 tablespoons unsalted butter, cut into small pieces

*M*ake the court bouillon: In a large sauté pan or shallow metal casserole, combine the onion, carrot, *bouquet garni*, water, and salt. Cover the pan, bring the water to a boil, then reduce the heat and simmer for 15 minutes. Add the wine and continue simmering, covered, another 15 minutes.

Add the fish and peppercorns and bring the court bouillon back to a simmer. Cover and reduce the heat to low. Poach the fish until opaque through, 3 to 5 minutes. Remove the fish and drain on paper towels. Discard the bouillon.

Meanwhile, make the sauce: In a heavy medium saucepan, bring the cream, shallots, and a little salt to a simmer. Reduce the heat to very low and gradually whisk in the butter to make a smooth sauce. Add the pepper and taste the sauce for seasoning. Keep it warm in a water bath.

Spoon some of the sauce on warmed plates and spread it with the back of a spoon to cover the bottom. Arrange the fish on the sauce. Pass any remaining sauce separately.

RAIE AU BEURRE NOISETTE

(NORMANDY)

Skate with Brown Butter and Capers

4 SERVINGS

COURT BOUILLON
1 onion, halved and thinly sliced
1 carrot, thinly sliced
1 bouquet garni (1 branch fresh thyme, or ½ teaspoon dried thyme leaves;
*   6 parsley stems; 1 bay leaf; and 3 leek or scallion greens, tied in a*
*   bundle with kitchen string or cheesecloth)*
1½ teaspoons salt
6 cups water
2 cups dry white wine

One 2-pound skate wing, with skin on
1 teaspoon crushed black peppercorns
8 tablespoons (1 stick) unsalted butter, cut into pieces
2 tablespoons small capers, drained
Salt and freshly ground pepper

This recipe comes from the Auberge du Trou Normand, a pretty, unpretentious restaurant in the seaside village of Pourville-sur-Mer. At the auberge, only three miles from Dieppe (Normandy's major fishing port), Fabien Duchêne prepares tempting fish dishes, and the few tables here are always crowded with regulars at lunchtime. Raie au beurre noisette is found throughout France, but made with good Norman butter and locally caught skate, it seems to belong in Normandy. Try the fish with its traditional accompaniment, steamed potatoes.

Make the court bouillon: In a large sauté pan or shallow metal casserole, combine the onion, carrot, *bouquet garni*, salt, and water. Set the lid on top, bring the water to a boil, then reduce the heat and simmer for 15 minutes. Add the wine and continue simmering, covered, for another 15 minutes.

Add the skate wing and peppercorns and bring the liquid to a simmer. (Add boiling water if the court bouillon doesn't completely cover the skate wing.) Cover and reduce the heat to low. Poach the skate until cooked through, 10 to 15 minutes.

Meanwhile, in a small saucepan, melt the butter. Add the capers and cook until the butter begins to brown, 2 to 3 minutes. Take the pan from the heat, add salt and pepper, and taste for seasoning. Keep warm.

Drain the skate well, scrape off the skin and any jellylike gristle, and pat the skate dry with paper towels. Cut the skate wing lengthwise into 4 even pieces. Transfer it to a warmed platter or plates. Pour the sauce over the skate and serve.

RAIE SAUCE MOUTARDE FALLOT

(BURGUNDY)

Poached Skate with Mustard Sauce

4 SERVINGS

COURT BOUILLON
1 onion, halved and thinly sliced
1 carrot, thinly sliced
1 bouquet garni (1 branch fresh thyme or ½ teaspoon dried thyme leaves;
*   6 parsley stems; 1 bay leaf; and 3 leek or scallion greens, tied in a*
*   bundle with kitchen string or cheesecloth)*
1½ teaspoons salt
6 cups water
2 cups dry white wine

One 2-pound skate wing, with skin on
1 teaspoon crushed black peppercorns
1 cup heavy (whipping) cream
½ cup plus 1 tablespoon imported Dijon mustard, or to taste
Salt and freshly ground pepper
1½ teaspoons yellow or black mustard seeds

This recipe takes its name from Edmond Fallot, whose little factory in Beaune still prepares Dijon-style mustard the old-fashioned way. Today, Monsieur Fallot's son-in-law and grandson, Messieurs Desarménien, watch over the time-tested steps of mustard making: Black mustard seeds are soaked in good Burgundy vinegar and then ground between millstones to a fiery paste.

In this recipe, given to me by the newest generation of Fallot mustard makers, skate poaches in a court bouillon, and a quick sauce is made separately with cream and mustard. To boost the mustard theme, toasted mustard seeds are sprinkled over the top before serving.

Make the court bouillon: In a large sauté pan or shallow metal casserole, combine the onion, carrot, *bouquet garni*, salt, and water. Set the lid on top, bring the water to a boil, then reduce the heat and simmer for 15 minutes. Add the wine and continue simmering, covered, for another 15 minutes.

Add the skate wing and peppercorns and bring the liquid to a simmer. (Add boiling water if the court bouillon doesn't completely cover the skate wing.) Cover and reduce the heat to low. Poach the skate until cooked through, 10 to 15 minutes.

Meanwhile, in a heavy medium saucepan, combine the cream and mustard and a little salt . Simmer the sauce, stirring from time to time, until it thickens, 5 to 10 minutes. Add pepper, taste for seasoning, and, if needed, add more mustard, pepper, or salt until the sauce is as pungent as you like. Keep warm.

Drain the skate well, scrape off the skin and any jellylike gristle, and pat the fish dry with paper towels. Cut the skate wing lengthwise into 4 even pieces. Transfer it to a warmed platter or plates and keep warm.

Put the mustard seeds in an ungreased frying pan and set over low heat until toasted, but not until they pop.

Pour the sauce over the skate and serve, sprinkled with the toasted mustard seeds.

MATELOTE DE ROUSSETTE

(NORMANDY)

Dogfish Stew

4 SERVINGS

3 tablespoons unsalted butter
2 large onions, halved and thinly sliced
2 large shallots, thinly sliced
Salt and freshly ground pepper
2 tablespoons all-purpose flour
2 cups imported dry French cider
1 bouquet garni (1 branch fresh thyme, or ½ teaspoon dried thyme leaves;
  6 parsley stems; and 1 bay leaf, tied in a bundle with kitchen string or
  cheesecloth)
One 2-pound skinned piece of dogfish, bone in, cut into 2-inch pieces
¼ cup chopped fresh flat-leaf parsley

*I*n a medium metal casserole, melt the butter. Add the onions, shallots, and a little salt, and cook, stirring occasionally, until tinged with brown, 8 to 10 minutes.

Sprinkle the flour over the onions and shallots and cook until it browns lightly, 1 or 2 minutes. Gradually stir in the cider, scraping up the browned juices. Add the *bouquet garni*. Cover the pot, bring the liquid to a boil, then reduce the heat to low and cook at a bare simmer for 30 minutes.

Add the fish to the pot, cover, and bring back to a boil. Reduce the heat to low and cook at a bare simmer for 30 minutes. Discard the *bouquet garni*. Add pepper and taste for seasoning. Serve the fish with its cooking liquid in a warmed serving dish or plates, sprinkled with parsley.

Frankly, I'd rather keep this one under my hat. The dining room at Le Drakkar is spare, but this spotless restaurant with rooms in Le Quinéville, Normandy, just north of Utah Beach, oozes good ole hospitality. And the fish, served simply (as at La Chaumière in Le Quettehou, run by the same Orange family), matches the best I have tasted anywhere.

This recipe from Le Drakkar calls for dogfish, a member of the shark family. Though you may not have heard of dogfish, your fishmonger probably carries it. If it's out of season or you just can't find it, substitute a different shark or other white, lean fish such as monkfish. (Use 1½ pounds skinned fillets.)

With the matelote, *serve peeled new potatoes. Says Madame Orange, "The potatoes are much better when they cook in the* matelote." *If you do cook the potatoes in the stew, leave out the flour and add them at the same time as the fish. One more hint from Madame Orange: "A reheated* matelote *is always better."*

ROUGETS À LA VINAIGRETTE DE TAPENADE

(PROVENCE)

Pan-Fried Red Snapper with Tapenade Vinaigrette

4 SERVINGS

VINAIGRETTE
1 tablespoon red-wine vinegar
½ cup extra-virgin olive oil
1 tablespoon Tapenade (page 30)

2 tablespoons olive oil
1½ pounds red snapper fillets, with skin on
Salt and freshly ground pepper

*M*ake the vinaigrette: In a small bowl, whisk together the vinegar, oil, and tapenade.

In a large frying pan, heat the oil over moderately high heat. (Or use 2 smaller frying pans, splitting the ingredients between the pans.) Add the fish, sprinkle with a little salt, and cook until opaque through, 2 to 3 minutes on each side. Add a grinding of pepper and remove to warmed dinner plates. Drizzle the vinaigrette over the fish and serve as soon as possible.

Elegant and earthy, this snapper dish typifies the way French restaurant chefs update regional classics. This recipe, inspired by one from Pascal Renaud of restaurant Lou Marquès in Arles, perks up plain vinaigrette with tapenade, a feisty blend of capers, black olives, and anchovies. Pair it with a local fish and—voilà—a new Provençal dish.

Steamed potatoes or Swiss Chard with Bacon and Tomatoes is all you need add. Or you might double the vinaigrette in this recipe and use half to dress a mixed green salad and the other half for the fish. Besides salad, try the tapenade vinaigrette with hot pasta. Or serve it alongside cold roast meat or poultry.

If you wanted to create a menu of modern Provençal dishes, you could start with Salad Greens with Warm Goat Cheese in a Hazelnut Crust and serve Warm Raspberry Tartlets for dessert.

Monkfish in Aromatic Shellfish Sauce

4 SERVINGS

With a name like lotte à l'armoricaine (armor *means "land by the sea" in Breton), the Brittany lineage here seems beyond question. But this dish—or a twin made with lobster or squid—is also a fixture on classic menus in coastal Provence, where it's called* lotte à l'américaine.

At Le Goyen in Audierne, a fishing port on Brittany's southwestern shore, Adolphe Bosser prepares two versions. The time-honored recipe appears on his price-fixed menu with the usual accompaniment of steaming rice pilaf. It's a heady blend of pounded lobster shells, flamed Cognac, white wine, vegetables, and tomato paste. The other, an elaborate affair, belongs to the realm of fancy-restaurant cooking. Still, if you like, add to the plate mussels and small clams opened over high heat and pulled from their shells, plus steamed fingerling potatoes and strips of sautéed squid.

Some recipes for lotte à l'armoricaine *leave out the lobster shells entirely. You could also substitute a pound of small blue crabs for the lobster shells. Cut them in half crosswise and sauté in the oil for about 2 minutes until their shells turn red, then add the vegetables and proceed with the recipe.*

ARMORICAINE SAUCE
1 pound lobster shells or lively blue crabs (optional, see headnote)
3 tablespoons olive oil
1 large onion, finely chopped
1 carrot, finely chopped
2 garlic cloves, crushed
2 tablespoons Cognac or brandy
½ cup dry white wine, such as Muscadet
2 cups water
1 tablespoon tomato paste
Salt and cayenne pepper
1 bouquet garni (1 branch fresh thyme, or ½ teaspoon dried thyme leaves; 6 parsley stems; 1 bay leaf; and 3 leek or scallion greens, tied in a bundle with kitchen string or cheesecloth)
1 branch fresh tarragon, or ½ teaspoon dried tarragon (optional)

1½ pounds skinned monkfish fillet
2 tablespoons olive oil
Salt and freshly ground pepper
2 tablespoons Cognac or brandy

*M*ake the *armoricaine* sauce: First pound the lobster shells in a sturdy bowl with the end of a rolling pin until crushed. In a medium lidded sauté pan or shallow metal casserole, heat the oil. Add the crushed lobster shells and the onion and garlic, and cook, stirring, until the onion is translucent, 3 to 5 minutes. Heat the Cognac or brandy in a small saucepan and light it. (It will flare up so take care.) Pour it into the vegetable pan and shake until the flames subside. Stir in the wine, water, and tomato paste. Add a little salt and cayenne pepper and tuck in the *bouquet garni* and tarragon. Set the lid on top, bring the liquid to a boil, then reduce the heat to low and simmer for 15 to 20 minutes.

Discard the herbs and lobster shells from the pan. Purée the *armoricaine* in batches in a food processor and, using a rubber spatula, scrape it into a medium saucepan. For extra smoothness, work the sauce through a fine sieve or a food mill into the saucepan. Taste for seasoning.

Cut the fish fillet into 1-inch-thick rounds. With the flat part of a heavy knife, lightly pound the fish rounds to flatten them to about ½ inch. Heat the oil in a frying pan. Add the fish, sprinkle with salt and pepper, and cook over moderately high heat just until opaque or lightly browned on both sides, 2 to 3 minutes in all. Heat the Cognac or brandy in a small saucepan and light it. (It will flare up so be careful.) Pour it into the fish pan and shake until the flames subside. Add the fish to the sauce.

Cover the *armoricaine* pan and bring to a boil, then reduce the heat and gently simmer the fish until opaque through, 3 to 5 minutes.

Transfer the fish to a warmed platter or plates and spoon the *armoricaine* over it. Serve a rice pilaf as accompaniment.

MARMITE DE CABILLAUD AUX HARICOTS BLANCS

(BRITTANY)

Golden Gratin of Cod with White Beans

4 SERVINGS

1¼ cups dried white beans, such as cannellini or Great Northern (the younger the better)
2 branches fresh thyme, or 1 teaspoon dried thyme leaves
2 bay leaves
Salt and freshly ground pepper
3 tablespoons unsalted butter
2 medium onions, chopped
3 garlic cloves, chopped
3 ripe medium tomatoes (about 1½ pounds), peeled, seeded, and chopped; or 1½ cups chopped canned Italian plum tomatoes, with their juice
¾ cup crème fraîche (page 368) or heavy (whipping) cream
1½ pounds skinned cod fillet

Soak the beans in plenty of cold water for at least 6 hours or overnight.

After soaking, pour off the water. Put the beans in a large saucepan and cover generously with fresh water. Bring them to a boil and boil vigorously, skimming, for 5 minutes. Drain and rinse.

Return the beans to the pan with half the thyme and 1 bay leaf, cover again with cold water, and bring to a boil. Lower the heat and gently simmer the beans, uncovered, until tender, 1 to 1½ hours, depending on the age of the beans. Toward the end of the cooking time, add 1 teaspoon of salt. Drain the beans and set aside.

While the beans are cooking, make the tomato sauce. In a large saucepan, melt the butter. Add the onions and garlic with a little salt and stir until evenly coated with the butter. Cover the pan and cook over low heat, stirring occasionally, until tender, about 10 minutes. Add the tomatoes, the remaining thyme and bay leaf, and cook, partly covered, until thick, about 30 minutes. Stir the tomatoes now and then during cooking.

Heat the oven to 450°F.

Stir the beans into the tomato sauce along with half the *crème fraîche* or cream. Add pepper and taste for seasoning. (The bean-

Nathalie Pelletier got creative sparks off a Breton mainstay—gigot à la bretonne—for her dish of cod and white beans. Codfish, not exactly a newcomer but untested in this combination, stands in for the roasted lamb, and it mingles happily with the creamy beans, tomatoes, and garlic. There are always new ways to see.

Start the meal with Nathalie's Gratin of Cockles with Spinach, Tomatoes, and Herbs and try her Golden Peach Gratin for dessert. While this makes three gratins, each one is so different that you don't get the feeling of déjà vu.

and-tomato sauce mixture can be made a day ahead and chilled. It tastes even better.)

Spoon the beans into a large gratin dish. Sprinkle the fish fillets with salt and pepper. Make indentations in the beans for the fish, and lay the fish on top. Spread the remaining cream evenly over the top.

Bake the *marmite* in the preheated oven until lightly browned and bubbling, 10 to 15 minutes. Serve as soon as possible.

IN BRITTANY, SEAFOOD FOR ALL

Assiduously fresh seafood is the prerogative of Breton home cooks as well as high-profile restaurant chefs. The following menu draws on various sources for recipes—the appetizer comes from a mussel farmer in northeastern Brittany; the main course is a signature dish at Nathalie Pelletier's restaurant in Lorient—but both show the same healthy respect for the natural flavor of seafood and for Brittany's uncomplicated cooking. For dessert, it's only normal to dip into the recipes of the *argoat* (inland Brittany). Even if you're new to prune *far*, you'll find it as comfortable as an old shoe. Serve a chilled Muscadet.

Moules Vivaraise (page 160)
Garlicky Mussels in Wine Sauce

Marmite de Cabillaud aux Haricots Blancs (page 186)
Golden Gratin of Cod with White Beans

Far Breton (page 346)
Brittany Prune Flan

BRANDADE PATIN COUFFIN

(PROVENCE)

Salt Cod Purée with Herbs, Olive Oil, and Garlic

6 TO 8 SERVINGS

1¼ pounds salt-cod fillet, with skin on

COURT BOUILLON
1 onion, halved and thinly sliced
1 carrot, thinly sliced
1 bouquet garni (1 branch fresh thyme, or ½ teaspoon dried thyme leaves;
*   6 parsley stems; and 1 bay leaf, tied in a bundle with kitchen string or*
*   cheesecloth)*
4 cups water
2 cups dry white wine
1 teaspoon crushed black peppercorns

1 large baking potato, unpeeled (optional)
24 to 32 thin slices narrow French baguette
3 fat garlic cloves, or to taste, peeled
¾ cup extra-virgin olive oil
½ cup whole milk
¼ cup heavy (whipping) cream
2 cups chopped fresh herbs, such as parsley, chives, and tarragon
Freshly ground white pepper

*I*n a shallow casserole, soak the fish in cold water to cover and chill, changing the water several times, for 2 to 3 days. Drain and rinse.

Make the court bouillon: In a medium sauté pan or shallow metal casserole, combine the onion, carrot, *bouquet garni*, and water. Set a lid on top, bring the water to a boil, then reduce the heat and simmer for 15 minutes. Add the wine and continue simmering, covered, another 15 minutes.

Add the soaked, drained cod and the peppercorns. Cover the pan and bring the liquid to a simmer, then reduce the heat to low. Poach the fish for 10 minutes, then drain. Discard the skin and bones. Put the fish in the bowl of a food processor.

Meanwhile, if you are adding the potato, put it in a medium saucepan, cover with water, and bring to a boil. Simmer until tender, 20 to 25 minutes. Drain. While the potato is still warm,

---

In nice weather at Patin Couffin in Fayence, tables are set up on the front porch so you can keep your eye on life on the steep, cobbled street as well as your food. Meanwhile, in her kitchen, burly Virginie Bandelier turns out rustic Provençal fare that's never quite what you expect. Her brandade, *for instance, is flecked with green (from piles of fresh herbs) instead of snowy white.*

Some restaurants prepare an addictive recipe for brandade *using potatoes. It's like the best garlicky mashed potatoes you've ever had. But if you want to hew to* brandade *tradition as it's done in Nîmes, forgo the potato. Keep in mind that salt cod that hasn't soaked long enough isn't worth eating. When in doubt, dunk it longer. If you don't want to bother with the court bouillon, poach the fish in 2 cups of milk and water to cover.*

peel and cut it into chunks. Add to the bowl of the food processor.

Heat the broiler. Toast the bread slices on a baking sheet under the broiler, turning once, until golden, 2 to 3 minutes. Rub the toasts with 1 or 2 of the garlic cloves and set aside.

In a small saucepan, heat the oil until hot but not smoking. At the same time, in a medium saucepan, heat the milk and cream together until bubbles appear around the edge. Pour the hot oil into the fish in a thin stream, pulsing to avoid overmixing. When all the oil is incorporated, gradually add the hot milk and cream, pulsing again until fluffy and smooth. Add 2 garlic cloves to the mixture with the herbs and pepper. Pulse to mix. Taste for seasoning. Add more garlic or pepper as needed, remembering that the garlic toasts will boost the garlic flavor.

With a rubber spatula, scrape the *brandade* into a warmed serving bowl. Arrange some of the garlic toasts around the *brandade* and serve as soon as possible. Pass the remaining toasts separately.

GREEN GOLD
AT YOUR FEET

Roscoff, Brittany—Sun worshippers at this seaside resort pick their way through the seaweed littering the beach. But where some perceive a nuisance, Michel Perzinsky sees a golden opportunity.

With all the gusto of youth, Monsieur Perzinsky, a jack-of-all-trades here at the seaweed-harvesting company Algomarine, regards seaweed as a hot new profession and he's itching to do business.

While the Japanese consider marine algae a dietary staple (each Japanese consumes four pounds of it a year), the French government did not authorize harvesting it for food until February 1990.

Sniffing a new trend, companies like Algomarine popped up along the north coast of Brittany, gathering seaweed to sell to the food industry as well as to such traditional markets as agriculture and the cosmetics industry. Today 100,000 tons of seaweed are carted away from French coasts between March and October.

Gamely, Monsieur Perzinsky grabs the *Indicateur des Marées*, the local timetable of tides, and checks the date and times. "It's almost low tide," he announces. "Let's get us some seaweed."

In contrast to his go-getter pitch, Michel Perzinsky's harvesting style could hardly be more low-key. After driving past the hordes of August tourists, past the Church of Our Lady of Kroaz-Baz to the beach, he unloads his tools: a wheelbarrow and a pile of potato sacks. Wearing jeans and high rubber boots, he stoops to his task. He wades out into the harbor in the warm afternoon sun and fills the potato sacks with armfuls of the abundant sea crop.

To be sure, not all seaweed gathering is so primitive. Since different species of seaweed come into view at different depths, harvesters also use tractors and boats equipped with hydraulic lines. On a good day, harvesters can pull in 1,300 to 1,500 pounds of seaweed, in the different varieties, in the space of two hours.

SEAWEED CUISINE

Back at the Algomarine plant, the seaweed is sorted, washed, and dried or, for some edible kinds like samphire, pickled. The seaweed turns up on tables around Brittany, often in the form of seaweed bread, flecked with green, as at the Maison de Bricourt, Olivier Roellinger's two-star restaurant in Cancale. And at the Hôtel de la Plage, on the beach in Sainte-Anne-la-Palud, Chef J. P. Gloanec adds alaria (a variety of seaweed also called wakame) to a mayonnaise sauce (recipe follows).

Edible seaweed fits right in with the work of restaurant chefs, who chase down new and novel ideas. Not so for the home cook. Michel Perzinsky sees the real challenge as making inroads into traditional French cooking. So he plays up the nutrition angle, calling seaweed a "healthful treasure."

But what cooks really want to know is what to do with the stuff. To break the barrier and introduce seaweed into the average diet, Monsieur Perzinsky suggests everyday uses such as adding it to *court bouillon*, an aromatic liquid for poaching fish.

He gives cooks a gastronomic grip on this unfamiliar ingredient by comparing it to something perfectly commonplace. Says Michel Perzinsky: "Think of it like parsley, but from the sea."

GRIBICHE DE LOTTE À LA CRÈME D'ALGUES

(BRITTANY)

Monkfish in Seaweed Sauce

4 SERVINGS

What's the best accompaniment to fish and shellfish? Why, briny seaweed, naturally. Recently, Breton chefs have been experimenting with the seaweed left behind by ebbing tides. J. P. Gloanec, for one, blends it with cream and mayonnaise to make a gribiche *that tastes of the sea. (Regulation* gribiche, *an oily, mayonnaiselike sauce also served with fish, gets its punch from capers, mustard, tangy chopped pickles, and herbs.)*

At the Hôtel de la Plage, on the beach in Sainte-Anne-la-Palud, Chef Gloanec adds his gribiche *to a warm salad entrée of steamed, sliced monkfish and raw vegetables, all topped with slivers of fried leeks. Look for dried seaweed in health-food shops and Japanese grocery stores.*

¼ cup alaria or wakame (dried seaweed)
2 cups water
½ cup crème fraîche *(page 368) or sour cream*
½ cup mayonnaise, prepared or homemade *(page 53)*
Salt and freshly ground pepper
Vegetable oil, for frying
1 small leek, white part only, or 2 scallions, cut into 2-inch matchstick strips
1¼ pounds skinned monkfish fillets, cut into ¼- to ½-inch slices
4 cups torn salad greens, such as baby spinach, oak-leaf lettuce, and purslane
1 small tomato, peeled, seeded, and diced
1 small carrot, cut into 2-inch julienne

*I*n a small bowl, soak the wakame in the water until reconstituted, 1 or 2 minutes, and drain. Pat dry with paper towels. In another bowl, combine the seaweed with the *crème fraîche* or sour cream and the mayonnaise. Add pepper and taste for seasoning. Chill.

In a small heavy saucepan, heat ½ inch of oil. Add the leek or scallion strips, a small handful at a time, to the oil, and fry until tinged with brown, 30 seconds to 1 minute. Using a skimmer, remove the strips to paper towels.

Sprinkle the fish with salt and pepper. In a steamer or a steaming basket, steam the fish until opaque through, 2 to 3 minutes.

Arrange the greens on plates. Strew the tomato and carrot on top of the greens. Arrange the slices of fish on spoonfuls of the seaweed sauce in a ring around the salad. Scatter the fried leeks or scallions over all and serve at once. Pass any remaining sauce separately.

POULTRY, RABBIT, AND FEATHERED GAME

ost chickens today never scratch in a barnyard, and pheasants hop around under netting on specialized farms. "I used to have chickens and ducks at home," says Jean-Pierre Clauzel. "No more." Monsieur Clauzel, a rancher in Les Saintes-Maries-de-la-Mer, explains, "To raise them cost me three times what I could buy them for."

But until 1955, the date of the first battery chickens in France, barnyard animals and game were the sole choices. And country folk won the right to hunt only after the Revolution. Prior to 1789, when the forest land and all the creatures in it belonged to the nobility or the church, stalking wild animals was poaching, and punishable.

In such prosperous regions as Normandy, the midday meal for all but the poorest always included a meat dish, usually one of the small farm animals—a roasting chicken, stewing hen, rabbit, duck, or guinea hen—and when the harvest had to come in and there were small hordes of workers to feed, geese and turkeys. But in less-favored places, the lower classes seldom ate meat. "A chicken was Sunday dinner," says poultryman Jean-Claude Miéral. "It was costly and looked forward to."

Why does Henri IV remain one of France's most beloved kings when he reigned for only five years? Because he promised a chicken in every pot on Sunday. At the end of the sixteenth century, when Henri IV came to power, farmers routinely went to bed hungry (or worse) when crops failed, and the nourishing potato hadn't yet been introduced to France.

At the same time, ordinary people were sooner left to starve than allowed to shoot game. You begin to understand the staying power in the Frenchman's love of hunting. Far more than a woodland chase, it's a symbol of equality and the right to feed oneself.

If you do buy poultry from a farmer, you'll come close to the old-time experience, both in terms of the quality of the bird and its jolt to the pocketbook—farm birds are no bargain. ✒

BRESSE POULTRY FARMING, A PROFESSION OF FAITH

Montrevel-en-Bresse, Burgundy—The way Jean-Claude Miéral sees it, there are four professions that attract passionate sorts of people: the priesthood, teaching, baking, and farming.

For this poultryman, who ferrets out and champions the men who raise the finest Bresse chickens, young hens, capons, and turkeys in the countryside around Montrevel, there's something almost holy about a farmer. "Bresse peasants," says Monsieur Miéral with a catch in his voice, "they're sages."

Before the 1950s, when technology standardized the chicken and turned it into food for the masses, each region of France had its own breed of chicken, like Bresse's famous bird. In the Bresse region in eastern Burgundy, farmers held ten hectares (about twenty-four acres) or less, and everyone had a cow, raised a few birds, and grew corn to feed them.

But mass-produced chicken got a toehold in Bresse after World War II when France was hungry. It was cheap. It required no dedication or mystical sense on the farmer's part. You didn't have to pay attention to the seasons. And you got Sunday roast chicken any day of the week.

The direction in which things were pointed seemed like progress. Mass-produced chicken arrived along with the democratization of French society and the advent of paid vacations for workers. Farmers' sons traded in the family hoe for a wrench at the Renault factory.

SAVE OUR BIRDS

Yet this farm exodus and the threat to his gastronomic heritage goaded Jean-Claude Miéral's father, and other single-minded farmers, into action. They could not imagine giving up the native poultry for one that could be raised anywhere, and they lobbied the government to affix an official appellation to their celebrated birds.

On August 1, 1957, René Coty, the President of the Republic, signed into law the defining criteria for *volaille de Bresse appellation d'origine contrôlée*, making this local poultry the first in the world to benefit from an AOC.

The AOC guarantees that this poultry is of the Bresse race, characterized by its white feathers, blue feet, and red cockscomb. In fact, as Monsieur Miéral explains, the Bresse race also produces gray and black birds. And the gray variant doesn't always have blue feet (*pattes bleues*). But by law, the only acceptable birds are the blue, white, and red variety. To emphasize these striking colors—also the colors of the French flag—authentic Bresse poultry sports a blue, white, and red label.

Another condition for AOC status requires that the birds come only from the Bresse countryside on Burgundy's eastern border, including the three *départements* of Ain, Jura, and Saône-et-Loire. Together they represent some 865,000 acres of farmland. About 650 farmers here raise 1 million chickens by the book.

These farmers buy day-old chicks from authorized breeders and then coddle the newborns in comfy, warm sheds until, after 35 prescribed days, they are strong enough to run in the fresh air. AOC rules stipulate that each bird must have at least ten square meters (about thirty-three square feet) to scratch around in.

Chickens strut for a spell of 9 weeks to wear a Bresse AOC label. Young hens run free in Bresse barnyards for 11 weeks, and capons waddle for a leisurely 23 weeks. Besides pecking at the tasty grass, worms, and insects in the yard, all the birds feed on a luxury diet of corn, wheat, and milk products. Medicines and additives are strictly forbidden except by medical prescription, and in any case never during the final weeks.

For the finishing touch, the birds spend their last days (10 to 15 days for chickens) sequestered in an *"épinette,"* or special cage, where they fatten up to minimum regulation size before their slaughter: 3½ pounds for a chicken, a hefty 4½ pounds for a young hen, and over 8 whopping pounds for a plump capon.

As a result of the good life, the best Bresse poultry has marbled flesh, making it self-basting from the inside out. The meat is firm yet it still cuts like butter. And it has the taste of a real barnyard bird.

It also takes longer to cook than an ordinary bird. "People gripe because it takes an hour and a quarter to cook a Bresse chicken for six people," says Monsieur Miéral. But he bristles at this impatient attitude: "In the time it takes to drink an aperitif, the chicken's done."

FIGHTING THE GOOD FIGHT

More important than the cooking time to Monsieur Miéral is that even with high breeding standards you can wind up with an ordinary chicken. For instance, he scoffs at the bylaw requiring ten square meters of land per chicken. The appropriate footage, he feels, is double or treble that amount.

"The problem with the AOC is that it does too little," he snaps. "The least-good chicken should at least be good. As it is, you can still be within the law and not have know-how."

In other words, you can't legislate a farmer's knack for doing things. "Peasants are instinctive," he explains. "It's insulting to give them rules and regulations."

For Monsieur Miéral, the quality of Bresse poultry depends more on the character of the farmer than on government decree. "If you don't know the man behind the chicken, what do you know?" he asks. "Like wine, the quality of poultry varies from one patch of land to another. It also depends on the passion and intuition of the farmer."

Monsieur Miéral regularly travels an hour or more to the tranquil farms in the Bresse countryside to see his poultry farmers. Here, away from roads, crowds, and noise, sixty farmers raise Bresse chickens just for him. He rarely buys at the poultry markets in Louhans and Pont-de-Vaux, where he can't see for himself the conditions in which the animals were raised.

When Jean-Claude Miéral talks about his work he sounds every bit the preacher he so admires. "I feel like I am pestering everybody," he says. "I don't accept compromise." ✍

POULET SAUTÉ À L'AIL

(BURGUNDY)

Chicken Sauté with Garlic

4 SERVINGS

4 tablespoons unsalted butter
One 3½-pound chicken, cut into 8 serving pieces; or 3 pounds chicken
*   pieces*
Salt and freshly ground pepper
10 fat garlic cloves, unpeeled
1 cup dry white wine

To clarify the butter, melt it in a small saucepan over low heat. Skim the froth from the surface and let the melted butter cool to tepid. Pour the butter into a small bowl, leaving the milky sediment at the bottom of the pan.

Sprinkle the pieces of chicken with salt. In a sauté pan or a shallow metal casserole just big enough to hold the pieces of chicken in a single layer, heat the clarified butter. Add the chicken, skin side down, to the pan in batches. Brown lightly all over, about 10 minutes, then remove.

Add the garlic to the same pan and cook, shaking the pan often, until the cloves brown lightly, 2 to 3 minutes.

Put the chicken, skin side down, with any juices, back into the pan with the garlic. Cover the pan, reduce the heat to low, and cook until the chicken is tender, 20 to 30 minutes. Remove the chicken to a warmed serving dish.

Stir the wine into the pan, scraping up the browned pan juices. Simmer until the wine reduces by two thirds and the flavor is concentrated. Add pepper and taste the sauce for seasoning.

Pour the sauce and garlic cloves over the chicken and serve, allowing each diner to peel the garlic.

THE TRUTH ABOUT CHICKEN

A chicken in every pot marks a valuable achievement. Still, gentle supermarket prices won't produce the quality of a barnyard bird. (Haven't you noticed the water and fat a supermarket chicken throws off during cooking? Doesn't it taste like wet cotton?) Now and then it's worth paying a premium to taste a better chicken—say, in any of these recipes. If you do buy a free-range chicken, note that the farm bird takes longer to cook than the mass-produced variety.

Poultryman Jean-Claude Miéral's garlicky chicken dish comes from Burgundy, not Provence. Farmers in the South of France haven't cornered the garlic market; northern farmers also cultivate the stinking rose. But in Burgundian cooking, the taste of garlic is insinuated, not declaimed as it is in that of Provence.

In Monsieur Miéral's chicken sauté, for instance, slow cooking and sweet butter—standing in for olive oil—both help take the edge off the garlic's pungency. And he calls for only 10 cloves. The famous Provençal version of this recipe counts a whopping 40. Also, the relatively small amount of garlic here makes it a condiment instead of a serious ingredient. With the chicken, serve a creamy potato gratin or try the Potato Pancakes from Burgundy.

POULARDE À L'ESTRAGON

(BURGUNDY)

Poached Chicken in Tarragon Sauce

4 SERVINGS

Says Jean-Claude Miéral, poulterer to France's great chefs: "If you really like chicken, you like it poached. But poaching takes no pity on inferior birds." Monsieur Miéral contributed this recipe from France's poultry capital, the Bresse area of Burgundy, and it shows up the best, and worst, qualities of a chicken.

The preparation will give you no trouble. The chicken cooks gently in an aromatic court bouillon until tender and juicy. Separately, a sauce is made with a cup of crème fraîche *(Monsieur Miéral's original recipe calls for 2 cups) and a handful of fresh tarragon.*

Now I'm not suggesting you serve Monsieur Miéral's creamy poached chicken every week or even every month. But, at least once, try this truly noble recipe. And when you do, track down the best free-range chicken you can find. If local stores don't stock crème fraîche, *make a batch for the occasion. If your greengrocer runs out of tarragon, then reschedule the dinner. It's worth the wait. This deserves a lovely white Burgundy and a simple rice pilaf.*

1 veal bone (optional)
One 3½-pound chicken, trussed, with neck and giblets (save the liver for another recipe)
2 carrots, thinly sliced
2 onions, quartered and studded with 2 cloves total
1 branch fresh thyme, or ½ teaspoon dried thyme leaves
2 imported bay leaves
2 branches fresh tarragon, plus 2 tablespoons chopped
12 cups water
Salt and freshly ground white pepper
1 cup crème fraîche *(page 368)*

*I*f using the veal bone, put it in a small saucepan, cover with cold water, and bring to a boil. Simmer for 5 minutes, skimming, then drain and rinse. In a metal casserole just big enough to hold all the ingredients, combine the chicken neck and giblets, optional blanched veal bone, the carrots, onions, thyme, bay leaves, branches of tarragon, and the 12 cups of water. Season lightly with salt. Cover the pot, bring the water to a boil and simmer for 15 minutes.

Add the chicken, breast side up, to this court bouillon. Bring the water back to a boil, then reduce the heat to low. Gently poach the chicken, covered, until tender, 45 minutes to 1 hour.

Leave the chicken in its poaching liquid, off the heat, while preparing the sauce. In a heavy medium saucepan, combine the *crème fraîche*, chopped tarragon, and a little salt. Bring the sauce to a boil, stirring, then lower the heat. Simmer the sauce, stirring from time to time, until it thickens slightly, 5 to 10 minutes. Add pepper and taste the sauce. If needed, add more tarragon, salt, or pepper until the sauce is flavored to your liking.

With a two-pronged fork, lift the chicken out of the poaching liquid, letting it drain into the pot. Transfer the chicken to a carving board with a well. Remove the strings from the chicken and carve it, discarding the skin.

Arrange the chicken pieces on a warmed platter or plates. Pour any juices from the chicken back into the poaching liquid. (Strain this liquid and keep it to use like stock.) Spoon some of the sauce over the chicken and serve. Pass the remaining sauce separately.

SECOND-CHANCE TARRAGON CHICKEN

If you consider this recipe an impossibility as long as headlines yell "cholesterol," don't reject poached chicken with tarragon altogether.

For another version, practically fat-free but no less good—only different—add a fistful of fresh tarragon, stems and all, when making the court bouillon. When the chicken is done, simmer the poaching liquid until it reduces by half or until well flavored, and strain instead of saving it for another recipe. Omit the *crème fraîche* sauce. Season to taste with salt and pepper. To accompany the chicken, in the reducing liquid cook carrots and zucchini, both halved lengthwise and cut into 2-inch pieces, and peeled new potatoes, until tender. Serve the chicken and vegetables in soup plates with some of the delicate poaching liquid and, if you want contrast, pass imported Dijon mustard alongside.

POULE SAUCE VERTE

(BURGUNDY)

Poached Chicken with Herbed Potato Salad

4 SERVINGS

One 3½-pound chicken, trussed, with neck and giblets (save the liver for
   another recipe)
2 carrots, thinly sliced
2 turnips, quartered
2 onions, quartered and studded with 2 cloves total
1 rib celery, thinly sliced
2 leeks, white and light green parts only, thinly sliced
1 bouquet garni (1 branch fresh thyme, or ½ teaspoon dried thyme leaves;
   6 parsley stems; 1 bay leaf; and 3 leek or scallion greens, tied in a
   bundle with kitchen string or cheesecloth)
12 cups water
Salt
1¼ pounds boiling potatoes, unpeeled

SAUCE VERTE
1 raw egg yolk, at room temperature, or hard-cooked if you prefer
2 tablespoons wine vinegar
1 tablespoon imported Dijon mustard
1 garlic clove, peeled
2 shallots, halved
Salt and freshly ground pepper
¾ cup vegetable oil
1 cup mixed fresh herb leaves, such as parsley, chives (snipped into 2-inch
   lengths), chervil, and tarragon

*I*n a metal casserole just large enough to hold all the ingredients, combine the chicken neck and giblets, the vegetables, *bouquet garni*, and the water. Season lightly with salt. Cover the pot, bring the water to a boil, and simmer for 15 minutes.

Add the chicken, breast side up, to this court bouillon, and when the water returns to a simmer, reduce the heat to low. Gently poach the chicken, covered, until tender, 45 minutes to 1 hour.

Meanwhile, put the potatoes in a large saucepan, cover with water, add salt, and bring to a boil. Simmer until tender, 15 to 20 minutes, and drain. While the potatoes are still warm, peel them and cut into ¼- to ½-inch slices. Arrange the potatoes in the bottom of a warmed shallow serving dish.

Make the sauce: In a food processor, whir together the egg

A friendly, funky spot (the menu is in comic-strip form), Coum' Chez Eux in Dijon offers a simple omelet and daily specials from Burgundy, especially the Morvan, the harsh country south of Vézelay. The day I ate there a handwritten note stuck on the menu said: "Today poule sauce verte." Not exactly typical Morvan fare, but so what? Good is good.

When trying this dish at home I found it every bit as tasty at room temperature, when the chicken and potatoes had absorbed the pungent herb sauce, as it was just out of the pot. Don't worry if the water doesn't entirely cover the breast of the chicken during poaching, because the meat still cooks beautifully. For the sauce, the choice of red- or white-wine vinegar is moot— use whatever's at your elbow—the herbs color the sauce a vibrant green in any case.

*If you prefer not to put an egg yolk in the sauce, the consistency will be considerably thicker than a vinaigrette but not as thick as mayonnaise.
A yolkless sauce eventually breaks if not used soon after it is made.*

yolk, vinegar, mustard, garlic, shallots, salt, and pepper. Slowly add a tablespoon of the oil and whir until incorporated. With the blades turning, add the remaining oil in a thin stream. Add the herbs and pulse to blend. Taste and add more mustard, vinegar, salt, or pepper until the mayonnaise is seasoned as you like. However, if you have not used an egg yolk, the emulsion will break if you add more vinegar.

With a two-pronged fork, lift the chicken out of the poaching liquid, letting it drain back into the pot. Transfer to a carving board with a well. Remove the strings from the chicken and cut into serving pieces. Discard the skin.

Arrange the chicken pieces on the potatoes. Pour any juices from the chicken back into the court bouillon. (Strain this liquid and keep it to use like stock.) Spoon some of the sauce over the chicken. Pass any remaining sauce separately. Serve the chicken warm or at room temperature.

COQ AU VIN

(BURGUNDY)

Chicken Simmered in Red Wine

4 SERVINGS

There are as many versions of coq au vin *as there are cooks in Burgundy. At the Moulin du Plateau, a retreat in the Morvan forest for families and the odd hiker, lavish amounts of wild mushrooms, tracked down under pine trees, replace run-of-the-mill button mushrooms in the garnish.*

Coq au vin *traditionally involves a marinade to tenderize tough old rooster meat. But the barnyard rooster, star of Burgundy's famous stew, is fast disappearing, and ordinary chickens don't need tenderizing. Recipes today tend to skip the marinating.*

For the full Burgundy treatment, start with a Beet Salad with Vinaigrette, Jellied Ham with Parsley, or Savory Cheese Pastries from the Morvan. For dessert, try Poached Pears with Cassis and Vanilla Ice Cream, Caramelized Pumpkin Pudding with Black-Currant Sauce, or, if you haven't chosen corniottes *to begin the meal, Apple Pastries with Black-Currant Sauce.*

3 tablespoons vegetable oil
5 ounces slab bacon, cut into lardons *(page 56); or 5 slices bacon, cut across into ⅜-inch strips*
One 3½-pound chicken, cut into serving pieces; or 3 pounds chicken pieces
Salt and freshly ground pepper
2 carrots, thinly sliced
1 large onion, halved and thinly sliced
1 fat garlic clove, crushed
3 cups young red wine, preferably a Burgundy
1 bouquet garni *(1 branch fresh thyme, or ½ teaspoon dried thyme leaves; 6 parsley stems; and 1 bay leaf, tied in a bundle with kitchen string or cheesecloth)*
¼ cup marc de Bourgogne *(the local brandy) or Cognac*
2 tablespoons unsalted butter
2 tablespoons all-purpose flour

GARNISH
7 ounces pearl onions
Salt
3 tablespoons unsalted butter
Pinch of sugar
7 ounces mushrooms (button, oyster, or a wild variety), halved or quartered if large

*I*n a sauté pan or a shallow metal casserole just big enough to hold the pieces of chicken in a single layer, heat the oil over low heat. Add the bacon, slowly cook it until golden, 5 to 8 minutes, then remove to paper towels.

Sprinkle the pieces of chicken with salt. Increase the heat under the pan to moderate and add the chicken, skin side down. Lightly brown all over, about 10 minutes, then remove. Discard all but 2 tablespoons of fat from the pan.

Add the carrots, onion, and garlic with a little salt and cook over low heat, stirring occasionally, until lightly browned, 8 to 10 minutes. Discard any fat from the pan.

Gradually stir in the wine, scraping up the browned pan juices. Add the chicken and tuck in the *bouquet garni*. In a small saucepan, heat the *marc* or Cognac and light. (It will flare up so take care.)

Pour the flaming liqueur into the chicken pan and shake until the flames subside. Cover the pan and bring the liquid to a boil. Reduce the heat to low and gently simmer the chicken until tender, 20 to 30 minutes. (The *coq au vin* can be made a day or two ahead to this point and chilled in its cooking liquid. Reheat before proceeding.)

Meanwhile, make the garnish: In a medium saucepan of boiling water, blanch the onions for 1 minute, drain, and peel them—the skins will strip away easily. Trim the roots and stalks of the onions carefully so they will not fall apart during cooking. Put the onions back in the saucepan and add salt, a tablespoon of the butter, the sugar, and water barely to cover. Bring to a boil and simmer, uncovered, until the onions are tender and the liquid evaporates to a shiny glaze, 10 to 15 minutes.

In a frying pan, melt the remaining 2 tablespoons of butter. Add the mushrooms with salt. Toss them in the butter over moderately high heat until they lose all their moisture, about 5 minutes, and remove. Press a piece of foil on top and cover the pan if the mushrooms look dry to start.

Remove the chicken to a warmed serving dish and keep warm. Discard the *bouquet garni*. Whir the remaining mixture in a food processor until mostly puréed. Pour through a fine strainer, pressing on any vegetable pieces to extract all their juice, back into the same pan. Discard any vegetables.

In a small bowl, mash together the butter and flour. Bring the sauce to a boil and skim off the fat. Whisk in just enough of the butter-and-flour paste, a little at a time, to thicken the sauce lightly. Add the reserved onions, mushrooms, and bacon and simmer for 10 minutes. Add pepper and taste for seasoning. Pour the sauce over the chicken and serve.

AUMONIÈRE
DE POULET BAJOCASSE

(NORMANDY)

Sautéed Chicken in Crispy Filo Packages

4 SERVINGS

AUMONIÈRES

4 skinless, boneless chicken-breast halves, each cut across into 2 pieces
½ cup Calvados
8 tablespoons (1 stick) unsalted butter
1 tablespoon vegetable oil
Salt and freshly ground pepper
8 sheets filo dough
1 egg, beaten to mix with a little salt

DUXELLES

2 tablespoons unsalted butter
2 shallots, finely chopped
10 ounces mushrooms, finely chopped
½ cup chopped fresh parsley
1 tablespoon crème fraîche (page 368) or heavy (whipping) cream
Salt and freshly ground pepper

SAUCE

2 cups chicken stock, preferably homemade (page 369) or low-salt canned
  broth
1 cup crème fraîche or heavy (whipping) cream
Salt and freshly ground pepper
2 tablespoons unsalted butter
2 tablespoons vegetable oil
10 ounces mushrooms, thinly sliced
2 firm apples, cut into ⅜-inch dice

Even in its marinated, pan-fried, souped-up state, Christophe Chabredier's chicken recipe from the Lion d'Or hotel-restaurant in Bayeux harks back to plain Norman cooking. (The original uses a whole chicken, boned; the carcass goes to making the stock. Anything else would be wasteful.) At its core, what you have is a version of dyed-in-the-wool poulet vallée d'auge —chicken with cream and Calvados sauce.

But every so often simply comforting is simply not enough. Try this dish when you want to surprise and enchant yet stay within the French country idiom. For a complete meal of haute cuisine à la normande, start with Lamb's Lettuce with Grilled Oysters and Preserved Gizzards, Swiss Chard Custard with Sautéed Chicken Livers, or Molded Chitterling Sausage with Potatoes and Cabbage, then after the chicken segue into a Gratin of Pears and Raspberries in Sabayon.

*F*or the *aumonières:* In a deep dish, marinate the chicken in the Calvados for at least 1 hour.

Meanwhile, make the *duxelles:* In a medium saucepan, melt the butter. Add the shallots and cook over moderate heat until translucent, 1 or 2 minutes. Raise the heat to moderately high, add the mushrooms, parsley, *crème fraîche* or cream, and salt and pepper, and cook, stirring, until most of the moisture evaporates, 2 to 3 minutes. Set aside.

Make the sauce: In a heavy medium saucepan, simmer the chicken stock over moderately high heat until it reduces to a syrupy glaze, about 30 minutes. Skim regularly during cooking. Stir in the *crème fraîche* or cream and simmer until it thickens slightly, 5 to 10 minutes. Add pepper and taste for seasoning.

In a frying pan, heat 1 tablespoon of the butter and 1 tablespoon of the oil over moderately high heat. Add the mushrooms with a little salt and pepper and toss them until the moisture evaporates, about 5 minutes. Press a piece of foil on top and cover the pan if the mushrooms look dry to start.

In a small saucepan, heat 2 tablespoons of the Calvados used to marinate the chicken and light it. (It will flare up so take care.) Pour the flaming liqueur over the mushrooms and shake until the flames subside. Add the mushrooms to the cream sauce.

In the empty frying pan, heat the remaining tablespoon of butter and tablespoon of oil over moderately high heat. Add the diced apples with a little salt and pepper and toss them until golden, 3 to 5 minutes.

In a small saucepan, heat 2 more tablespoons of the Calvados used to marinate the chicken and light it. (Remember, it will flare up.) Pour the flaming liqueur over the apples and shake until the flames subside. Add the apples to the cream sauce. Set the sauce aside. Reheat and taste for seasoning before serving.

Heat the oven to 425°F.

Finish the *aumonières:* In the same frying pan used to sauté the mushrooms and apples, melt 1 tablespoon of the butter and the oil over moderately high heat. Pat the pieces of chicken dry with paper towels. Sprinkle the chicken with salt and pepper, lightly brown on both sides, about 1 minute in all, then remove.

In a small saucepan, melt 4 tablespoons of the butter. Unroll the filo dough. Count out 8 sheets and save the remaining dough for another recipe. Brush the top sheet with some melted butter. Fold the top sheet across in half, butter side in. Brush the top with more butter. Put ½ tablespoon of *duxelles* in the center of the sheet. Set a piece of chicken on top. Add ½ tablespoon of *duxelles* and 1 teaspoon of the remaining butter. Fold the sheet over the chicken so the filling is completely enclosed. Remove to a baking sheet. Brush the top with beaten egg. Repeat the procedure until you've made 8 packages.

Bake the *aumonières* in the heated oven until a knife inserted in the center of one comes out hot to the touch, 20 to 25 minutes.

Set each *aumonière* in the center of a warmed plate. Spoon some of the sauce around it and serve as soon as possible. Pass any remaining sauce separately.

FRICASSÉE DE VOLAILLE AU VINAIGRE DE CIDRE

(NORMANDY)

Chicken in Cider Vinegar Sauce

4 SERVINGS

At Chez Octave in La Ferté-Macé, the food is faultless in its own traditional way. In this chicken fricassee, there are unsalted butter for frying the pieces of chicken, chicken stock for moistening, and a healthy dose of cider vinegar, which, together, give the dish its undeniable Norman identity. Serve sautéed apple slices alongside, or try Baked Carrots in Cream and a crisp potato cake.

One 3½-pound chicken, cut into 8 serving pieces; or 3 pounds chicken pieces
Salt and freshly ground pepper
4 tablespoons clarified unsalted butter (page 199)
4 shallots, finely chopped
1 cup cider vinegar
1 cup chicken stock, preferably homemade (page 369)
1 tablespoon unsalted butter

Sprinkle the pieces of chicken with salt. In a sauté pan or shallow metal casserole just big enough to hold the pieces of chicken in a single layer, heat the clarified butter. Add the chicken, skin side down, to the pan in batches. Brown lightly all over, about 10 minutes, then remove.

Reduce the heat to low, add the shallots to the same pan, and cook until translucent, 1 or 2 minutes.

Gradually stir in the vinegar, scraping up the browned pan juices. Simmer until reduced by half. Stir in the stock. Return the chicken to the pan and bring the liquid to a boil. Cover the pan, reduce the heat to low, and cook at a bare simmer until tender, 20 to 30 minutes. Remove the chicken to a warmed platter.

Simmer the cooking liquid until it lightly coats a spoon and then strain it. Add the butter and whisk over low heat so the butter softens creamily. Season with pepper and taste. Pour the sauce over the chicken and serve.

BLANC DE POULET AUX ÉCHALOTES

(BRITTANY)

Sautéed Chicken Breast with Shallots and Garlic

4 SERVINGS

2 tablespoons unsalted butter
1 tablespoon vegetable oil
4 skinless, boneless chicken-breast halves
Salt and freshly ground pepper
3 shallots, finely chopped
2 garlic cloves, finely chopped
½ cup dry white wine, such as Muscadet
1 cup chicken stock, preferably homemade (page 369)
¾ cup heavy (whipping) cream

Fast and fussless, Jean-Marie Le Gall's chicken recipe is wonderful with a Warm Salad of Green Beans and Tomatoes. Begin the meal with Mussels in Buttery Broth or Tuna, Egg, and Potato Salad, and, for dessert, serve Baked Apples with Cider Eau de Vie.

In a medium sauté pan or a shallow metal casserole, warm the butter and oil over moderately high heat until the butter foams. Sprinkle the chicken breasts with a little salt and cook them in the pan until lightly browned on both sides, 2 or 3 minutes. Remove the chicken from the pan.

Reduce the heat to fairly low, add the shallots to the same pan, and cook, stirring, until translucent, 1 or 2 minutes. Add the garlic and cook until fragrant, about 1 minute. Raise the heat and pour in the wine and stock, stirring to dissolve the browned pan juices. Boil until the liquid reduces to about ½ cup, 5 to 10 minutes. Stir in the cream and bring to a boil. Return the chicken with any accumulated juices to the pan. Cover the pan, reduce the heat to low, and cook until the meat has lost all trace of pink, 10 to 15 minutes. Add pepper and taste for seasoning before serving.

PINTADE SAUTÉE
AU CHOU VERT

(BURGUNDY)

Guinea Hen with Savoy Cabbage and Bacon

4 SERVINGS

About the time you first notice hunters' spent orange cartridges mixed with split chestnut pods and other fall detritus, Burgundy cooks start adding this recipe to their list of daily specials. Every so often pheasant takes the place of guinea hen. Turkey drumsticks could also substitute for the guinea hen, in which case you would cook them, covered, until tender (about 2¾ hours).

There's a trick to blending these earthy ingredients so the flavors meld in a relatively short time—blanching the cabbage and, if needed, the bacon. Emphatically smoky or salty bacon overwhelms here. Fry a small piece first to see if it needs taming. To mellow strongly flavored bacon, put it in a pan of cold water, bring it to a boil, and simmer for 5 minutes. Drain and proceed with the recipe.

2 tablespoons vegetable oil
½ pound slab bacon, cut into lardons (page 56); or 8 slices bacon, cut across into ⅜-inch strips
One 3½-pound guinea hen, cut into 4 serving pieces
Salt and freshly ground pepper
3 small onions, chopped
2 carrots, chopped
1 cup dry white wine
1 cup chicken stock, preferably homemade (page 369)
1 bouquet garni (1 branch fresh thyme, or ½ teaspoon dried thyme leaves; 6 parsley stems; and 1 bay leaf, tied in a bundle with kitchen string or cheesecloth)
One 1-pound wedge Savoy cabbage, shredded

Heat the oven to 350°F.

In a shallow metal casserole just big enough to hold the pieces of guinea hen in a single layer, heat the oil over a low flame. Add the bacon and cook it slowly until the fat runs but the bacon is not yet crisp, then remove to paper towels.

Sprinkle the guinea hen with salt. Increase the heat under the casserole to moderate and add the guinea hen, skin side down. Lightly brown all over, about 10 minutes, then remove. Discard all but 1 tablespoon of fat from the casserole.

Add the onions and carrots with the bacon and a little salt, and stir until the vegetables are evenly coated with the fat. Cook over low heat, stirring occasionally, until lightly browned, 7 to 10 minutes. Discard any fat from the casserole. Gradually stir in the wine and stock, scraping up the browned pan juices. Return the pieces of guinea hen to the pan and tuck in the *bouquet garni*.

Bring the liquid to a boil on the stove. Transfer the casserole to the heated oven and cook, uncovered, for 15 minutes. Turn the guinea hen and cook for 15 minutes longer.

Meanwhile, cook the cabbage in plenty of boiling salted water (as for pasta) for 10 minutes, and drain. Rinse it in cold water and drain again thoroughly. Firmly press out most of the water with your hands. Set aside the cabbage.

Remove the pieces of guinea hen from the casserole and keep warm. Simmer the cooking liquid on the stove until well flavored, 8 to 10 minutes. Discard the *bouquet garni*. Add the cabbage and a few grindings of pepper and heat through. Taste the cabbage for seasoning.

Mound the cabbage on a warmed platter or plates. Arrange the guinea hen on the cabbage and serve.

PINTADE AUX POIVRONS ROUGE

(PROVENCE)

Roast Guinea Hen in Sweet Red Pepper Sauce

4 SERVINGS

One 3½-pound guinea hen, trussed
4 tablespoons olive oil
Salt

RED PEPPER SAUCE
¼ cup extra-virgin olive oil
1 large onion, chopped
4 fat garlic cloves, crushed
Salt and freshly ground pepper
4 ripe medium tomatoes (about 2 pounds), chopped; or one 28-ounce can
   Italian plum tomatoes, chopped, with their juice
2 large red bell peppers, cut into 1-inch pieces

*H*eat the oven to 425°F. Spread 2 tablespoons of the oil in a roasting pan just big enough to hold the bird. Set the bird in the pan. Sprinkle it inside and out with salt and rub with the remaining 2 tablespoons of oil.

Roast the bird for 25 minutes. Then continue cooking, basting every 10 minutes, until the juice runs clear when an inner thigh is pierced, 30 to 40 minutes longer.

While the hen roasts, begin the sauce: In a large saucepan, heat the oil. Add the onion and garlic with a little salt and stir until the vegetables are evenly coated with the oil. Cover the pan and cook over low heat, stirring occasionally, until tender, about 10 minutes. Add the tomatoes and red peppers and cook, partly covered, until the sauce is thick, about 45 minutes. Stir the tomatoes now and then during cooking. Work the sauce through a food mill into another saucepan to remove skin and seeds. Add pepper and taste the sauce for seasoning.

Remove the hen to a carving board when done, and let it stand, covered loosely with foil, while finishing the sauce, at least 10 minutes.

Discard the strings and carve the hen. Spoon some of the sauce onto a warmed platter or plates and spread it with a back of a spoon to cover the bottom. Arrange the pieces of guinea hen on the sauce. Pass any remaining sauce separately.

While I can't recommend the food at the Bistro Latin in Aix-en-Provence wholeheartedly—the menu promises more than it delivers—the combinations are still appealing. I worked with one of their ideas until I came up with a simple recipe that pulls together the lusty flavors of guinea hen and red bell peppers.

With the guinea hen, serve Lemony Orzo with Black Olives. The red pepper sauce is also delicious over fresh sausages, pasta, grilled tuna, and monkfish—pan-fried, baked, or poached.

BEYOND WINE IN BURGUNDY

In France, when you want a good chicken, you go to the poultryman and buy a chicken from Bresse, in northeast Burgundy.

But Burgundy is better known for wine than poultry. In this major wine-producing area, wine often replaces water (or cider or stock) in cooking. To be sure, you find *coq au vin* and *boeuf à la bourguignonne*, local stews made with local wines, but also *jambon persillé*, chunks of ham simmered in white wine and then jellied with chopped parsley, and *oeufs en meurette*, eggs in a red-wine sauce. For dessert, sweetened red wine serves as a poaching liquid for pears and, once reduced, as a sauce.

HOME OF INTENSE TASTES

Along with grapevines, winegrowers often cultivate shade-loving berries; principally, black currants, pressed to make full-flavored cassis liqueur. Dijon is the black-currant capital of France, and the sweet black-currant liqueur is stirred with local wine to make the aperitif *kir*, drizzled over poached peaches, and poured over ice cream for a quick dessert.

Another specialty associated with Dijon is *pain d' épices*, a moist, dense honey cake flavored with the sweet spices that once traveled through Dijon on the spice route.

To make Dijon mustard, mustard makers now import mustard seeds (most come from Canada). But the pungent condiment still plays an important role in local fare. Bistro standbys like rabbit *à la moutarde*, pork *dijonnaise*, and chitterling sausage *sauce moutarde* depend on mustard.

Besides mustard, Burgundy also produces two more of France's favorite condiments, tart *cornichon* pickles and pickled onions, both essential for enjoying typical French foods like pot-au-feu.

To partner Burgundy wines, cheese makers produce dozens of memorable varieties, including creamy Chaource; Charolais, a goat or mixed goat and cow cheese; strong-smelling, washed Epoisses; Aisy Cendré, a similar ash-covered cheese; and Cîteaux, still made by monks at the abbey here.

Burgundy cooks use cheese in their recipes, too. For the favorite appetizer *gougère*, rings or, sometimes, mounds of choux pastry are baked with Gruyère cheese, an import from nearby Savoie. To make the easy dessert, *fromage blanc à la crème*, cooks sweeten fresh, smooth cheese and fold in *crème fraîche*.

Farmers in southwest Burgundy raise Charolais cattle, a synonym for quality beef when it appears on a restaurant menu. It is so popular throughout France that it is replacing many other regional breeds of cattle.

To the north lies the Regional Nature Park of the Morvan. In this rugged terrain, cooks take advantage of trout from fast-flowing rivers, forest mushrooms, and low-bush blueberries.

OLD FAVORITES STILL PLEASE

Surprisingly, some of the ingredients that originally made Burgundy cuisine famous no longer come from Burgundy. Besides imported mustard seeds, the snails on your plate probably come from Greece. Since most of Burgundy's vineyard snails have succumbed to insecticides, the local supply is limited.

Imported or homegrown, these products continue to be a vital part of the cooking repertoire. Even today everyone enjoys snails smothered in garlicky herb butter and served sizzling hot, just as their grandparents did.

CUISSES DE DINDE AU VIN ROUGE

(BURGUNDY)

Turkey Drumsticks in Red Wine

4 SERVINGS

4 turkey drumsticks (about 3 pounds in all)
Salt and freshly ground pepper
¼ cup all-purpose flour
3 tablespoons clarified unsalted butter (page 199)
1 tablespoon vegetable oil
2 shallots, or 1 small onion, finely chopped
1 carrot, finely chopped
3 cups red wine, preferably a Burgundy
1 bouquet garni (1 branch fresh thyme, or ½ teaspoon dried thyme leaves;
    6 parsley stems; and 1 bay leaf, tied in a bundle with kitchen string or
    cheesecloth)

Pierre Landau, who is attached to Burgundy by marriage, has a way with food. He prepares a version of coq au vin *without a complicated garnish, using turkey drumsticks, a few vegetables, and a bottle of Burgundy. Turkey, once reserved for Christmastime in France, is now readily available throughout the year. You might want to try it with Pierre's Autumn Fruit Sauté.*

Sprinkle the turkey drumsticks with salt. Dredge them in the flour, patting off any excess. In a black iron skillet or a shallow metal casserole just big enough to hold the drumsticks in a single layer, heat the butter and oil. Brown the drumsticks on all sides, about 10 minutes, and remove. Reduce the heat to low, add the shallots or onion and the carrot to the same pan, and sauté until tender, about 5 minutes. Discard any fat from the pan.

Gradually stir the wine into the skillet, scraping up the browned juices. Add the drumsticks and tuck in the *bouquet garni.* Cover the skillet, bring the wine to a boil, then reduce the heat to low and cook the turkey at a bare simmer until very tender, 2 to 3 hours.

Remove the turkey to a carving board and cover loosely with foil. Simmer the cooking liquid until it lightly coats a spoon. Discard the *bouquet garni.* Add pepper and taste the sauce for seasoning. Slice the meat off the bone and arrange on a warmed platter or plates. Pour the sauce over the meat and serve.

RÔTI DE DINDE FARCIE AUX CHÂTAIGNES

(PROVENCE)

Provençal Christmas Turkey with Chestnut Stuffing

6 TO 8 SERVINGS

One 6- to 6½-pound turkey, with neck and giblets
7 tablespoons unsalted butter
Salt and freshly ground pepper
½ cup marc de Provence *(the local brandy) or Cognac*
¼ cup chopped fresh flat-leaf parsley
3 fat garlic cloves, sliced
⅓ cup finely chopped onion
1½ pounds peeled, cooked chestnuts
2 tablespoons olive oil
2 cups chicken stock, preferably homemade (page 369)

*H*eat the oven to 425°F. Cut the turkey giblets into 3 or 4 pieces.

In a frying pan, melt 1 tablespoon of the butter. Add the giblets with a little salt and cook them over moderately high heat until they are brown on all sides but still pink in the center, 1 or 2 minutes in all. In a small saucepan, heat ¼ cup of the *marc* or Cognac and light it. (It will flare up so take care.) Pour it into the frying pan and shake until the flames subside.

Transfer the giblets to the bowl of a food processor and add the parsley, garlic, onion, more salt, and pepper. Pulse until coarsely chopped. Add 20 to 25 of the chestnuts and pulse until broken into bite-size pieces. Sauté a small piece of the mixture and taste. Adjust the seasoning in the rest as needed. Stuff the turkey with the chestnut mixture, but don't pack it tightly. Truss the turkey.

In a roasting pan large enough to hold the turkey with room to spare, spread 2 tablespoons of the remaining butter and the oil. Set the turkey in the pan. Sprinkle it with salt and rub with the remaining 4 tablespoons of butter. Add the neck to the pan.

Roast the turkey in the preheated oven for 30 minutes. Then continue cooking, basting every 10 minutes, until the juices run clear when an inner thigh is pierced, and a meat thermometer inserted into the thickest part of the thigh reads 180°F., 1½ to 2 hours longer. After 1 or 1½ hours of cooking, add the remaining chestnuts to the turkey pan.

It's Christmas Eve at La Table de Nicole in Valaurie, and Nicole Vernerey and her kitchen crew are finishing the preparations for le gros souper, Christmas Eve dinner in Provence. "Who's basting the turkey?" Nicole wants to know. "Every 10 minutes," she chants. "You've got to baste the turkey every 10 minutes."

This hard-nosed taskmaster turns out a moist, brown bird. Nicole's stuffing, made with the giblets, persillade (the Provençal "masala" of chopped parsley and garlic), onion, brandy, and chestnuts, is more condiment than starchy filler. It adds a rich, pungent note to the plate and sets off the plain chestnuts roasted in the pan alongside the bird. Two tablespoons a person is all you want.

Instead of peeling raw chestnuts or using the shelled variety that come in a jar or can, don't hesitate to buy the roasted chestnuts street vendors sell. You will need 2 pounds of the unshelled kind. But even canned chestnuts will taste good after cooking in the turkey juices.

Remove the cooked turkey to a carving board with a well and let it stand, covered loosely with foil, at least 20 minutes. Using a slotted spoon, transfer the chestnuts to a bowl and keep warm.

Meanwhile, set the roasting pan over high heat. Stir in the remaining ¼ cup of *marc* or Cognac and the chicken stock, scraping up the browned pan juices. Simmer the cooking juices until reduced by half to concentrate the flavor. Season to taste.

Discard the strings from the turkey and carve it. Pour any juices from the turkey into the reduced cooking juices. Mound some of the stuffing and additional chestnuts on one side of a warmed platter. Arrange the turkey next to them. Spoon some of the cooking juices over the turkey. Pass the remaining cooking juices, stuffing, and additional chestnuts separately. Serve as soon as possible.

CHRISTMAS DINNER IN PROVENCE

This menu is the spiritual equivalent of a Christmas pilgrimage to the South of France. The soup fortifies you without spoiling your appetite, whether you're dealing with the Mistral wind that blows down the Rhône valley or with snow drifts. *Noël* wouldn't be *Noël* without roast turkey and chestnuts. Likewise, something would be missing without cardoons, although they are regularly eaten throughout the chilly months. *Oreillettes*, fresh and dried fruits, and nuts offer a sampling of the standard finish to a Provençal Christmas dinner—the thirteen desserts.

You can make the soup a day or two ahead. The dough for the pastries can also be prepared in advance, leaving only the rolling out and deep-frying for Christmas Eve. With the meal, serve a red wine from the southern Rhône, such as a Châteauneuf-du-Pape, Gigondas, or Beaumes de Venise.

Soupe à l'Ail de Nicole (page 14)
Nicole's Garlic and Herb Soup

Rôti de Dinde Farcie aux Châtaignes (page 216)
Provençal Christmas Turkey with Chestnut Stuffing

Cardons au Gratin (page 138)
Braised Cardoons with Cheese

Oreillettes (page 306)
Deep-Fried Christmas Pastries
and
*Fresh clementines, dried dates and figs,
raisins, almonds, hazelnuts, and walnuts*

CIVET DE CUISSES DE CANARD

(NORMANDY)

Marinated Duck Stew with Bacon

4 SERVINGS

This is the dish to prepare when you feel deeply deserving of a good meal. The recipe comes from the Moulin de Villeray near Condeau in the Norman Perche region, where you can go when you want to be served a good meal, with the Huisne River purling in the background.

The duck legs marinate overnight in red wine with vegetables, then they are braised, slowly, to a rich, robust stew. Traditionally, duck blood thickens and flavors the sauce. But since blood is hardly a standard or favored food item in America, I've left it out. With the duck, serve Creamy Cubed Celery Root.

4 duck legs (about 12 ounces each); or one 4½-pound duck, cut into 8 serving pieces

MARINADE
1 large onion, halved and thinly sliced
1 carrot, thinly sliced
2 fat garlic cloves, crushed
1 branch fresh thyme, or ½ teaspoon dried thyme leaves
2 imported bay leaves
½ tablespoon juniper berries, crushed
3 cups full-bodied red wine
3 tablespoons red-wine vinegar

Salt and freshly ground pepper
3 tablespoons vegetable oil
1 tablespoon tomato paste
5 ounces slab bacon, cut into lardons (page 56); or 5 slices bacon, cut across into ⅜-inch strips
2 tablespoons unsalted butter

A day before you plan to serve the duck, cut each duck leg, if using, in half through the joint, between the thigh and drumstick, using the line of white fat on the inside as a guide.

Make the marinade: Combine the ingredients in a bowl (not aluminum). Add the pieces of duck, cover, and leave to marinate overnight in a cool place, stirring once or twice.

The next day, heat the oven to 325°F. With a slotted spoon, lift each piece of duck out of the marinade, letting it drip back into the bowl, and pat the duck dry with paper towels. Sprinkle the pieces of duck with salt. In a black iron casserole or another heavy pot just big enough to hold the pieces of duck in a single layer, heat the oil over a moderate flame. Add the duck, skin side down, to the oil in batches. Brown it all over, about 10 minutes, then remove.

Drain all the vegetables from the marinade (saving the seasonings and the liquid), add them to the pot, and cook over moderate heat, stirring, until they are light brown, 8 to 10 minutes.

Discard any oil from the pot. Gradually stir in the marinade liquid and seasonings, and the tomato paste, scraping up the browned juices. Return the duck to the pot, cover with a lid, and bring the liquid to a boil on top of the stove. Transfer to the oven and bake until the duck is tender, about 1½ hours. (The duck can be cooked a day ahead and chilled in the cooking liquid; reheat it before proceeding. When chilled, the fat rises to the surface and can easily be removed. Otherwise, skim off as much fat as you can.)

In a frying pan, render the bacon slowly until golden, about 5 minutes, and drain on paper towels.

Remove the duck to a warmed serving dish and keep it warm. Strain the cooking liquid into a medium saucepan and add the bacon. Bring the cooking liquid to a boil, reduce the heat, and simmer it, skimming regularly, until it lightly coats a spoon, 10 to 15 minutes.

Whisk in the butter over very low heat so the butter doesn't melt completely but softens to form a smooth sauce. Add pepper and taste for seasoning. Pour the sauce over the duck and serve.

LAPIN AUX QUETSCHES

(NORMANDY)

Rabbit with Italian Prune Plum Sauce

4 SERVINGS

It's cold outside, but it's warm next to the crackling fire at the Auberge du Vieux Puits in Pont-Audemer, Normandy. And to eat, Chef Denis Geffroy always keeps at least one homey, restorative dish on the menu.

Here, a stock is made with rabbit bones and used first as a poaching liquid for the plums then, reduced, as a sauce. The rabbit meat is flamed with quetsch eau-de-vie, reinforcing the plum theme, and simmered in white wine. The result is a rich, full-flavored recipe without the addition of butter, egg, or cream. With it, serve fresh buttered pasta.

One 2½- to 3-pound rabbit, cut into serving pieces
5 tablespoons vegetable oil
1 carrot, finely chopped
2 onions, finely chopped
4 cups water
1 pound Italian prune plums, halved and pitted
Salt and freshly ground black pepper
3 tablespoons quetsch or plum eau-de-vie or Cognac
1½ cups dry white wine
1 bouquet garni (1 branch thyme; or ½ teaspoon dried thyme leaves; 6 parsley stems; 1 bay leaf; and 3 leek or scallion greens, tied in a bundle with kitchen string or cheesecloth)
1 teaspoon arrowroot mixed with 1 tablespoon cold water, if needed

*F*irst make a rabbit stock: Bone the pieces of rabbit by cutting and scraping the meat from the bones. Reserve the bones. Don't worry about doing this perfectly or about scraping the bones clean; the meat still attached to the bones will help flavor the stock. Cut the meat into 1½-inch pieces.

In a medium saucepan, heat half the oil over moderately high heat. Add the rabbit bones, brown them, turning often, 10 to 12 minutes, and remove. Reduce the heat to moderate, add the carrot and onions, and cook them until the onions are tinged with brown, 8 to 10 minutes. Return the rabbit bones to the pan, add the water, and bring to a boil over high heat. Reduce the heat to moderate and simmer the stock, uncovered, until it reduces by half, about 30 minutes. Skim the sauce regularly during cooking. Strain the stock into another saucepan.

Poach the plums in the stock until tender, 8 to 10 minutes. With a slotted spoon, remove them until ready to use. Reserve the stock.

Sprinkle the pieces of rabbit with salt. In a sauté pan or shallow metal casserole just big enough to hold the rabbit in a single layer, heat the remaining oil. Add the rabbit to the oil and lightly brown all over.

Heat the eau-de-vie in a small saucepan and light it. (It will flare up so take care.) Pour the flaming liqueur into the rabbit pan and shake until the flames subside. Stir in the wine and tuck in the *bouquet garni*. Cover the pan, bring the liquid to a boil, then reduce the heat to low, and cook at a bare simmer until the rabbit is tender, 35 to 45 minutes. (The rabbit can be cooked a day ahead and refrigerated in the cooking liquid; reheat it before proceeding.)

Remove the rabbit to a warmed serving dish and keep warm. Discard the *bouquet garni*. Stir the reserved stock into the rabbit cooking juices. Bring the sauce to a boil, reduce the heat to low, and simmer, skimming regularly, until the sauce reduces to ¾ cup. The sauce should be thick enough to coat a spoon lightly, so, if necessary, whisk enough of the arrowroot mixture into the simmering sauce to thicken it slightly. Reheat the plums in the sauce. Add pepper and taste the sauce for seasoning. Pour the sauce and plums over the rabbit and serve.

PRIX-FIXE PERFECTION

Even lavish restaurants in the French countryside offer bargains at lunchtime. Like François Lagrue at the Moulin de Villeray, chefs often turn to regional fare, creative or not, for the modest set menu. They save pure invention for the à la carte selection.

While I couldn't afford to wake up to the sound of a millstream under my window at the Moulin de Villeray, on limited funds I did hear it during my meal. Here is the same menu (minus the platter of local cheeses) I enjoyed at this restored Normandy mill one Saturday in early spring. Since Normandy produces no grapes, there are no traditional food-and-wine alliances to respect. Try one of the fuller-bodied reds from the Loire, like Chinon or Saint-Nicolas-de-Bourgueil.

Salade de Boudin Noir aux Pommes (page 66)
Green Salad with Blood Pudding–and–Apple Crown

Civet de Cuisses de Canard (page 218)
Marinated Duck Stew with Bacon

Céléri à la Crème (page 134)
Creamy Cubed Celery Root

Beignets aux Pommes (page 305)
Melt-in-Your-Mouth Apple Fritters

CUL DE LAPIN
À LA NANTAISE

(BRITTANY)

Marinated Rabbit in Muscadet Wine

4 SERVINGS

One 3-pound rabbit, cut into serving pieces
Salt and freshly ground pepper
3 tablespoons vegetable oil
¼ pound slab bacon, cut into lardons *(page 56); or 4 slices bacon, cut*
*   across into ⅜-inch strips*
6 shallots, finely chopped
½ pound button mushrooms, halved or quartered if large
¼ cup finely chopped fresh flat-leaf parsley
7 tablespoons lightly salted butter, cut into pieces (optional)

MARINADE
1 carrot, finely chopped
6 shallots or 1 large onion, finely chopped
1 branch fresh thyme, or ½ teaspoon dried thyme leaves
2 cups dry white wine, preferably Muscadet

*A*t least a day before you plan to serve the dish, make the marinade by combining the ingredients in a bowl (not aluminum). Add the rabbit pieces, cover, and set aside to marinate in a cool place overnight or up to 2 days, stirring once or twice.

The next day, heat the oven to 425°F. With a slotted spoon, lift each piece of rabbit out of the marinade, letting it drip back into the bowl, and pat the rabbit dry with paper towels. Reserve the marinade. Sprinkle the meat with salt, then rub with 1 tablespoon of the oil. Arrange in a shallow metal casserole just big enough to hold the pieces in one layer. Roast the rabbit, basting once after 20 minutes, for 30 minutes.

Reduce the oven temperature to 325°F. In a medium saucepan, bring the marinade to a boil on the stove and skim the foam from the surface. Pour the boiling marinade over the rabbit. Cover with the lid and bake the rabbit, turning it once, until it is tender, 20 to 30 minutes. (The rabbit can be cooked a day ahead and refrigerated in the cooking liquid; reheat it before proceeding.)

Meanwhile, for the garnish, heat the remaining 2 tablespoons of oil in a frying pan. Add the bacon, render it slowly until golden,

Mon Rêve, a villa near the mouth of the Loire river, makes a plush and sober backdrop for Gérard Ryngel's classic food with solidly Breton underpinnings. (Monsieur Ryngel with his roly-poly belly, is a chef straight out of central casting.) Here in Brittany's southeastern wine-producing Nantes region, the local Muscadet is the drink most often found in the glass and in the pot. In the northeast of Brittany, cider replaces the wine in virtually the same dish. Salted butter makes this recipe doubly Breton.

With the rabbit, serve fresh buttered pasta for catching the parsley-flecked sauce. If the idea of rabbit conjures up a cuddly bunny for you, try the recipe with chicken.

about 5 minutes, then push it to one side of the pan. Add the shallots and cook until translucent, 1 or 2 minutes. Raise the heat to moderately high, add the mushrooms, and toss them with the other ingredients in the pan until the moisture evaporates, about 5 minutes. Press a piece of foil on top and cover the pan if the mushrooms look dry to start.

Remove the rabbit to a warmed serving dish and keep warm. Bring the cooking liquid to a boil on the stove, reduce the heat and simmer it, skimming regularly, until it thickens enough to lightly coat a spoon, 5 to 10 minutes. Strain it into a small saucepan. Add the garnish, pepper, and parsley. If adding the butter, bring the cooking liquid to a boil, then reduce the heat to very low and gradually whisk in the butter so it doesn't melt completely but softens to form a smooth sauce. Taste the sauce for seasoning. Pour the sauce over the rabbit and serve.

DIJON MUSTARD: WHAT'S IN A NAME?

Dijon, Burgundy—In a country that safeguards the territorial specificity of its food and wines by law, one becomes accustomed to matching the unique character of a specialty to a distinct parcel of land, or, for that matter, body of water.

So it comes as a shock to learn that the French government doesn't hold one of its most prominent foods, Dijon mustard, to its habitual jurisdictional high-mindedness: France actually permits the manufacture of *moutarde de Dijon* outside Dijon. The mustard seeds come from abroad in any case. What's more, certain mustard made in Dijon may not be entitled to "Dijon mustard" status.

In fact, the particule *de Dijon* designates a procedure and, consequently, a style rather than a motherland. Simply, Dijon mustard (aka *moutarde forte* and *moutarde blanche*) is the fiery, smooth kind. Mention of Dijon in the name is purely honorary. To this day, the city produces about 70 percent of France's mustard.

MUSEUM HONORS MUSTARD

For those who thrill to the pungency of allyl senevol, the irritating essential oil released when mustard seeds are macerated and crushed, a visit to Dijon's Musée Amora is a must. Amora, one of France's largest mustard makers, gives free tours of its private mustard museum by appointment. While the tour (in French) is largely Amora boosterism, it still opens the door to a treasure trove of mustard facts, folklore, and ephemera.

You learn, for instance, how Dijon came to be France's mustard capital. First, the Burgundy court, headquartered in Dijon, hungered for the piquant condiment. Second, and essential to the mustard equation, proximity to vineyards sparked a thriving vinegar trade. Meanwhile, in the city's vast outlying forests, *charbonniers*, who made charcoal to feed Dijon's furnaces, also cultivated mustard plants as a sideline on the land made fertile by successive fires. The *charbonniers* sold the mustard seeds to the vinegar makers and *voilà*—mustard.

My favorite literary mustard snippet, gleaned at the Musée Amora, comes from Rabelais' *Gargantua*. The author reported that in order to satisfy a mustard habit,

Gargantua employed four servants whose task it was to shovel mustard into his mouth continually while he dined.

THE MUSTARD SELL

In any serious chronology of significant mustard events in Dijon, as at the Musée Amora, mention is made of the creation in 1634 of the Guild of Vinegar and Mustard Makers of Dijon, an early version of *appellation d'origine contrôlée* thinking. Local mustard makers hoped the new guild, whose regulations were stricter and more precise than any existing rules, would shore up their sagging image and win back customers who were shunting mustard aside in favor of new spices and condiments from India.

Despite improved standards, however, the mustard business in Dijon continued to falter. But in 1750 a mustard alchemist, Jean-Baptiste Naigeon, helped reverse the downturn. He replaced vinegar with verjuice, the juice of unripe grapes, an innovation that apparently swept the fickle Dijonnais off their feet.

As you are being fed the history of mustard making in Dijon at the Musée Amora, it becomes abundantly clear that other mustard centers flourished at the same time. In addition to Dijon, the towns of Bordeaux, Yvetot, Orléans, Meursault, and Beaune (to name a few) also kept mustard makers employed.

In fact, one of Beaune's family-owned mustard factories still churns out mustard the old-fashioned way. Établissements Edmond Fallot exemplifies the simple process of making Dijon-style mustard.

Here, black mustard seeds, imported primarily from Canada—French farmers haven't grown mustard seriously since 1945—are sifted to remove any foreign matter. The cleaned seeds go into vats where they macerate in a brew of vinegar (sometimes white wine), water, and salt.

THE UNHURRIED METHOD

To crush the seeds and release all the burning pleasure of allyl senevol, the seeds are ground between slow-moving flint millstones. This is significant. Using a heavy-duty industrial grinder, which by its speed heats up the mustard paste, destroys some of the flavor. As a practical corollary, mustard added to food at the beginning of cooking loses most of its punch and usually needs a fresh dose before serving.

At Fallot, the mustard paste is then pushed through a sieve to remove the hulls and produce a smooth paste. Most large mustard factories separate out the hulls by centri-fusion. By comparison, in *moutarde à l'ancienne*, also called *moutarde de Meaux* or *moutarde douce*, some of the seeds are left whole, producing a relatively tame, grainy mustard.

After sieving, ground turmeric is added to boost the canary-yellow color, along with citric acid and an antioxidant. For specialty mustards, such flavorings as green pepper-corns, tarragon, basil, and lemon are added at this point.

TRUFFLE MUSTARD, ANYONE?

Although we cynically think of designer mustard as a product of our own materialist times, mustard makers in the nineteenth century were already turning out gourmet fla-vors. The way Alexandre Dumas *père* reports on the mustard industry in an essay in *Le Grand Dictionnaire de Cuisine*, he could be talking about perfumery. Master *moutardiers* developed a following of mustard fanciers devoted to such kinky varieties as rose, vanilla, nasturtium, and truffle.

Besides chronicling weighty happenings in mustard history, the Musée Amora dis-plays whimsical mustard-related ephemera: postcards, posters, labels, and mustard pots in every size and shape. Sometimes mustard is touted as a flavor enhancer in connec-tion with a dubious lineup of foods: One poster features a lobster clutching a tumbler of mustard.

Anyone intrigued by mustard pots will be interested to know that before 1700, mustard was kept only in barrels, and shopkeepers and itinerant merchants sold it by the scoop. Customers supplied their own containers. Mustard packed in glass tumblers didn't appear until the 1950s.

The museum's array of mustard pots reflects popular culture. My favorite was a natty pig dressed in black tie seated with a matching black umbrella.

Also, those mad about mustard pots will not want to miss the Grey-Poupon shop on rue de la Liberté in downtown Dijon. This flagship store sells keepsake mustard pots, many reproductions of Grey-Poupon's own museum-quality collection displayed around the shop. The staff will refill your pot with mustard, too, if you already have one, just as *moutardiers* have done in Dijon for centuries.

FRENCH FIRE

For the record, Dijon mustard manufactured in France is hotter than any Dijon-style mustard made in the USA. If you can't find imported Dijon mustard and you want the authentic, nose-assaulting experience, the American equivalent to look for is extra-strong.

In France, mustard remains an enduring favorite, both as a major ingredient in dishes prepared *à la dijonnaise* and as a peppy condiment with *choucroute garnie*, pot-au-feu, and other poached fare like Potée Bourguignonne (see page 280), Burgundy's boiled dinner.

A retired English teacher from Dijon on the Musée Amora tour for the umpteenth time told me she never tires either of the tour or the condiment. Then she proceeded to give me her favorite, easy mustard recipe—you smear a pork loin with vast amounts of mustard and roast it. "We use lots of mustard," she confessed. "We buy it by the kilo."

LAPIN À LA CRÈME DE MOUTARDE

(BURGUNDY)

Rabbit in Creamy Mustard Sauce with Mushrooms

4 SERVINGS

One 2½- to 3-pound rabbit, cut into serving pieces
4 tablespoons imported Dijon mustard, or to taste
2 cups dry white wine, preferably a Burgundy
2 tablespoons unsalted butter
½ pound mushrooms, halved if large, thinly sliced
Salt and freshly ground pepper
2 shallots, finely chopped
1 cup crème fraîche (page 368) or heavy (whipping) cream
1 tablespoon chopped fresh flat-leaf parsley

Rabbit in a nose-tingling mustard sauce remains a regular blue-plate special in the bistros of Burgundy. I think the secret of its popularity lies in the rich yet tangy sauce. In this version, the rabbit is first smeared with fiery mustard and baked in the oven, then white wine is added to finish the cooking. A quick sauce is made in the same pan with a little cream, fresh Dijon mustard, and sautéed mushrooms.

A whole roast loin of pork on the bone (cooked to 150°F. on a meat thermometer) and duck, cut into serving pieces, are also good this way. With the rabbit, serve a plain rice pilaf or buttered noodles. Or, if you're willing to mix regions, try one of the creamless vegetable recipes from Normandy. To drink, uncork more of the white wine used for cooking, or another white Burgundy.

Smear the rabbit pieces with 2 tablespoons of the mustard and put them in a shallow metal casserole just big enough to hold the pieces of rabbit comfortably. If you have the time, chill the rabbit for an hour or two and bring it back to room temperature before cooking.

Heat the oven to 425°F.

Roast the rabbit in the preheated oven for 30 minutes. Reduce the oven temperature to 325°F. Remove the rabbit to a plate. Stir the wine into the casserole, scraping up the browned juices. Return the rabbit to the casserole, cover with the lid, and cook in the oven, turning once, until tender, 30 to 40 minutes.

Meanwhile, in a frying pan, melt the butter over moderately high heat. Add the mushrooms with a little salt to the same pan and toss them until the moisture evaporates, about 5 minutes. Press a piece of foil on top and cover the pan if the mushrooms look dry to start. Push the mushrooms to one side of the pan. Reduce the heat to moderate, add the shallots, and cook until translucent, 1 or 2 minutes. Set aside.

Remove the rabbit to a warmed serving dish. Set the casserole over high heat and boil the cooking liquid until it reduces by half, 5 to 10 minutes. Stir in the *crème fraîche* or cream, the remaining 2 tablespoons of mustard, and a little salt. Simmer the sauce until it thickens slightly, 5 to 10 minutes. Add the mushroom mixture and pepper and taste. Add additional mustard, salt, or pepper, if needed.

Pour the sauce over the rabbit and serve, sprinkled with parsley.

À LA BOURGUIGNONNE

Ingredients that Make a Dish Typically Burgundian

Bresse poultry

Black currants

Black-currant liqueur (cassis)

Spice bread

Dijon mustard

Cornichons (tart pickles)

Pickling onions

Chaource cheese

Charolais cheese

Epoisses cheese

Aisy Cendré cheese

Cîteaux cheese

Fromage blanc (fresh curd cheese)

Charolais beef

Snails

Côte de Nuits wines

Côte de Beaune wines

Auxerrois wines

Mâconnais wines

Chalonnais wines

FAISAN AU CALVADOS

(NORMANDY)

Roasted Pheasant with Calvados and Cream

2 SERVINGS

2 tablespoons unsalted butter
1 young pheasant (about 2 pounds), trussed
Salt and freshly ground pepper
2 tablespoons Calvados
½ cup crème fraîche (page 368) or heavy (whipping) cream

*H*eat the oven to 375°F. Spread 1 tablespoon of the butter in a roasting pan just big enough to hold the bird. Set the bird in the pan. Sprinkle it inside and out with salt and rub the breast with the remaining tablespoon of butter.

Roast the bird in the preheated oven for 20 minutes. Then continue cooking, basting every 10 minutes, until the juices run slightly pink when the bird is lifted with a two-pronged fork, 25 to 35 minutes longer. For a well-done bird, continue roasting until the juices run clear, 5 to 10 minutes more.

Transfer the roasting pan with the bird to the top of the stove. In a small saucepan, heat the Calvados and light it. (It will flare up so take care.) Pour the flaming liquor over the bird and shake until the flames subside.

Remove the bird to a carving board and let it stand, covered loosely with foil, while finishing the sauce, at least 10 minutes.

Stir the *crème fraîche* or cream into the roasting pan and simmer until it thickens slightly, 2 to 3 minutes. Add pepper and taste for seasoning.

Discard the strings from the bird and carve it. Pour any juices into the sauce. Arrange the pheasant on a warmed platter and spoon the sauce over it. Serve as soon as possible.

If the ferme-auberge Le Haut de Crouttes were any more authentic a farm, you'd have to leave your muddy boots at the door. As it is, you wend your way through the preserves of free-running ducks, chickens, guinea hens, pheasants, quails (close the gate behind you so they don't wander off), and caged ornamental birds to get to the dining room.

Here, Madame Guidez serves up Normandy farm cooking, and birds of every variety are her stock-in-trade. Her roast pheasant is a variation of a favorite in these parts—poulet vallée d'auge—with pheasant standing in for the chicken. The pheasant roasts until the juice runs slightly rosy for connoisseurs of game meat pink at the bone, or cooked through, and then it's flamed with Calvados. For a sauce, the pan is washed out with crème fraîche. With the pheasant, Madame Guidez sets out plain baked apple halves, but you could also try Apples Stuffed with Oyster Mushrooms or Baked Endives with Apple and Clove.

DOWN ON THE FARM IN NORMANDY

This dinner could be a meal stop on a tour of rural Normandy.
On some farms, the repast would also include homemade terrines,
a course of crepes and assorted farm cheeses, capped by a shot of
Calvados. All you need is a hammock for a snooze.
The following menu pares down the number of courses and offers
only one cheese. The Calvados *digestif* is up to you. With the meal,
serve a dry imported French cider or a dry white wine from the
Loire such as a Savennières or Pouilly-Fumé.

Salade Paysanne (page 59)
Potato, Celery, and Ham Salad

Faisan au Calvados (page 230)
Roasted Pheasant with Calvados and Cream

Endives et Pommes au Clou de Girofle (page 135)
Baked Endives with Apple and Clove

Camembert cheese

Tarte aux Pommes et Rhubarbe (page 313)
Rhubarb and Apple Tart
or
Crème à l'Ancienne (page 333)
Old-Fashioned Vanilla Custard

Gérard Agu, whose butcher shop opens onto Nice's outdoor market, does a brisk business with the stylish restaurants on the Côte d'Azur. Yet he calls himself a justified pessimist. "Most people go to the supermarket," he announces, keeping his eyes on the crown roast of lamb he is preparing. Looking up he adds, "I wouldn't tell my son to go into this line of work."

The lamb Monsieur Agu is working on is *agneau de Sisteron*, three- or four-month old lamb that grazes in the *garrigues*, the wild herb-covered pastures in the foothills of the French Alps. But most home cooks pass over this native, fine-textured meat for cheaper lamb. At the same time, they ignore the neck, shoulder, and shank—stewing meat—in favor of tender, quick-cooking cuts. "A lamb has only so many ribs," a butcher recently told me. "But that's all anyone wants."

What about *daube* and *estouffade*, *potée* and pot-au-feu, the long-simmered dishes of the French countryside? "Traditional recipes are too much trouble to make on a daily basis," says Germaine Papo, a grandmother in Nice. "We make them for special family gatherings."

Everything changed in the 1950s. After World War II, lifestyles modernized even in the countryside, and the standard of living improved. Until the 1950s, farmers who raised cattle and lambs could rarely afford to buy the meat of the animals they reared. And when they did, they bought the cheap cuts requiring hours of cooking. More than beef or lamb, though, ordinary people ate pork, largely salted or smoked. Most people kept a pig for themselves, and when it was time for slaughtering they called in the local butcher.

Today restaurants, *charcuteries*, and other eateries are taking over the housewife's repertoire, and preserving it. The recipes in this chapter offer a glimpse of the meat dishes still lovingly prepared by home cooks and professionals in the French countryside. ❧

KIG HA FARS

(BRITTANY)

Breton Pot-au-Feu

6 TO 8 SERVINGS

Unlike a traditional pot-au-feu, Thierry Rannou's version from northwestern Brittany includes poitrine salée (a meaty kind of salt pork, which I replace with corned beef) and salt-cured ham hock as well as beef. But what really makes it special is the raisin-studded buckwheat pudding, or fars, which poaches in the broth alongside the meats and vegetables.

If you're expecting the fars to be a lead sinker, you're in for a surprise. Once poached, the pudding is rolled in its cloth sack and crumbled. The final texture more nearly resembles fluffy couscous than dense polenta. And it tastes wonderful. Rich with butter, cream, yogurt, and eggs, fars beautifully sets off the delicate broth.

Thierry puts the fars on the table still in its rough sack (it looks like a doll-size pillow case), and everyone digs in with a spoon. But with a makeshift bag, as here, it's easier to transfer it to a bowl. Traditionally, cooks make two or three times the recipe I've given for the pudding, leftovers to be sautéed in butter or poached in milk for future meals.

1½ pounds carrots, peeled and cut into 2-inch pieces
1 pound turnips, peeled and quartered
1 leek, white part only
4 onions, peeled and stuck with 2 cloves total
1 fat bouquet garni (2 branches fresh thyme, or 1 teaspoon dried thyme leaves; 12 parsley stems; 2 imported bay leaves; and 6 leek or scallion greens, tied in a bundle with kitchen string or cheesecloth)
7 quarts water
Salt
1 pound corned beef
1 pound boneless beef rump
1 salt-cured or smoked ham hock or picnic shoulder, presoaked if needed (see headnote page 24)
1 white cabbage, cut into 6 or 8 wedges and cored

FARS
2 cups buckwheat flour
1 tablespoon granulated sugar
½ tablespoon salt
½ cup raisins, plumped in warm water and drained
2 eggs
⅓ cup crème fraîche (page 368) or heavy (whipping) cream
¼ cup plain yogurt
⅓ cup cooking liquid from the meat
7 tablespoons lightly salted butter, melted and cooled
½ to 1 cup milk

Sliced, toasted baguette or country bread, to accompany (optional)

*I*n a metal casserole large enough to hold all the ingredients with room to spare, combine the carrots, turnips, leek, onions, *bouquet garni*, water, and a little salt. Bring the water to a boil, skimming, then add the meats. Reduce the heat to low and barely simmer the ingredients, uncovered, for 2 hours. Skim the fat and foam from the pot regularly. (*Kig ha fars* can be made to this point a day ahead and chilled. Wait more than a day, though, and the vegetables become waterlogged. Discard the fat from the surface and reheat gently before proceeding.)

While the meat cooks, prepare the *fars:* Drape a scalded kitchen towel in a narrow mixing bowl, with the middle of the towel touching the bottom.

Sift the flour with the sugar and salt into another mixing bowl and add the raisins. Make a well in the center. Break the eggs into the well and add the *crème fraîche* or cream and the yogurt. With a whisk, beat the wet ingredients to mix. Gradually beat the flour into the wet ingredients while pouring in the cooking liquid, butter, and the smaller amount of milk. Add as much of the remaining milk as needed until the *fars* batter is as thick as pancake batter. Pour this into the prepared towel and tie firmly with kitchen string, leaving a little room at the top for the batter to swell during cooking.

When the meat has cooked for 2 hours, add the cabbage and bring the liquid to a simmer. Push the ingredients in the pot to one side and add the bag of *fars*. Reduce the heat to low and barely simmer for 1½ hours. Skim from time to time.

Discard the onions, leek, and *bouquet garni*. Skim off any fat, and taste the broth for seasoning. If you like, you can put the toasted bread in warmed soup bowls, ladle some broth over them, and serve this as a first course.

Lift the bag of *fars* out of the pot and transfer it to a carving board. Tap it all over with a rolling pin, then roll the bag back and forth with your hands like a rolling pin to crumble the *fars*. Open the bag and spoon the *fars* into a bowl.

Transfer the meats to a carving board with a well and cut them into medium-thick slices. Arrange the meats in a warmed serving dish and surround with the carrots and turnips. Moisten with some of the broth. Pass the *fars* separately.

POTÉE BOURGUIGNONNE

(BURGUNDY)

Burgundian Boiled Dinner

6 TO 8 SERVINGS

2 cups dried white beans, such as cannellini or Great Northern (the
   younger the better)
Salt
5 quarts water
2¾ pounds corned beef, cut into 2-inch pieces
1 leek, white and light green parts only, trimmed
2 onions, peeled, each stuck with a clove
2 celery ribs, trimmed
1 fat bouquet garni (2 branches fresh thyme, or 1 teaspoon dried thyme
   leaves; 12 parsley stems; and 2 imported bay leaves, tied in a bundle
   with kitchen string or cheesecloth)
1½ pounds carrots, peeled and cut into 2-inch pieces
3 turnips, peeled and quartered
1 white cabbage, cut into 6 wedges and cored
1½ pounds new potatoes, peeled, halved or quartered depending on size
Imported Dijon mustard

One of the few places you can still find a good bowl of potée *is on a farm in central Burgundy, not far from Arnay-le-Duc. At the Ferme-Auberge de Laneau, Françoise Doret makes hers (if you order ahead) with hunks of homegrown cabbage, carrots, turnips, and home-cured pork (I substitute corned beef). This* potée *is similar to the* kig ha fars *from Brittany, but instead of a rich buckwheat pudding, potatoes and dried white beans add bulk. (Brittany also has a* potée, *which most of the time includes smoked pork.)*

Served with a dollop of hot Dijon mustard, it's the perfect answer to flagging spirits and raging appetites.

Soak the beans in plenty of cold water for at least 6 hours or overnight.

After soaking, pour off the water. Put the beans in a large saucepan and cover generously with fresh water. Bring them to a boil and boil vigorously, skimming, for 5 minutes. Drain and rinse.

Return the beans to the pan, cover again with cold water, and bring to a boil. Lower the heat and gently simmer, uncovered, until the beans are tender, 1 to 1½ hours, depending on the age of the beans. Toward the end of the cooking time, add 1¼ teaspoons of salt. Drain the beans and set aside. Five minutes before serving, add the beans to the *potée*.

Put the 5 quarts water in a large metal casserole and bring to a boil. Reduce the heat to low and add the salt pork or corned beef. Barely simmer the meat, uncovered, for 30 minutes. Skim the fat and foam from the pot regularly. Add the leek, onions, celery, and *bouquet garni*. Cook for 30 more minutes, skimming, then add the carrots and turnips. Cook for another hour. (The *potée* can be made to this point a day ahead and chilled. Wait more than a day, though, and the vegetables will become waterlogged. Discard the fat from the surface and reheat gently before proceeding.)

When the *potée* has cooked for 2 hours, add the cabbage and potatoes and cook for 1 hour longer.

To serve, discard the leek, onions, celery, and *bouquet garni*. Skim off any fat and taste the broth for seasoning. Transfer the meat and remaining vegetables to a warmed serving dish. Moisten with some of the broth. Pass the mustard separately.

BURGUNDY BARNYARD MENU

If you wanted to open a *ferme-auberge* in Burgundy, you could start by serving this much-copied menu. Sometimes chicken in a cream sauce replaces the *potée*, but in any case, farmwives in Burgundy are onto a good thing. They set a superb table with homegrown produce while the star ingredients scratch in the yard. On the other hand, the wine offerings at most of these farmsteads need some attention. You can do much better at home with one of the uncomplicated young reds from Yonne—Irancy, Épineuil, or Coulanges-les-Vineuses.

Salade Bressane (page 48)
Warm Salad of Greens, Chicken Livers, Croutons, and Eggs

Potée Bourguignonne (page 238)
Burgundian Boiled Dinner

Fromage Blanc aux Herbes (page 326)
Fresh Farmer Cheese with Herbs, Shallots, and Garlic

DINNER CHEZ THIERRY RANNOU

I thought no one made *kig ha fars* (pronounced keek´ ha farce) anymore. Then I heard about Thierry Rannou, a young man come back to the Monts d'Arrée, a folded, twisting patch of Brittany where people still talk half-jokingly about goblins.

Join the communal table in Brézéhant for a meal of Thierry's *kig ha fars*, based on his grandmother's recipe. First, though, Thierry offers everyone a *"kir breton,"* an aperitif made with crème de cassis and home-brewed sparkling cider. For a first course, Thierry sets out tureens of broth, fragrant with the scent of herbs and vegetables, meats, and buckwheat pudding. Guests add crusts of bread to their plates of broth. The *kig ha fars* itself is about as authentic and soulful fare as you will find. To finish, there's a mousse, made with the wild elderberries Thierry collects in the woods around his farmhouse. With the meal, serve an imported dry French cider.

Bouillon (page 236)
Broth from the kig ha fars

KIG HA FARS (page 236)
Breton Pot-au-Feu

MOUSSE DE SUREAU (page339)
Elderberry Mousse

DAUBE À LA NIÇOISE
(PROVENCE)

Beef Stew with Wild Mushrooms

6 SERVINGS

2 ounces dried cepes or other boletus mushrooms
2 cups boiling water
2¾ pounds boneless stewing beef, cut into 1½-inch pieces
Salt and freshly ground pepper
¼ cup olive oil
4 medium carrots, thinly sliced
3 medium onions, halved and thinly sliced
2 tablespoons all-purpose flour
2 cups young red wine, such as a Côtes de Provence
¾ cup tomato paste
1 branch fresh thyme, or ½ teaspoon dried thyme leaves
2 imported bay leaves

*P*ut the mushrooms in a heatproof bowl and pour the boiling water over them. Set a small saucer that just fits inside the bowl on top to keep the mushrooms submerged. Set aside for 30 minutes. When you are ready to use the mushrooms, pour them and their liquid into a fine strainer lined with a double layer of damp cheesecloth and set over a bowl. Save the mushroom liquid. Wash the mushrooms well to remove all the grit. Chop the mushrooms.

Sprinkle the pieces of meat with salt. In a black iron casserole or other heavy pot just big enough to hold the meat in a single layer, heat the oil over moderate heat. Add the meat to the oil in batches, brown it all over, 5 to 7 minutes, then remove.

Add the carrots and onions to the same pot and cook, stirring, until they are tinged with brown, 8 to 10 minutes.

Discard any fat from the pot. Sprinkle the flour over the vegetables and cook until it browns lightly, 1 or 2 minutes. Gradually stir in the wine, scraping up the browned pan juices. Add the meat, tomato paste, the plumped mushrooms, and their strained soaking liquid to the pot and tuck in the thyme and bay leaves. Cover the pot, bring the liquid to a boil, then reduce the heat to low and cook at a bare simmer until the meat is very tender, 3 or 4 hours. (The *daube* can be cooked a day or two ahead and chilled; the flavor improves with time.)

If you have the time, chill the *daube* until the fat rises to the surface and can easily be removed. Otherwise, skim off as much fat as you can. Reheat the *daube* gently, if necessary. Add pepper and taste the sauce for seasoning before serving.

When Michel Vergnaud sent his recipe for Baked Cannelloni Filled with Daube, it came with this subrecipe. Intensely flavored, thick, and bosky (there are heaps of dried cepes), this version of Provençal beef stew from Lou Pistou reminds me of Mexican mole.

At his pint-size restaurant near Nice's Cours Saleya market, Monsieur Vergnaud prepares the daube in a pressure cooker. This gadget slashes cooking time by about two thirds. Even though the following recipe gives a more traditional method, by all means, use a pressure cooker if you'd like. Follow the general advice in the instruction booklet, and cook the daube 1 hour and 10 minutes.

Boiled potatoes go well with the stew, as does pasta. For a complete dinner à la niçoise, start with a Flat Swiss Chard Omelet with Garlic and Parmesan, known as la trouchia, and serve Warm Raspberry Tartlets for dessert.

BOEUF À LA BOURGUIGNONNE

(BURGUNDY)

Burgundy Beef Stew

4 SERVINGS

"Demain on fait du bourguignon," *said Denise Lagelée when asked about the upcoming dinner menu. "Tomorrow it's Burgundy beef stew." For Madame Lagelée, who runs a no-name café-bar-restaurant in Evelle known mostly to an odd mix of roustabouts and well-heeled wine buyers,* boeuf à la bourguignonne, *as it's properly known, is simply "bourguignon."*

Despite its plain nickname, Burgundy's famed dish is more refined than other stews, such as the homely daubes *of Provence. The wilted carrots, onions, and herbs that have given up their flavor to the cooking liquid, are strained out and fresh, shapely button mushrooms, pearl onions, and cubes of bacon are added. With the* bourguignon, *Denise Lagelée serves buttered elbow macaroni, but boiled potatoes are good here, too.*

MARINADE
2 large onions, halved and thinly sliced
2 large carrots, thinly sliced
1 fat garlic clove, crushed
1 bouquet garni *(1 branch fresh thyme, or ½ teaspoon dried thyme leaves; 6 parsley stems; and 1 bay leaf, tied in a bundle with kitchen string or cheesecloth)*
3 cups young red wine, preferably a Burgundy

1¾ pounds boneless stewing beef, cut into 1½-inch pieces
3 tablespoons vegetable oil
5 ounces slab bacon, cut into lardons (page 56); or 5 slices bacon, cut across into ⅜-inch strips
Salt and freshly ground pepper
2 tablespoons all-purpose flour
¼ cup marc de Bourgogne *(the local brandy)* or Cognac

GARNISH
7 ounces pearl onions
Salt
3 tablespoons unsalted butter
Pinch of sugar
7 ounces button mushrooms, halved or quartered if large
12 thin slices narrow French baguette
1 fat garlic clove, peeled
1 tablespoon chopped fresh parsley

*A*t least a day before you plan to serve the stew, make the marinade: In a bowl (not aluminum), combine the ingredients. Add the meat, cover, and leave to marinate in a cool place overnight or up to 2 days, stirring once or twice.

The next day, in a black iron casserole or other heavy pot just big enough to hold the meat in a single layer, heat the oil over low heat. Add the bacon, slowly cook it until golden, 8 to 10 minutes, then remove it to paper towels and set aside. With a slotted spoon, lift the meat out of the marinade, letting it drip back into the bowl, and pat the meat dry with paper towels. Sprinkle the pieces of meat with salt. Increase the heat under the pot to moderate. Add the meat in batches, brown it all over, 5 to 7 minutes, then remove.

Drain all the vegetables from the marinade (saving the *bouquet garni* and the liquid), add them to the pot, and cook over moderate heat, stirring, until tinged with brown, 8 to 10 minutes.

Discard any oil from the pot. Sprinkle the flour over the vegetables and cook until it browns lightly, 1 or 2 minutes. Return the meat to the pot. Gradually stir in the marinade liquid with the *bouquet garni*, scraping up the browned juices. Heat the *marc* or Cognac in a small saucepan and light it. (It will flare up so take care.) Pour the flaming liqueur into the pot and shake until the flames subside. Cover the pot, bring the liquid to a boil, then reduce the heat to low and cook at a bare simmer until the meat is very tender, 3 to 4 hours. (The stew can be cooked a day or two ahead to this point and chilled. Reheat before proceeding.)

While the stew cooks, make the garnish: In a medium saucepan, blanch the onions in boiling water for 1 minute. Drain, and peel them—the skins will strip away easily. Trim the roots and stalks of the onions carefully so they will not fall apart during cooking. Put the onions back in the saucepan and add salt, a tablespoon of butter, the sugar, and water barely to cover. Bring to a boil and simmer, uncovered, until the onions are tender and the liquid evaporates to a shiny glaze, 10 to 15 minutes.

In a frying pan, melt the remaining 2 tablespoons of butter. Add the mushrooms with salt. Toss them in the butter over moderately high heat until they lose all their moisture, about 5 minutes, and remove. Press a piece of foil on top and cover the pan if the mushrooms look dry to start.

Heat the broiler. Toast the bread slices on a baking sheet under the broiler, turning once, until golden, 2 or 3 minutes. Rub the toasts with the garlic and set aside.

To finish, remove the meat to a warmed serving dish. Discard the *bouquet garni*. Pour the sauce through a fine strainer into a saucepan, pressing on the vegetables to extract all their juice. Discard the vegetables. Add the reserved bacon, onions, and mushrooms to the sauce. If needed, simmer the sauce, uncovered, until it thickens enough to lightly coat a spoon. Add pepper and taste for seasoning.

Pour the sauce and garnish over the meat, set some of the garlic toasts around the stew, and sprinkle the parsley over the top. Pass the remaining toasts separately. Serve as soon as possible.

THE ART OF THE STEW

Unfortunately, the knack for stew making isn't encoded in our DNA. You have to learn this art essential to country cooking. If you didn't catch on to the basics of *blanquette, estouffade, daube, ragoût,* or *fricassée* at your mother's knee, here are some pointers to remedy the situation:

Seek out fat, gristle, bone, and sinew. (The fat we're looking for here is the marbled kind. Trim off visible fat.) The very best cuts of stewing meat include short ribs, shanks, chuck, rump, and brisket for beef; Boston butt, picnic shoulder, and meaty neck bones for pork; breast, shank, neck, and shoulder for veal; neck, shoulder, shank, and riblets for lamb.

Portions: Allow 7 ounces per person for boneless meat, 10 ounces for meat on the bone. The recipes here call for 1¾ pounds of boneless stewing meat for four servings.

Choice of pot: A big black iron pot browns the best. For white stews, like *blanquettes,* where the meat is not browned, choose an enameled cast-iron casserole. A heavy, tight-fitting lid ensures that liquid stays in the pot, keeping the meat moist.

Browning the meat: Pat it dry with abundant paper toweling, whether marinated or not. Don't crowd the pot; leave sufficient room for moisture to escape, allowing the meat to brown.

Salt and pepper: Unless you have hypertension, please salt to taste. I add pepper from the mill at the end of cooking where it does some good. Even perfect technique can't repair lack of flavor. Tasting and seasoning, however, can change "What's wrong here?" to something very right.

Bouquet garni: Don't forget to use it. Don't forget to throw it out.

Wine for the pot: You should be able to drink it without wincing.

Never say boil. Stews cook to perfection at a bare simmer.

In the oven or on the stove? Your choice. If you need the stove space while the dish cooks, move the pot to a 300° or 325°F. oven once the contents have arrived at a simmer.

Don't skip the skimming. Skim off fat and foam before serving. If you have the time, chill the stew until the fat rises to the surface and can easily be removed.

Don't stint on the cooking time. Ample cooking time makes the difference between an ordinary stew and a memorable one. Hours of gentle heat transform tough, gelatinous cubes of meat into tender morsels. You should be able to cut them with a fork. If your meat is still tough after what seems like an eternity of cooking, cook it some more.

Saving a drowned stew: It's almost impossible to match up every time the amount of added liquid (whether water, stock, or wine) to the chosen cooking method, cooking time, quirks of individual stoves, ovens, and cooking utensils. If the meat is swimming in liquid, lift out all the solids and boil the liquid to reduce it. *Do not reduce the cooking liquid if you plan to hold the stew a day or two. It will thicken on reheating.*

Saving a dry stew: Rescue a dry stew by stirring in water or stock, and scrape up any bits stuck to the bottom of the pot. At this stage, I don't recommend adding wine, which needs time for its flavor to mellow.

The benefits of aging: Only good things happen when a stew is set aside for a day or two.

What do you serve with your soulful stew? Rice pilaf, steamed potatoes, fried polenta, fresh buttered gnocchi, or pasta sprinkled with Parmesan all make good accompaniments, depending on the dish's home ground.

TAUREAU À LA GARDIANE

(PROVENCE)

Marinated Beef Stew

4 SERVINGS

MARINADE

3 large onions, halved and thinly sliced
6 fat garlic cloves, crushed
1 bouquet garni (1 branch fresh thyme, or ½ teaspoon dried thyme leaves;
    6 parsley stems; and 1 bay leaf, tied in a bundle with kitchen string or
    cheesecloth)
3 cloves
3 cups red wine, such as Vacqueyras or Costières du Gard
½ cup red-wine vinegar

1¾ pounds boneless stewing beef, cut into 1½-inch pieces
3 tablespoons olive oil
¼ pound slab bacon, cut into lardons (page 56); or 4 slices bacon, cut
    across into ⅜-inch strips
Salt and freshly ground pepper
¼ cup Cognac or brandy

A day before you plan to serve the stew, make the marinade: In a bowl (not aluminum), combine the ingredients. Add the meat, cover, and leave to marinate overnight in a cool place, stirring once or twice.

The next day, heat the oven to 325°F. In a black iron casserole or other heavy pot just big enough to hold the meat in a single layer, heat the oil over low heat. Add the bacon, cook it slowly until the fat runs but the bacon is not yet crisp, 3 to 5 minutes, then remove it to paper towels.

With a slotted spoon, lift the meat out of the marinade, letting it drip back into the bowl, and pat the meat dry with paper towels. Sprinkle the pieces of meat with salt. Increase the heat under the pot to moderate, add the meat in batches, brown it all over, 5 to 7 minutes, then remove.

Drain all the vegetables from the marinade (saving the seasonings and liquid), add them to the pot, and cook over moderate heat, stirring, until tinged with brown, 8 to 10 minutes.

Discard any oil from the pot. Return the meat to the pot. In a

Rough and hearty, this stew from the ranches of the Camargue has none of the frivolous olives and strips of orange zest found in some Provençal dishes. (This is not olive or orange country.) The honest-to-goodness version calls for the local athletic taureau, *or bull, whose meat is tougher and has a gamier taste than that of ordinary pampered steer. The stew is a hungry man's dish, first made by the steward's wife to feed a crew of shepherds and* gardians, *as cowboys are still called in the Rhône delta.*

Still, over time, cooks have refined some of the stew's rugged qualities. Pierre Milhaud, the butcher in Arles who gave me this recipe, adds the polish of brandy, and includes a day of marinating.

The wine and vinegar tenderize the stewing beef, and the aromatic seasonings flavor the meat as it marinates. With the stew, serve boiled potatoes, dried noodles, or fresh pasta.

small saucepan, heat the Cognac or brandy and light it. (It will flare up so take care.) Pour it into the pot and shake until the flames subside.

Gradually stir in the marinade liquid, seasonings, and bacon, scraping up the browned juices. Cover the pot with a lid, bring the liquid to a boil on top of the stove, then transfer it to the preheated oven and bake until the meat is very tender, 3 to 4 hours. Skim the sauce to remove as much fat as possible. Discard the *bouquet garni*. Add pepper and taste the sauce for seasoning. (The stew can be cooked a day or two ahead and chilled.)

JOUE DE BOEUF EN DAUBE PROVENÇALE

(PROVENCE)

Reine Sammut's Beef Stew with Lemon

4 SERVINGS

At her pretty and elegant village restaurant, La Fenière in Lourmarin, Reine Sammut cooks up some of the most appealing food in Provence. Her menu draws on the cooking of the region but not slavishly. Rather, she uses the traditional as a springboard for her imagination, developing a personal, subtle cuisine, like this lemony version of beef daube. Madame Sammut serves the stew with Polenta with Wild Mushrooms, stamped into flower shapes with a cookie cutter.

MARINADE
2 large onions, halved and thinly sliced
2 large carrots, thinly sliced
1 bouquet garni (1 branch fresh thyme, or ½ teaspoon dried thyme leaves; 6 parsley stems; and 1 bay leaf, tied in a bundle with kitchen string or cheesecloth)
3 cups red wine, such as a Côtes de Provence
Juice of 1 lemon (about 3 tablespoons)

1¾ pounds boneless stewing beef, cut into 1½-inch pieces
¼ cup olive oil
Salt and freshly ground pepper
4 fat garlic cloves, crushed

A day before you plan to serve the stew, make the marinade: In a bowl (not aluminum), combine the ingredients. Add the meat, cover, and leave to marinate for 5 hours or overnight in a cool place, stirring once or twice.

The next day, in a black iron casserole or other heavy pot just big enough to hold the meat in a single layer, heat the oil over moderate heat. With a slotted spoon, lift the meat out of the marinade, letting it drip back into the bowl, and pat the meat dry with paper towels. Sprinkle the pieces of meat with salt. Add the meat to the pot in batches, brown it all over, 5 to 7 minutes, then remove.

Drain all the vegetables from the marinade (saving the *bouquet garni* and the liquid), add them and the garlic to the pot, and cook over moderate heat, stirring, until tinged with brown, 8 to 10 minutes.

Discard any oil from the pot. Return the meat to the pot. Gradually stir in the marinade liquid with the *bouquet garni*, scraping up the browned juices. Cover the pot, bring the liquid to a boil, then reduce the heat to low and cook at a bare simmer, until the meat is very tender, 3 to 4 hours. Skim the sauce to remove as much fat as possible. Discard the *bouquet garni*. Add pepper and taste the sauce for seasoning. (The stew can be cooked a day or two ahead and chilled.) Serve from the pot or in a large serving dish.

THE TRIPE TRIALS

Courseulles-sur-Mer, Normandy—When she's in her dining room during business hours, Annick Collette keeps the communicating door to her butcher shop slightly open just in case a customer strolls in, lured by the smells of her award-winning *tripe à la mode de Caen*.

Like a parent who hears what the childless are deaf to, Madame Collette sprints through the door while you strain to catch a sound. In the nice weather, when Parisians come to Courseulles-sur-Mer, a seaside resort on the Calvados coast, they stop at the Collette *boucherie* for tripe. "When you have an award it makes a big difference," says Madame Collette. "Parisians trust you. They trust your product."

Madame Collette is only the second woman ever to beat out her competitors (more than 280 in 1989 when she won) and land the *tripière d'or*, the traveling trophy awarded each year for one plate of tripe prepared in the Caen fashion.

HOMEY, NOT HAPHAZARD

What makes her tripe worth a detour? "It's nothing sophisticated," Madame Collette warns. She uses four kinds of beef tripe (remember, cattle have four-compartment stomachs for digesting grass and hay) cut into squares, cow heel, carrots, onions, leeks, a bundle of herbs, salt, and pepper. No cider, no Calvados, no white wine, no water. After twenty-four hours of gentle cooking, the dish produces its own delicious juices.

No one knows for sure who invented *la tripe à la mode de Caen*. But as the Confrérie de Gastronomie Normande, a brotherhood devoted to the promotion of Norman specialties, realizes, it helps to have a creation story if you want to keep alive a humble piece of gastronomic history.

The stock figure in this version of Genesis is Sidoine Benoit. Tripe folklore credits Brother Sidoine, a monk-cook in the kitchen of Caen's Abbey for Men, built by William the Bastard (later the Conqueror) in penance for marrying his cousin, with whipping up the first batch of Caen-style tripe in the sixteenth century.

A BOOST TO HUMBLE FARE

To spread the renown of this regional dish and maintain high standards, every October or November since 1952 the Confrérie de Gastronomie Normande has staged a contest in Caen, the Calvados capital set inland on the Orne river and a mecca for tripe enthusiasts. Dressed in robes trimmed in red and blue, members taste their way through the entries—two hundred is an average number—making preliminary judgments, then retasting before arriving at the final selection of the world's best tripe.

Prior to tasting, to ensure that each recipe is sampled anonymously, an independent commissioner assigns secret identifying numbers to the entries, which come from France, of course, but also from as far away as Belgium, Sweden, Colombia, Portugal, the United States, and China.

Everything is geared to fair play. To guarantee that all entries are shown in the best possible light, they are first warmed in giant water baths to optimum eating temperature. Every dish of tripe is sampled by a triumvirate of judges called a *"triplette."* Each judge in the *triplette* writes down his or her score and submits it to the commissioner, who calculates the average of the three under the watchful eye of a bailiff.

WHAT IS GOOD?

But what critical parameters do they use? How do you know a good bowl of tripe when you see one? Tripe judges first use their noses. "The odor of good tripe," says Madame Collette, "that's what attracts you right off."

While everybody can recognize yummy smells, only a trained nose can distinguish the remembered scent of perfectly prepared tripe in which no one odor dominates. The aroma wafting up from each dish is worth anything from 0 to 20 hefty points.

Next the judges consider a dish's appearance. The meat should be cut in regular squares, 2½ by 2½ inches. Also, there's the thickness to assess. The pieces of meat shouldn't be too thin or too thick. The overall color must be characteristic and pleasing. And the ratio of meat to sauce should be proportionate: The dish should be neither drowning in sauce nor dry-looking. Based on this checklist, an entry can rack up a maximum of 20 more points.

Still, it's the taste that counts most—making up a possible 40 whopping points. The best *tripe à la mode de Caen* is rich but not heavy, fragrant with aromatic vegetables and meat, and not at all fatty. The tripe itself should have a chickeny taste and a texture and succulence similar to that of perfectly cooked squid.

At this point the entries with a score of 50 or better are sampled again and new tallies reckoned. The five best bowls of tripe undergo a final evaluation, and of these, just one earns the title *"Meilleure Tripe du Monde."* To win the most prestigious tripe title in the world, the dish must log over 75 points. Dishes in the 70 to 75-point range carry away the lesser *"Grand Prix International."*

To bolster their high standards, the judges don't always award a *Meilleure Tripe du Monde*. If no entry hits the mark, as was the case already in nine contests, no world winner is announced.

OLD FAVORITE, NEW HABITS

While tripe used to be the epitome of home cooking—it was cheap and required little attention during the long hours of simmering—today it's left to professionals like Annick Collette. In Normandy, most *tripiers*, or tripe dressers, prepare the old favorite from scratch a couple of times a week. That's when the tempting smells draw customers into the shop. On other days, *tripe à la mode de Caen* is sold cold, by the slice or wedge—the cow heel provides natural gelatin—and you warm it up at home.

Madame Collette talks about the time when men gathered to eat a bowl of tripe washed down by dry cider or white wine in the morning before heading out to fish or to the hunt. It was soul food to share with buddies. Today tripe fanciers normally chow down at lunch or dinner with the family.

With her hand in the making of *la tripe à la mode de Caen* several days a week, does Madame Collette still enjoy eating it? "Oh, yes, enormously. I don't eat a lot of it," she explains, "but I taste what I make all the time." ⌣

TIAN AUX COURGETTES

(PROVENCE)

Zucchini and Meat Loaf from Provence

This main dish of zucchini, meat, herbs, and rice (for absorbing juices you don't want to lose) has long been baked in the village bread ovens of Provence. The following recipe comes from the casual hotel-restaurant-café Les Arcades in Biot, where I enjoyed it one summery September afternoon. A cross between squash pudding and meat loaf, tian *should* please all lovers of rustic cooking. A serving will keep you going all day.

At Les Arcades, Mimi serves her loaf with boiled or steamed potatoes. To flesh out the menu, serve Salade Niçoise to start, and Pine-Nut Tartlets for dessert.

3 pounds unpeeled zucchini, preferably summer squash, chopped
Salt and freshly ground pepper
1 tablespoon olive oil
1 onion, halved and thinly sliced
2 shallots, sliced
2 fat garlic cloves, finely chopped
¾ cup raw rice
1 pound mixed ground meats, including beef, pork, and veal
½ cup mixed chopped fresh herbs, such as basil, parsley, and tarragon
2 eggs, beaten to mix
Pinch of grated nutmeg, or to taste
1 cup freshly grated Gruyère or Parmesan cheese

TOMATO SAUCE
½ cup extra-virgin olive oil
2 large onions, chopped
8 fat garlic cloves, chopped
Salt and freshly ground pepper
8 ripe medium tomatoes (about 4 pounds), chopped; or two 28-ounce cans
    Italian plum tomatoes, chopped, with their juice

*I*f using winter zucchini, arrange a layer of chopped zucchini in a colander set over a plate and salt generously. Continue layering until all the zucchini is used. Set aside for 2 or 3 hours, then rinse and pat dry with paper towels.

In a large metal casserole, heat the oil. Add the onion, shallots, and garlic with a little salt and stir until evenly coated with the oil. Cover the pot and cook over low heat, stirring occasionally, until tender, 10 to 15 minutes. Stir in the zucchini and the rice with a little salt and cook, uncovered, over moderate heat, stirring often, until the zucchini is soft, 15 to 30 minutes. (With summer zucchini, you may need to add a lid if it seems dry.)

Meanwhile, heat the oven to 350°F. Oil an 8-cup loaf pan or a deep baking dish.

Into the zucchini mixture, beat the meats, herbs, eggs, nutmeg, and ½ cup of the cheese. Cook a small piece of the mixture in a frying pan and taste. Adjust the seasoning in the rest of the mixture as needed. Pack it into the prepared pan and sprinkle the remaining

½ cup of cheese over the top. Bake the *tian* in the preheated oven until firm and a knife inserted in the center is hot to the touch, about 1 hour.

Meanwhile, make the sauce: In a large saucepan, heat the oil. Add the onions and garlic with a little salt and stir until evenly coated with the oil. Cover the pan and cook over low heat, stirring occasionally, until tender, 10 to 15 minutes. Add the tomatoes and cook, partially covered, until the sauce is thick, about 45 minutes. Stir the tomatoes now and then during cooking. Work the sauce through a food mill into another saucepan to remove skin and seeds. Add pepper and taste for seasoning. (The sauce can be made a day or two ahead and chilled.)

Serve the *tian* warm or at room temperature, cut into slices or wedges. Pass the tomato sauce separately.

On my last visit to Lou Pistou (it was the second time in one week), I passed an aggressively trendy couple in front of La Mérenda, the eatery next door. They were obviously put out because, it being Monday, Nice's spot for slumming was closed. By default, they checked out the menu at Lou Pistou (the offerings at both restaurants are similar) and glanced in the window. They plainly found it wanting because soon they headed off into the night, in search of something more rakish I suppose.

Lou Pistou may not be a player in Nice's night scene, but, oh, how I wish I could drop in for Michel Vergnaud's cannelloni whenever the mood strikes. Anyone used to Italian cannelloni has a surprise in store with this version from Nice. It's stuffed with a fusion of leftover stew meat and Swiss chard leaves.

There's no getting around the fact that if you want bona fide cannelloni in the Nice style, you have to start by making daube—using Monsieur Vergnaud's own recipe or an alternate. But that's looking at things backward. If you make a generous daube one day, you'll have all the fixings for a cannelloni dinner some other time. Note that instead of using dried pasta for the cannelloni, you can substitute 6 ounces of fresh pasta in sheets, cut into 3½-x-3¼-inch rectangles.

CANNELLONI LOU PISTOU

(PROVENCE)

Baked Cannelloni Filled with Daube

6 SERVINGS

TOMATO SAUCE
3 tablespoons extra-virgin olive oil
1 small onion, chopped
2 fat garlic cloves, chopped
Salt and freshly ground pepper
3 ripe medium tomatoes (about 1½ pounds), chopped; or 1½ cups chopped canned Italian plum tomatoes, with their juice
¼ cup leftover daube sauce (preceding recipe), with mushrooms

10 ounces coarsely chopped Swiss chard leaves (8 cups)
1¼ cups leftover drained daube meat (preceding recipe)
2 eggs
Salt and freshly ground pepper
¼ cup leftover daube sauce (preceding recipe), with mushrooms
3 tablespoons olive oil
18 dried cannelloni pasta rectangles (¼ pound)
1 cup freshly grated Parmesan cheese, plus additional for the table

*M*ake the tomato sauce: In a medium saucepan, heat the oil. Add the onion and garlic with a little salt and stir until evenly coated with the oil. Cover the pan and cook over low heat, stirring occasionally, until tender, 10 to 15 minutes. Add the tomatoes and cook, partly covered, until the sauce thickens, about 30 minutes. Stir the tomatoes now and then during cooking. Work the sauce through a food mill into a bowl to remove the skin and seeds. Stir in the daube sauce. Add pepper and taste for seasoning. (The sauce can be made a day or two ahead and chilled.)

Heat the oven to 350°F.

Cook the Swiss chard in plenty of boiling salted water (as for pasta) until wilted and tender, 5 to 10 minutes, and drain. Rinse in cold water and drain again thoroughly. Press out the water by handfuls.

Combine the daube meat and Swiss chard in the bowl of a food processor and pulse until coarsely chopped. Add the eggs, salt, and pepper, and pulse until blended. Transfer the mixture to a bowl and beat in the daube sauce. Cook a small piece of the mixture in a frying pan and taste. Adjust the seasoning in the rest of the mixture.

Bring a large pan of water to the boil and add salt and 2 tablespoons of the oil. Add the pasta, cook until al dente, and drain.

Coat a large gratin dish with the remaining tablespoon of oil. Put a heaped tablespoon of *daube* mixture on each pasta square and roll it up. Arrange the cannelloni in a single layer in the prepared dish. Spoon the sauce over the top and sprinkle with the cheese.

Bake the cannelloni in the upper third of the preheated oven until golden and a knife inserted in a cannelloni is hot to the touch, about 30 minutes. Pass additional cheese separately.

SOU FASSUM

(PROVENCE)

Provençal Stuffed Cabbage

6 TO 8 SERVINGS

*Maître Boscq's rustic yet
dramatic stuffed cabbage will
be heated through after a good
hour of cooking, but in his
eponymous restaurant in
Grasse, he poaches it a
leisurely 3 hours until meltingly
tender. This is not nouvelle
cuisine with its bright palette
and crisp textures, but
heirloom cooking all in faded
colors with rounded flavors.*

*If any stuffed cabbage remains
after a meal, put the leftovers
in a gratin dish, spoon any
extra tomato sauce over it, and
sprinkle with grated Parmesan
cheese. (Maître Boscq, who
always refers to himself in the
third person, says tomato sauce
isn't authentic, but it is tasty.)
Bake it in a 350°F. oven until
a knife inserted in the center is
hot to the touch, about 30
minutes. For the full flavor of a
meal à la grassoise, serve
Maître Boscq's Snails in Basil
and Garlic Sauce to start.*

1 medium Savoy cabbage (2½ to 3 pounds)
1¼ cups leftover drained *daube* meat (page 241, 246, or 248)
10 ounces coarsely chopped Swiss chard leaves (8 cups)
5 ounces lean salt pork with skin, coarsely chopped
1 medium onion, quartered
3 fat garlic cloves, peeled
½ cup fresh herb leaves, such as basil, parsley, and sage
2 eggs
1 tablespoon extra-virgin olive oil
Salt and freshly ground pepper
Grating of nutmeg, or to taste
5 ounces shelled fresh or thawed frozen peas
½ cup raw rice
8 cups beef stock

TOMATO SAUCE

½ cup extra-virgin olive oil
2 large onions, chopped
8 fat garlic cloves, chopped
Salt and freshly ground pepper
8 ripe medium tomatoes (about 4 pounds), chopped; or two 28-ounce cans
    Italian plum tomatoes, chopped, with their juice

*D*iscard any damaged outer leaves from the cabbage and trim the stalk. Immerse the whole cabbage in plenty of boiling salted water (as for pasta), cook until the outer leaves can easily be bent, 15 to 20 minutes, then drain. Rinse the cabbage in cold water and drain again thoroughly. Peel back the outer leaves to reveal the heart. Carefully cut out the cabbage heart and reserve it, leaving a pocket for stuffing. Set the cabbage aside.

Shred the reserved cabbage heart, discarding the core. Combine the *daube* meat, shredded cabbage, Swiss chard, salt pork, onion, garlic, and herbs in the bowl of a food processor and pulse until coarsely chopped. Add the eggs, oil, and a little salt, pepper, and nutmeg. Pulse to blend. Transfer the mixture to a bowl and beat in the peas and rice. Cook a small piece of the mixture in a frying pan and taste. Adjust the seasoning in the rest of the mixture.

Drape a scalded kitchen towel in a colander. Set the cabbage in the colander, stalk side down. Peel back the cabbage leaves and stuff the pocket with about ¼ cup of the *daube* mixture. Fold a layer of cabbage leaves over the stuffing, covering it entirely, and pat on about 1 cup of the remaining stuffing. Continue layering cabbage and stuffing until all the ingredients are used, finishing with several layers of plain cabbage leaves. Gather the towel over and tie it with string to make a tight ball.

Put the stuffed cabbage in a metal casserole just big enough to hold it comfortably. Pour in the stock and, if needed, add enough water to completely cover the cabbage. Cover the pot, bring the liquid to a boil, then reduce the heat to low and barely simmer the cabbage for 3 hours. (The cabbage can be cooked a day ahead and chilled in the cooking liquid. Reheat it before proceeding.)

Meanwhile make the sauce: In a large saucepan, heat the oil. Add the onions and garlic with a little salt and stir until evenly coated with the oil. Cover the pan and cook over low heat, stirring occasionally, until tender, 10 to 15 minutes. Add the tomatoes and cook, partly covered, until the sauce is thick, about 45 minutes. Stir the tomatoes now and then during cooking. Work the sauce through a food mill into another saucepan to remove skin and seeds. Add pepper and taste the sauce for seasoning. (The sauce can be made a day or two ahead and chilled.)

Lift the cabbage out of the cooking liquid and transfer it to a colander. (Save the cooking liquid for another recipe.) Unwrap the cabbage, set a large plate on top, and invert the cabbage onto the plate. Remove the towel. Set a warmed serving dish on top and invert the cabbage, core side down, onto the dish. Spoon some of the sauce around the cabbage. Serve the cabbage cut in wedges. Pass the remaining sauce separately.

TAUREAU À LA CAMARGUAISE

(PROVENCE)

Pot Roast with Cloves, Cinnamon, and Nutmeg

4 SERVINGS

There's pot roast in the Camargue, too, that flat sweep of land where the Rhône empties into the Mediterranean Sea. Here, small but fierce black bulls graze in semi-liberty between sessions in the ring. Clear up the Rhône to Arles, locals are as fond of bullfighting as they are of bull meat, called taureau *or* toro.

Homey and fragrant with sweet spices, this pot roast (made with beef not bull) fills your kitchen with heavenly smells. It's good served with boiled carrots, turnips, and potatoes; or steamed green beans and rice pilaf; or fresh pasta.

1¾ pounds boneless beef rump, in one piece, tied
Salt and freshly ground pepper
3 tablespoons olive oil
4 large onions, each cut into 8 wedges and stuck with 2 cloves total
4 fat garlic cloves, crushed
One 3-inch cinnamon stick
¼ teaspoon freshly grated nutmeg, or to taste
1 branch fresh thyme, or ½ teaspoon dried thyme leaves
2 imported bay leaves
2 to 3 tablespoons water

Sprinkle the meat with salt. In a black iron casserole or other heavy pot just big enough to hold the meat and onions, heat the oil over moderate heat. Add the meat, brown it on all sides, 5 to 7 minutes, and remove.

Add the onions and garlic to the same pot and cook, stirring, until they are tinged with brown, 8 to 10 minutes. Discard any fat from the pot. Stir in the spices and herbs. Push the onions to the side and return the meat to the pot. Cover the pot and cook at a bare simmer on top of the stove or in a 325°F. oven until the meat is tender, about 2 hours. (The pot roast can be cooked a day or two ahead and chilled; the flavor improves with time. Reheat it before proceeding.)

Transfer the meat to a carving board and cover it loosely with foil. Discard any fat and the cinnamon stick, bay leaves, cloves, and thyme branch, if using them, from the pot.

Transfer the onion mixture to a blender or food processor and whir until it makes a smooth gravy, then remove it to a saucepan. Rinse the blender with the water and add this to the saucepan. Reheat the gravy. Sprinkle it with pepper and taste for seasoning, adding salt, pepper, or nutmeg until you're satisfied.

Discard the strings from the roast and carve the meat into thin slices. Arrange the slices, overlapping, on a warmed platter. Spoon some of the gravy over the meat and serve. Pass any remaining gravy separately.

GRILLADES À L'ARLÉSIENNE

(PROVENCE)

Layered Pot Roast with Anchovies, Capers, and Garlic

4 SERVINGS

1 large onion, finely chopped
2 garlic cloves, finely chopped
2 tablespoons capers, drained and chopped
¼ cup fresh chopped parsley
4 cured anchovy fillets packed in oil, drained and chopped
4 tablespoons olive oil
1¾ pounds boneless beef rump, cut across into 8 slices

In a bowl, combine the onion, garlic, capers, parsley, and anchovies.

Add 2 tablespoons of the oil to a small shallow casserole, preferably ovenproof earthenware. Arrange a layer of meat slices in the bottom of the casserole and spread with the onion mixture. Cover with a second layer of meat and continue layering meat and onion mixture until all the ingredients are used, finishing with a layer of onions. Pour the remaining 2 tablespoons of oil over the meat and cover with a lid.

Cook the *grillades* at a bare simmer over very low heat or in a 325°F. oven until the meat is tender, about 2 hours. (This can be cooked a day or two ahead and refrigerated in the cooking liquid; the flavor improves with time.)

Like any respectable French butcher, Pierre Milhaud in Arles dispenses recipes along with each order. For this dish, famous along the Rhône and sometimes called Rhône ferryman's stew, slices of pot roast are spread with a pungent mixture of finely chopped garlic, capers, and anchovies, then baked in the oven until the meat is very tender and the flavors are mellow. (Curiously, it also resembles boeuf miroton, *for which Menon gave a recipe in* La Cuisinière bourgeoise *(1746), the culinary bible of eighteenth- and nineteenth-century French households.) Still, it's not for timid eaters. Serve with baked potatoes or a rice pilaf.*

Between the salted peanuts for sale at Acchiardo's bar (two francs a handful) and the Indian corn dangling from the ceiling, this hangout for blue-collar workers would never make the cover of a swanky "shelter" magazine. You first have to feel at home with (or at least tolerate) sharing a table with the real citizenry of Nice—a crowd that enjoys smoking and cacophony—before you can begin to appreciate the food here.

In places like this, Niçois cooking comes closest to the dishes of Italy's trattoria. (Until 1873, in fact, Nice was Ligurian.) So if you like scaloppine, you will also enjoy Acchiardo's escalope, stuffed with mozzarella, basil leaves, and ham, then fried in a bread-crumb coating.

To suit Provençal sensibilities, the veal is served with a vegetable sauce, really a kind of ratatouille. Sauce provençale is also good with Thyme-Crusted Lamb Chops; Layered Pot Roast with Anchovies, Capers, and Garlic; and Roast Guinea Hen in Sweet Red Pepper Sauce.

ESCALOPE MAISON SAUCE PROVENÇALE

(PROVENCE)

Stuffed Veal Cutlets with Provençal Vegetable Sauce

4 SERVINGS

VEGETABLE SAUCE
6 tablespoons olive oil
1 medium onion, chopped
2 garlic cloves, chopped
½ teaspoon dried herbes de Provence
Salt and freshly ground pepper
3 ripe medium tomatoes (about 1½ pounds), chopped; or 1½ cups chopped canned Italian plum tomatoes, with their juice
¼ pound small mushrooms, trimmed, or medium mushrooms, quartered
¼ pound small, young zucchini, cut into ½-inch dice
¼ pound eggplant, cut into ½-inch dice

4 veal cutlets (about 1 pound total), cut across the grain from the top round
2 thin slices best-quality boiled or baked ham
4 ounces mozzarella cheese, cut into 8 slices
12 large basil leaves
Salt and freshly ground pepper
¼ cup all-purpose flour, spread on a soup plate
2 eggs, beaten in a soup plate with ¼ teaspoon salt
1 cup dry white bread crumbs, spread on a soup plate
2 tablespoons unsalted butter
¼ cup plus 2 tablespoons olive oil

Make the sauce: In a medium saucepan, heat 1½ tablespoons of the oil. Add the onion, garlic, and herbes de Provence with a little salt and stir until evenly coated with the oil. Cover the pan and cook over low heat, stirring occasionally, until the onion is tender, about 10 minutes. Add the tomatoes and cook, partly covered, until the sauce is thick, about 30 minutes. Stir the tomatoes now and then during cooking. Work the sauce through a food mill into a large saucepan to remove skin and seeds.

Meanwhile, in a frying pan, using 1½ tablespoons of oil for each vegetable, sauté the mushrooms, zucchini, and eggplant, one at a time, with a little salt. Cook, stirring now and then, over moderate heat until tender, 5 to 15 minutes, depending on the vegetable. Press a piece of foil on top and cover the pan if the vegetables look dry to begin.

Stir the vegetables into the strained tomato sauce, cover, and cook gently for 10 minutes to blend the flavors. Add pepper and taste for seasoning.

If necessary, gently pound the cutlets with a mallet or the flat of a heavy knife until they are thinner. Then, pressing one hand flat on top of a cutlet, slice the cutlet from side to side with a very sharp, large knife, cutting the meat almost in half horizontally and leaving one side joined. Open the cutlet and cover one side with half a slice of ham, cutting to fit, if necessary. Top with 2 slices of cheese and 3 basil leaves. Sprinkle with salt and pepper. Close the cutlet. Repeat for the remaining cutlets.

One at a time, dredge the stuffed cutlets in the flour, patting off any excess. Dip them in the beaten eggs, then coat with bread crumbs. Press the bread crumbs firmly onto the cutlets.

In a large cast-iron skillet or a heavy frying pan, melt the butter with the oil over moderate heat until hot but not smoking. (If the oil is too hot the cutlets will brown without cooking through.) When hot, slip in the breaded cutlets, without crowding the pan. Fry for 1 or 2 minutes on one side, then turn and fry for a minute or so on the other side. As they are ready, remove the cutlets to paper towels and keep the drained cutlets warm in a 200°F. oven while frying the rest. Serve as soon as possible, with the sauce on the side.

Like his father and grandfather, Victor Letouzé grows carrots and leeks in Créances, on Normandy's western coast. Though the average holding in Créances amounts to only nine hectares, growing vegetables is a skilled business and a thriving way of life here. While farmers everywhere are losing their shirts, in Créances they are bucking that trend. Monsieur Letouzé, president of the Coopérative Maraîchère de Créances, the local vegetable coop, sums it up: "The young people stay."

What makes these carrots sell like hot cakes? Carottes de Créances grow in fields by the sea, tucked between sand dunes. There's no need for chemical fertilizers. Iodine-rich seaweed nourishes the sandy soil. And the pest-and pebble-free earth produces a straight, unblemished carrot so there's no waste.

While Créances and six other nearby communes grow the world's only carrots with an appellation d'origine contrôlée, nobody makes any special dishes with them. "We grate them for carottes rapées," says Monsieur Letouzé. "And of course you add them to pot-au-feu." Monsieur Letouzé also offered this home classic of veal, carrots, and tomatoes braised in white wine. As do most hearty soups and stews, these braised veal shanks taste even better the next day when the bright flavors have melded into fuzzy harmony. Serve rice or noodles alongside.

JARRETS DE VEAU AUX CAROTTES

(NORMANDY)

Braised Veal Shanks with Carrots

4 SERVINGS

Four ¾- to 1-pound veal shanks
Salt and freshly ground pepper
¼ cup vegetable oil
1½ pounds carrots, cut on the diagonal into ¾-inch pieces
3 onions, halved and thinly sliced
1 cup dry white wine
1 cup chicken stock, preferably homemade (page 369), or additional white wine
4 small tomatoes, peeled, seeded, and chopped
1 bouquet garni (1 branch fresh thyme, or ½ teaspoon dried thyme leaves; 6 parsley stems; and 1 bay leaf, tied in a bundle with kitchen string or cheesecloth)

Sprinkle the veal shanks with salt. In a heavy metal casserole just big enough to hold the shanks, heat the oil over moderate heat. Add the meat to the oil, lightly brown it all over, 5 to 7 minutes, then remove. Add the carrots and onions to the pot and cook, stirring, until they are tinged with brown, 8 to 10 minutes.

Discard any fat from the pot. Gradually stir in the wine and stock, scraping up the browned pan juices. Return the meat to the pot, add the tomatoes, and tuck in the *bouquet garni*. Cover the pot and bring the liquid to a boil. Reduce the heat to low and cook at a bare simmer until the meat is very tender, 1½ to 2 hours. Discard the *bouquet garni*. Skim the sauce to remove as much fat as possible. Add pepper and taste for seasoning. (This dish can be cooked a day or two ahead and chilled.)

Serve the veal shanks surrounded by the carrots. Pour some of the sauce over all. Pass the remaining sauce separately.

MAGNIFICENT MARROW

Not only do veal shanks make a tender stew, they contain marrow, divine stuff when cooked, which you dig out with a knife or spoon. If marrow conjures up bland, greasy, gray matter for you, try it once on little toasts, sprinkled with sea salt, then see what you think.

COLOMBO DE VEAU

(NORMANDY)

Curried Veal Stew

4 SERVINGS

1¾ pounds boneless veal shoulder, cut into 1½-inch pieces
Salt and cayenne pepper
¼ cup vegetable oil
3 onions, halved and sliced
2 garlic cloves, crushed
3 cups water
1 branch fresh parsley
2 carrots, sliced
2 medium new potatoes, peeled and cut into 1-inch chunks
1 eggplant, cut into 1-inch chunks
1 red bell pepper, cut into 1-inch squares
1 green bell pepper, cut into 1-inch squares
2 tablespoons fresh prepared curry powder, or to taste

*H*eat the oven to 325°F.

Sprinkle the veal with salt. In a heavy metal casserole just big enough to hold the meat in a single layer, heat the oil. Lightly brown the veal in batches, and remove. Add the onions and cook, stirring, until they are lightly browned, 8 to 10 minutes. Add the garlic and cook, stirring, until fragrant, about 1 minute.

Gradually add 2 cups of the water, scraping up the browned juices. Return the meat to the casserole, and add the parsley and remaining vegetables. In a small bowl, slowly stir the remaining cup of water into the curry powder mixed with a little cayenne until blended. Add this curry water to the pot. Cover the casserole and bring the water to a boil on the stove. Transfer to the preheated oven and bake until the veal is very tender, 1½ to 2 hours. Taste for seasoning. (The *colombo* can be cooked a day or two ahead and chilled; the flavor only improves.)

If you have the time, chill the *colombo* until the fat rises to the surface and can easily be removed. Otherwise, skim off as much fat as you can. Reheat the *colombo* gently, if necessary. Taste the sauce for seasoning before serving.

A moment of relief from the delicate flavors of northern French cuisine. Viviane Maignan and her husband run a dairy farm in southern Normandy. What could be more unoriginal? But the Maignans are originally from the French Antilles, and at La Rajellerie, they prepare the spicy country cooking of their homeland.

Madame Maignan's directions call for throwing all the vegetables into the pot at the same time as the meat, so the vegetables soften into a velvety stew after hours of cooking. If you prefer to have recognizable chunks of vegetables, add the potatoes, eggplant, and peppers after an hour of cooking. Serve with boiled rice or a gratin of mashed potatoes.

BLANQUETTE DE VEAU À L'ANCIENNE

(BURGUNDY)

Old-Fashioned Creamy Veal Stew

4 SERVINGS

1¾ pounds boneless veal shoulder, cut into 1½-inch pieces
1 veal bone
2 onions, halved and thinly sliced
2 carrots, thinly sliced
2 leeks, white and light green parts only, halved lengthwise and thinly
    sliced across
2 fat garlic cloves, crushed
1 rib celery, sliced
1 clove
1 bouquet garni (1 branch fresh thyme, or ½ teaspoon dried thyme leaves;
    6 parsley stems; and 1 bay leaf, tied in a bundle with kitchen string or
    cheesecloth)
3 cups water
Salt

GARNISH

7 ounces pearl onions
Salt
1 tablespoon unsalted butter
Pinch of sugar
7 ounces small button mushrooms, halved or quartered if large
½ lemon

SAUCE

3 tablespoons unsalted butter
3 tablespoons all-purpose flour
¼ cup crème fraîche (page 368) or heavy (whipping) cream
1 egg yolk
Fresh lemon juice, to taste
Salt and freshly ground white pepper

Burgundy can't claim blanquette as its own (it's a staple in the classic repertoire). But Burgundy cooks, using the outstanding local Charolais veal, probably make the best. If you're looking for a warming experience in the vein of traditionally unhealthy French cooking, try Jérôme Besancenot's blanquette. (Really, though, 5 tablespoons of butter, ¼ cup of cream, and 1 egg yolk is not wildly excessive for 4 people.)

To accompany the stew at the Auberge des Brizards, Monsieur Besancenot serves its usual partner: plain rice. He cooks it like pasta, boiling it for 15 to 20 minutes in plenty of salted water, then draining it and tossing in a little butter and salt to taste. I don't recommend substituting noodles or potatoes for the rice; anything else just doesn't seem right.

*I*n a mixing bowl, soak the pieces of veal in plenty of cold water for 1 hour.

Meanwhile, put the veal bone in a medium saucepan, cover the bone with cold water, and bring to a boil. Simmer for 5 minutes, skimming, then drain and rinse.

After soaking the veal, pour off the water. Put the veal in a large saucepan and cover with fresh water. Bring to a boil and boil vigorously, skimming, for 1 or 2 minutes. Drain and rinse.

In a large, heavy metal casserole, combine the veal, veal bone, vegetables, clove, *bouquet garni*, water, and a little salt. Cover the pot with the lid and bring the liquid to a boil. Reduce the heat to low and barely simmer until the veal is very tender, 1½ to 2 hours. (The *blanquette* can be cooked to this point a day or two ahead and chilled. Reheat before proceeding.)

While the veal cooks, make the garnish: Blanch the onions in a small saucepan of boiling water for 1 minute. Drain and peel them—the skins will strip away easily. Trim the roots and stalks of the onions carefully so they will not fall apart during cooking. Put the onions back in the saucepan and add the salt, butter, sugar, and water barely to cover. Bring to a boil and simmer, uncovered, until the onions are tender and the liquid evaporates to a shiny glaze, 10 to 15 minutes.

In another saucepan, combine the mushrooms, a squeeze of lemon juice, a little water, and salt. Cover and boil for 1 minute, then drain.

Remove the veal to a warmed serving dish. Add the onion and mushroom garnish to the veal.

Discard the *bouquet garni* and the clove, if you can find it. Whir the veal cooking liquid and vegetables in a food processor until mostly puréed. Pour it through a fine strainer, pressing on the vegetables to extract all their juice, back into the cooking pot. Discard the vegetables.

Make the sauce: In a heavy medium saucepan, melt the butter over low heat. Whisk in the flour and cook for 30 seconds without letting it color. Gradually whisk in the strained purée, and bring to a boil. Lower the heat and simmer the sauce, skimming regularly, until it reduces to 2 cups. Whisk the *crème fraîche* or cream into the egg yolk. Whisk a little of the hot sauce into the egg yolk mixture and then whisk this mixture into the sauce in the pan over very low heat. Add lemon juice and pepper and taste the sauce for seasoning.

Pour all the sauce over the veal and serve as soon as possible.

PETITS FARCIS

(PROVENCE)

Stuffed Provençal Vegetables

6 SERVINGS

2 small eggplants (about 1 pound in all)
3 small onions, peeled
2 large zucchini, trimmed
3 small round tomatoes
2 medium red bell peppers
3 tablespoons extra-virgin olive oil
Salt and freshly ground pepper
2½ slices sourdough or other country bread, crusts removed (1 cup fresh
*   bread crumbs)*
½ pound veal roast leftovers, chopped
1 garlic clove, peeled
¼ cup chopped fresh basil
¼ cup chopped fresh parsley
3 eggs
2 tablespoons freshly grated Parmesan cheese

*H*eat the oven to 400°F.

Trim and peel the eggplants. Cut them into 1-inch chunks and steam until tender, 5 to 7 minutes. Set aside.

Cut the onions in half crosswise and steam until tender, about 5 minutes.

Cut each zucchini crosswise into 3 even lengths. Cut the tomatoes crosswise in half. Using a melon baller or a grapefruit knife, hollow out the onions, zucchini, and tomatoes, leaving a thin yet sturdy cup. Save the vegetable insides.

Cut the peppers crosswise into three pieces. Trim the core and discard the ribs and seeds.

Coat a large shallow baking dish or 2 smaller ones just big enough to hold the vegetable "cups" (the middle pepper cup will be bottomless) with 1 tablespoon of the oil. Arrange the "cups" in the dish. Sprinkle them with salt and a little pepper.

Tear the bread into pieces. Drop them into the bowl of a food processor, and pulse into small crumbs. Set aside.

Combine the vegetable insides, the eggplant chunks, veal, garlic, and herbs in a bowl. Pulse batches of this mixture in the food processor until finely chopped. Add the eggs, cheese, salt, and pepper, and pulse until blended. Cook a small piece of the mixture in a

Before tasting Michel Vergnaud's petits farcis, I plodded through a lot of stuffed-vegetable dinners I wouldn't like to sample a second time. In many renditions of this classic Niçois dish, the vegetable "cups" are undercooked or acrid, the stuffing hard as a squash ball or tasteless.

Since the dish is time-consuming (though not complicated), I wanted to find a recipe worth the fuss. At Lou Pistou, Monsieur Vergnaud takes advantage of the wonderful vegetables in the Nice open market, including a round zucchini perfect for stuffing. And he uses just the right amount of bread (not rice) to make a stuffing that holds together without becoming compact.

If you don't happen to have ½ pound of leftover veal roast sitting in the fridge, substitute the same amount of uncooked, boneless veal shoulder or breast. Grind the meat in the food processor, then, in a frying pan, sauté it in a little olive oil until cooked through.

Michel Vergnaud's petits farcis are so moist that he serves them without a sauce. But if you would like one, try the tomato sauce that accompanies Cannelloni Lou Pistou.

frying pan and taste. Adjust the seasoning in the rest of the mixture.

Spoon the vegetable mixture into the prepared "cups," mounding it slightly. Sprinkle the bread crumbs on top and drizzle with the remaining 2 tablespoons of oil. Bake the *farcis*, uncovered, in the preheated oven until the vegetables are tender and a knife inserted in the stuffing comes out hot to the touch, about 45 minutes.

Arrange 4 *farcis* on each warmed plate. Serve hot, warm, or at room temperature.

A TIME FOR SEASONING

What else makes Monsieur Vergnaud's *petits farcis* so good? Tasting and seasoning for one thing. While this is true for all recipes, even experienced cooks tend to throw up their hands when it comes to seasoning a raw mixture. When dealing with any raw mixture (this includes terrines, stuffings, mousses), first pinch off a bite and sauté it in a frying pan until cooked through. Taste the morsel and, if needed, add salt and pepper, herbs, cheese, whatever, to the remaining mixture until the food is flavored to your liking.

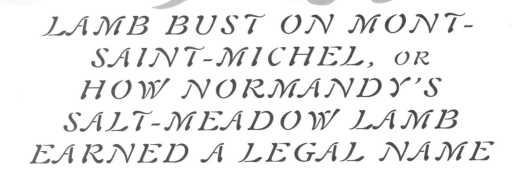

LAMB BUST ON MONT-SAINT-MICHEL, OR HOW NORMANDY'S SALT-MEADOW LAMB EARNED A LEGAL NAME

Mont-Saint-Michel, Normandy—An agent from the *services de la consommation et des prix*, the French equivalent of the department of consumer affairs, scrutinized restaurant menus here on the morning of July 17, 1984, hunting down mention of lamb grazed in the salt grasses around the Mont.

But this tracker of salt-meadow lamb, called variously *pré-salé des grèves* and *pré-salé du Mont-Saint-Michel*, as well as *agneau rôti à la montoise*, was not pursuing a special lunch deal. When he flashed his badge at chefs gearing up for the noontime service, he asked to inspect the cold storage room.

In six restaurant kitchens advertising the regional lamb, sleuthing turned up lamb from Maine-et-Loire, Vienne, Vendée, Charente-Maritimes, Ille-et-Vilaine—all French *départements* outside Normandy—and from as far away as Ireland. The *services de la consommation et des prix* slapped the purchasing managers with charges of false advertising.

If the Archangel Michael perched atop the abbey bell tower here had let drop his sword, the blow to this tiny island at the border of Normandy and Brittany could not have been greater.

In a show of goodwill, the erring restaurateurs immediately rejigged their menus to list plain lamb, not the native *pré-salé* variety. But Eric Vannier, the mayor of Mont-Saint-Michel, was bitter about the rotten publicity. For him, the crackdown was yet another in a series of unfair checks and controls aimed at a tourist attraction with a high profile.

Despite efforts among the restaurateurs to rally, bad feelings did well up. Many resented the accusation of false advertising when no ruling even existed legally to define salt-marsh lamb from Mont-Saint-Michel. With lamb as much of a draw as the abbey itself or La Mère Poulard's famous Puffy Omelet (see page 120), the island's other gustatory attraction, and with not enough locally grazed salt-marsh lambs to meet demand, the restaurateurs argued that good lamb is good lamb, no matter where it comes from, and that's what they serve. For their ultimate justification, they said that, anyway, nobody ever complained.

CALL YOUR LAWYER

But at the hearing, the prosecutor, Madame Roche-Eyssautier, swept aside defense claims. As she pointed out, authentic salt-marsh lambs do have a special taste and texture and cost more to raise than the ordinary sheepfold variety, qualities that are reflected by the justifiably higher prices they bring at the butcher's and on restaurant menus.

In the end, the court ordered four purchasing managers to pay stiff fines ranging from 10,000 to 20,000 francs ($2,000 to $4,000), and to foot the bill for the printing of the judgment in a legal journal.

Meanwhile, salt-marsh lamb farmers around the Mont found the attitude of the restaurateurs worrisome. For them, all lambs are not equal. "Normandy's salt-marsh lamb is the best lamb in France," states Bernard Adam, a lamb farmer in Bricquebec. "I'm not the one who says it. *Gault Millau* [the French food magazine] says so."

Farmers discriminate between lambs pastured in the salt marshes and those grazed on hillsides or reared in the sheepfold. As an antidote to vagueness, they joined with other salt-marsh lamb farmers on the west coast of Normandy (besides Mont-Saint-Michel, Normandy counts salt marshes in Regnéville, Geffosses, Portbail, and Bricquebec) to form the *association des producteurs d'agneaux de pré-salé de la baie du Mont-Saint-Michel et de l'Ouest Cotentin.*

ORIGINS OF AOC

This group, with just twenty members, began looking into an *appellation d'origine contrôlée* (AOC), the legal construct created in 1919 and unique in the world that defines and regulates the production of French foods and wines.

Today, the Institut National des Appellations d'Origine (INAO) legally protects the area of fabrication, select varieties and breeds, production techniques, and characteristic attributes of four hundred wines and thirty cheeses as well as certain oysters, lentils, walnuts, carrots, olives and olive oil, chicken, turkey, guinea hen, butter, and cream. Originally conceived to weed out fakes, in the current industrially oriented climate, the AOC now serves to promote foods that are still crafted the old-fashioned way.

But some foods don't qualify for an AOC on account of scarceness. Once an *appellation d'origine contrôlée* is bestowed on a carrot or chicken, for instance, INAO feels there should be enough of it to go around—even if that means a diluted result. Sometimes INAO's guidelines for an AOC expand original geographic boundaries of production or cut and paste faithful techniques.

CONSUMER PROTECTION

For provincial specialties that can't be reshaped to AOC standards, like Normandy's salt-marsh lambs, there are regional labels and *marques* with less clout than that of the national AOC. In the end, the Normandy association of *pré-salé* lamb farmers went after, and won, a "Grévin" label, named for the *grèves*, or salt-meadow shores of Normandy. This regional label means, finally, a set of regulations for all farmers wanting to market Normandy *pré-salé* lambs and an end to mix-ups on restaurant menus. To be a Grévin, lambs must graze in the salt meadows from the age of six to eight weeks until four or five months old.

For the first time, a plastic label distinguishes Normandy's salt-marsh lambs from imposters. It indicates the name of the farmer, the lamb's date of birth, its number, and the date of slaughter. An agent from the *services de la consommation et des prix* can easily tell when information checks out or not, as, for instance, when the same number has been used twice.

"Thanks to the label," says Bernard Adam, the association's president, "consumers will know what they are getting."

GIGOT D'AGNEAU DE PONTORSON

(NORMANDY)

Roast Lamb on a Potato Gratin

4 SERVINGS

4 tablespoons unsalted butter
One 2¾-pound half leg of lamb, bone in, trimmed
Salt and freshly ground pepper
2 pounds all-purpose potatoes, peeled and thinly sliced
1½ cups chicken stock, preferably homemade (page 369)

*H*eat the oven to 400°F. Butter a 6-cup shallow baking dish with 1 tablespoon of the butter.

Rub the leg of lamb all over with salt, pepper, and the remaining 3 tablespoons of butter. Insert a meat thermometer deep into the thickest part of the leg without touching the bone. Position the thermometer so that it can be easily read.

Arrange the potatoes in layers, slices overlapping, in the bottom of the baking dish. Season each layer with salt and pepper.

Pour the stock over the potatoes and set the lamb on top. Cook the lamb until the thermometer reads 135° to 140°F. At this temperature the lamb is pink. For medium lamb, continue cooking until the meat thermometer reads 150°F.

Remove the lamb from the baking dish to a carving board with a well and let it sit, loosely covered with foil, for 20 to 30 minutes. While the lamb rests, return the potatoes to the oven to continue cooking until they are perfectly tender and the juices have reduced, 20 to 30 minutes. Pour any juices that collect from the lamb over the potatoes.

To serve, carve the lamb into thin slices and arrange on a warmed platter or plates. Pass the potato gratin separately.

Jean-Robert Tiercelin is one of only two butchers in Pontorson who still buy lambs, on the hoof, from farmers who graze them in the grèves, or salt meadows, around Mont-Saint-Michel. When asked about his favorite lamb recipe, Monsieur Tiercelin hesitates. "We like to do as little as possible to our lamb," he says. "My wife just roasts it. We want to taste the meat. It has such a nice flavor."

Even if you cannot find the salt-marsh variety, Monsieur Tiercelin's recipe shows off any good-quality lamb. And cooking the lamb atop thinly sliced potatoes infuses them with a wonderful meaty flavor. Accompany with Baked Carrots in Cream or Café des Sports' Flageolet Beans.

If you want more of a culinary jaunt to Normandy's Mont-Saint-Michel, start the meal with La Mère Poulard's Puffy Omelet and serve Apple Feuilletés with Calvados, Rhubarb and Apple Tart, or Apple-Bavarian Charlotte for dessert.

GIGOT À LA
CRÈME D'AIL

(PROVENCE)
Roast Leg of Lamb with Creamy Garlic Toasts

6 SERVINGS

One 4-pound half leg of lamb, bone in, trimmed
Salt and freshly ground pepper
1 branch fresh thyme, or ½ teaspoon dried thyme leaves
3 tablespoons extra-virgin olive oil, plus additional for drizzling
1½ cups chicken stock, preferably homemade (page 369)
15 garlic cloves, unpeeled
12 thin slices narrow French baguette or small slices country bread

*H*eat the oven to 400°F.

Rub the leg of lamb all over with salt, pepper, and thyme.

In a heavy metal casserole just big enough to hold the lamb, heat the 3 tablespoons oil over moderate heat. Lightly brown the lamb on all sides, 5 to 7 minutes. Insert a meat thermometer deep into the thickest part of the leg without touching the bone. Position the thermometer so that it can be easily read. Discard any fat from the pot.

Pour ½ cup of chicken stock over the lamb and add the garlic to the pot. Cover the pot, bring the stock to a boil on the stove, then transfer to the preheated oven. Cook the lamb, covered, until the meat thermometer reads 135° to 140°F. At this temperature the lamb will be pink. For medium lamb, continue cooking until the meat thermometer reads 150°F.

Remove the lamb to a carving board with a well and let stand for 15 to 20 minutes, covered loosely with foil.

Stir the remaining cup of stock into the pot, scraping up the browned juices. Simmer until the sauce reduces to ½ cup, 5 to 10 minutes. Taste for seasoning. Remove the cloves of garlic with a slotted spoon.

Peel the garlic cloves. In a small bowl, mash the soft garlic with salt to taste.

Heat the broiler. Toast the bread slices on a baking sheet under the broiler, turning once, until golden, 2 or 3 minutes. Drizzle olive oil over the toasts and spread them with the mashed garlic.

Carve the lamb and arrange the slices of meat on a warmed platter. Set the garlic toasts around the lamb. Spoon the gravy over the lamb and serve.

Toasts spread with soft garlic traditionally accompany Provençal roasts and stews. Here, the garlic cloves are pot-roasted with a leg of lamb so they absorb all the meaty juices. As always with garlic, cooking takes the pungency away, leaving a subdued, almost sweet flavor. With the lamb, serve buttered green beans, Swiss Chard with Bacon and Tomatoes, or Golden Garlicky Tomatoes.

As a change from lamb in this recipe, you might try pork roast or a hindquarter roast of turkey—an idea from a rôtisseur at the open market in Les Saintes-Maries-de-la-Mer in the Camargue region of Provence. Instead of pan-roasting the meat, as here, he rubs tied roasts with a blend of salt, pepper, herbs, mashed garlic, olive oil, and curry powder, then sets them to turn slowly on a rotisserie and baste each other with dripping fat. Cook a pork roast to 150°F. on a meat thermometer; cook turkey until a meat thermometer inserted into the thickest part of the thigh reads 180°F.

CÔTES D'AGNEAU PANÉES AU THYM

(PROVENCE)

Thyme-Crusted Lamb Chops

4 SERVINGS

2 slices sourdough or other country bread, crusts removed (¾ cup fresh
    bread crumbs)
¼ cup snipped fresh thyme, or 1 tablespoon dried thyme leaves
Eight 4-ounce thick loin lamb chops
Salt and freshly ground pepper
¼ cup all-purpose flour, spread on a soup plate
2 eggs, beaten in a soup plate with ¼ teaspoon salt
2 tablespoons unsalted butter
6 tablespoons olive oil

*T*ear the bread into pieces. Drop them into the bowl of a food
processor and pulse into large crumbs. Add the thyme and pulse
until everything is finely chopped. Transfer to a soup plate.

Sprinkle the lamb chops with salt and pepper. Dredge a lamb
chop in the flour, patting off any excess. Dip it in the beaten eggs,
then coat with herbed bread crumbs. Press the bread crumbs firmly
onto the lamb chop. Repeat for the remaining chops.

In a large cast-iron skillet or heavy frying pan, melt the butter
with the oil over moderate heat. (If the fat is too hot the lamb
chops will brown without cooking through.) When hot, add the
breaded lamb chops without crowding the pan. Fry until golden on
the outside but still pink in the middle, 3 or 4 minutes per side. As
they are ready, remove the lamb chops to paper towels. Keep the
drained lamb chops warm in a 200°F. oven while frying the rest.
Serve as soon as possible.

As a change from plain broiled lamb chops, try Gérard Praillet's lamb chops in a thyme-and-fresh-bread-crumb crust. In a display of pure ingenuity, Monsieur Praillet, chef at the Hostellerie du Moulin de la Foux in Draguignan, sautés the chops in a mixture of butter and olive oil. The olive fragrance and buttery flavor enhance one another, with the lamb chops the winner. Keep this unconventional pairing in mind for when you want to add a whiff of Provence to anything fried or basted.

Monsieur Praillet serves these thyme-scented lamb chops with Golden Garlicky Tomatoes, a potato gratin, and buttered green beans. But if you find the bread crumbs in the tomatoes repetitious, Braised Artichokes with Onions and Garlic would go well here.

ESTOUFFADE DE GIGOT D'AGNEAU

(PROVENCE)

Marinated Lamb Stew with Tomatoes and Olives

6 SERVINGS

No one could accuse Bernard Dumas' estouffade of inappropriate flights of fancy. Even if this Provençal chef does call for tender leg of lamb instead of ordinary stewing lamb, his recipe for the local lamb stew couldn't be more down to earth.

As it's prepared at Brasserie Nord-Pinus in Arles, which Monsieur Dumas oversees in addition to his own restaurant, Le Vaccarès (the two restaurants sit catty-corner on a square dominated by a statue of Provençal poet Frédéric Mistral), the lamb steeps overnight in the marinade ingredients and then the mixture cooks gently in the oven until the lamb is very tender. That's all. Monsieur Dumas does away with the extra step of browning the meat and vegetables before braising. The resulting stew is sprightlier than the usual rib-sticking variety.

Monsieur Dumas offers an enduring favorite, creamy garlic toasts, as an accompaniment. Try a rice pilaf here instead of potatoes.

MARINADE

4 ripe medium tomatoes (about 2 pounds), peeled, seeded, and chopped; or 2 cups chopped canned Italian plum tomatoes, drained
3 large onions, halved and thinly sliced
2 large carrots, thinly sliced
5 garlic cloves, crushed
1 fat bouquet garni (2 branches fresh thyme, or 1 teaspoon dried thyme leaves; 12 parsley stems; and 2 imported bay leaves, tied in a bundle with kitchen string or cheesecloth)
1 clove
4 cups full-bodied red wine, preferably one from Provence
¼ cup marc de Provence (the local brandy) or Cognac
⅓ cup extra-virgin olive oil

2¾ pounds boneless leg of lamb, cut into 1½-inch pieces
½ pound salt pork or slab bacon, preferably unsmoked, cut into lardons (page 56); or 8 slices bacon, cut across into ⅜-inch strips
¾ cup black olives, preferably from Nyons, pitted or not
Salt and freshly ground pepper
15 garlic cloves, peeled
12 slices narrow French baguette or small slices country bread
1 tablespoon extra-virgin olive oil, or to taste

A day before you plan to serve the stew, make the marinade: In a bowl (not aluminum), combine the ingredients. Add the lamb, cover, and set aside to marinate overnight in a cool place, stirring once or twice.

The next day, heat the oven to 325°F. Put the salt pork or bacon in a pan of cold water. Bring it to a boil, simmer for 5 minutes, and drain.

In a large metal casserole, combine the blanched pork or bacon, the marinade ingredients, and the lamb. Cover the pot, bring the liquid to a boil on top of the stove, then transfer the casserole to the oven and bake for 1 hour. Add the olives and continue cooking until the lamb is very tender, about 1 hour longer. Discard the *bouquet garni*. Skim the sauce to remove as much fat as possible. Add pepper and taste the sauce for seasoning. (The stew can be cooked a day or two ahead and chilled. Reheat it before proceeding.)

While the stew bakes, cook the garlic cloves in plenty of boiling salted water (as for pasta) until very tender, 20 to 25 minutes. In a small bowl, mash the soft garlic with salt to taste.

Heat the broiler. Toast the bread slices on a baking sheet under the broiler, turning once, until golden, 2 or 3 minutes. Add a drop of olive oil to each toast and spread with the mashed garlic. Pass the garlic toasts separately from the stew.

RAGOÛT D'AGNEAU AUX OLIVES

(PROVENCE)

Braised Lamb with Potatoes and Olives

4 SERVINGS

1¾ pounds boneless stewing lamb, cut into 1½-inch pieces; or 2¾ pounds
    stewing lamb with bone, cut into pieces
Salt and freshly ground pepper
¼ cup olive oil
3 onions, halved and thinly sliced
2 fat garlic cloves, crushed
2 tablespoons all-purpose flour
3 cups water
1 bouquet garni (1 branch fresh thyme, or ½ teaspoon dried thyme leaves;
    6 parsley stems; and 1 bay leaf, tied in a bundle with kitchen string or
    cheesecloth)
1 pound boiling potatoes, peeled and halved or quartered, depending on
    size
½ cup black olives, preferably from Nyons, pitted or not

When Josiane Autrand-Dozol comes home after a day a the family olive mill in Nyons, she often makes this lamb stew with her olives. "I ate it for dinner last night," this fourth-generation olive oil-maker said.

Some of the best Provençal olives grow in Nyons and environs (this region claims the only olive appellation d'origine in the world), and the town's three olive mills press a mildly fruity oil. Josy, who manages the Moulin Autrand down by the Pont Romain, adds a final instruction to her recipe: "Don't forget to brown the meat in olive oil." With potatoes cooked in the same pot, it's practically a meal in itself.

Sprinkle the pieces of meat with salt. In a black iron casserole or other heavy pot just big enough to hold the meat in a single layer, heat the oil over a moderate flame. Add the meat to the oil in batches, lightly brown it all over, 5 to 7 minutes, then remove. Add the onions and garlic to the pot and cook, stirring, until they are tinged with brown, 8 to 10 minutes.

Discard any fat from the pot. Sprinkle the flour over the onions and cook until it browns lightly, 1 or 2 minutes. Gradually stir in the water, scraping up the browned pan juices. Return the meat to the pot and tuck in the *bouquet garni*. Cover the pot, bring the liquid to a boil, then reduce the heat to low and cook at a bare simmer for 1 hour. Add the potatoes and olives and continue cooking until the lamb is very tender, about 1 hour longer. (The ragout can be cooked a day or two ahead and chilled; the flavor only improves.)

If you have the time, chill the ragout until the fat rises to the surface and can easily be removed. Otherwise, skim off as much fat as you can. Reheat the ragout gently, if necessary. Add pepper and taste the sauce for seasoning before serving.

OLIVES PIQUÉES

In December and January, Josiane Autrand-Dozol adds fresh *olives piquées*, quick-cured, ripe black olives, to her lamb ragout. Instead of being pickled in brine for months, these olives are pricked all over with a sterilized pin, then layered in a basket with salt (2 pounds of salt to 4½ to 6½ pounds of olives, according to one *olives piquées* recipe.) The salt makes the olives wrinkle and "weep" their bitter juices. The mixture is tossed three or four times a day for a week; then the olives are washed and ready to eat.

IN THE SHADOW OF MONT-SAINT-MICHEL, HOME ON THE RANGE

Saint-Broladre, Brittany—Like Brigadoon, a cutout of Mont-Saint-Michel suddenly appears off to the east in the late overcast afternoon. But when the road to Brittany's salt meadows twists away, the Mont vanishes. Once out in the meadows, with an unencumbered view, the Mont still looks unearthly. Along a low green horizon, the wind chases a bank of clouds past the abbey's pinnacle.

While Mont-Saint-Michel seems like a fixture, if a disembodied one, on the Brittany landscape, technically it belongs in Normandy. Sometime in the past, the Couësnon River, which separates the two provinces, charged off to the west, leaving the Mont behind in Normandy. Bretons consider this one of fate's little tricks.

Even for thirty-one-year-old Yves Fantou, who's known the *grèves*, this patch of land by the sea, since boyhood, being here is magical. Wondering aloud, Yves says, "It's really a pleasure to come out here." Now his work in Saint-Broladre as a butcher specializing in salt-marsh lamb brings him back to this otherworldly place. He scans the landscape for signs of his aunt and uncle's flock heading home after a day's roaming.

For August it's been unusually stormy, and the ground has turned to soggy cement, sucking up his booted feet. For the sheep and lambs that pasture here, such sticky conditions can be fatal. Some get stuck in the mud and die of exposure or drown in the rising tide. But today the flock returns wet yet intact. The sheep come into view beyond the shepherd's hut—the only hint of human life out in the salt meadows. The son of a butcher and grandson of a sheep farmer, Yves used to spend summers out here, earning money as a shepherd and sleeping in the same tumbledown dwelling.

CHOOSING TRADITION

As part of his upwardly mobile generation, Yves might have left the land like his friends, who went into the professions. He even married a lawyer. Yet Yves stuck with the family trade. "You have to love what you do," he says. "I try to run my little business. It's a personal kind of thing."

Although farmers in Normandy also graze sheep in the salt grasses around the

Mont, customs change from one side of the Couësnon River to the other. Ille-et-Vilaine, the Breton *département* bordering the Mont, counts ten ranches each with flocks of 500 sheep (flocks are calculated by the number of *brebis* or mothers). But Manche, the *département* across the river in Normandy has fifty sheep ranches of about 100 sheep each.

Besides keeping larger flocks, sheep farmers in Brittany still employ shepherds. Even today, two shepherds lead their flocks to the meadows in the morning, aided by their sheep dogs. Each day the shepherds cover nine or ten miles along with the athletic sheep, who scour the *grèves* in search of tasty, sea-washed grasses, or *herbu*.

Not so in Normandy where shepherds have become a luxury farmers cannot afford. As a result, Norman sheep graze unchaperoned. During the day, flocks from different farmers mingle in the pastures. At nightfall, they sort themselves out and head home.

Behind the flock making its way back to the sheepfold tonight, sweeping up the rear, comes Noel Louves and his dog Belle. Louves has minded sheep for twenty-five years, alone all day in the meadows under a big sky. Bundled in a green waterproof parka, with a rain hat pulled down over his head and his feet stuck in knee-high rubber boots, Louves seems to blend into the scenery.

SALT-MARSH MASS

Apart from the shepherds and their sheep, no one comes out here much. But on the first Sunday in August, for the *"pardon d'agneau,"* or parish pilgrimage, mass takes place on the *herbu*, drawing large crowds. In the 1960s, Bretons home from Algeria brought back with them a taste for *méchoui*, a whole spit-roasted lamb, and in an unusual fusion of traditions, the congregation celebrates with a local version of the North African specialty—spit-roasted salt-marsh lamb.

Noel Louves and Belle guide the black-faced sheep from the meadows up a packed-dirt road, over the dike and past planted fields to the sheepfold. The dike protects the surrounding low-lying fields, reclaimed from the sea and turned over to cultivation.

Like most salt-marsh lamb farmers, Thérèse and Christophe Anger, Yves' aunt and uncle, combine lamb farming with other activities. They also grow carrots and onions on the polder and raise Charolais cattle.

And like relatives everywhere, they won't let Yves go home empty-handed. Thérèse Anger calls after him as he walks to the car, "You can't leave without taking some onions home to your wife."

AILLADE D'AGNEAU AUX AUBERGINES

(PROVENCE)

Casserole of Lamb and Eggplant with Garlic

6 SERVINGS

2¾ pounds boneless lamb shoulder, cut into 1½-inch pieces
Salt and freshly ground pepper
½ cup olive oil, more as needed
2 medium onions, halved and thinly sliced
2 pounds eggplant, peeled and cut into 1-inch cubes
1 cup chicken stock, preferably homemade (page 369)
1 bouquet garni (1 branch fresh thyme, or ½ teaspoon dried thyme leaves;
    6 parsley stems; and 1 bay leaf, tied in a bundle with kitchen string or
    cheesecloth)

TOPPING
2 slices sourdough or other country bread, crusts removed (¾ cup fresh
    bread crumbs)
3 fat garlic cloves, peeled
½ cup chopped fresh parsley
2 tablespoons unsalted butter
2 tablespoons extra-virgin olive oil

If they made cassoulet *in Provence it might taste like this. Paul Salvador of the Vintage Café prepares a succulent stew with lamb, eggplant, and onions (no beans or* confit*), then he adds a topping of bread crumbs, garlic, and parsley, and browns the casserole under the broiler. It's both meat and vegetable in one dish and needs no accompaniment.*

Heat the oven to 375°F.

Sprinkle the pieces of lamb with salt. In a cast-iron skillet or heavy frying pan, heat the oil over moderate heat. Add the pieces of lamb to the oil in batches, brown them all over, 5 to 7 minutes per batch, then transfer to a large casserole, preferably ovenproof earthenware.

Add the onions to the same pan and cook, stirring, until they are tinged with brown, 8 to 10 minutes. Add them to the lamb in the casserole. In the same skillet, brown the eggplant in batches with a little salt and add it to the lamb. Add oil while cooking the eggplant if it looks too dry.

Pour the stock into the lamb casserole and tuck in the *bouquet garni*. Transfer the casserole to the oven and bake, uncovered, until the lamb is tender, about 1½ hours. Stir the mixture 2 or 3 times during baking. Discard the *bouquet garni*. Add pepper and taste for seasoning. (The casserole can be cooked a day or two ahead and chilled. Reheat, covered, in a low oven before proceeding.)

While the lamb cooks, make the topping: Tear the bread into pieces. Drop them into the bowl of a food processor and pulse into large crumbs. Slice the garlic into the food processor. Pulse until the garlic is coarsely chopped. Add the parsley and pulse until everything is finely chopped. In a frying pan, melt the butter with the oil. Add the bread-crumb mixture and toss until evenly coated with the butter.

Heat the broiler. Sprinkle the topping over the lamb mixture. Put the casserole on an oven rack so the topping is about 2 inches from the heat and broil until lightly browned, 3 to 5 minutes. Watch carefully, and turn the casserole as necessary so the topping browns evenly and doesn't burn. Serve as soon as possible.

JAMBON À LA CRÈME

(BURGUNDY)

Gratin of Creamy Ham with Cheese

8 SERVINGS

One 6- to 7-pound semiboneless country ham
4 carrots, peeled and cut into 2-inch pieces
3 onions, halved and stuck with 2 cloves total
2 leeks, trimmed
6 garlic cloves, crushed
1 fat bouquet garni (2 branches fresh thyme, or 1 teaspoon dried thyme
    leaves; 12 parsley stems; and 2 imported bay leaves, tied in a bundle
    with kitchen string or cheesecloth)
½ tablespoon black peppercorns
½ tablespoon crushed coriander seeds
4 cups dry white wine
4 cups water

SAUCE
2 tablespoons tomato paste, or to taste
Reserved ham cooking liquid
1 cup red Rivesaltes, or other fortified red wine
2 cups crème fraîche (page 368) or heavy (whipping) cream
Salt and freshly ground pepper

GARNISH
4 tablespoons unsalted butter
1 pound mushrooms, sliced
Salt
1 cup freshly grated Gruyère or other Swiss-type cheese

*I*n a metal casserole just big enough to hold all the ingredients, combine the ham, vegetables, seasonings, wine, and water. Set the lid on top, bring to a boil, then lower the heat and barely simmer for 6 hours.

Lift the ham out of the pot and transfer it to a carving board with a well. Trim all the skin and fat and reserve.

Make the sauce: In a cup, thin the tomato paste with 1 cup of the ham cooking liquid. Add this thinned tomato paste, the reserved skin and fat, and the fortified wine to the remaining cooking liquid. Bring to a boil, then lower the heat and simmer until the liquid reduces to 2½ cups, 45 minutes to 1 hour. Skim regularly

La Bouzerotte in Bouze-lès-Beaune calls no attention to itself. This small restaurant in wine country a short drive from Beaune is neither new nor old. And it's not the kind of place you'd spontaneously want to photograph for its Burgundian charm.

But inside, Olivier and Christine Robert's openheartedness is displayed on the sideboard for all to see: a pâté en croûte still on its baking sheet, and six different homemade tarts and cakes. Their menu offers a repertoire of oldies but goodies, including jambon à la crème.

And the ham is good. Monsieur Robert cooks it himself, in a broth of wine and vegetables for six hours. Both the ham and the sauce can be made a day or two ahead so there's only assembling and gratinéeing to do before you sit down to dinner. With the ham, Monsieur Robert serves boiled unpeeled new potatoes in cream with chopped fresh herbs.

during cooking. (Both the ham and sauce can be cooked a day or two ahead.)

While the sauce reduces, make the garnish: In a large frying pan, melt the butter over moderately high heat. Add the mushrooms with a little salt to the pan and toss them until the moisture evaporates, about 5 minutes. Press a piece of foil on top and cover the pan if the mushrooms look dry to start. Set aside.

Strain the reduced ham cooking liquid into a large saucepan. Add the *crème fraîche* or cream. Bring to a boil, then reduce the heat and simmer until the sauce reduces by a third, 15 to 20 minutes. Taste for seasoning.

Heat the oven to 450°F.

Cut the ham into slices ¼ to ½ inch thick. Arrange them overlapping in a large gratin dish. Add the mushrooms and sauce and sprinkle the cheese on top. Bake in the preheated oven until the topping is lightly browned and bubbling, 10 to 15 minutes. Serve as soon as possible.

RÔTI DE PORC AU CARAMEL DE CIDRE

(NORMANDY)

Juicy Pork Roast with Caramel-Cider Sauce

4 SERVINGS

Philippe Potignon cooks pork roast—sometimes a whole fresh ham—with a Norman touch. That is, at La Crémaillère, his small family restaurant in Saint-Sylvain, he makes a cider-flavored caramel with sugar and cider vinegar. The meat cooks in the mixture, throwing off abundant juice while absorbing the apple-caramel taste.

Of course, Monsieur Potignon cooks the pork until well done. But while it may go against the grain to serve pork that is still slightly pink, this way the meat remains moist and flavorful yet perfectly safe to eat. It's a new habit worth cultivating.

Serve Monsieur Potignon's roast with mashed potatoes and Brussels sprouts tossed in butter. Or try the Baked Carrots in Cream, Savory Baked Apples, or Stuffed Endives with Apple and Clove.

1 tablespoon vegetable oil
One 1¾-pound boneless pork roast, tied; or one 2¾-pound center-cut pork loin on the bone
Salt and freshly ground pepper
3 tablespoons dark brown sugar
¼ cup cider vinegar
1½ cups imported dry French cider
2 carrots, finely chopped
1 rib celery, finely chopped
1 large onion, finely chopped
1 bouquet garni (1 branch fresh thyme, or ½ teaspoon dried thyme leaves; 6 parsley stems; 1 bay leaf; and 3 leek or scallion greens, tied in a bundle with kitchen string or cheesecloth)
2 tablespoons unsalted butter, cut into pieces
1 tablespoon snipped chives or scallion greens (optional)

*H*eat the oven to 350°F.

In a heavy metal casserole just big enough to hold the meat, heat the oil over moderate heat. Sprinkle the pork with salt, and brown it on all sides, 5 to 7 minutes, in the oil. Remove the pork and discard the fat from the pot.

In the same pot, simmer together the brown sugar and vinegar until the mixture reduces by half, 2 to 3 minutes. Stir in the cider, scraping up the browned juices. Add the vegetables and a little salt. Set the meat on top and tuck in the *bouquet garni*. Insert a meat thermometer deep into the meat. Position the thermometer so that it can be easily read. Cover the pot, bring the liquid to a boil on top of the stove, then transfer to the heated oven. Cook the meat until the thermometer reads 150°F. The meat will still be slightly pink but perfectly safe to eat.

Transfer the meat to a carving board with a well and let it stand for 15 to 20 minutes, covered loosely with foil.

Simmer the cooking liquid until it reduces enough to coat a spoon, 7 to 10 minutes. Strain the sauce into a small saucepan, pressing on the vegetables to extract all the juices. Add the butter and whisk over low heat so the butter softens creamily. Add pepper and taste the sauce for seasoning.

Discard the strings from the roast and add any juices to the sauce. Carve the meat into thin slices and arrange them on a warmed platter. Spoon some of the sauce over the meat and serve, sprinkled with chives or scallion greens, if you like. Pass any remaining sauce separately.

SAUTÉ DE PORCELET À LA SAUGE

(BURGUNDY)

Braised Pork Tenderloin with Sage

4 SERVINGS

1 large onion, halved and thinly sliced
1 large carrot, quartered lengthwise and thinly sliced
2 cloves
1 bouquet garni (1 branch fresh thyme, or ½ teaspoon dried thyme leaves; 6 parsley stems; and 1 bay leaf, tied in a bundle with kitchen string or cheesecloth)
4 cups water
Salt and freshly ground white pepper
1¾ pounds pork tenderloin, cut into 1½-inch pieces
2 tablespoons vegetable oil
1 tablespoon walnut oil
½ pound wild, oyster, or button mushrooms, cut into ⅜-inch slices

SAUCE
3 tablespoons unsalted butter
3 tablespoons all-purpose flour
Reserved court bouillon
½ cup heavy (whipping) cream
¼ cup fresh sage leaves
Salt and freshly ground white pepper

Nestled in Burgundy's Cousin valley near Avallon, the Moulin des Ruats is a secluded, enchanting spot—especially in summer when tables are set up outside along a gurgling stream. Here, Gérard Fillaire offers contemporary fare grounded in the classics.

His braised pork dish, for instance, is like a speedy blanquette de veau. *If you love that traditional white veal stew, you will also appreciate the following recipe: It's just this side of old-fashioned. Instead of cooking a tough piece of meat for hours to melting tenderness, Chef Fillaire poaches tenderloin until just cooked through but still juicy.*

Then he transforms the aromatic broth into a velvety sage-infused sauce. With the pork, serve fresh, wide egg noodles or a rice pilaf for soaking up the fragrant sauce.

*I*n a sauté pan or shallow metal casserole just big enough to hold the pork in a single layer, combine the onion, carrot, cloves, *bouquet garni*, and water. Season lightly with salt. Cover the pan, bring the water to a boil, then reduce the heat and simmer for 15 minutes.

Add the meat to this court bouillon. Bring the water back to a boil, then reduce the heat to low and cook at a bare simmer, covered, until the pork is cooked through but still juicy, 10 to 15 minutes.

Remove the meat to a plate. Discard the *bouquet garni* and cloves, if you can find them. Whir the remaining mixture in a food processor until mostly puréed. Pour through a fine strainer, pressing on any vegetable chunks to extract all their juice, back into the cooking pot. Discard any vegetables.

Make the sauce: In a large heavy saucepan, melt the butter over low heat. Whisk in the flour and cook for 30 seconds without letting it color. Gradually pour in the strained, reserved court bouillon, whisking, and bring it to a boil. Lower the heat and simmer the sauce, skimming regularly, until the liquid reduces to 2 cups. Add the cream and sage and simmer for another 5 to 10 minutes. Add pepper and taste the sauce for salt.

While the sauce simmers, prepare the mushrooms: In a frying pan, heat the oils over moderately high heat. Add the mushrooms and a little salt and toss them until their moisture evaporates, about 5 minutes. Press a piece of foil on top and cover the pan if the mushrooms look dry to start.

Reheat the meat gently in the sauce. Serve on a warmed platter or plates with the mushrooms.

CÔTES DE PORC EN PAPILLOTE

(BURGUNDY)

Pork Chops with Mustard and Canadian Bacon

4 SERVINGS

In his charcuterie on Beaune's pedestrian shopping street, Roger Batteault sells not only umpteen sausages, hams, pâtés, terrines, salads, and savory pastries—all made on the spot—but cuts of best-quality fresh pork, too. "I'd eat rosette every day if my figure allowed it," says Josette Batteault referring to her husband's salami, which takes two months of drying to achieve its award-winning taste and texture. Instead she creates low-calorie recipes like this one in the kitchen behind the shop.

For her porc en papillote, Madame Batteault smears a pork chop with mustard—from Beaune's one remaining moutarderie, or mustard factory, naturally—adds fresh thyme and a slice of lean Canadian bacon, then bakes it in foil to make a juicy dish with no added fat. With the pork chop, serve string beans and mashed potatoes.

Four ½-pound pork chops, 1 inch thick
Salt and freshly ground pepper
2 tablespoons imported Dijon mustard
4 sprigs fresh thyme, or ½ teaspoon dried thyme leaves
4 slices Canadian bacon (about 2½ ounces in all)

*H*eat the oven to 400°F.

Set each pork chop on a square of foil large enough to wrap it in. Sprinkle both sides of the pork chops with salt and pepper, then spread one side with the mustard. Press a sprig of thyme on top of the mustard or sprinkle with dried thyme, and top with a slice of Canadian bacon.

Wrap the pork chops, set the parcels on a baking sheet, bacon side down, and bake them in the preheated oven until the pork is still slightly pink in the center yet perfectly safe to eat, 25 to 30 minutes. Remove the baking sheet from the oven and let the pork chops sit in their wrapping for 3 to 5 minutes so they are juicy. Discard the foil before serving.

IN BURGUNDY, WHAT'S FOR DINNER?

In addition to the demands of full-time work, Colette Giraud, Josette Batteault, and Françoise Choné answer the "What's for dinner?" call every night. This meal composed of their recipes is not exactly the thing for a formal dinner party when you set aside a day to shop, peel, and chop, but it is a sensible menu sensitive to the food that grows at one's doorstep (in Burgundy, that is) and the everyday problems of getting a meal on the table. In Burgundy, an assortment of local cheeses would automatically follow the main course. For the wine, stay in simple territory with an unpretentious white Mâcon. But if you're serving a cheese course, you might want to uncork a red Burgundy, too.

Tarte Colette Giraud (page 88)
Goat-Cheese Tart with Leeks

Côtes de Porc en Papillote (page 288)
Pork Chops with Mustard and Canadian Bacon

Buttered String Beans and Mashed Potatoes

Gâteau au Chocolat de Madame Choné (page 298)
Madame Choné's Chocolate Cake

CAKES
AND
PASTRIES

Bundled in wool sweaters with aprons knotted on top, two farmers' wives work side by side on this freezing Sunday in February. The two women share a trestle table, and each has a vat of hot oil in front of her, set on a portable gas burner. They fry batter-dipped apple slices, then sprinkle them with sugar and sell the warming snack to visitors here at the apple market in Sainte-Opportune-la-Mare, Normandy.

Besides the treat of hot apple fritters, farmers bring their apples, for sale by the crate. Wives and daughters have baked up a storm in farmhouse kitchens, and they now look up expectantly from behind their fresh apple pies, cakes, and tartlets, all arranged on red-and-white checked tablecloths. Everything looks wholesome and shows the quirks of home ovens and the baker's hand.

As unpredictable as modern home ovens can be, though, they are more reliable and certainly easier to use than the old bread ovens. It should be remembered that in the countryside, farmers once heated the oven with wood or vine clippings every two weeks or so, and most cakes and tarts, often merely enriched versions of bread, cooked in the diminishing heat after the bread. Some kitchens did also have pots with lids, which were filled with coals for cooking pies in the hearth.

French country cakes and pastries include all those confections that somehow taste better when made at home. Flavor counts more than looks. These alluringly homespun cakes and pastries are not difficult to prepare, and they follow the seasons, using what is produced and grown nearby.

Accordingly, in this chapter you will find Brittany Pound Cake, made with the slightly salted butter that Breton cooks favor, Sweet Swiss Chard Tart from Provence, and a Norman farmer's version of Rhubarb and Apple Tart, for when the first rhubarb hits the market.

One sign of the times: Puff pastry has invaded every nook and cranny of the French baking landscape. Even housewives use the store-bought version routinely. You see it pressed into service for tarts, wrapped around whole fruit for dumplings—anywhere you might once have seen bread dough or *pâte brisée*, the basic pastry dough.

LINGOT AUX NOIX

(BRITTANY)

Walnut Loaf

8 TO 10 SERVINGS

⅔ cup chopped walnuts
2 teaspoons dried instant coffee dissolved in ½ cup water, or ½ cup strong
    brewed coffee
½ cup all-purpose flour
3 tablespoons rye flour
½ cup plus 2 tablespoons granulated sugar
½ tablespoon baking powder
3 tablespoons unsalted butter, cut into small pieces
1 egg

*H*eat the oven to 350°F. Butter a 4-cup loaf pan and line the bottom with wax paper. Butter the paper also and coat the pan with flour.

Grind the walnuts to a powder in a food processor and transfer them to a bowl. Combine the coffee with the walnuts.

Sift both flours with the sugar and baking powder onto wax paper and pour it into the bowl of a food processor. Add the butter and egg and process to blend. Whir in the walnut mixture.

Using a rubber spatula, scrape the cake batter into the prepared pan. Bake in the preheated oven until a cake tester inserted in the center of the cake comes out clean, 40 to 45 minutes. Cool the cake briefly in the pan, then turn out onto a rack and discard the wax paper. Let the cake cool completely before slicing. (This cake can be made a day or two ahead and wrapped in plastic without harm.)

If you looked for cakes only in France's big-city pastry shops, you'd come away dazzled by the pâtissiers' sleight of hand but also, possibly, miffed. Who wants art and butter cream all the time? Doesn't anyone make good cake, plain and simple?

But visit any regional farmers' market or country bakery and you'll happen on an array of home-wrought baked goods. Pierre-Jan Indekeu, veteran mathematician and farmer turned jam maker and baker, makes a specialty of them at La Cours d'Orgères in Saint-Pierre-de-Quiberon.

Monsieur Indekeu points out that there's nothing Breton about his crumbly loaf (typical of nut cakes). No matter. With a nutty flavor enhanced by bitter coffee, it's wonderful at brunch, at five o'clock, or for dessert. At the dinner hour, serve the lingot *(French for "gold ingot") with sweetened whipped cream.*

PAIN D'ÉPICES,
A HONEY OF A CAKE

Massigny-lès-Vitteaux, Burgundy—Pascal Dupas loves honeybee talk. The ability of bees to gather pollen and nectar, turn it into nourishment, and squirrel it away in the honeycomb fascinates him. "Pascal is driven by beekeeping," says Marie-Colette Dupas about her apiarist husband. "And by *gourmandise.*"

Key to Pascal and Marie-Colette Dupas' success in the honey business is the popularity of *pain d'épices,* a local favorite for breakfast or at teatime. Despite its name, literally "spice bread," *pain d'épices* is long on honey and short on the spices that recall Dijon's strategic position astride the spice route in Gallo-Roman times.

Several specialty shops in Dijon, twenty-six miles southeast of Massigny, have earned a name in *pain d'épices.* But today these institutions, which churn out a mass-produced sweetmeat, face growing competition from a cottage industry of makers like the Dupases who whip up small batches of *pain d'épices* made with their own honey and sell them still fresh at the market in Dijon and other nearby communities.

Although *pain d'épices* has long enjoyed a reputation around Dijon and, when Pascal was growing up, every family kept a beehive, few would have considered the honey business as career material.

RISK AND OPPORTUNITY

It was only when an expanding interest in beekeeping began to encroach on his regular job that Pascal saw his hobby as a possible vocation, with all the rewards and snags of striking out in a new direction. "I had a tough choice," he says. "First on my mind was making it work as a business. Were we going to have enough money to live?"

Today Pascal keeps twenty-five beehives, which he moves around according to the seasons. April to early July the bees find ample pollen and nectar in Burgundy's flowers. But when the supply of nectar dwindles with the dry summer weather, Pascal closes the hives with the honeybees inside, stows them in a truck, and hauls them twenty miles northeast to the lush hunting grounds in the Jura mountains. Here the bees forage until the end of September.

Spring, acacia, forest: Pascal Dupas' various honeys reflect the diversity of the nectar that his bees suck. Exposing them to different blossoms allows him to offer several *crus*, or varieties of honey. A good hive will often produce more than a hundred pounds of honey in a summer season.

RECIPE FOR SUCCESS

To expand their business, Marie-Colette joined her skills as a baker to those of her husband. Today she sells sixty *pains d'épices* a week. But first she had to find the right formula. "I tried many, many recipes," Marie-Colette recalls. "Finally I got one from a little grandfather."

Fifty or sixty years ago, people still made *pain d'épices* at home for Christmas. According to spice-bread lore, the *pain d'épices* sponge was kept from one annual baking to another. For a new loaf, the rock-hard sponge was broken and kneaded into the new dough.

Today, besides using baking soda instead of a sourdough starter in most recipes to leaven the *pain d'épices*, cheap sugar now replaces much of the expensive honey. "*C'est une histoire financière*," Marie-Colette says. "It's a money thing." Even Marie-Colette makes two recipes for varying pocketbooks: a deluxe version with 100 percent honey and an ordinary cake with 60 percent honey and 40 percent sugar.

Which spices to add seems more a matter of taste than tradition. Marie-Colette spikes hers with aniseed. Other bakers season with clove and cinnamon. Whichever spices are preferred, they add a subtle taste, reminiscent of the flavorings in Jewish honey cake. *Pain d'épices*, while denser than honey cake, does not have the full-blown spiciness of gingerbread either.

Most *pain d'épices* comes in large rectangular or square loaves spread with a sugar icing. "You never see it round," says Marie-Colette. "That just isn't *pain d'épices*." Still, the cake does appear in miniature versions and in frivolous shapes, especially at Christmastime. Also, embellished spin-offs, some draped with chocolate glaze, others holding dried fruits or candied orange peel, fill out the *pain d'épices* line.

Children like slices of *pain d'épices* still warm from the oven, when it's very moist. But Marie-Colette thinks it's best when ripened for at least a day. Still, there's aged and aged. Industrial *pain d'épices*, which often sits on the shelf too long, can be dry and hard.

SOUVENIR TO SAVOR

Profiting from its status as an icon of childhood food memories, restaurant cooks flagrantly indulge adults in *pain d'épices* nostalgia. They let the crumbs melt away in a warm custard or ice-cream mixture. When added as a flavoring to other desserts, *pain d'épices* rises from homeyness to regional sophistication.

Even with *pain d'épices* available year-round, Marie-Colette sells more of the cake in the cold weather. "Summer's too hot for *pain d'épices*," says Marie-Colette. "People still live according to the seasons."

GÂTEAU AU CHOCOLAT DE MADAME CHONÉ

(BURGUNDY)

Madame Choné's Chocolate Cake

6 TO 8 SERVINGS

¼ pound bittersweet chocolate, broken into pieces
1 tablespoon water
4 tablespoons unsalted butter, cut into pieces
½ cup plus 2 tablespoons granulated sugar
3 large eggs, separated
½ cup all-purpose flour
Confectioners' sugar, for dusting (optional)

*H*eat the oven to 425°F. Butter and flour a 9-inch round layer-cake pan.

In a large, heavy saucepan, combine the chocolate, water, and butter, and stir constantly over low heat until it all melts creamily.

Take the pan from the heat and stir in all but 1 tablespoon of the sugar. Beat in the egg yolks, one at a time, then the flour. Do not overbeat.

In a mixing bowl, whip the egg whites with the remaining tablespoon of sugar until they hold stiff peaks. Stir a quarter of the egg whites into the chocolate mixture, working until it is smooth. Using a large rubber spatula, gently fold this lightened mixture into the remaining egg whites.

Pour the batter into the prepared pan. Put the pan in the oven, reduce the temperature to 350°F., and bake until a cake tester inserted in the center of the cake comes out clean, 25 to 30 minutes. Take the cake from the oven and let it stand for 15 minutes before turning it out onto a rack to cool. If you like, sift confectioners' sugar over the cake before serving.

In Venoy between Auxerre and Chablis, Françoise Choné runs a B&B at her large and comfortable home, the Domaine de Montpierreux— not your average Burgundian farmhouse. In the cheery breakfast room containing the estate's original bread oven, she sets out slices of her slim chocolate cake with the other breakfast offerings. "I've been making this cake for over 20 years," Madame Choné wrote when she sent the recipe. It comes from the grandmother of a friend."

This dependable recipe, passed from friend to friend, is made by beating the dry ingredients with the chocolate, butter, and egg yolks and then folding the batter into air-filled (whipped) egg whites. It's more tea cake than decadent dessert.

AVOCAT AU MARRON ET AU CHOCOLAT

(BRITTANY)

Chocolate and Chestnut Cake

8 TO 10 SERVINGS

¾ cup all-purpose flour
½ cup plus 2 tablespoons granulated sugar
1 tablespoon baking powder
6 tablespoons unsalted butter
4 ounces bittersweet chocolate, broken into pieces
1 tablespoon rum
2 eggs
8 ounces sweetened chestnut purée

Heat the oven to 350°F. Butter and flour a 4-cup loaf pan.

Sift the flour with the sugar and baking powder into a mixing bowl.

In a heavy medium saucepan, combine the butter, chocolate, and rum and stir constantly over low heat until it all melts creamily.

Break the eggs into the dry ingredients, add the sweetened chestnut purée, and beat together with an electric mixer for 1 minute. Add the chocolate mixture to the bowl and beat again until smooth.

Pour the cake batter into the prepared pan and bake in the preheated oven until a cake tester inserted in the center of the cake comes out clean, 45 minutes to 1 hour. Cool the cake briefly in the pan, then unmold it onto a rack to cool before slicing. (This cake can be made a day or two ahead and wrapped in plastic without harm.)

Here's a treasure from Pierre-Jan Indekeu of La Cours d'Orgères in southern Brittany. This cake is not so insufferably rich that you can eat it only once in a blue moon. Rather, it's a homey loaf I'd put on the menu at my dream tea room. Monsieur Indekeu's avocat is moist (from the chestnut purée) with a hint of rum and not too sweet.

You can find sweetened chestnut purée—usually the Faugier label imported from France—in the fancy-foods section of the supermarket. Also, it's worth checking chocolate labels for one with a minimum of 50 percent cocoa, such as Lindt's extra-bitter chocolate. Lesser amounts of cocoa don't give the same chocolatey taste.

Please add the rum even if you're not fond of liquor in desserts. While the flavor of rum dominates the batter, you barely taste it in the finished cake: A friend who actively dislikes liquor-scented confections asked for a second slice. (The rum flavor does, however, develop with time.) I can't imagine this cake without a dollop of whipped cream.

QUATRE-QUARTS BRETON

(BRITTANY)

Brittany Pound Cake

MAKES ONE 9-INCH TUBE CAKE

What gives Régis Mahé's pound cake Breton flavor is the lightly salted butter, locally preferred in all cooking—even baking. This old-fashioned cake uses no artificial leaveners such as baking powder. Instead, whole whisked eggs provide the lift. In another twist on the usual recipe, the butter is melted instead of creamed, then folded into the puffy egg-sugar mixture. If you want a customary pound cake, use sweet (unsalted) butter and beat in ½ teaspoon salt and 1 teaspoon pure vanilla extract with the eggs and sugar.

At his restaurant in Vannes, Monsieur Mahé serves the not-too-sweet pound cake as a foil for an array of lush strawberry desserts. It's the French answer to strawberry shortcake.

Set out slices of the cake with such accompaniments as strawberry sorbet or ice cream, strawberry jam, Fresh Strawberries in Red Wine, Strawberry Sauce (recipes follow), and whipped sweetened cream or crème fraîche.

This cake tastes even better after it has ripened a couple of days, so keep it in mind as a dessert to prepare ahead.

½ pound (2 sticks) lightly salted butter, cut into pieces
6 eggs
1¼ cups granulated sugar
2 cups all-purpose flour

*H*eat the oven to 350°F. Butter a 9-inch tube pan and dust it with flour.

In a medium saucepan, melt the butter. Pour it into a mixing bowl and let it cool to room temperature.

In a large stainless-steel bowl, beat the eggs and sugar with a hand-held electric mixer until blended. Set the bowl over a pan of barely simmering water, making sure the water does not touch the bowl. Whip at high speed for 10 to 15 minutes, until the mixture falls from the beaters in a thick ribbon and doesn't melt away immediately but holds a ribbon trail for 4 or 5 seconds. Take the bowl from the heat and continue beating until the mixture cools.

Sift the flour over the fluffy egg mixture in 3 batches and fold together as lightly as possible using a large rubber spatula.

Stir a quarter of this batter into the melted butter, working until it is smooth. Gently fold this lightened mixture into the remaining batter.

Pour the batter into the prepared pan. Bake it in the preheated oven until the cake is golden and pulls away from the sides of the pan, 50 to 60 minutes. Take the cake from the oven and let it stand for 15 minutes before turning it out onto a rack to cool completely. Once thoroughly cooled, wrap the cake tightly in plastic for at least a day before slicing. (Pound cake keeps up to a week tightly wrapped.)

FRAISES AU VIN ROUGE
(BURGUNDY)

Fresh Strawberries in Red Wine

4 SERVINGS

1 pound fresh strawberries, hulled, and halved lengthwise
1 to 2 tablespoons granulated sugar, depending on the sweetness of the
*   strawberries*
1 cup fruity red wine (see headnote)

*I*n a medium bowl, stir together the strawberries and 1 tablespoon of the sugar. Taste and add more sugar, if needed, until the strawberries are as sweet as you like. Chill for 1 or 2 hours before serving, until the berries ooze their flavorful juice.

Spoon the strawberries into wineglasses or dessert dishes. Pour the wine over the berries and serve.

To complement his pound cake, Régis Mahé draws on the food of other regions, namely French wine territory, where these strawberries make a familiar and easy dessert. In Brittany, vines grow only around Nantes, and the wines are exclusively white. The advantage of being wine-poor—and thus unfettered by viticultural loyalties—is complete freedom in choosing what to drink. With the berries, try any fruity red wine such as Beaujolais, Chinon, a young Burgundy, or a California Zinfandel.

COULIS DE FRAISES

Strawberry Sauce

MAKES 1 CUP

½ pound fresh or thawed frozen strawberries
Confectioners' sugar, to taste

*P*urée the strawberries in a food processor or blender. Add a little sugar, if needed, until the purée is as sweet as you like. Work the purée through a fine sieve if you want to remove the seeds. Chill the sauce.

A basic recipe from the French sweet repertoire, this sauce will dress up any down-home or store-bought dessert. Try it with Old-Fashioned Apple Pudding, Elderberry Mousse, angel-food cake, rice pudding, or cheesecake. Raspberries could replace the strawberries. You'll notice that some frozen strawberries come already sweetened; these need only defrosting and puréeing.

GÉNOISE CARAMELISÉE AUX FRAMBOISES

(BURGUNDY)

Luscious Raspberry Cake

8 TO 10 SERVINGS

If you've peered into enough French pastry shop windows, Olivier Robert's raspberry cake needs no introduction. It's the one filled with pastry cream (or butter cream or whipped cream, depending on the baker), and you can see the red berries in profile between the layers of cake.

Monsieur Robert makes his dessert using génoise, the whisked cake made with whole eggs, and raspberries. In fancy pastry shops, the top of the cake is often draped with a thin sheet of pale green or pink almond paste. Homier variations are simply dusted with confectioners' sugar. At his restaurant, La Bouzerotte, in Burgundy, Monsieur Robert picks the second option, but then dresses it up with a caramelized crosshatch design in the sugar.

PASTRY CREAM
6 egg yolks
½ cup granulated sugar
¼ cup all-purpose flour
2 cups whole milk
½ teaspoon pure vanilla extract
Confectioners' sugar, for dusting

CAKE
4 eggs
½ cup plus 2 tablespoons granulated sugar
1 cup cake flour
¼ teaspoon salt

SYRUP
⅓ cup water
⅓ cup granulated sugar
¼ cup kirsch

1¼ cups raspberries
Confectioners' sugar, for topping

Heat the oven to 350°F. Butter and flour a 9-inch round layer-cake pan.

Make the pastry cream: In a mixing bowl, whisk the egg yolks and granulated sugar until light, 1 or 2 minutes, then whisk in the flour. In a saucepan, heat the milk until bubbles appear around the edge. Pour the hot milk into the yolk mixture, whisking until smooth. Pour this mixture back into the pan and bring to a boil, whisking until it thickens, 1 or 2 minutes. Take the pan from the heat. Whisk in the vanilla extract. Transfer the pastry cream to a shallow dish and dust the surface with confectioners' sugar to discourage a skin from forming. Chill until completely cooled. (The pastry cream can be made a day ahead.)

Make the cake: In a large stainless-steel bowl, beat the eggs and sugar with a hand-held electric mixer until blended. Set the bowl over a pan of barely simmering water, making sure the water does not touch the bowl. Whip at high speed for 5 to 10 minutes, until the mixture falls from the beaters in a thick ribbon and doesn't melt away immediately but holds a ribbon trail for 4 or 5 seconds. Take the bowl from the heat and continue beating until the mixture cools. Sift the flour with the salt over the fluffy egg mixture in 3 batches and fold together as lightly as possible using a large rubber spatula.

Pour the batter into the prepared pan and bake in the preheated oven until the cake shrinks slightly and the top springs back when lightly pressed with a fingertip, about 20 minutes. Take the cake from the oven and let it stand for 2 or 3 minutes before turning it out on a rack to cool.

Make the syrup: Combine the water and sugar in a saucepan, and set over low heat. Heat the mixture, stirring, until the sugar dissolves. Take the pan from the heat and cool slightly before stirring in the kirsch.

Cut the cooled cake in half horizontally with a long serrated knife to make 2 layers. Brush the cut side of each layer with sugar syrup to moisten.

Assemble the cake: Using a thin-bladed spatula, spread the cut side of 1 layer with half the pastry cream. Cover with all the raspberries, stem side down. Spread the remaining cream over the cut side of the second layer. Set the second cake layer, cream side down, on the raspberries and press lightly to flatten.

Just before serving, sift confectioners' sugar over the cake. Heat a stainless-steel skewer over a flame until burning hot, then make a caramelized crosshatch pattern in the sugar by applying the whole skewer to the top of the cake.

LA GÂCHE

Norman Tea Cake

Compact and crumbly, Pascal Bernou's gâche *reminds me of one of those Italian cakes served at the end of a meal for dunking in sweet fruity wine. Known properly as* la gâche amendaée—*or "improved"* gâche—*in western Normandy, and as* la fallue *to the near east, this cake is prepared like a firm bread dough, but enriched with eggs, butter, and* crème fraîche. *It's even shaped into flattened oval loaves, recalling plain* gâche, *the flat regional bread of Cherbourg.*

At La Verte Campagne, Monsieur Bernou sets out slices of this cake for breakfast, along with brioche and croissants, and for five o'clock tea. It also traditionally accompanies rice pudding and vanilla custard.

¼ cup whole milk
1 envelope active dry yeast
2 eggs, lightly beaten
4 cups all-purpose flour
½ cup granulated sugar
1 teaspoon salt
8 tablespoons (1 stick) unsalted butter
¼ cup crème fraîche *(page 368)* or sour cream

*I*n a small saucepan, heat the milk until bubbles appear around the edge, then let it cool to lukewarm. Sprinkle the yeast over the milk and set aside until the mixture is foamy, 5 to 10 minutes.

Reserve 1 tablespoon of the beaten eggs to use for a glaze.

Sift the flour with the sugar and salt into a large bowl and make a well in the center. Add the yeast mixture, the remaining eggs, the butter, and the *crème fraîche* or sour cream to the well and work with your fingertips until the dough is thoroughly mixed. Gradually draw in the flour. Knead the dough on a work surface for 5 to 10 minutes. Shape the dough into a ball. Put the dough back in the bowl, cover it with plastic wrap, and let it rise for 1½ to 2 hours. (It will not double in bulk like other yeast doughs.)

Punch the dough down and divide it in half. Shape each half into a flattened sausagelike loaf 10 to 12 inches long. Transfer the loaves to a heavy baking sheet. Cover with a floured kitchen towel and let rise again until puffy, 1 to 2 hours. (For a slower rise, chill the dough for at least 12 hours or up to 3 days.)

Heat the oven to 350°F. Brush each loaf with reserved egg glaze. Bake in the preheated oven until they brown and sound hollow when tapped with a knuckle, 20 to 25 minutes. Cool the loaves completely on a rack. Once thoroughly cooled, wrap tightly in plastic for at least a day before slicing.

BEIGNETS AUX POMMES

(NORMANDY)

Melt-in-Your-Mouth Apple Fritters

4 SERVINGS

BATTER

1 cup all-purpose flour
Pinch of salt
1 tablespoon granulated sugar
1 egg
¼ cup warm water
½ cup imported dry French cider or beer, or as needed, at room temperature
2 tablespoons unsalted butter, melted and cooled

4 apples, cored, peeled, and cut across into ⅜-inch rounds
¼ cup granulated sugar
¼ cup Calvados
¼ teaspoon ground cinnamon
4 cups vegetable oil, for frying
Confectioners' sugar, for sprinkling
4 scoops vanilla ice cream (optional)
1 cup applesauce, preferably homemade (page 330, optional)

François Lagrue's fritters melt away in your mouth, leaving the delicious tastes of apple, Calvados, and cinnamon. Funny as it may seem, Chef Lagrue uses beer in his batter at the Moulin de Villeray in Normandy. The bubbly drink makes a featherweight fritter. But, as it's a Norman specialty, I couldn't resist trying the recipe with sparkling apple cider. After a marathon day of testing apple recipes, the following was voted the hands-down favorite. If you do use cider, chill any left over and offer it with the fritters.

*M*ake the batter: Sift the flour with the salt and sugar into a mixing bowl and make a well in the center. Break the egg into the well and add the water. With a whisk, beat the egg and water to mix. Gradually beat the flour into the central ingredients while pouring in the cider or beer and the butter. Let the batter stand for 1 hour. If the batter thickens dramatically on standing, thin it with a tablespoon or so of cider or beer before adding the apples.

While the batter rests, combine the apples, granulated sugar, Calvados, and cinnamon in a mixing bowl. Toss gently and set aside for 15 to 30 minutes. In a deep-fat fryer, heat the oil to 375°F.

Pat the apples dry with paper towels as you use them. Dip the dried apples, one at a time, in the batter. Using a wire skimmer or wooden chopsticks, slip the batter-dipped apple slices into the hot oil without crowding the pan. Fry them until golden brown on one side, then turn them and brown on the other side, 1 to 3 minutes in all. As they are ready, remove them to paper towels or brown paper bags to drain. Keep the drained *beignets* warm in a 200°F. oven while frying the rest.

To serve, sprinkle the warm *beignets* with the confectioners' sugar and arrange them, overlapping, on plates. If you like, add a scoop of ice cream and a dollop of applesauce to each plate.

OREILLETTES

(PROVENCE)

Deep-Fried Christmas Pastries

MAKES ABOUT 5 DOZEN PASTRIES

2 cups all-purpose flour
3 tablespoons unsalted butter, at room temperature, cut into pieces
¼ cup granulated sugar
3 eggs
2 tablespoons rum, orange-flower water, or Cognac
½ teaspoon salt
4 cups vegetable oil, for frying
Confectioners' sugar, for dusting

Oreillettes *count among the hotly debated 13 desserts of Provençal Christmas. (No one can quite agree on the significance of the number 13, which desserts should be included—there are some 17 or 18 contenders—or even whether this custom is authentic. But no one wants to do without it.) Made from a simple, sweetened dough, rolled thin and then deep fried, these pastries often appear as broad sheets instead of small squares. They come into view at about the same time as the first crèches in Provence.*

Besides Christmastime, these light, crisp pastries can also be served whenever you'd like a crunchy cookie—with ice cream, poached fruit, baked apples, a mousse. Like anything deep-fried, their charm lasts only as long as they're warm.

Sift the flour into a mixing bowl and make a well in the center. Add the butter, sugar, eggs, flavoring, and salt to the well and work the ingredients in the well with your fingertips until thoroughly mixed. Draw in the flour, tossing, to form coarse crumbs. If the crumbs seem too dry, add a little water. Press the dough into a ball and knead on a floured work surface until smooth, 2 or 3 minutes. Transfer the dough to plastic wrap, flatten it into a disc, and wrap well. Chill for at least 30 minutes or overnight.

Just before serving, heat the oil in a deep-fat fryer to 360°F.

Divide the dough in half. Roll out each half on a floured surface to a sheet as thin as possible. Using a pastry wheel, cut the dough into 3- × 2-inch rectangles. As the rectangles are cut, transfer them to a floured kitchen towel until ready to use. Chill, reroll, and cut any scraps.

Drop a few *oreillettes* into the hot oil without crowding the pan. Fry them until golden brown on one side, then turn them, using a metal skimmer or wooden chopsticks, and brown on the other side, 30 seconds to 1 minute in all. As they are ready, remove them to paper towels or brown paper bags to drain. Keep the drained *oreillettes* warm in a 200°F. oven while frying the rest.

Sprinkle the *oreillettes* generously with the confectioners' sugar, arrange them, overlapping, on a napkin-lined plate, and serve as soon as possible.

TARTE AUX NOIX

(PROVENCE)

Walnut Tart

8 SERVINGS

Sweet Buttery Pastry Dough for one 9- to 10-inch tart shell (page 362)
½ cup granulated sugar
3 tablespoons water
1 cup crème fraîche *(page 368) or heavy (whipping) cream*
2 tablespoons strong-flavored honey, or to taste
2½ cups walnut halves

*R*oll out the dough on a floured surface to a round 2 inches wider than a 9- to 10-inch tart pan and about ¼ inch thick. Line the pan with the dough. Prick the tart shell all over with a fork about every ½ inch. Chill until firm, at least 30 minutes.

Heat the oven to 400°F.

Blind bake the tart: Line the tart shell with foil and fill almost to the top with dried beans. Bake for 15 minutes. Remove the foil and beans and continue baking until the shell just begins to brown and is fully cooked, 8 to 12 minutes. Let the shell cool completely on a rack before filling.

Have ready a basin of cold water for the caramel. In a heavy medium saucepan, combine the sugar and water. Heat gently until the sugar dissolves, stirring often. Raise the heat to moderately high, set a lid ajar on top of the pan, and continue cooking, undisturbed, until the syrup turns a deep amber color, 8 to 10 minutes. Check the color of the boiling syrup frequently during cooking. When done, dip the bottom of the pan into the cold water to stop the cooking.

Pour the *crème fraîche* or cream into the caramel. (It will sputter so take care.) Set the caramel mixture over moderate heat and melt it, stirring to combine the cream thoroughly. Cook until the mixture thickens slightly, 5 or 10 minutes. Add the honey, stirring until it melts. Taste and add more honey if you'd like. Stir in the walnuts and let cool to room temperature.

Pour the filling into the cooled tart shell and chill until the filling is firm enough for slicing, about 1 hour. Bring back to room temperature before serving.

A half-dozen desserts are temptingly displayed at Escalinada in Nice so that even before you finish your main dish, you mentally reserve a slice of tart, or a portion of chocolate mousse.

With its amber-colored, sugary filling and crunchy nut halves, this walnut tart reminds me of pecan pie. But here the filling, a blend of homemade caramel, crème fraîche, *and honey, clings like butterscotch sauce to the walnuts. The filling is not baked with flour and eggs; it sets in the refrigerator. The high butterfat content of the* crème fraîche *or heavy cream helps bind the mixture. Don't use light cream or you'll wind up with a runny (but tasty) mess. Serve the tart with unsweetened whipped cream or additional tangy* crème fraîche.

TARTELETTES ARLÉSIENNES

(PROVENCE)

Pine-Nut Tartlets

MAKES SIX 4-INCH TARTLETS

Sweet Buttery Pastry Dough for one 9- to 10-inch tart shell (page 362)
¾ cup pine nuts

ALMOND-CREAM FILLING
1¼ cups sliced blanched almonds
¾ cup granulated sugar
3 eggs, separated
8 tablespoons (1 stick) unsalted butter, cut into pieces
1 tablespoon rum

When in Arles, make time to visit the Musée Arlaten, the town's local history museum. Frédéric Mistral, the bard of Provençal folk life, launched this museum in 1899, and other grass-roots curators have followed his lead throughout France. Then at five, when you are shown the door, walk up the cobbled rue de la République for a late afternoon snack of tartelette arlésienne. *All the pastry shops along this pedestrian street offer a version, or several, of this almond-cream tartlet studded variously with pine nuts (as here), almonds, or raisins.*

*B*utter and flour six 4-inch round tartlet pans. Arrange the pans close together on a work surface. Roll out the dough on a floured surface to a rectangle about ¼ inch thick. Wrap the dough around the rolling pin, then unroll it over the pans, letting it drape loosely into the pans. Press the dough into the corners of the pans. Roll the pin over the tops of the pans to trim the dough. With your fingers, press the dough up the sides of each pan. Prick the tartlet shells all over with a fork about every ½ inch. Chill until firm, at least 30 minutes. If the sheet of dough doesn't cover all the tartlet pans, gather the dough scraps, reroll, line the remaining pans, and chill.

Heat the oven to 350°F. Spread the pine nuts on a baking sheet and bake until the nuts brown lightly, 3 to 5 minutes. Set aside.

Make the almond-cream filling: Whir the sliced almonds and all but 1 tablespoon of the sugar in a food processor or blender until the nuts are finely chopped. Add the egg yolks, butter, and rum, one at a time, puréeing until smooth after each addition. Transfer the mixture to a bowl.

In a mixing bowl, whip the egg whites with the remaining tablespoon of sugar until they hold stiff peaks. Stir a quarter of the egg whites into the almond mixture, working until it is smooth. Using a large rubber spatula, gently fold this lightened mixture into the remaining egg whites.

Pour the filling into the shells. (You may not need all the filling.

Do not overfill.) Gently press 2 tablespoons of the toasted pine nuts into the filling of each shell.

Set the tartlets on a baking sheet and bake in the bottom third of the heated oven for 10 minutes. Raise the tartlets to the middle of the oven and continue baking until the filling sets and is golden, 20 to 25 minutes. Let the tartlets cool slightly on a rack. Serve warm or at room temperature.

TOURTE DE BLETTES

(PROVENCE)

Sweet Swiss Chard Tart

8 SERVINGS

½ cup raisins
¼ cup marc de Provence *(the local brandy)* or Cognac

PASTRY DOUGH
4 cups all-purpose flour
¾ cup granulated sugar
1½ teaspoons salt
12 tablespoons unsalted butter, cut into pieces
2 eggs, beaten
½ cup plus 2 tablespoons ice water

⅔ pound coarsely chopped Swiss chard leaves (12 cups)
¾ cup light brown sugar
1 tablespoon extra-virgin olive oil
3 eggs
¾ cup pine nuts
4 firm apples, cored, peeled, and thinly sliced
Granulated sugar, for sprinkling

Most Swiss chard tarts sold at bakeries in Provence, even if they don't taste as weird as you'd think, still don't leave you hankering for more. But don't jettison the idea until you've tasted Mimi's recipe.

From six in the morning until a little before noon, Mimi tends to the cooking at Les Arcades, a refuge for denizens of terribly touristy Biot. Now in her eighties, Mimi has had plenty of time to perfect her tourta de bléa. *She tucks chard leaves, raisins, and pine nuts (a typical Arabic blend), plus a layer of apples and a shot of local brandy, between layers of sweet pastry dough. It makes a beguiling tart that you think about long after it's finished.*

*I*n a bowl, soak the raisins in the *marc* or Cognac, stirring once or twice, for at least 1 hour.

Make the pastry dough: Whir the flour, sugar, and salt in a food processor until mixed. Add the butter and pulse until the mixture resembles coarse crumbs. Add the eggs and ice water and pulse until the dough holds together when you pinch it with your fingers. Add another tablespoon or so of water if the dough looks too dry. Press into a ball and knead on a floured work surface for 1 or 2 minutes. Transfer the dough to wax paper, flatten it into a disc, wrap well, and chill until firm, at least 1 hour.

Cook the Swiss chard leaves in plenty of boiling salted water (as for pasta) until they are wilted and tender, 10 minutes. Drain, rinse in cold water, and drain again thoroughly. Press out as much water as possible by handfuls.

In a mixing bowl, beat together the light brown sugar, raisins with their brandy, the olive oil, 2 of the eggs, and the pine nuts. Beat in the cooked Swiss chard leaves.

Roll out two thirds of the dough on a floured surface to a

round 2 inches wider than a 10- or 11-inch tart pan. Line the pan with the dough, leaving the dough overhanging. Prick the tart shell all over with a fork about every ½ inch. Chill until firm, at least 30 minutes.

Heat the oven to 450°F.

Spoon the Swiss chard filling in an even layer into the bottom of the chilled tart shell. Cover with the apples.

Roll out the remaining dough to a round that fits just inside the tart pan. Place on top of the apples. Beat the remaining egg to mix and brush some of it on the *tourte*. Fold the overhanging dough up and over the top of the *tourte* and press to seal. Brush this flap with more of the beaten egg. Make 4 slits in the top of the *tourte* to allow steam to escape during cooking.

Bake the *tourte* in the preheated oven until it begins to brown, about 15 minutes. Cover with foil and continue baking for 15 to 20 minutes longer. Let the *tourte* cool slightly on a rack before sprinkling it with granulated sugar and slicing.

BLESSED BENEDICTINE

Benedictine doesn't number among Normandy's *produits du terroir*— edibles, like Livarot cheese, that take their character from the soil and their environment and are prepared exclusively with local ingredients. But the liqueur has been made in Fécamp on Normandy's Alabaster Coast for so long that it's been adopted as a Norman specialty.

Dom Bernardo Vincelli, a Venetian monk, first introduced this herbal liqueur to the Benedictines of Fécamp in the sixteenth century. The local monks concocted it according to Vincelli's recipe for almost three centuries. But they scattered during the Revolution and the secret formula disappeared.

The lost recipe was "rediscovered" by a marketing genius named Alexandre Le Grand, who started manufacturing Benedictine in 1863. He boosted the liqueur's religious aura by collecting sacred objects and building a Neo-Gothic, Neo-Renaissance palace in Fécamp to house them as well as the thriving liqueur factory.

It's fascinating to visit this dusty museum and contemplate one man's vision of free enterprise. You stroll from a timber-framed Gothic hall, crammed with priests' robes, liturgical ornaments, and books of hours, to an abbots' hall-cum-modern-conference-room, to rooms hung with old-time Benedictine posters by such artists as Mucha and Sem. Visitors may touch and sniff the twenty-seven component herbs and spices and visit the fragrant distillery and cellars.

TARTELETTES AUX FRAMBOISES

(PROVENCE)

Warm Raspberry Tartlets

MAKES EIGHT 4-INCH TARTLETS

Sweet and Crumbly Pastry Dough for one 10- to 11-inch tart shell (page 363)
⅓ cup raspberry jam, melted and strained, or black- or red-currant jelly
2 tablespoons water
1½ cups (¾ pint) fresh or thawed, frozen raspberries

Oh, those Provençal raspberries! In season, nearly every small family restaurant in Nice offers these tartlets, called cryptically tartelettes maison *or more explicitly* tartelettes aux framboises minute. *According to the local drill, you order this dessert at the same time as the rest of your meal—not later—so that at the appropriate moment the tartlet arrives in front of you still warm from the oven. The Nice formula for raspberry tartlet skips the usual pastry-cream filling. What you taste is pure berry flavor mixed with a cookie crust.*

*B*utter and flour eight 4-inch round tartlet pans. Arrange the pans close together on a work surface. Roll out the dough on a floured surface to a rectangle about ¼ inch thick. Wrap the dough around the rolling pin, then unroll it over the pans, letting it drape loosely into the pans. Press the dough into the corners of the pans. Roll the pin over the tops of the pans to trim the dough. With your fingers, press the dough up the sides of each pan. Prick the tartlet shells all over with a fork about every ½ inch. Chill until firm, at least 30 minutes. If the sheet of dough doesn't cover all the tartlet pans, gather the dough scraps, reroll, line the remaining pans, and chill.

Heat the oven to 400°F.

Blind bake the tartlets: Line the tartlet shells with foil and fill almost to the top with dried beans. Set the pans on a baking sheet and bake for 15 minutes. Remove the foil and beans and continue baking until the shells just begin to brown and are fully cooked, 8 to 12 minutes.

While the shells bake, make the glaze: In a small saucepan, stir together the jam or jelly and the water. Bring to a boil and simmer gently for 3 minutes.

Remove the tartlet shells from the oven and from their pans. Snugly fit the raspberries, stem side down, into the warm shells. While the tartlets are still warm, brush the raspberries with melted jam or jelly. Serve warm.

TARTE AUX POMMES ET RHUBARBE

(NORMANDY)

Rhubarb and Apple Tart

8 SERVINGS

*Sweet and Crumbly Pastry Dough for one 10- to 11-inch tart shell
(page 363)*
½–¾ cup granulated sugar
2 tablespoons all-purpose flour
3 cups diced rhubarb
2 pounds firm apples, cored, peeled, and thinly sliced into wedges
3 tablespoons unsalted butter, cut into small pieces

Roll out the dough on a floured surface to a round 2 inches wider than a 10- or 11-inch tart pan. Line the pan with the dough. Prick the tart shell all over with a fork about every ½ inch. Chill until firm, at least 30 minutes. Heat the oven to 400°F.

In a large bowl, stir together the sugar and flour. Add the rhubarb and toss well. Set aside for 15 minutes, stirring occasionally.

Spoon the rhubarb mixture into the bottom of the chilled tart shell in an even layer. Arrange the apples, rounded side up and overlapping, in concentric circles on the rhubarb. Dot the top with the butter.

Bake the tart in the preheated oven for 1 hour. Let it cool slightly on a rack before slicing.

Gérard and Lilliane Gosselin fatten ducks and geese for a living (typical of many enterprising farmers today who are making a go of untypically Norman occupations). But they also cook at the Ferme du Perrier in the Perche for groups of four or more, who come on horseback, bicycle, and foot as well as in their cars to share a farmhouse meal.

In rhubarb season, Lilliane turns out this tart, loaded with rhubarb and apples. Overlapping slices of apple hide the juicy rhubarb beneath, so the pretty dice of pink and green comes as a surprise. For a tarter fruit taste, use the lesser amount of sugar. If you are working with frozen rhubarb, note that it throws off more liquid than when fresh. A baking sheet under the tart pan will save a major clean-up job on your oven.

TARTES AUX POMMES CARAMELISÉES

(BRITTANY)

Caramelized Apple Tartlets

4 SERVINGS

½ pound best-quality puff-pastry dough

ALMOND CREAM
¼ cup sliced blanched almonds
3 tablespoons granulated sugar
1 small egg
2 tablespoons unsalted butter, cut into pieces
1 tablespoon all-purpose flour
½ teaspoon rum

4 small apples
2 tablespoons unsalted butter
Confectioners' sugar, for dusting

Sprinkle a baking sheet with water. Roll out the dough on a floured surface to a sheet ⅛-inch thick. Using a pan lid as a guide, cut the dough into 4 rounds about 5½ inches across. Transfer the rounds to the baking sheet. Prick them all over with a fork about every ½ inch, and chill until firm, at least 15 minutes. Heat the oven to 425°F.

Make the almond cream: Whir the sliced almonds and sugar in a food processor or blender until finely chopped. Add the egg, butter, flour, and rum, one at a time, puréeing until smooth after each addition. Spread about 2 tablespoons of the almond cream on each chilled dough round, mounding it slightly and leaving a narrow border of plain dough all around the edge.

Core and peel one of the apples, then halve it lengthwise. Set an apple half, rounded side up, on a cutting board and cut it lengthwise into thin slices. Slip a narrow spatula under the sliced apple half and, keeping the slices together, set it on one side of a dough round. Press the slices gently to flatten them a little. Rearrange the slices to follow the shape of the dough round. Slice the other apple half and set it on the empty side of the dough round in the same way. Dot with ½ tablespoon of butter. Repeat with the

True to everyone's expectations, restaurants and pastry shops all over Normandy and Brittany offer an apple tart or two. At a table d'hôte *the version will be homey, probably a large single tart. Fancy restaurants, on the other hand, specialize in complicated individual specimens made to order and served just-out-of-the-oven hot.*

These tartlets, from Brittany's Le Goyen restaurant, are eye-catching and easy. They're also amazingly delicious for something so simple. What's more, you don't need special tartlet pans, a pan lid will do just fine to measure the pastry rounds. These minimum-fuss tartlets can be assembled several hours ahead of time for a company dinner.

remaining apples and dough rounds. (The tartlets can be prepared to this point 2 or 3 hours ahead of time and chilled.)

Bake the apple tartlets in the preheated oven until the pastry has risen around the edge and is golden brown, about 15 minutes. Remove the tartlets from the oven. Heat the broiler.

Dust each tartlet with confectioners' sugar. Put the baking sheet with the tartlets on a rack about 3 inches from the heat and cook until the tops are lightly caramelized, 3 to 4 minutes. Watch carefully, turning the tartlets as necessary so they brown evenly and don't burn. Serve as soon as possible.

CRAZY FOR KIR

Dijon, Burgundy—In what must be the highest compliment ever paid by one region of France to another, Normandy and Brittany have both filched Burgundy's most popular aperitif, the *kir*.

On home ground, a classic *kir* consists of one-third crème de cassis, the black-currant liqueur (for a recipe see page 367), and two-thirds Bourgogne Aligoté, an unpretentious white wine. Today, however, most bartenders ease up on the expensive liqueur, so the average drinker would now find the original formula overly sweet. Moreover, it's not unheard of to find a variant, called a *communard*, made with red Burgundy wine instead of white. A *kir* made with *crémant de Bourgogne* or another sparkling wine takes the name *kir royal*.

It is this effervescent version that kindled Norman and Breton interest in *kir*. But in the natural process of adapting something foreign into something familiar, the Normans and Bretons replaced the ersatz champagne with native sparkling cider. The usurpers do at least cite their sources: The drink is called a *kir breton* or *kir normand*.

HOME SWEET HOME

Kir may be made all over France, but its cradle remains the town of Dijon, where *cassis de Dijon appellation d'origine contrôlée* is made. One version of the *kir* story has it that black-currant liqueur originated in the nineteenth century from a home recipe for *ratafia*, which calls for infusing nuts or fruit in brandy.

Folklore credits Denis Lagoute with starting the manufacture of crème de cassis (called plain cassis for short) in Dijon. By 1860, thirty establishments in Dijon were producing black-currant liqueur.

Even though making black-currant liqueur evolved into a business, the procedure remained simple. Black currants were crushed, then macerated in oak (later metal) casks with alcohol. The berries lent color, flavor, and aroma to the alcohol. Afterward, the black currant-infused alcohol was siphoned off, and granulated sugar and water were added to make a liqueur with 16- to 18-proof alcohol.

Cassis growing got an unexpected push in 1865 from the phylloxera epidemic that devastated Burgundy's vineyards. While waiting for a cure, winegrowers planted *noire de Bourgogne*, the preferred variety of black currant, and the shrub thrived in the cool climate of the Côte d'Or.

By the end of the nineteenth century, however, *vin blanc cassis*, as *kir* was first known, faced stiff competition from the many quinine drinks, such as gin and tonic, offered in bars and cafés. A decree issued by the appellate court of Dijon in 1923 gave local cassis makers another shot in the arm by creating *cassis de Dijon appellation d'origine contrôlée* and restricting its manufacture to Dijon.

POLITICAL PUNCH

But it was Canon Kir, Dijon's mayor from 1946 to 1968, who gave *kir* its name and launched it as a favorite drink all over France by serving it at official receptions.

In 1976, a European court once again established Dijon as the crème de cassis capital. In the meantime, cassis growing has moved from the precious wine slopes around Dijon to southeast of Beaune. Also, many independent winegrowers around Beaune have small productions of outstanding crème de cassis de Bourgogne without legal laurels.

Dijon still benefits from the cassis AOC, but only until 1996, when the court will review the question of whether Dijon alone deserves the right to produce *crème de cassis de Dijon.*

CORNIOTTE BOURGUIGNONNE AUX POMMES SAUCE CASSIS

(BURGUNDY)

Apple Pastries with Black-Currant Sauce

4 SERVINGS

Jean-Pierre Silva at the Hostellerie du Vieux Moulin understands that no matter how much we want to be coddled with the familiar, we also crave something new. His version of a sweet corniotte gives us both Burgundian innovation and tradition. Instead of using a sweetened cheese filling, Silva swaddles a whole apple, stuffed with almond cream, in puff-pastry dough.

His black-currant sauce, a sweetened blend of red wine, cinnamon, orange, lemon, and black currants, is one of the best things ever to have happened to cassis. Keep any extra for pouring over ice cream, poached pears and peaches, french toast, or, believe it or not, pumpkin pie.

BLACK-CURRANT SAUCE
2 cups red wine, preferably a Burgundy
¼ cup plus 2 tablespoons granulated sugar
1 orange slice
1 lemon slice
One 3-inch piece of cinnamon
40 black currants or blueberries

FILLING
1 egg yolk
1½ tablespoons granulated sugar
1 tablespoon all-purpose flour
½ cup milk
¼ teaspoon pure vanilla extract
3 tablespoons unsalted butter, softened
⅓ cup ground almonds

4 smallish apples, cored and peeled
½ pound best-quality puff-pastry dough
1 egg, beaten

Make the sauce: In a medium saucepan, combine the wine, sugar, orange, lemon, and cinnamon. Bring to a boil, then reduce the heat and simmer the sauce, uncovered, until reduced by half, 15 to 20 minutes. Strain the sauce into another saucepan, add the black currants or blueberries, and boil until they burst, about 5 minutes. Set aside to cool to room temperature, then discard the cinnamon and slices of orange and lemon.

Make the filling: In a mixing bowl, whisk the egg yolk and sugar until thick and light, 1 or 2 minutes, then whisk in the flour. In a medium saucepan, heat the milk until bubbles appear around the edge. Pour the hot milk into the yolk mixture, whisking until smooth. Pour this mixture back into the pan and bring to a boil, whisking until the mixture thickens, 1 or 2 minutes. Take the pan from the heat and whisk in the vanilla, butter, and almonds. (The sauce and filling can be made a day ahead and chilled.)

Spoon some of the filling into the core of each apple. You may not need all the filling.

Roll out the dough on a floured surface to a 12-inch square ⅛ inch thick. Cut the dough into four 6-inch squares and set a filled apple on each. Brush the dough around the apple with beaten egg. Bring the dough up to enclose each apple and pinch together the edges. Set the *corniottes*, seam side up, on a baking sheet and chill until firm, at least 15 minutes. Meanwhile, heat the oven to 425°F.

Brush beaten egg over the *corniottes* and bake them in the preheated oven until the pastry begins to brown, about 15 minutes. Reduce the oven temperature to 350°F. and continue baking until the pastry is brown and the apples are very tender when pierced with a knife, 10 to 15 minutes longer.

Remove the *corniottes* from the oven and set each on a plate. Pour some of the sauce around each pastry and serve. Pass the remaining sauce separately.

FEUILLETÉS À LA POMME ET CALVADOS

(NORMANDY)

Apple Feuilletés with Calvados

4 SERVINGS

Layers of puff pastry sandwich baked apple halves filled with a lightened pastry cream. Daniel Touchais's dessert fits the image of the Hôtel-Restaurant Montgomery in Pontorson, where a meal brings back moments gone by—culinary as well as historic—and Norman ingredients. With its building-block recipes of pastry cream, custard sauce, and whipped cream, the feuilleté draws on classical French cooking, but apples and Calvados give it unmistakable regional overtones.

LIGHT PASTRY CREAM
1 egg yolk
1½ tablespoons granulated sugar
1 tablespoon all-purpose flour
½ cup milk
1 teaspoon Calvados, or to taste
1 teaspoon confectioners' sugar, plus additional for dusting
¼ cup plus 2 tablespoons heavy (whipping) cream

CALVADOS CUSTARD SAUCE
1 cup milk
2 tablespoons granulated sugar
3 egg yolks
2 teaspoons Calvados, or to taste

APPLES AND FEUILLETÉS
½ pound best-quality puff-pastry dough
¼ cup granulated sugar
4 small, firm apples, peeled, halved lengthwise, and cored
1 egg white, beaten

*M*ake the light pastry cream: In a mixing bowl, whisk the egg yolk and the granulated sugar until thick and light, 1 or 2 minutes, then whisk in the flour.

In a small saucepan, heat the milk until bubbles appear around the edge. Pour the hot milk into the yolk mixture, whisking until smooth. Pour this mixture back into the pan and bring to a boil, whisking until the cream thickens, 1 or 2 minutes. Take the pan from the heat. Whisk in the Calvados and taste, adding more Calvados if needed. Transfer the pastry cream to a shallow dish, dust with confectioners' sugar to discourage a skin from forming, and chill until completely cooled. (The light pastry cream can be made a day ahead to this point.)

Make the custard sauce: In a medium saucepan, heat the milk with the sugar until the sugar dissolves and bubbles appear around the edge. Take the pan from the heat. Beat the egg yolks in a bowl and slowly whisk in the hot milk. Pour this custard back into the pan and cook over low heat, stirring constantly with a wooden spoon, until the sauce thickens enough to coat the spoon, 18 to 20 minutes. Strain the sauce and chill. When chilled, add the Calvados; taste and add more if needed. (This sauce can be made a day ahead and chilled.)

Heat the oven to 425°F.

Prepare the apples and feuilletés: Sprinkle a baking sheet with water. Roll out the dough on a floured surface to a sheet ¼ inch thick. Cut the dough into 4 rectangles about 4 × 3 inches. Transfer the rectangles to the baking sheet and chill until firm, at least 15 minutes.

Put the sugar in a shallow dish. Dredge the apples in the sugar, patting off the excess. Put the sugared apples in a roasting pan and bake them until they are tender when pierced with a knife but still hold their shape, 20 to 30 minutes, depending on the size and variety of the apples. Take them from the oven.

Brush the dough rectangles lightly with beaten egg white but be careful not to get any on the edges. (The egg white would seal the layers of puff pastry and prevent them from separating and flaking.) Bake the dough rectangles until puffed and brown, about 15 minutes.

Meanwhile, finish the light pastry cream: In a mixing bowl, whip the cream with the teaspoon of confectioners' sugar until it holds firm peaks. Fold the cold pastry cream into the whipped cream. Scoop this lightened cream into a pastry bag and pipe it into the apple cores. Or spoon the cream into the cores.

Remove the feuilletés from the baking sheet with a palette knife. Cut each feuilleté in half horizontally. Set 2 stuffed apple halves, cream side up, on the bottom half of each feuilleté. Cover with the top half of the pastry.

Set each feuilleté on a plate. Pour some of the custard sauce around it and serve. Pass any remaining sauce separately.

DESSERTS

For the apple-charlotte contest in Athis-de-l'Orne, a village in western Normandy, not just anything goes. Homely applesauce charlottes with bread crusts are turned away, for instance. A prizeworthy recipe for this competition consists of an apple-Bavarian mixture packed into delicate but sturdy ladyfingers. Says Raymond Lelouvier, grand master of the *Confrérie des Gouste Bourdelots du Bocage Athisien:* "We look for the polished examples."

Country bake-offs like the one in Athis-de-l'Orne help keep regional specialties alive. But such elaborate preparations have always been exceptional in the French provinces. Traditionally, countryfolk didn't eat dessert in the everyday course of things. And the few sweet endings around needed little or no culinary fuss: Home cooks offered a piece of fruit or fresh cheese—made with cow, sheep, or goat milk, depending on the region—accompanied perhaps by cream, berries, jam, or herbs.

Anything more complicated than applesauce, baked apples, or, in wine-producing areas, strawberries in red wine, would have been saved for a *repas de fête*, or special meal. For weddings, religious festivals, births, and other events, country cooks typically whipped up custards and puddings. Normandy had its *crème aux oeufs*, an old-fashioned vanilla custard, and burnt rice pudding. Breton *cuisinières* cracked eggs for *far*, a flan made with store-bought prunes—pure luxury. In Burgundy, cooks mixed pumpkin purée with semolina to make a Burgundian flan.

Today, with the longing people seem to have for the simple things in life, even trendy chefs emulate these rustic desserts. Throughout the French countryside you find such desserts, as well as their upscale equivalents—fruit gratins, mousses, frozen soufflés, all prepared with time-honored flavorings and combinations in mind.

FROMAGE BLANC
AUX HERBES

(BURGUNDY)

Fresh Farmer Cheese with Herbs, Shallots, and Garlic

4 SERVINGS

You're in a pickle every time the cheese course arrives at a restaurant in Burgundy: Do you want the tray of local aged cheeses? Or do you try the fresh *fromage blanc, served either with thick ivory cream and sugar or (as here) with herbs, shallots, and garlic?*

If you opt for the fromage blanc aux herbes, *it comes, sometimes, thick as sour cream, sometimes, completely drained and firm, resembling farmer or pot cheese. The embellishments are set out in little bowls to add according to taste. In the hands of arty cooks, the platter looks like a still life, adorned with nuts, fruit, leaves, flowers, and other found objects. It's hard to imagine the pleasure in something as simple as mashing together soft cheese with aromatic seasonings and then spooning it into your mouth. But try it once and a light goes on in your head.*

½ pound soft farmer or pot cheese
¼ cup snipped fresh chives
¼ cup chopped fresh tarragon
⅓ cup chopped fresh parsley
¼ cup finely chopped shallots
2 garlic cloves, finely chopped (optional)

Set out the cheese on a plate and each herb, the shallots, and garlic in ramekins or other cups. Put salt and the pepper grinder on the table, too, and let your guests go to it.

CALISSONS,
SWEETS TO MAKE EVEN
A SAD QUEEN SMILE

Aix-en-Provence, Provence—For those who don't already love almonds, the charm of this city's almond-paste candy, the *calisson*, often remains elusive. Maybe it's the celebrity factor. Everyone knows that if you go to Aix-en-Provence you have to eat *calissons*. To say you don't especially care for them can be a rare form of one-upmanship.

As for those who forswear truffles and *foie gras* after one try ("They're really not worth all the fuss"), rejection confers the status of independent thinker. What a pity. This diamond-shaped sweetmeat rumored to have teased a smile from a dejected bride, has everything to please.

In Aix, the legend of a candy maker's wedding gift to Provence's new queen, Reine Jeanne, has been told for generations. One sweet shop here even takes its name from the young queen, while another carries her husband's name, Roy René, who is a beloved figure in his own right.

According to Maurice Farine, an inexperienced palate might confuse a *calisson* with a piece of marzipan. Monsieur Farine, Roy René's third-generation director, can sympathize with the costly let down: "Why buy something at twice the price when you can't tell the difference?"

WHAT'S THE BIG DEAL?

But in fact, *calissons* are made using roughly one-third almonds, one-third candied melon, one-third sugar, plus a small amount of candied orange peel. Marzipan consists of 40 percent almonds and 60 percent sugar. To anyone who has grown up eating *calissons*, the distinction is obvious and addictive.

For Monsieur Farine, what determines the best *calissons* is the quality of the ingredients. He buys Valencia almonds from Spain because he finds them closest to Provence's native almond, a crop too scarce to tap. His candied melons come from Apt, Provence's traditional candied-fruit capital.

To make *calissons*, the whole almonds are first skinned by boiling them and then sorted by hand. Granite rollers grind the skinned nuts to a powder, which is mixed with sugar syrup and the candied fruit to make a paste. The paste is spread on thin sheets of edible rice paper, stamped into little diamonds, and then spread with a thin sugar coating before the molds are removed.

Still, freshness is everything. Superior ingredients make only potentially good *calissons*. All *calissons* left to languish on a shelf turn dry and disappointing. The best bet is to go to a factory where they are made or to a shop that does a brisk business. At Christmastime, the most popular season for *calissons*, the candies are always just out of the mold. "Don't keep *calissons* more than five days," cautions Monsieur Farine. "The fresher the better." ✍

FROMAGE DE CHÈVRE AU MIEL

(PROVENCE)

Fresh Goat Cheese with Honey and Pollen

4 SERVINGS

6 ounces fresh (soft) goat cheese log, cut across into 4 rounds
2 tablespoons pourable honey, or to taste
2 teaspoons pollen, or to taste

*A*rrange each round of cheese in the center of a dessert plate. Spoon ½ tablespoon of honey on each and sprinkle with ½ teaspoon of pollen. Pass additional honey and pollen separately.

If now and then the kitchen gets too ambitious at Le Mas de Cotignac, there's always something on the menu that sticks with the Provençal basics yet makes you look at them again—like this simple cheese dessert. Michel Lecuyer takes local goat cheese (or brousse, fresh sheep-milk cheese), pours on the herb-infused honey, and adds a pollen crunch. You wonder why no one thought of it before.

COMPOTE DE POMMES

(NORMANDY)

Homemade Applesauce

MAKES ABOUT 4 CUPS

3½ pounds apples, unpeeled, quartered, and cored

Cut any large pieces of apple in half. Leave the skin on, but cut away any bruised spots.

Put the apples in a large, heavy, metal casserole. Cover the pot and set it over the lowest possible heat. Cook the apples, stirring occasionally, until they are very soft and falling apart, 1 to 1¼ hours. If the apples begin to catch and burn at the start of cooking, reduce the heat even more and add a little water. When done, work the applesauce through a food mill to remove the skins.

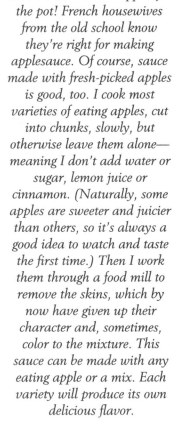

Save those wrinkled apples for the pot! French housewives from the old school know they're right for making applesauce. Of course, sauce made with fresh-picked apples is good, too. I cook most varieties of eating apples, cut into chunks, slowly, but otherwise leave them alone— meaning I don't add water or sugar, lemon juice or cinnamon. (Naturally, some apples are sweeter and juicier than others, so it's always a good idea to watch and taste the first time.) Then I work them through a food mill to remove the skins, which by now have given up their character and, sometimes, color to the mixture. This sauce can be made with any eating apple or a mix. Each variety will produce its own delicious flavor.

POMMES AU LAMBIG

(BRITTANY)

Baked Apples with Cider Eau-de-Vie

4 SERVINGS

4 tablespoons unsalted butter, softened
3 tablespoons granulated sugar
2 tablespoons lambig (the local brandy) or Calvados
1 teaspoon grated orange zest
4 apples, cored and peeled

*H*eat the oven to 350°F.

In a small bowl, mash together the butter, sugar, *lambig* or Calvados, and orange zest.

Put the apples in a shallow baking dish just big enough to hold them. Stuff bits of the butter mixture into the cores and dot the tops with any remaining butter.

Bake the apples, basting them every 10 minutes with the melted stuffing, until tender, 45 minutes to 1 hour, depending on the size and variety of the apples. Serve hot, warm, or at room temperature.

Lambig *is the name for Brittany's cider eau-de-vie, which does not share the Calvados name. For one thing, Breton apple varieties differ from those in Normandy, next door (fount of France's Calvados). But most of all, Breton terroir—the sum of climate, soil, and exposure— makes good but not great eau-de-vie. Still, Brittany's landscape encourages the growing of apple trees, and so we have cider and* lambig.

Soft, fruity, and sweet, baked apples can't be improved upon, only adapted to local taste. Here's a Breton version with its whiff of cider eau-de-vie and citrus. And, being a French recipe, the apples are peeled. If you prefer, leave the skins on or peel a wide strip from just around the top.

Use any baking apple here. Cortland has the advantage of its flesh staying white after cutting longer than most varieties. Or moisten the apples with lemon juice to discourage browning. With the apples, serve crisp butter cookies, or try Norman Tea Cake or Deep-Fried Christmas Pastries.

POIRES À LA DIJONNAISE

(BURGUNDY)

Poached Pears with Cassis and Vanilla Ice Cream

4 SERVINGS

When speaking of dessert, dijonnaise *means black currant. Even though the cassis belt has moved from Dijon to southeast of Beaune, the name Dijon still conjures up these intense purple-black berries.*

Some cooks recommend green pears for poaching, but in my experience the unripe fruit stays hard unless cooked for hours. I prefer pears at their peak, still firm and ready to eat out of hand. To poach them, find a saucepan just big enough to stand the pears in snugly so they don't bob wildly in the poaching liquid but stay mostly submerged.

Adding a cream topping here may seem like gilding the lily, but that's the custom. It's hard to go wrong whether you opt for the whipped cream or not: Ice cream and cassis liqueur without the pears also tastes good. And the poached pears are terrific on their own.

Poach the pears up to three days ahead, if you like, but they're also good eaten the day they're cooked. Unlike pears poached in red wine, where marinating is essential for the fruit to absorb the vibrant red color, here, leaving the pears in the syrup is up to you.

SYRUP
3 cups water
⅔ cup granulated sugar
1 vanilla bean, split lengthwise; or ½ teaspoon pure vanilla extract

4 firm ripe pears (about 1¼ pounds in all)
1 lemon, halved
½ cup heavy (whipping) cream
½ tablespoon confectioners' sugar
4 scoops vanilla ice cream
4 tablespoons crème de cassis, store-bought or homemade (page 367), or to taste

*M*ake the syrup: In a medium saucepan, combine the ingredients and set over low heat. Heat the mixture, stirring, until the sugar dissolves.

Peel each pear and remove the stem. Core the pears through the bottom with a paring knife. As you work, moisten the pears with lemon juice to discourage browning.

Add all the pears to the syrup along with the used lemon halves and bring the syrup just to a simmer. Reduce the heat to low and poach the pears, covered, until tender, 20 to 25 minutes. Take the pan from the heat but leave the pears to cool in the syrup. (The pears can be cooked up to 3 days ahead and chilled in the syrup.)

In a mixing bowl, whip the cream with the confectioners' sugar until it holds firm peaks. Chill.

To serve, put a scoop of ice cream in each of 4 small bowls. With a slotted spoon, lift each cooled pear out of the sugar syrup, letting it drip into the pan, and set it in a bowl. Pour a tablespoon of crème de cassis over each pear. Scoop the whipped cream into a pastry bag and pipe rosettes of cream to cover the pear, or spoon a dollop of cream on each.

CRÈME À L'ANCIENNE

(NORMANDY)

Old-Fashioned Vanilla Custard

6 SERVINGS

2 cups whole milk
½ cup granulated sugar
3 eggs
½ teaspoon pure vanilla extract

*H*eat the oven to 325°F.

In a medium saucepan, combine the milk and sugar and heat, stirring once or twice, until the sugar dissolves and bubbles appear around the edge. In a mixing bowl, beat the eggs to mix. Pour the hot milk, whisking, over the eggs. Add the vanilla.

Pour this custard into six individual ¾-cup soufflé dishes or custard cups. Put the dishes in a roasting pan. Carefully add enough water to the pan to reach halfway up the sides of the dishes. Bring the water to a boil on top of the stove, then transfer the lot to the preheated oven. Bake until the custards just set, 35 to 45 minutes. (Check the custards during cooking; if small bubbles appear, reduce the oven temperature to 300°F.) Remove the custards from the oven and their water bath and set aside to cool slightly. Serve warm (my preference) or at room temperature.

Before crème brûlée *was part of our vernacular, even before* crème caramel, *there was* crème aux oeufs *(today known as* crème à l'ancienne)*. You may have forgotten how good the plain-Jane version can be.*

Madame Mottier makes hers at the family ferme-auberge *in Normandy for people who need a fix of farm cooking. Serve Madame Mottier's custard while it holds a bit of warmth from the oven.*

CRÈME D'AVOINE CARAMELISÉE

(BRITTANY)

Caramelized Oatmeal Cream

4 SERVINGS

Crème brûlée *still reigns as nearly everyone's favorite dessert. And it's no surprise, for who can resist the sweet, egg-rich custard set off by a slightly bitter brown-sugar crust? Today, however, cooks are tampering with the original vanilla flavoring.*

This recipe from Jacques Thorel of L'Auberge Bretonne, one of Brittany's most creative chefs, draws on the humble oat porridge that was once a staple in the Breton peasant diet. But in this upscale pudding, the oats, roasted to bring out their nutty taste, are used only for flavoring.

½ cup whole oats (not rolled)
1½ cups whole milk
6 egg yolks
¼ cup plus 2 tablespoons light brown sugar
½ cup heavy (whipping) cream
Dark brown sugar, for sprinkling

Heat the oven to 425°F. Spread the oats on a baking sheet and toast them in the oven until deep brown, 5 to 10 minutes.

In a medium saucepan, heat the milk until bubbles appear around the edge, then take from the heat. Add the toasted oats to the milk, cover, and set aside to steep at room temperature for 3 hours.

Heat the oven to 300°F.

In a mixing bowl, beat the egg yolks with the light brown sugar until light. Reheat the milk to boiling and strain the hot milk, whisking, into the sugar and yolk mixture. Discard the oats. Whisk in the cream.

Pour this custard into 4 individual gratin dishes. Put the dishes in 1 or 2 roasting pans. Carefully add enough water to the pan to reach halfway up the sides of the baking dishes. Bring the water to a boil on top of the stove, then transfer the lot to the preheated oven. Bake until the custards just set, about 30 minutes. Cool to room temperature and then refrigerate for at least 3 hours or overnight.

Just before serving, heat the broiler. Sift dark brown sugar evenly over the cold custards. Put the gratin dishes on a baking sheet about 3 inches from the heat and broil until the sugar melts and forms a firm crust, 3 or 4 minutes. Watch the browning carefully, turning the dishes as necessary so the sugar melts evenly and doesn't burn. Serve at once.

GRATIN DE POIRES ET FRAMBOISES

(NORMANDY)

Gratin of Pears and Raspberries in Sabayon

4 SERVINGS

SYRUP
1 cup water
¼ cup granulated sugar

2 pears
Juice of ½ lemon
½ cup heavy (whipping) cream
4 teaspoons granulated sugar
2 egg yolks
7 ounces fresh or thawed frozen raspberries

*M*ake the syrup: In a medium saucepan, combine the water and sugar and set the mixture over low heat. Heat, stirring, until the sugar dissolves.

Peel the pears and halve them lengthwise. To discourage browning, moisten the cut pears with lemon juice as you work. Core them and cut each half lengthwise into 4 slices. Add all the pears to the saucepan and bring the sugar syrup just to a simmer. Reduce the heat to low, cover, and poach the pears until just tender, 8 to 10 minutes. Take the pan from the heat but leave the pears in the warm syrup.

In a mixing bowl, whip the cream with 2 teaspoons of the sugar until it holds soft peaks. Chill.

To finish, heat the broiler. In a large stainless-steel bowl, beat the egg yolks with a hand-held electric mixer or a whisk until creamy, about 30 seconds. Beat in the remaining 2 teaspoons of sugar. Set the bowl over a pan of simmering water, making sure the water does not touch the bowl. Whip at high speed until the sabayon holds soft peaks, 3 to 5 minutes. Take the bowl from the heat and keep beating until cool. Fold the whipped cream into the sabayon with a large rubber spatula.

Divide the pears, drained, and the raspberries among individual gratin dishes. Spoon the sabayon over the fruits. Put the gratin dishes on a baking sheet about 3 inches from the heat and cook until the tops are lightly browned, 3 or 4 minutes. Watch the browning carefully, turning the dishes as necessary so the sabayon browns evenly and doesn't burn. Serve as soon as possible.

Orne is Normandy's land of pear (cider) orchards and tangled hedgerows of berry bushes. This pretty, warm dessert combines sweet poached pears with slightly tart raspberries and fluffy sabayon. Then the mixture browns under the broiler.

Serving the gratin family-style from one dish doesn't do it justice. You need individual gratin dishes here. The poached pears and whipped cream can be prepared a couple of hours ahead, leaving only the sabayon making and browning for the last minute.

STRAWBERRIES FROM PLOUGASTEL, A TASTE FOUND AND LOST

Plougastel-Daoulas, Brittany—The Plougastel strawberry still thrives on a reputation it hasn't deserved since the 1950s. "Today's strawberries are hard as rocks," Jean-Marie Le Gall confesses ruefully. Monsieur Le Gall, president of SAVEOL, a farmers' cooperative in this favored patch of farmland on Brittany's western coast, says, "We have to rediscover the taste of real strawberries."

The flavor Monsieur Le Gall is talking about harks back to the Chilean strawberry plants brought here in 1714 by François Frézier, a Breton botanist. They flourished in ivory-tower splendor at the nearby botanic garden in Brest until 1820, when cuttings were transplanted to Plougastel with the aim of producing a strawberry crop.

Soon the *Fragaria chiloensis* covered the sunny southern slopes of the Plougastel peninsula down to the sea. With an Arcadian setting nurtured by the Gulf Stream, the farmers of Plougastel could satisfy the English taste for strawberries with an early variety that hit the market weeks before England's own berries. From this strawberry, farmers moved to other varieties ever more precocious, large, high-yielding, and sturdy.

ENGLISH AS A SECOND LANGUAGE

Besides developing a strawberry to please their English customers, many Bretons from Plougastel learned the English language in order to trade easily across the Channel. While the French are infamous for speaking nothing but their mother tongue, Monsieur Le Gall's grandfather studied English on the island of Jersey to be able to sell his sweet peas and strawberries abroad.

Large families supplied the many hands needed for this labor-intensive crop. In Plougastel life, women and children traditionally tended the strawberries while the men fished, often dragging nets along the ocean floor off Brest for scallops. These fishermen also harvested seaweed to fertilize the soil for their crops.

Today, strawberry production is floundering precisely because it depends on manual labor. A typical yield in Plougastel used to weigh in at six or seven thousand tons a year. Now the harvest has plummeted to a thousand tons.

"Girls used to come for a month or two to help harvest the strawberries in the spring," Monsieur Le Gall explains. "Today no one will do it."

The remaining strawberry crop grows in hothouses where everything can be controlled, instead of on Plougastel's beneficent slopes. "In the hothouses everything's easy," Monsieur Le Gall says. "You don't have to go out in the rain. Nobody grows strawberries in the open fields anymore. It's a question of culture. Times change."

COMING AROUND AGAIN

Still, Monsieur Le Gall is heartened by some new trends. He says he's noticed a turn-around in the last two or three years, spurred by chefs who want old-fashioned strawberry flavor.

When asked about his favorite strawberry recipe, Monsieur Le Gall breaks into a broad smile. This farmer from a long line of strawberry farmers spurns strawberry cake and strawberry mousse, even strawberries sprinkled with sugar or ladled with fresh cream. "*Je ne les aime que nature,*" he says. "I only like them plain and simple." ✎

GRATIN DE PÊCHES

(BRITTANY)

Golden Peach Gratin

4 SERVINGS

4 small ripe peaches

SYRUP
1 cup water
¼ cup granulated sugar

¼ cup sliced blanched almonds
3 tablespoons granulated sugar
1 egg
2 tablespoons unsalted butter, cut into pieces
½ teaspoon rum
4 scoops peach sorbet or vanilla ice cream

*P*eel and prepare the peaches: Immerse them whole in a large saucepan of simmering water for 10 to 30 seconds, depending on the ripeness of the fruit. Transfer them briefly to ice water and drain. Run a knife around the peaches, following the natural division. Twist the halves and discard the pit. Peel the skin from the flesh. Cut the peaches into ¼-inch slices.

Make the syrup: In a medium saucepan, combine the water and sugar and set over low heat. Heat the mixture, stirring until the sugar dissolves. Add all the peaches to the saucepan and bring the sugar syrup just to a simmer. Reduce the heat to low, cover, and poach the peaches until just tender, 8 to 10 minutes. Take the pan from the heat but leave the peaches in the warm syrup.

Whir the sliced almonds and the sugar in a food processor or blender until finely chopped. Add the egg, butter, and rum, one at a time, puréeing until smooth after each addition. Heat the broiler.

Drain the peaches and divide them among 4 individual gratin dishes. Spoon the almond cream over the peaches. Put the dishes on a baking sheet about 3 inches from the heat and cook until the tops are lightly browned, 3 or 4 minutes. Watch the browning carefully, turning the dishes as necessary so the topping browns evenly and doesn't burn. Serve hot. Pass individual bowls of sorbet or ice cream separately.

When Nathalie Pelletier started out on her own as a cook, she relied on her mother's surefire dessert recipes. "Now my mother calls me when she wants something good," says 28-year-old Nathalie, chef-owner of Le Jardin Gourmand in Lorient, Brittany.

For this warm fruit gratin, Madame Pelletier tops poached peach slices with almond cream. Then she runs individual gratins of the mixture under the broiler until warm and brown. For contrast, the talented young cook pairs this hot dessert with icy homemade peach sorbet, but any good vanilla ice cream is delicious, too. Vary the recipe by substituting poached plums or apricots for the peaches.

MOUSSE DE SUREAU

(BRITTANY)

Elderberry Mousse

6 SERVINGS

1 pound fresh wild elderberries (about 3 heaped cups), reserving a handful
    for decoration
½ cup water
¾ cup granulated sugar, or to taste
Juice of 2 lemons (about 6 tablespoons)
1 cup heavy (whipping) cream
1 tablespoon powdered unflavored gelatin

Discard the stems from the berries. In a medium saucepan, combine the berries with ¼ cup of the water and bring to a boil. Simmer the berries until they burst, 5 to 7 minutes.

Purée the berries in a food processor. Work the purée through a food mill into a bowl. Using a rubber spatula, scrape the purée back into the saucepan. Add ½ cup plus 2 tablespoons of the sugar and heat gently, stirring, until the sugar dissolves. Take the pan from the heat and add the lemon juice. Taste and add more sugar if needed. The purée should be sweet and intensely flavored, like sorbet.

In a mixing bowl, whip the cream with the remaining 2 tablespoons of sugar until it holds soft peaks. Chill.

In a small metal bowl, sprinkle the gelatin over the remaining ¼ cup of water and set it aside until spongy, about 5 minutes. Set the bowl in a barely simmering water bath and heat until the gelatin melts, shaking it gently without stirring. Stir it into the fruit purée and set the purée in a bowl of ice water. Stir the purée until it is completely cool and starts to set, 3 to 5 minutes.

When the purée thickens, showing it has start to set, fold it into the whipped cream using a large rubber spatula. Spoon this mousse into a serving bowl and smooth the top. Chill until it sets, at least 3 hours or overnight. Decorate each serving with a few whole elderberries.

Testing the culinary acumen of his guests, Thierry Rannou quizzes: "Can you guess the flavoring in this mousse?" Thierry, who runs a backcountry B&B and table d'hôte in northwestern Brittany, adds neither blackberries nor myrtilles, the small European blueberries, to his deep-purple dessert. He prepares the mousse with the wild elderberries he collects in late August and September in the rugged Monts d'Arrée.

If you like to stalk the woods for edibles, you'll appreciate a simple recipe using these tart berries. Boil them until they burst, then work them through a food mill and sweeten to taste. (At this point, the elderberries make a delicious sauce for pouring over pancakes or ice cream.) Thierry then blends the purée with whipped cream and sets the mixture lightly with gelatin.

If you're not a gatherer type, substitute raspberries, blackberries, or even blueberries for the elderberries. Accompany the rich mousse with a peach salad or another fresh fruit.

CHARLOTTE AUX POMMES

(NORMANDY)

Apple-Bavarian Charlotte

8 SERVINGS

APPLES AND LADYFINGERS
1½ pounds apples, cored, peeled, and thinly sliced
¾ cup water
¼ cup Calvados
Approximately 30 ladyfingers

BAVARIAN CREAM
1 cup milk
2 tablespoons granulated sugar
3 egg yolks
1 tablespoon powdered unflavored gelatin
¼ cup water
½ cup heavy (whipping) cream
2 teaspoons confectioners' sugar
2 tablespoons Calvados, or to taste
2 tablespoons lemon juice, or to taste

SAUCE AND DECORATION
Calvados Custard Sauce (page 320, replacing the Calvados with ½
    teaspoon pure vanilla extract) or Strawberry Sauce (page 301)
½ cup heavy (whipping) cream whipped with 1 teaspoon confectioners'
    sugar and 1 teaspoon Calvados (optional)

*P*repare the apples and ladyfingers: Put the apples in a heavy metal casserole, cover, and set over the lowest possible heat. Cook the apples, stirring occasionally, until they are very soft and falling apart, 25 to 30 minutes. Add a little water if necessary to discourage the apples from catching and burning. Mash any large pieces with a fork. Chill thoroughly.

In a soup plate, combine the water and Calvados. Briefly dip a few ladyfingers at a time in this mixture. If the ladyfingers are left too long in the Calvados mixture, they will fall apart into soggy crumbs. Cut each in half crosswise and trim each half into a long triangle resembling a flower petal to fit in the bottom of a 5-cup charlotte mold. Arrange the trimmed ladyfingers in a flower shape, rounded sides down, in the bottom of the mold. Use as many as

Anxious to spark renewed interest in native desserts and, especially, in the local Calville baking apple, the Confrérie des Gouste Bourdelots du Bocage Athisien *launched a* bourdelot *(apples baked in pastry) contest in 1977. Then in 1990, encouraged by the talents of local bakers with this double-crusted apple pie, the gastronomic brotherhood based in the Norman village of Athis-de-l'Orne, sponsored the first apple-charlotte contest.*

In all categories (there are separate divisions for apprentice bakers, full-fledged bakers, and home bakers), jury members single out just the right Calvados-laced blend of cooked apples, vanilla custard, and whipped cream, lightly set with gelatin, all packed in a case of ladyfingers. Even though the rules limit entries to Normandy, the following auslander *recipe would fit right in.*

will fit comfortably, without overlapping. Fit the trimmings into any gaps.

Briefly dip more ladyfingers in the Calvados mixture and stand them upright, rounded sides out, around the sides of the mold, packing them as close together as possible. Trim the tops of the ladyfingers level with the top of the mold, if necessary. Set aside the prepared charlotte mold and the Calvados mixture.

Make the bavarian cream: In a medium saucepan, heat the milk with the sugar until the sugar dissolves and bubbles appear around the edge. Take the pan from the heat. In a mixing bowl, beat the egg yolks and slowly whisk in the hot milk. Pour this custard back into the pan and cook over low heat, stirring constantly with a wooden spoon, until the sauce thickens enough to coat the spoon, 15 to 18 minutes. Take the custard from the heat.

In a small metal bowl, sprinkle the gelatin over the water and set aside until the gelatin is spongy, about 5 minutes. Set the bowl in a simmering water bath and heat until the gelatin melts, shaking it gently without stirring.

Stir the melted gelatin into the custard. Add the chilled apples and set the pan in a bowl of ice water. Set aside, stirring occasionally, until the mixture is completely cool and starts to set, about 5 minutes.

Meanwhile, in a mixing bowl, whip the cream with the confectioners' sugar until it holds soft peaks. Chill.

When the custard thickens, showing it has start to set, fold it into the whipped cream. Gently stir in the Calvados and lemon juice and taste, adding more lemon juice or Calvados if needed.

Assemble the charlotte: Spoon the bavarian cream into the prepared charlotte mold. Dip more ladyfingers in the reserved Calvados mixture and cover the bavarian cream completely, cutting the ladyfingers to fit as necessary. Gently press them into the cream and chill the charlotte until it sets, at least 5 hours or overnight.

To serve, run a knife around the mold to loosen the charlotte and turn it out onto a platter. Pour some of the vanilla custard sauce or strawberry sauce around the base and pass the remaining sauce separately. If you like, scoop the whipped cream into a pastry bag and decorate the charlotte with rosettes of cream.

APPLE-CHARLOTTE CHICANERY

A letter distributed to all competitors in Athis-de-l'Orne's apple-charlotte contest spells out the regulations: In addition to listing deadlines and entrance fees, the letter urges hopefuls to "pack their confections with particular care since grievances regarding deterioration during shipping will not be heard." And in an effort to discourage prizewinning bakers from later pawning off inferior merchandise on unsuspecting customers, the rules state: "It is understood that, for a year, the same high quality as that of the winning entry will be maintained."

MARMELADE DE POMMES

(NORMANDY)

Old-Fashioned Apple Pudding

4 TO 6 SERVINGS

4 tablespoons unsalted butter
2 pounds apples, cored, peeled, and thinly sliced
2 tablespoons lemon juice, or to taste
2 tablespoons Calvados, or to taste
½ cup plus 2 tablespoons granulated sugar, or to taste
2 large eggs

*H*eat the oven to 350°F. Butter a 4-cup terrine mold.

In a medium metal casserole, melt the butter over moderate heat. Add the apples, lemon juice, Calvados, and sugar. Cover and cook, stirring occasionally, until the apples are very soft and falling apart, 25 to 30 minutes. Uncover, increase the heat, and continue cooking, stirring frequently, until the juices evaporate and the apples are thick, about 10 minutes. Mash any large pieces of apple with a fork. Taste and add more lemon juice, Calvados, or sugar, if needed.

Take the pot from the heat and cool the mixture slightly. Break the eggs into the apple mixture and beat to combine. Spoon the pudding into the prepared mold and smooth the top. Set the mold in a roasting pan and fill the pan halfway with water. Bring to a boil on top of the stove.

Transfer the lot to the preheated oven and bake until the pudding is firm to the touch and a knife inserted in the center comes out hot, 45 minutes to 1 hour. Remove from the oven and cool to slightly warm or room temperature before serving, 30 to 45 minutes. Serve warm or at room temperature, in slices. Pass the fruit sauce or vanilla custard sauce separately.

Roland Rougeolle, the last old-time basketmaker in eastern Normandy, sits weaving at the apple market in Sainte-Opportune-la-Mare. He's made a nest for himself amid his wares woven in wild chestnut and rattin cane. Around him farmwives peel apples for fritters and sell home-baked goods and crates of apples. This market takes place the first Sunday of each month from November to April, on the grounds of the Maison de la Pomme.

Suitably ensconced in an eighteenth-century school complete with neat straw roof, the "Apple House" provides a clearinghouse for information on apples, for eating as well as cider making. I even found this old-time recipe tucked amongst odd cider-making facts and legends.

With the pudding, serve Strawberry Sauce, Black-Currant Sauce, Black-Currant Liqueur, or Calvados Custard Sauce (replacing the Calvados with ½ teaspoon pure vanilla extract).

FLAN DE COURGE AU COULIS DE CASSIS

(BURGUNDY)

Caramelized Pumpkin Pudding with Black-Currant Sauce

8–10 SERVINGS

The story on Jean-Pierre Billoux's (Le Bistrot des Halles in Dijon) semolina-based pudding is this: The more you taste, the more you want to taste. With a textured, homespun appearance, it's every bit the Burgundy country dessert. But the combined flavors of pumpkin, caramel, and black currant take it into another realm. (The color scheme—orange, purple, and amber—launches it into orbit.)

Be sure the pumpkin dries thoroughly before you add it to the semolina mixture. If you can't find black currants, blueberries are a good second choice. Pumpkin flan is the perfect sequel to Chicken Simmered in Red Wine or Burgundy Beef Stew.

CARAMEL
¾ cup granulated sugar
¼ cup water

One 1¼-pound wedge pumpkin or other hard-shelled squash, peeled and
    cut into 2-inch chunks
4 cups whole milk
1 cup granulated sugar
½ cup Cream of Wheat (semolina)
6 eggs, beaten to mix

BLACK-CURRANT SAUCE
½ pound black currants
¼ cup water
¼ cup plus 2 tablespoons granulated sugar, or to taste
Juice of 1 lemon (about 3 tablespoons), or to taste

*H*eat the oven to 350°F. Have ready a 1½- or 2-quart soufflé or other deep baking dish.

Make the caramel: In a small, heavy saucepan, combine the sugar and water. Heat gently until the sugar dissolves, stirring often. Raise the heat to moderately high, partially cover the saucepan, and continue cooking, undisturbed, until the sugar syrup turns a deep amber color, 8 to 10 minutes. Check the color of the boiling syrup frequently during cooking. As soon as the caramel reaches the desired color, pour all of it into the soufflé dish. Quickly turn the dish to coat the bottom and sides with the caramel. Set aside.

Boil or steam the pumpkin or squash until very tender, 10 to 15 minutes, and drain if necessary. Transfer it to a medium saucepan and mash. If the pumpkin is watery, set the pan over moderate heat and cook, stirring, until the pumpkin dries, about 10 minutes.

In a large saucepan, combine the milk and sugar. Heat the milk, stirring, until the sugar dissolves and bubbles appear around the edge. Reduce the heat to low and stir in the cream of wheat in a thin stream. Cook, uncovered, stirring from time to time to avoid lumps, until thickened, about 10 minutes. Stir in the mashed pumpkin. Take the pan from the heat and cool slightly. Beat in the eggs. Pour this mixture into the prepared soufflé dish.

Bake in the preheated oven until a knife inserted in the flan comes out clean, about 45 minutes. Remove from the oven and cool to slightly warm or room temperature before serving, 1 to 1½ hours.

Meanwhile, make the sauce: Discard the stems from the berries. In a medium saucepan, combine the berries and water and bring to a boil. Simmer the berries until they burst, 5 to 7 minutes. Purée the berries in a food processor, scrape them back into the saucepan, and add the sugar. Heat gently, stirring, until the sugar dissolves. Take the pan from the heat and add the lemon juice. Let the sauce cool to room temperature. Taste the cooled sauce and add more sugar or lemon juice if needed. (Both the flan and sauce can be made a day ahead and chilled. Bring them to room temperature before serving.)

To serve, run a knife around the flan and turn it out onto a round platter. Spoon some of the sauce around the base and serve. Pass the remaining sauce separately.

FAR BRETON

(BRITTANY)

Brittany Prune Flan

6 TO 8 SERVINGS

If you wrinkle your nose at the mention of this quintessential Breton flan, it's because either you've never had far *or you haven't tasted the best. The really good examples are solid (this is not the ethereal cooking of* haute cuisine) *without being heavy or pasty. Luscious, humble, with a trace of rum,* far *occupies the same exalted place in the gastronomic order of things as, say, brownies or carrot cake.*

Granted, unless you're Breton you probably need only one recipe for far *in your repertoire. Make it this one from Pierre-Jan Indekeu, who bakes the flan to order for his customers at La Cours d'Orgères in Saint-Pierre-de-Quiberon. Monsieur Indekeu offered me his* far *when I requested a couple of other recipes. "Would you like to try it?" he asked. "I think I've got it right." He's too modest. It deserves a prize.*

If you don't have whole milk in the house you can use 1¾ cups partially skimmed milk and ¼ cup heavy (whipping) cream. I've tried this far breton *with Armagnac, too, and it's not at all bad.*

12 large prunes (¼ pound unpitted), pitted or not; or ⅔ cup dark raisins
¼ cup rum or Armagnac
1 cup all-purpose flour
½ cup plus 2 tablespoons granulated sugar
Pinch of salt
3 eggs
2 cups whole milk
⅓ cup unsalted butter, melted and cooled to tepid

*I*n a bowl, soak the prunes or raisins in the rum or Armagnac, stirring occasionally, for at least 2 or 3 hours; overnight is better. The dried fruit will absorb most of the liqueur.

Heat the oven to 400°F. Butter a 6-cup shallow baking dish.

Sift the flour with the sugar and salt into a mixing bowl and make a well in the center. Break the eggs into the well and add a little milk. With a whisk, beat the eggs and milk to mix. Gradually beat the flour into the central ingredients while pouring in the remaining milk and the butter.

Strain this batter into the prepared baking dish and add the prunes or raisins here and there. Bake the *far* in the preheated oven until it is set and the top is golden, 25 to 35 minutes. Cool to lukewarm before eating (my preference), or serve at room temperature.

RIZ À LA PALETTE

(NORMANDY)

Burnt Rice Pudding

4 TO 6 SERVINGS

½ cup white rice, preferably short-grain
3 cups whole milk
½ cup granulated sugar
⅓ cup dark brown sugar

*H*eat the oven to 325°F. Put the rice in a bowl, wash it in several changes of water until the water is clear, then drain. Spread the rice evenly in a 4- or 6-cup shallow casserole or baking dish.

In a medium saucepan, combine the milk and granulated sugar. Set it over moderate heat and cook, stirring, until the sugar dissolves and bubbles appear around the edge. Pour the hot milk over the rice. Smooth the top with the back of a spoon. Set a lid on top or cover tightly with foil and bake in the preheated oven, undisturbed, until nearly all the liquid is absorbed, 1¾ to 2 hours. (The pudding can be made to this point a day ahead and chilled. Let it come to room temperature before proceeding.)

Just before serving, heat the broiler. Sift the brown sugar evenly over the top of the pudding. Put the pudding on a rack about 3 inches from the heat and cook until the sugar melts and forms a firm crust, 3 or 4 minutes. Watch the browning carefully, turning the dish as necessary so the sugar melts evenly and doesn't burn.

Madame Mottier still makes the caramelized crust on her rice pudding by heating a palette, a kind of iron, in the hot embers of her farm's wood-burning bread oven and pressing the scalding metal on the sugar topping. Even today at La Nocherie, an isolated ferme-auberge in Normandy's Orne département, much of the food cooks in the farm's old bread oven.

While I have adapted Madame Mottier's technique for a modern kitchen, I have stuck with the rural spirit of the recipe, which doesn't lavish good eggs on a frivolous dessert. If this sounds stingy, remember that on the farm, milk isn't skimmed of its cream, except to make butter, and even then it's richer than low-fat milk. That's why I specify whole milk. (Light cream would not be out of place here.) But if you want a more luxurious pudding, cook the rice, milk, and sugar, covered, in a medium saucepan over low heat until nearly all the liquid is absorbed, then beat in 3 egg yolks. Spread this mixture into a 4- or 6-cup shallow casserole or baking dish and bake in a simmering water bath for 30 minutes before making the burnt sugar topping.

COFFEE WITH A KICK

Today's Calvados makers don't like to talk about *calva*, the 70-proof moonshine that dragged the name of Normandy's cider eau-de-vie through the mud. It was this rough brew, also called *la goutte*, that was routinely poured into coffee to make *café-calva*. *Calva* tipplers drove French legislators to advocate uprooting entire apple orchards, which practically wiped out the cider-apple crops in the 1950s.

Having been rehabilitated into a blended, aged, 40- to 45-proof spirit, and rebaptized "Calvados," the brandy now ranks up there with Armagnac and Cognac as one of France's finest *digestifs*, worthy of the usual high-minded debate.

But old habits die hard in the countryside. If you stop for a chat with a Norman farmer at ten o'clock in the morning, you'll automatically be offered a reheated cup of coffee. Even today it's not unusual for your host to top up the cup with *la goutte* once you've taken a few sips. If you balk at brandy before lunch, you may be admonished. "*C'est l'eau de la vie, pas de la mort,*" teases Victor Letouzé, a farmer in Créances. "It's the water of life, not of death."

SOUFFLÉS GLACÉS CAFÉ ET CALVADOS

(NORMANDY)

Frozen Coffee and Calvados Soufflés

4 SERVINGS

3 tablespoons very strong coffee, or 1½ tablespoons instant coffee dissolved
   in 3 tablespoons water
3 tablespoons Calvados
½ cup heavy (whipping) cream
4 eggs, separated, 1 egg white discarded
1 cup granulated sugar
½ cup water
Chocolate coffee-bean candies (optional)

These cool and airy soufflés are a whimsical nod to a hallowed Norman pairing—the café-calva, or black coffee spiked with Calvados. Régis Lecomte, one of several young chefs helping to revive the languishing local cuisine, serves a version of these at his restaurant Le Dauphin in Le Breuil-en-Auge. Here, I've freely interpreted Monsieur Lecomte's idea.

Wrap a sturdy foil or wax-paper collar around four individual ¾-cup soufflé dishes or custard cups, extending it about 2 inches above the rim. Snugly tape the collars closed.

Combine the coffee with the Calvados in a small bowl and chill.

Whip the cream until it holds soft peaks, and chill.

Beat the 3 egg whites until they hold stiff peaks. Beat in 2 tablespoons of the sugar until the whites are glossy to make a light meringue, about 30 seconds. Set aside.

In a heavy medium saucepan, heat the remaining sugar and the water, stirring, until the sugar dissolves. Bring to a boil and cook, undisturbed, to the soft-ball stage, 238° to 240°F. on a sugar thermometer.

Meanwhile, in a large bowl, beat the 4 egg yolks. While beating constantly with an electric mixer, gradually pour the hot syrup into the yolks—avoid the beaters which would spray the hot syrup all over the place. Beat at high speed for 5 minutes, then reduce the speed to low and continue beating until the mixture cools and forms a thick mousse, about 10 minutes.

Lightly fold the whipped cream and the meringue into the mousse along with the coffee and Calvados mixture.

Spoon the mousse into the prepared dishes and smooth the tops. Freeze until firm, at least 5 hours or overnight. (Because of the alcohol, these soufflés don't freeze rock solid.) Remove the collars and serve the soufflés, decorated with the coffee beans, if you like.

With the aid of a paper collar, a frozen soufflé stands above the rim of its dish like a traditional hot soufflé. But, buoyed by a frozen blend of meringue, egg yolks, and whipped cream, this soufflé mixture won't fall. You won't need an ice-cream churn for this dessert, and it can be held in the freezer a day or two before serving.

BREAD, BEVERAGES, PRESERVES, AND BASIC RECIPES

What could be more fundamental to eating than bread? What could be more useful than a pastry shell when you have a family and farmhands to feed? What more essential to soups and stews than stock, the simmered scraps of finished meals? In vintage provincial life, what was more vital than a pantry stocked with preserves?

And yet, the recipes in this chapter—more than any others in this book—are fading from the farmwife's repertoire. Bakers have virtually taken over the task of bread baking. Most of the French look upon a home-baked loaf as a freakish thing. They are determined to believe that bread can't be made at home. And why would you want to bake, anyway, when bread from the *boulangerie* is pretty good? (Only those who have tasted homemade bread would understand.)

While tarts still make quintessential dining here, the dough (made with butter) often comes from the supermarket, if not the entire tart. And French housewives are handy with bouillon cubes. Sound familiar? Only jams, fortified wines, and other edible gifts still draw reluctant cooks into the kitchen.

You could make all the other recipes in this book without consulting this chapter. But if you cook for a hobby, or if you want to know how French country cooks got on in the kitchen until the 1950s, here's basic reading. ✍

FOUGASSE AUX OLIVES

(PROVENCE)

Lacy Olive Bread

MAKES 1 LOAF

Provence, known for its olives and olive oil, has also given us fougasse. *A flat bread, it's sometimes called "ladder bread" in English as an attempt to describe the characteristic openings. Here's the* fougasse *you see at the* boulangerie, *this one studded with black olives. (They also come plain and with pork cracklings.) Once you make this at home, Provence won't seem so far away.*

¼ cup coarsely chopped black olives, preferably from Nyons
1 recipe French Bread Dough (page 357) made with bread flour, through
   the first rising
Olive oil, for brushing

*K*nead the olives into the dough. On a floured surface, roll out the dough to an oval 8 × 12 inches and about ¼ inch thick. Transfer the dough to a heavy baking sheet. Using a sharp knife, make 6 slits to resemble the veins of a leaf, cutting all the way through the dough. Gently pull the slits open so the bread retains its lacy look when baked. Cover with a floured kitchen towel for about 1 hour, until the dough gets puffy.

Heat the oven to 450°F. Fill a roasting pan half full with hot water and put it on the oven floor.

Brush the top of the *fougasse* with olive oil. Bake in the middle of the heated oven until crisp and light brown, 25 to 30 minutes. Cool on a rack before serving.

FROM THE MEDITERRANEAN, SALT GROUNDED IN TECHNOLOGY

Aigues-Mortes, Provence—At night they look like some kind of flying machine with unusually long wings. Landing lights on, they taxi down a snowy runway. But these giant contraptions are earthbound salt harvesters. In September, when it's time for the salt to come in, they run day and night, scooping up the sea salt that crystallizes in salt pans the size of football fields.

In sight of Aigues-Mortes' thirteenth-century ramparts and set in the marshy Camargue, where the Rhône River twists its way through the flatlands south of Arles, the Salins du Midi harvests 450,000 tons of salt, more than half the table salt consumed in France.

"Wind, sun, warmth, and the right kind of soil," says Jean-Pierre Brun, an executive with the Salins du Midi, "that's what you need to make salt." But it takes more than passive energy to produce these colossal amounts of sea salt.

High technology also figures in the equation at the Salins du Midi. Eleven miles south of the salt fields, a pumping station pumps 10 cubic meters (about 33 square feet) of sea water a second from the Mediterranean into a canal leading to the salt fields. From here the water's flow is regulated by computer and given a push by twenty-three intermediate pumping stations through a forty-two-mile circuit of shallow clay canals and ponds—an area the size of Paris.

During this journey, the breeze off the coast and the warm Provençal sun do indeed act jointly to evaporate nine tenths of the water. By the time the water reaches the salt pans, the concentration of salt has risen from about 1 ounce per quart to over 8 ounces for the same volume of water, and the salt crystallizes.

Between the months of April and September, salt season in Provence, a four-inch layer of sea salt piles up in each pan. Before the autumn rains begin, the big-gun salt harvesters are called in, and for an entire month they plow up the salt continuously, with only a Sunday break. On an average day, 15,000 tons of salt are weighed in.

With a single harvest in September, the *fleur de sel*, or the fine, naturally white salt that floats on the surface of the salt pan, simply mixes into the remaining salt instead of being skimmed off, as in Brittany (see page 165).

TECHNOLOGY VERSUS TRADITION

And unlike the resolutely traditional Breton harvest, in Provence, the salt is sorted and washed, taking away some of the inimitable sea flavor and all the impurities. (There's no scum when you use it in cooking as with natural sea salt.) Washing leaves a bleached, consistent, and, ultimately, more banal product. This snow-white salt is then stocked outside in the form of hills sixty feet high, giving the flat landscape an incongruous wintry, alpine look.

This is how salt dissolved in the Mediterranean comes to end up on tables in France, packaged in familiar blue saltshakers with a smiling whale, *la baleine.* As Jean-Pierre Brun describes it, trying to put into words a very particular kind of farming: "We cultivate sea water to make salt."

PÂTE À PAIN

French Bread Dough

MAKES ENOUGH FOR 1 LACY OLIVE BREAD OR
CRUSTY ONION, ANCHOVY, AND OLIVE PIZZA

½ envelope active dry yeast
¾ cup lukewarm water
1½ to 2 cups all-purpose or bread flour
½ teaspoon salt

*I*n a small bowl, sprinkle the yeast over the water and set the mixture aside until it becomes foamy, 5 to 10 minutes.

Sift 1½ cups of the flour with the salt into a large mixing bowl and make a well in the center. Add the yeast mixture to the well. With your fingertips, gradually draw the flour into the yeast mixture. Knead the dough on a work surface until smooth, about 10 minutes, working in up to ½ cup more flour, if needed, so that the dough is still soft but no longer sticky. Shape the dough into a ball. Put it back into the same mixing bowl, cover with plastic wrap, and set it aside until doubled in bulk, 1 to 1½ hours.

Punch down the dough, cover, and let it rise again, about 1 hour. (For a slower rise, chill the dough for at least 4 hours or up to 3 days.) Punch down the dough before shaping.

BACK-TO-THE-FARM CIDER

"This is the room I was born in," says forty-year-old Annie Lesur, as we sit talking in her kitchen. "My family has lived here since the Revolution." But the room looks barely ten years old and the modern heating keeps us all toasty on this cold February afternoon.

When her father retired in 1983, he offered Annie and her husband, René, the tumbledown family home and forty-six hectares of land in Noyer-en-Ouche, a village in southern Normandy. René quit his hospital job, fixed up the two-hundred-year-old house, and became a farmer.

"The land's not very rich here in the Pays d'Ouche," says Monsieur Lesur. "I couldn't graze cows for milk, for instance. I had a choice between cereal crops and apples, and I liked the idea of making cider. Cider always used to be made here. It seemed like the right thing to do."

Annie and René are part of a larger movement helping to reestablish cider in its homeland. The back-to-nature trend and a resurgence of interest in France's rural heritage are encouraging some farmers to replant their orchards.

Although we may think of cider as eternally Norman, the drink wasn't widespread in western Normandy until the fourteenth century, and not until the eighteenth century in eastern Normandy. Wine and beer were more common until cider was given a boost in the seventeenth century by Louis XIII, who imposed a vineyard tax. This spurred Norman farmers to replace their few existing vineyards with fruit trees.

From the 1800s until well into this century, cider became the traditional Norman drink. Every farmer made his own cider for his family and, especially, the four or five hired hands. These laborers worked up a thirst scattering seeds on soil they tilled, slashing ripened hay, and looking after the farm animals. Any extra apples were sold to the local cider factory or distillery.

FROM STANDBY TO OLD HAT

All this changed in the second half of the twentieth century. To stem the high rate of alcoholism (a result of tippling the Norman moonshine called *calva*, rather than cider), the French government paid farmers to uproot their apple trees. At the same time, other crops such as wheat, corn, and beetroot earned more in the marketplace. Also, the appearance of tractors and other machinery reduced the need for thirsty hired hands, who had become too expensive for the average farmer anyway. When farmers didn't convert their orchards to fields, they often abandoned them.

Even with farmers like Annie and René Lesur returning to traditional cider making, there's no turning the clock back to pre–World War II days. Today, agricultural experts counsel interested farmers to plant low-branch apple trees, which begin to yield fruit after only three or four years and produce twenty-five tons of apples a hectare at their peak. In addition, farmers can easily grow grains between the rows of trees while waiting for the apples. These are trees for the short term, when you know your children will probably leave the homestead and the taste for cider may dry up before the harvest is in.

By comparison, traditional *pommiers à haute tige* (high-branch apple trees) bear fruit after seven to ten years and reach a yield of only fifteen tons of apples per hectare after eighteen years. These trees live twice as long as the diminutive variety, however— forty years instead of twenty. They encourage mixed farming, too. Beneath their lofty branches, animals graze and hay grows in summer. But if demand drops, well, much is lost.

Today the Lesurs produce three thousand bottles of cider a year, a small production even by farm standards, most of which goes to local restaurants.

As we check on the cider's progress in René Lesur's cider cellar, our noses red from the cold, Monsieur Lesur says, "But you should be here in May when the apple trees blossom."

PAIN DE MIE AU CIDRE ET AUX CINQ CÉRÉALES

(BRITTANY)

Granary Cider Bread

MAKES 2 LOAVES

2 tablespoons applesauce, prepared or homemade (page 330)
1 envelope active dry yeast
4 cups all-purpose flour
1¼ cups 5-grain flour
2 teaspoons salt
2 cups imported dry French cider

*P*ut the applesauce in a small saucepan and warm over low heat. Let it cool to tepid. Sprinkle the yeast over the applesauce and set the mixture aside until it's foamy, 5 to 10 minutes.

Put both flours and the salt in a large mixing bowl and make a well in the center. Add the yeast mixture to the well. With your fingertips, gradually draw the flour into the yeast mixture while gradually pouring in the cider. Knead the dough on a work surface until smooth and elastic, about 10 minutes. Shape the dough into a ball. Put it back into the same mixing bowl, cover with plastic wrap, and let it rise until doubled in bulk, about 1½ hours.

Butter two 4-cup loaf pans. Punch down the dough and divide it in half. Shape each half into a sausagelike loaf and transfer the loaves to the prepared loaf pans. Cover them with a floured kitchen towel and let rise again until the dough fills the pans, 1½ to 2 hours. (For a slower rise, chill the dough in the pans for at least 8 hours or up to 3 days.)

Heat the oven to 375°F. Fill a roasting pan half full with hot water and put it on the oven floor.

Bake the loaves in the preheated oven until they brown and sound hollow when rapped with a knuckle, 50 to 60 minutes. Take the loaves from their pans and bake them for an additional 5 minutes. Cool the loaves completely on a rack before slicing. (Once thoroughly cooled, they can be wrapped tightly and frozen.)

Bread devotees will appreciate Patrick Jeffroy's 5-grain loaf in which, this being Breton fare, applesauce and cider find their way into the recipe. (They take the place of water.) Even if the apple flavor remains elusive, this loaf will remind you that 1) there is nothing like home-baked bread, and 2) bread isn't difficult to make.

Note that while Chef Jeffroy uses 5 grains, they are ground into flour and not left whole, so the loaf is smooth not chunky. You could offer this bread with any Norman or Breton meal. It also makes great toast.

PÂTE BRISÉE

Buttery Pastry Dough

MAKES ONE 10- TO 11-INCH TART SHELL

1½ cups all-purpose flour
½ teaspoon salt
8 tablespoons (1 stick) unsalted butter, cut into pieces
1 egg yolk
3 to 4 tablespoons ice water

MAKES ONE 9- TO 10-INCH TART SHELL

1 cup all-purpose flour
¼ teaspoon salt
5 tablespoons unsalted butter, cut into pieces
1 egg yolk
2 to 3 tablespoons ice water

*W*hir the flour and salt in a food processor until mixed. Add the butter and pulse until the mixture resembles coarse crumbs. Add the egg yolk and the lesser amount of water and pulse until the dough holds together when you pinch it with your fingers. Add another tablespoon of water if the dough looks too dry. Press it into a ball and knead it on a floured work surface for 1 or 2 minutes. Transfer the dough to wax paper, flatten it into a disc, wrap well, and chill until firm, at least 1 hour.

PÂTE SUCRÉE

Sweet Buttery Pastry Dough

MAKES ONE 10- TO 11-INCH TART SHELL

1½ cups all-purpose flour
1 tablespoon granulated sugar
½ teaspoon salt
8 tablespoons (1 stick) unsalted butter, cut into pieces
1 egg yolk
3 to 4 tablespoons ice water

MAKES ONE 9- TO 10-INCH TART SHELL

1 cup all-purpose flour
2 teaspoons granulated sugar
¼ teaspoon salt
5 tablespoons unsalted butter, cut into pieces
1 egg yolk
2 to 3 tablespoons ice water

*W*hir the flour, sugar, and salt in a food processor until mixed. Add the butter and pulse until the mixture resembles coarse crumbs. Add the egg yolk and the lesser amount of water and pulse until the dough holds together when you pinch it with your fingers. Add another tablespoon of water if the dough looks too dry. Press it into a ball and knead it on a floured work surface for 1 or 2 minutes. Transfer the dough to wax paper, flatten it into a disc, wrap well, and chill until firm, at least 1 hour.

PÂTE SABLÉE

Sweet and Crumbly Pastry Dough

1½ cups all-purpose flour
⅓ cup granulated sugar
½ teaspoon salt
8 tablespoons (1 stick) unsalted butter, cut into pieces
1 egg yolk
3 to 4 tablespoons ice water

1 cup all-purpose flour
¼ cup granulated sugar
¼ teaspoon salt
5 tablespoons unsalted butter, cut into pieces
1 egg yolk
2 to 3 tablespoons ice water

Whir the flour, sugar, and salt in a food processor until mixed. Add the butter and pulse until the mixture resembles coarse crumbs. Add the egg yolk and the lesser amount of water and pulse until the dough holds together when you pinch it with your fingers. Add another tablespoon of water if the dough looks too dry. Press it into a ball and knead it on a floured work surface for 1 or 2 minutes. Transfer the dough to wax paper, flatten it into a disc, wrap well, and chill until firm, at least 1 hour.

CONFITURE DE NOIX COCO

(NORMANDY)

Coconut Preserve

MAKES ABOUT 2 CUPS

At Viviane Maignan's table d'hôte, *La Rajellerie*, in Normandy, more sweet, spicy odors from the French Antilles wafted into the dining room even as we polished off her Curried Veal Stew. But it wasn't until the next morning that we tasted the source of those tantalizing coconut, caramel, and cinnamon smells. Madame Maignan served this coconut preserve instead of jam with toast and coffee. It's child's play to prepare (just don't burn the caramel) and makes an intriguing breakfast offering for overnight guests.

CARAMEL
½ cup granulated sugar
2 tablespoons water

2 cups grated coconut
3 cups water
½ cup granulated sugar
1 teaspoon pure vanilla extract
One 3-inch piece cinnamon

*M*ake the caramel: In a heavy medium saucepan, combine the sugar and water. Heat gently until the sugar dissolves, stirring often. Raise the heat to moderately high, partially cover the pan, and continue cooking, undisturbed, until the sugar syrup turns a deep amber color. Check the color of the boiling syrup frequently during cooking.

Take the caramel from the heat. Add all the coconut at once and beat with a wooden spoon to blend. Return the pan to moderately high heat and stir in the water. Cook, uncovered, stirring now and then, for 5 to 10 minutes. Stir in the sugar, vanilla, and cinnamon, and cook, stirring occasionally, until most of the liquid evaporates, 20 to 30 minutes.

Spoon the coconut into jars and cover. (Chilled, the preserve keeps for up to 2 months.) Or spoon the coconut into hot, sterilized canning jars, and seal according to the manufacturer's instructions.

CONFITURE DE POIRES

(BURGUNDY)

Fresh Pear Jam

MAKES ABOUT 5½ CUPS

3 pounds ripe pears (about 6), peeled, cored, and cut into ½-inch chunks
Juice of 1 lemon (about 3 tablespoons)
5 cups granulated sugar

*H*eat the oven to 300°F.

Put the pears and the lemon juice in a large, heavy metal casserole. Cover the pot and set it over the lowest possible heat. Cook the pears, stirring occasionally, until they are very soft and falling apart, 25 to 30 minutes. Purée in a food processor or food mill and return to the pot.

Warm the sugar in a heatproof bowl in the preheated low oven, stirring it occasionally, until heated through, about 10 minutes.

Bring the pear purée to a boil. As soon as it boils, remove it from the heat and add the warmed sugar all at once. Stir over moderate heat until the sugar dissolves. Bring to a boil, then boil rapidly, skimming the froth off the top, for 15 minutes. Take the pot from the heat and let sit for 3 minutes.

Ladle the jam into jars and seal. (Chilled, the jam keeps for up to 2 months.) Or ladle the jam into hot sterilized canning jars, and seal according to the manufacturer's instructions.

Marie-Thérèse Andriot's golden jam has a fresh taste and is not a typical firm-setting one. She serves it at her B&B in Monthélon just outside Autun in Burgundy, along with cream and butter from her dairy cows and general instructions on eating breakfast. Madame Andriot, who hasn't read the dire warnings in American health columns, urges her guests to eat: "You must try both the jam and the crème fraîche together on toast." Take care not to overcook the jam as the sugar will caramelize, changing the flavor of the fruit.

Besides breakfast toast, Madame Andriot's saucelike jam is delicious with Brittany Pound Cake and atop pancakes. Or try it poured over vanilla ice cream or Poached Pears with Cassis.

VIN D'ORANGES

(PROVENCE)

Fortified Orange Wine

MAKES ABOUT 9 CUPS

7 juice oranges (about 2½ pounds total)
7 cups fruity red wine, dry white wine, or rosé wine, preferably from
    Provence
Grated zest of 1 orange
1 cup granulated sugar
1 cup plain eau-de-vie or vodka

It's currently fashionable to run down manufacturers' recipe giveaways. But that doesn't stop people from using them in secret. This is one such recipe for a homemade aperitif, especially popular around Christmastime in Provence. Made with wine—red, white, or rosé—and chopped juicy oranges, it's like Provençal sangria.

Peel the oranges and chop the flesh into ¼-inch pieces on a cutting board with a well to catch the juices. You should have at least 3 cups chopped orange. Transfer with any juice to a 12-cup, wide-mouthed jar with a tight-fitting lid, or divide the ingredients between 2 smaller jars. Pour in the wine and seal. Set aside in a cool place for 10 days. Gently shake the jar once a day. On about the seventh day, the wine starts to ferment; this is normal.

On the tenth day, stir in the orange zest. On the eleventh day, strain the wine mixture into a large bowl, pressing on the oranges to extract all the juice. Discard the oranges. Add the sugar to the wine and stir until it dissolves. Add the eau-de-vie or vodka. Pour this fortified wine through a funnel into 3 wine bottles. Seal with corks and set aside in a cool place for 10 more days before using. Serve well chilled. (The wine keeps up to 3 months stored in a cool, dark place.)

CRÈME DE CASSIS

Black-Currant Liqueur

MAKES ABOUT 1 CUP

½ pound fresh black currants
1 cup fruity red wine, preferably a young Burgundy
1 cup granulated sugar
⅓ cup brandy

Discard the small stems from the berries. Put the berries in a bowl and crush them slightly with a fork. Pour in the wine and steep the berries, covered, for 2 days. (You do not need to chill the mixture.)

Pour the berries with the wine through a fine strainer into a measuring cup, pressing on the berries to extract all the juice. There should be about 1 cup of liquid.

Pour the wine into a saucepan and add the sugar. Heat gently, stirring, until the sugar dissolves, then simmer until it thickens and becomes syrupy, 3 to 4 minutes.

Let the liqueur cool and stir in the brandy. Seal tightly in a bottle and store at room temperature for up to a month. The flavor improves with time.

Almost any tart berry can be substituted here, for example blackberries or elderberries. You may need to adjust the sugar to the sweetness of the fruit. Whatever the berry, this liqueur is good poured over a fruit mousse, a simple cake, or crepes, as well as with ice cream and poached fruit. Try it, too, to make kir.

CRÈME FRAÎCHE

(NORMANDY)
MAKES 2 CUPS

2 cups heavy (whipping) cream, preferably not ultrapasteurized
2 tablespoons buttermilk, plain yogurt, or sour cream

*I*n a medium saucepan, combine the cream and buttermilk, yogurt, or sour cream and heat gently until tepid. Using a rubber spatula, scrape the mixture into a bowl, preferably earthenware, cover with plastic wrap, and set aside in a warm place until it thickens and tastes slightly acidic, 6 to 8 hours. Chill for up to 2 weeks; it will thicken further in the refrigerator.

Let's say you imported Norman cows, with their unmistakable spotted faces, and grazed them in clover at home. You still wouldn't get crème fraîche de Normandie. While it might be very good indeed, it wouldn't have the flavor of the genuine article, which comes from the Norman terroir, that hard-to-define admixture of soil and climate.

Nothing tastes like real crème fraîche made in Normandy. In the wetlands around Isigny, the crème fraîche has even been awarded an appellation d'origine contrôlée, legal praise and protection for Normandy's finest cream.

Traditionally, farmers simply left milk, straight from the cow, in a cool place for the cream to rise to the surface. The nubbly crust was skimmed off, then set aside to ripen and develop its unique tangy flavor. Today, virtually all the commercial crème fraîche in France is pasteurized, though the best cheese shops stock the raw, homemade variety, and farmers still ladle it out at local markets (bring your own jar).

Although not quite the same thing as France's crème fraîche, the formula below makes a thickened, slightly tart cream. If you would like a cream with more bite, add up to 1 cup of buttermilk, yogurt, or sour cream.

FOND DE VOLAILLE

Homemade Chicken Stock

MAKES ABOUT 3 QUARTS

4 pounds chicken carcasses, wing tips, skin, necks, thigh bones, drumsticks,
    giblets (except liver), and any other scraps
3 carrots, cut into 2-inch pieces
3 onions, quartered
2 ribs celery, cut into 2-inch pieces
1 fat bouquet garni (2 branches fresh thyme, or 1 teaspoon dried thyme
    leaves; 12 parsley stems; and 2 imported bay leaves, tied in a bundle
    with kitchen string or cheesecloth)
4 quarts water
Salt

*B*reak up the carcasses and put them in a stockpot along with the other scraps. Add the vegetables, *bouquet garni*, water, and a little salt. Bring to a boil, then reduce the heat to low and barely simmer, uncovered, for 3 to 4 hours. Skim the fat and foam regularly from the stock. Strain the stock into a large bowl and discard everything in the strainer.

If you have the time, chill the stock until the fat rises to the surface and can easily be removed. Otherwise, skim off as much fat as you can. (Stock keeps 2 or 3 days in the refrigerator and freezes well.)

In the French countryside, farmwives never throw away a roasted chicken carcass, hacked-off wing tips, or giblets. They collect them in the freezer until about 4 pounds accumulate or until a fresh batch of stock is needed, whichever comes first. The bones and such barely simmer in water (1 quart of water for every pound of chicken scraps) with a few vegetables for 3 or 4 hours, or until flavorful. Of course you could make stock with a fresh, uncooked chicken, but it wouldn't be as thrifty.

FRENCH COUNTRY COOKING IN FRANCE

Here is a personal list of addresses, mostly restaurants, with the spirit of the French countryside. All the entries are grouped by region, then arranged in alphabetical order by town or village name. Some burgs are too small to rate their own zip codes; these I list under the name of the nearest town where mail is distributed.

The eating establishments range from farmhouses and family restaurants to Michelin-starred restaurants. They all serve regional food or make creative use of local ingredients. Cooks at *fermes-auberges* and *tables d'hôtes* usually prepare meals only on request, and when you call you may be asked what you would like to eat. It is worth remembering that even lavish restaurants offer bargain price-fixed menus during the week at lunchtime. Often the most interesting regional fare appears on these set menus.

The following also includes a handful of food museums and addresses where you can find the local products mentioned in the text, such as candy shops, olive-oil mills, *charcuteries*, bakeries, canneries, oyster farms.

PARIS

LE RASCASSON
148 rue de Vaugirard
75015 Paris
Tel 47 34 63 45

CHEZ MARIE-LOUISE
52 rue Championnet
75018 Paris
Tel 46 06 86 55

NORMANDY

HÔTEL DE LA CHAINE D'OR
Place Saint-Sauveur
27700 Les Andelys
Tel 32 54 00 31

MANOIR DU LYS
Route de Juvigny-Croix-Gauthier
61140 Bagnoles-de-l'Orne
Tel 33 37 80 69

LE LION D'OR
71 rue Saint-Jean
14400 Bayeux
Tel 31 92 06 90

CAFÉ DES ARTS
4 place Colonel-Langlois
14950 Beaumont-en-Auge
Tel 31 64 18 78

AUBERGE DU DAUPHIN
14130 Le Breuil-en-Auge
Tel 31 65 08 11

LA BOURRIDE
15 rue Vaugueux
14000 Caen
Tel 31 93 50 76

DANIEL TUBOEUF
8 rue Buquet
14000 Caen
Tel 31 43 64 48

HÔTELLERIE DU MOULIN DU VEY
14570 Clécy
Tel 31 69 71 08

LE MOULIN DE VILLERAY
Villeray
61110 Condeau
Tel 33 73 30 22

BOUCHERIE COLLETTE
(*Tripe à la mode de Caen*)
31 rue de la Mer
14470 Courseulles-sur-Mer
Tel 31 37 45 02

HÔTEL FERME DE LA RANCONNIÈRE
Route Arromanches
14480 Crépon
Tel 31 22 21 73

FERME-AUBERGE DU HAUT DE CROUTTES
61120 Crouttes
Tel 33 35 25 27

RESTAURANT CHEZ OCTAVE
23 rue Saint-Denis
61600 La Ferté-Macé
Tel 33 37 01 19

GÉRARD CHATEL
31 rue Saint-Denis
61600 La Ferté-Macé
Tel 33 37 11 85

AUBERGE DU BEAU LIEU
Le Fossé
76440 Forges-les-Eaux
Tel 35 90 50 36

AUBERGE DU TROU NORMAND
Pourville-sur-Mer
76550 Hautot-sur-Mer
Tel 35 84 59 84

L'ASSIETTE GOURMANDE
2 quai Passagers
14600 Honfleur
Tel 31 89 24 88

AUBERGE DES GROTTES
Le Nez de Jobourg
50440 Jobourg
Tel 33 52 71 44

LA RAJELLERIE
(Bed and breakfast, *table d'hôte*)
Melleray
53110 Lassay-les-Châteaux
Tel 43 04 73 43

MUSÉE DU FROMAGE DE LIVAROT
(Cheese museum)
Manoir de l'Isle
68 rue Marcel-Gambier
14140 Livarot
Tel 31 63 43 13

AUBERGE DE L'OUVE
Village Longuerac
50360 Les Moitiers-en-Bauptois
Tel 33 21 16 26

LA MÈRE POULARD
Grande-Rue
50170 Le Mont-Saint-Michel
Tel 33 60 14 01

CHÂTEAU DE LA SALLE
50210 Montpinchon
Tel 33 46 95 19

LES DEUX TONNEAUX
14130 Pierrefitte-en-Auge
Tel 31 64 09 31

RESTAURANT DE LA MER
Rue Fernand-Desplanques
50770 Pirou
Tel 33 46 43 36

AUBERGE DU VIEUX PUITS
6 rue Notre-Dame-du-Pré
27500 Pont-Audemer
Tel 32 41 01 48

HOTEL-RESTAURANT MONTGOMERY
13 rue Couësnon
50170 Pontorson
Tel 33 60 00 09

LA CHAUMIÈRE
Place du Général-de-Gaulle
50630 Le Quettehou
Tel 33 54 14 94

LE DRAKKAR
Rue Havre
50310 Quinéville
Tel 33 21 24 90

LE BEFFROY
15 rue Beffroy
76000 Rouen
Tel 35 71 55 27

MUSÉE DES TECHNIQUES FROMAGÈRES
(Cheese museum)
Rue Saint-Benoit
14170 Saint-Pierre-sur-Dives
Tel 31 20 97 90

AUBERGE LA CRÉMAILLÈRE
Rue 18-Juillet
14190 Saint-Sylvain
Tel 31 78 11 18

LA VERTE CAMPAGNE
Le Hameau Chevalier
50660 Trelly
Tel 33 47 65 33

RESTAURANT LES VAPEURS
160 boulevard Fernand-Moureaux
14360 Trouville-sur-Mer
Tel 31 88 15 24

MUSÉE DU CAMEMBERT
(Camembert museum)
10 avenue du Général-de-Gaulle
61120 Vimoutiers
Tel 33 39 08 08

BRITTANY

HÔTEL-RESTAURANT DU GOYEN
Place Jean-Simon
29770 Audierne
Tel 98 70 08 88

MUSÉE DES MARAIS SALANTS
(Salt museum)
29 bis rue Pasteur
44740 Batz-sur-Mer
Tel 40 23 82 79

MAISON DE BRICOURT
1 rue Du Guesclin
35260 Cancale
Tel 99 89 64 76

THIERRY RANNOU
(Bed and breakfast, *table d'hôte*)
Brézéhant
29450 Commana
Tel 98 78 93 71

BOUCHERIE-CHARCUTERIE MICHEL GUILLEMOT
(*Andouille de Guémené*)
2 rue Joseph-Pérès
56160 Guémené-sur-Scorff
Tel 97 51 21 44

MAISON DES PALUDIERS
(Salt museum)
18 rue des Prés-Garniers
Saillé
44350 Guérande
Tel 40 62 21 96

RESTAURANT LE JARDIN GOURMAND
46 rue Jules-Simon
56100 Lorient
Tel 97 64 17 24

RESTAURANT MON RÊVE
Route des Bords de la Loire
44000 Nantes
Tel 40 03 55 50

AU CHAR À BANCS
22170 Plélo
Tel 96 74 13 63

MUSÉE DE LA POMME ET DU CIDRE
(Cider museum)
La Ville-Hervy
22690 Pleudihen
Tel 96 83 20 78

MUSÉE DE LA CRÊPE
(Crepe museum)
29700 Plomelin
Tel 98 52 91 92

LE DOMAINE DE KERCROC
(Oysters)
Didier and Michèle Militon
56720 Plouharnel
Tel 97 52 40 57

HÔTEL-RESTAURANT PATRICK JEFFROY
11 rue Bon-Voyage
22780 Plounérin
Tel 96 38 61 80

MOULIN DE L'ÉCLUSE
(Buckwheat mill)
29120 Pont-l'Abbé
Tel 98 87 08 37

LA BELLE-ÎLOISE
(Vintage sardines)
10 rue de Kervozès
56170 Quiberon
Tel 97 50 08 77

AUBERGE DE POUL-FÉTAN
Poul-Fétan
56310 Quistinic
Tel 97 39 72 82

ECOMUSÉE DU PAYS DE RENNES
(Farm museum)
La Bintinais
35000 Rennes
Tel 99 51 38 15

L'AUBERGE BRETONNE
2 place Duguesclin
56130 La Roche-Bernard
Tel 99 90 60 28

RESTAURANT ENTRE DEUX VERRES
1 rue Broussais
35400 Saint-Malo
Tel 99 40 01 46

LA COUR D'ORGÈRES
(Specialty bake shop)
156 rue Général-de-Gaulle
56510 Saint-Pierre-de-Quiberon
Tel 97 30 91 90

HÔTEL DE LA PLAGE
29550 Sainte-Anne-la-Palud
Tel 98 92 50 12

RESTAURANT RÉGIS MAHÉ
24 place de la Gare
56000 Vannes
Tel 97 42 61 41

BURGUNDY

FERME-AUBERGE DE LANEAU
Laneau
21320 Arconcey
Tel 80 84 11 18

LE QUAI
4 place Saint-Nicolas
89000 Auxerre
Tel 86 51 66 67

HOSTELLERIE DU MOULIN DES RUATS
Vallée du Cousin
89200 Avallon
Tel 86 34 07 14

DENISE LAGELÉE
Hameau d'Evelle
21340 Baubigny
Tel 80 21 70 38

CHARCUTERIE BATTEAULT
(*Jambon persillé, rosette*)
4 rue Monge
21200 Beaune
Tel 80 22 23 04

BRASSERIE LE FRANÇAIS
7 avenue Alsace-Lorraine
01000 Bourg-en-Bresse
Tel 74 22 55 14

LA BOUZEROTTE
21200 Bouze-lès-Beaune
Tel 80 26 01 37

AUBERGE LES TILLEULS
12 quai Yonne
Vincelottes
89290 Champs-sur-Yonne
Tel 86 42 22 13

LE BAREUZAI
Route Nationale 74
21200 Chorey-lès-Beaune
Tel 80 22 02 90

LE BISTROT DES HALLES
10 rue Bannelier
21000 Dijon
Tel 80 49 94 15

COUM' CHEZ EUX
68 rue Jean-Jacques-Rousseau
21000 Dijon
Tel 80 73 56 87

GREY-POUPON
(Mustard specialty shop)
32 rue de la Liberté
21000 Dijon
Tel 80 30 41 02

MUSÉE AMORA
(Mustard museum)
48 quai Nicolas-Rolin
21000 Dijon
Tel 80 44 44 40

AUBERGE DU CEP
Place de l'Eglise
69820 Fleurie
Tel 74 04 10 77

LE PETIT CAVEAU
4 rue de Richebourg
21220 Gevrey-Chambertin
Tel 80 34 32 83

LA RIVE GAUCHE
Chemin Port-au-Bois
89300 Joigny
Tel 86 91 46 66

LES GOURMETS
8 rue du Puits-de-Tet
21160 Marsannay-la-Côte
Tel 80 52 16 32

LES GRANGES
(Bed and breakfast)
71400 Monthélon
Tel 85 52 22 99

AUBERGE DE LA BEURSAUDIÈRE
Chemin de Ronde
Nitry
89310 Noyers
Tel 86 33 62 51

JEAN-BAPTISTE JOANNET
(Crème de cassis)
Rue Basse
Arcenant
21700 Nuits-Saint-Georges
Tel 80 61 12 23

LA STRADA
Marcigny-sous-Thil
21390 Précy-sous-Thil
Tel 80 64 52 34

AUBERGE DES BRIZARDS
Les Brizards
89630 Quarré-les-Tombes
Tel 86 32 20 12

COLETTE GIRAUD
(Goat-cheese maker)
Chèvrerie de la Pierre Longue
Saint-Germain-de-Modéon
21530 La Roche-en-Brénil
Tel 80 64 71 97

LA CÔTE D'OR
2 rue Argentine
21210 Saulieu
Tel 80 64 07 66

HOSTELLERIE DU VIEUX MOULIN
Bouilland
21420 Savigny-lès-Beaune
Tel 80 21 51 16

RESTAURANT-BAR DES MINIMES
39 rue de Vaux
21140 Semur-en-Auxois
Tel 80 97 26 86

DOMAINE DE MONTPIERREUX
(Bed and breakfast)
89290 Venoy
Tel 86 40 20 91

FERME-AUBERGE DU COLOMBIER
01560 Vernoux
Tel 74 30 72 00

LES RUCHERS DE L'AUXOIS
(*Pain d'épices* and honey)
Pascal and Marie-Colette Dupas
Massingy-lès-Vitteaux
21350 Vitteaux
Tel 80 49 63 78

L'ANCIENNE AUBERGE
Place du Marché
01540 Vonnas
Tel 74 50 11 13

PROVENCE

BRASSERIE NORD-PINUS
Place du Forum
13200 Arles
Tel 90 93 02 32

CALISSONS DU ROY RENÉ
(Candy shop)
7 rue Papassaudi
13100 Aix-en-Provence
Tel 42 26 67 86

RESTAURANT LOU MARQUÈS
Boulevard des Lices
13200 Arles
Tel 90 96 35 72

PIERRE MILHAUD
(Butcher shop)
11 rue Réattu
13200 Arles
Tel 90 96 16 05

RESTAURANT LE VACCARÈS
11 rue Favorin
13200 Arles
Tel 90 96 06 17

AUBERGE DU BEAUCET
82104 Le Beaucet
Tel 90 66 10 82

LES ARCADES
16 place des Arcades
06410 Biot
Tel 93 65 01 04

CONFISERIE BONO
(Candy maker)
26 rue de la Sous-Préfecture
84200 Carpentras
Tel 90 63 04 99

ÉTABLISSEMENTS CHARLES VIAN
(Preserved truffles)
316 rue Terradou
84200 Carpentras
Tel 90 63 04 23

RESTAURANT LE VERT GALANT
12 rue Clapies
84200 Carpentras
Tel 90 67 15 50

HOSTELLERIE DE L'ABBAYE
06480 La Colle-sur-Loup
Tel 93 32 66 77

RESTAURANT LE MAS DE COTIGNAC
Route de Carcès
83570 Cotignac
Tel 94 04 66 57

RESTAURANT PATIN COUFFIN
Placette Olivier
83440 Fayence
Tel 94 76 29 96

RESTAURANT CHEZ MAÎTRE BOSCQ
13 rue Fontette
06130 Grasse
Tel 93 36 45 76

RESTAURANT LA FENIÈRE
9 rue Grand-Pré
84160 Lourmarin
Tel 90 68 11 79

RESTAURANT LE PANORAMIQUE
06420 Marie
Tel 93 02 03 01

LES ARCENAULX
25 cours Honoré-d'Estienne-d'Orves
13001 Marseille
Tel 91 54 77 06

LE FOUR DES NAVETTES
(Bakery)
136 rue Sainte
13007 Marseille
Tel 91 33 32 12

COOPÉRATIVE OLÉICOLE VALLÉE BAUX
(Olive-oil mill)
rue Charloun-Rieu
13520 Maussanne-les-Alpilles
Tel 90 54 32 37

RESTAURANT OU RAVI PROVENÇAU
34 avenue Vallée-des-Baux
13520 Maussanne-les-Alpilles
Tel 90 54 31 11

LA GLORIETTE
(Restaurant and bakery)
26170 Mérindol-les-Oliviers
Tel 75 28 71 08

ALZIARI
(Olive oil)
14 rue Saint-François-de-Paule
06000 Nice
Tel 93 85 76 92

BAR-RESTAURANT ACCHIARDO
38 rue Droite
06000 Nice
Tel 93 85 51 16

RESTAURANT L'ESCALINADA
22 rue Pairolière
06000 Nice
Tel 93 62 11 71

LOU PISTOU
4 rue Terrasse
06000 Nice
Tel 93 62 21 82

LA MÉRENDA
4 rue Terrasse
06000 Nice
No telephone

VINTAGE CAFÉ
7 rue Bernis
30000 Nîmes
Tel 66 21 04 45

AUTRAND-GAUTRON
(Olive-oil mill)
Rue Bas Bourgs
26110 Nyons
Tel 75 26 02 52

BAR-RESTAURANT LOU CIGALOUN
83510 Saint-Antonin-du-Var
Tel 94 04 42 67

BISTROT DES ALPILLES
15 boulevard Mirabeau
13210 Saint-Rémy-de-Provence
Tel 90 92 09 17

LA TABLE DE NICOLE
Route de Grignan
26230 Valaurie
Tel 75 98 52 03

INDEX

and green beans in warm salad, 133

and greens, in bread salad, 70

mussels, shrimp, egg, and sardines, with oak-leaf lettuce, 46–47

and olives, with marinated lamb stew, 274–75

spicy marinated with fennel, red pepper, and olives, 82

spinach and herbs, in gratin of cockles, 167

Tarts with Garlic and Basil, 86–87

Tomato sauce
in Baked Cannelloni Filled with Daube, 254
in Provençal Stuffed Cabbage, 256–57
in Tomato Tarts with Garlic and Basil, 86
with vegetables and puff pastry, 28–29
in Zucchini and Meat Loaf from Provence, 252–53

Topping
in Casserole of Lamb and Eggplant with Garlic, 280–81
in Gratin of Crepes Stuffed with Ham and Cheese, 96–97

Tourte de Blettes, 310–11

Tripe, 249–51

Truffle mustard, 226

Truffles, 148–50

Tuna, Egg, and Potato Salad, 53

Turkey

Drumsticks in Red Wine, 215

Provençal Christmas, with chestnut stuffing, 216–17

Vadot, Jean-François, 35–36

Vanilla custard, old-fashioned, 333

Veal
cutlets, stuffed, with Provençal vegetable sauce, 260–61
shanks, braised, with carrots, 262
stew
creamy, old-fashioned, 264–65
curried, 263

Vegetable(s)
with Puff Pastry and Tomato Sauce, 28–29
salad (mixed), with ring mold of eggs, 57
soup
with Basil and Garlic, 12–13
green, with split peas, 10
stuffed Provençal, 266–67
See also Side dishes and vegetables

Vegetable sauce, Provençal, stuffed veal cutlets with, 260–61

Vergnaud, Michel, 119, 241, 254, 266, 267

Vernerey, Nicole, 14, 15, 138, 161, 216

Vian, Charles, 148–50

Vinaigrette, 44, 46, 48, 54, 55, 57, 64, 66, 70, 71, 75, 76, 79, 80, 81, 82, 133
beet salad with, 78

mashed potatoes with herbed, 145

Tapenade, with pan-fried red snapper, 183

See also Cider vinegar sauce

Vin d'Oranges, 366

Walnut(s)
with apples and beets in endive salad, 79
Loaf, 294
Tart, 307

Warm Raspberry Tartlets, 312

Warm Salad of Green Beans and Tomatoes, 133

Warm Salad of Greens, Chicken Livers, Croutons, and Egg, 48

White beans, with golden gratin of cod, 186–87

Wild mushrooms
in beef stew, 241
with polenta, 151

Wine, 213
with Burgundian cheese and garlic bread, 107
orange, fortified, 366
See also Muscadet wine; Red wine

Wine sauce
Brittany, salmon in, 176–77
garlicky mussels in, 160

Zucchini and Meat Loaf from Provence, 250–51